The Sporting Woman

THE SPORTING WOMAN

Mary A. Boutilier, Ph.D.
Seton Hall University

Lucinda SanGiovanni, Ph.D.
Seton Hall University

HUMAN KINETICS PUBLISHERS
Champaign, IL

Library of Congress Catalog Number: 82-83147

ISBN: 0-931250-35-8

9   8   7   6   5   4

Publications Director
Richard D. Howell

Production Director
Margery Brandfon

Editorial Staff
Robert Lange, Copyeditor
Dana Finney, Proofreader

Text Layout
Lezli Harris

Cover Design and Interior Art
Jack W. Davis

Human Kinetics Books
A Division of Human Kinetics Publishers, Inc.
Box 5076, Champaign, IL 61825-5076
1-800-747-4HKP

UK Office:
Human Kinetics Publishers (UK) Ltd.
P.O. Box 18
Rawdon, Leeds LS19 6TG
England
(0532) 504211

Contents

About the Contributors

Susan Birrell, Ph.D., is an assistant professor in the Department of Physical Education and Dance at the University of Iowa in Iowa City. A scholar, feminist, and athlete, Dr. Birrell has recently co-edited *Sport in the Sociocultural Process* (3rd ed.) with Marie Hart.

Susan Greendorfer, Ph.D., is an associate professor in the Department of Physical Education at the University of Illinois in Urbana-Champaign. An avid athlete, Dr. Greendorfer is the treasurer for the North American Society for the Sociology of Sport and has published articles in such journals as *Research Quarterly* and *Quest*.

Preface

During the past decade or so, women's participation in sport has witnessed unprecedented growth both in its range and depth of involvement. Simultaneously, the scientific study of sport has been established as a legitimate area of inquiry in a variety of disciplines, such as history, physical education, psychology, and sociology. In addition, feminist scholars have initiated a critical evaluation of women's place in sport. We wrote *The Sporting Woman* with the intention of combining these three themes into a single work that explores women's engagement in sport from the perspectives of social science and feminism.

Over the course of researching and writing this work we spoke with hundreds of women and men who differed greatly in their interest in and involvement with sport. A few of the women were professional or Olympic athletes; many were college and high school players; and the majority were physically active women whose range in age, social class, race, life style, and feminist commitment is considerably diverse. We also spoke with men who are professional athletes and trainers, college players and coaches, fans and recreational participants. We observed countless hours of play and athletic contests, and we ourselves remained active in sport, often as a relief from the demands of writing.

In addition to the use of intensive interviews and observation techniques, we also collected data by analyzing the contents of a wide range of written documents that derive from within the athletic and feminist communities. This book, therefore, results in an eclectic blend of new and existing data, of professional and lay literature, of scholarly theory and concrete experience.

Two central considerations are interwoven throughout *The Sporting Woman*, one that deals with the nature of social scientific inquiry, the other with the multiple approaches to feminism. We wish to speak briefly about each of these themes.

At the level of scientific scholarship, we offer a critical evaluation of the theories and research methods that presently dominate the scientific study of both sport and women's place in it. We identify what we believe to be the major weaknesses of mainstream social science—both in conceptualization and methodology—such as the insistence on value-neutrality, the functionalist assumptions of value and normative consensus, the overly determined view of individuals implied in much of social science, and the overemphasis on quantitative research techniques. We ask instead for a *humanist* sociology that combines the insights of symbolic interactionism with the contributions of conflict perspectives. Specifically, we offer a theoretical approach to sport and women's role in sport that identifies the constraints of power and social structure on women's involvement (as suggested by conflict theory) while asserting that individuals can choose to overcome these constraints (as suggested by symbolic interactionism). We also stress that such a humanist sociology is best generated by using *qualitative* research (e.g., participant observation, intensive interviews), which allows theory to emerge from the data itself rather than being imposed on it by preconceived ideas and structured techniques.

In terms of a *feminist* perspective, our book proposes a view of feminism as an overarching theoretical tree with many branches. We have used Jaggar and Struhl's (1978) classification of four models of feminism—liberal, Marxist, radical, and socialist—as a framework for our feminist analysis. Each model of feminism is developed in terms of its ability to identify, interpret, and resolve the many problems facing women as they enter into sport. We highlight the benefits and costs of adhering to different conceptions of feminism as each proposes a strategy for enhancing the capacity of sport to be a liberating experience for all women and men.

This book is organized into two parts, each consisting of four chapters. We created this division because we wanted to facilitate the difficult task of dealing simultaneously with both the theoretical problems and the more substantive issues that are involved in treatments of women's role in sport. Thus, in Part 1 we devote our attention to the philosophical, theoretical, and methodological dimensions of studying women in sport. We believe that a critical evaluation of the "conceptual maps" of a given area of inquiry—their assumptions, values, premises, concepts—is a prerequisite to the more specific treatment of a given topic.

Having explored these larger conceptual controversies and created a conceptual foundation, we proceed in Part 2 to the more substantive, concrete treatment of women's participation in sport. We pursue the implications of this framework for an understanding of how women's involvement in sport emerges and takes shape within different institutional contexts. We focus our attention here on four major social institutions—the family, the school, the mass media, and the government—which serve as dominant arenas within which women's sport is enacted.

The degree to which this book is successful in meeting its goals is due to the efforts of many individuals. A special acknowledgement must be given to the two contributors, Susan Birrell and Susan Greendorfer. Both women contributed substantially to this book in terms of expertise, energy, and empathy. Each, in her own voice, has been a source of insight and criticism and we hope that our joint venture has benefited them as well.

Obviously, it takes a certain type of publisher to produce a book of this nature—someone whose concern extends beyond "the bottom line" of profit. A book with an unknown market, an unorthodox approach, and an avowed ideology cannot give much comfort to a publisher. Rainer Martens and his associate editor Margery Brandfon accepted these challenges with enthusiastic courage, extending us a freedom seldom given to authors today.

Many others also deserve our gratitude. A special recognition goes to those who read our work or in other ways shared their ideas, especially Richard Adinaro, Sue Dilley, Bonnie Slatton, and Nancy Theberge. We also want to thank our playmates and friends who helped us enjoy the very experiences of which we are writing: Jo-Ann, Judy, Patsy and Muff, the Nutley Sun, Ro, Wessel, Marie, Kar, Meb, and Phil.

In terms of a unique form of spiritual support, we wish to recognize the part played in our lives by Maryann Gorman, Martha Courtot, Mark R. Mankoff, Sara A. Vogel, and Francine E. San Giovanni.

No book ever evolves without the dedication and effort of extraordinary women, women who type and retype, who collate, who correct, who counsel, who reassure. To Lucy Miller, Pat Parry, and Doris

Sura we say thank you while knowing that these words barely recognize your contribution.

Finally, we wish to thank the Research Council of Seton Hall University for a 1979 summer stipend granted to L. San Giovanni.

Prologue

Many people have asked us why we want to write a book about women and sport. As we answered this question posed by family, friends, colleagues, and editors, we were reminded of the feminist dictum that "the personal is political," that our private experience has public consequence, that the unique twists in our biographies shape our roles as citizens and professionals. Scholars have been able, and indeed encouraged, to hide themselves behind the veil of the disembodied, impersonal, "objective," and rational canons of science. While it is a safe place, it is also a false and dangerous place. It provides the illusion that our ideas, research emphases, and theories have no connection to our private world of feelings, experiences, and values. In speaking of the changing role of the sociologist, Alvin W. Gouldner (1971, p. 57) called for an increased awareness of who and what we are as members of a particular society at a specific time, and of how our social roles and personal life influence our professional work. We want to heed this call by sharing our motives in writing this book and some of the personal forces behind them.

Our wish to write about women and sport historically is anchored in our love of play and sport that began for one of us on the streets and alleys of an Italian-American community in Newark, New Jersey, for the other on a makeshift ballfield of a backyard in Houlton, Maine. As little girls, we perfected our skills at stickball, punchball, O-U-T, football, ice hockey, and baseball. We formed passionate allegiances to the Yankees and Dodgers. We honed our entrepreneurial talents collecting and trading baseball cards. We absorbed our scrapes and sprains with equanimity and pleaded with our parents to buy us that vital piece of sports equipment that would be the envy of our friends and the solution to our deficient performance.

We were vaguely aware of the fact that games and sports were for boys. Most of the time we were the only girls playing. We dismissed this with the rationalization that the rest of the girls just were not interested or talented enough while simultaneously we glowed with pride when the boys chose us among the first players to be on "their" teams.

It was as adolescents that we, like countless other "tomboys," were taught that the sweaty, vigorous, competitive world of sports had to be abandoned in order for us to lay claim to a "feminine identity." Despising the terms of this trade-off, we tried to forge a shaky compromise for ourselves and for others by shuttling between the roles of "young lady" and "jock," alternately feeling bewildered, frustrated, devious, and triumphant.

By the end of high school, we had created an acceptable resolution of the supposed duality of being female and being athletic, aided in large measure by our decision to pursue vigorous academic careers. The demands of college and the lure of social lives meant that sport would assume a more limited, but still passionate, place in our daily round. As graduate students we were absorbed in the intellectual controversies of the protest movements of the sixties, which gave us a language and an orientation that could inform our social activism. Out of this societal turmoil the women's movement surfaced again, and we quickly saw its power to describe and explain our seemingly private struggle to juggle the "contradictions" of being women, scholars, and athletes.

Our first years as university instructors were exhilarating, frightening, exhausting. We were finishing our dissertations, learning the art of college teaching, helping to form the first women's rights groups on campus, and playing on opposing teams in the women students' intramural program. It was on the playing fields of those games that we first met. One of us played on a team of militant, counter-culture, radical feminists whose high level of activists skills existed uneasily with meager levels of athletic skill and with an open disdain for even the rudimentary structure and goals of intramural competition. The other played on a departmentally based team of women students whose approach to feminism was a moderate, "equal rights" liberalism and whose skillful athleticism earned them first-place T-shirts and a reputation to be reckoned with. In our progression through seasonal intramural competition in different sports, we met teams composed of sorority members, commuters, dormitory mates, black women, and former high school varsity athletes. The intellectual and ideological issues of feminist athleticism were emerging in loosely formed and vaguely stated observations and complaints:

- Why did the jocks have to play so roughly, take the rules and score so seriously, and look so "butch"?
- Why did the sorority "sisters" play so indifferently, act so silly, and have male students to coach them?
- Why did the women's winning team only get T-shirts while the men got trophies, T-shirts, better playing fields, and coverage in the school paper?
- Why did the radical feminists see sexism *everywhere?* Why were they so angry, so unorganized, and so often the team with the most forfeits?
- Why did the black women stress racism as their major social problem, rather than joining the new "sisterhood" of oppressed women?
- Why did it take so long for all of us to meet each other, to celebrate our bodies and our games, and to begin to ask these questions?

These and other issues became more salient and consequential with the elaboration, in the early seventies, of feminist critiques of patriarchal culture and society.

Virtually every social institution was under attack. Sport would be no exception. Two events, one political and the other athletic, are often identified as originating forces that brought to public consciousness the debate over women's place in sport. We remember both of them clearly. In 1972, Congress passed the Higher Education Act, with its controversial Title IX provision. As members of the Title IX committee commissioned to study our university's compliance with the provisions of the act, we soon recognized that one of the prime areas of inequality was in the athletic programs of the university.

On September 20, 1973, Billy Jean King defeated Bobby Riggs in front of 30,000 spectators and millions of television viewers; we scrawled the score in chalk on our blackboards at our next class meetings. The ensuing classroom debate underscored the profound challenge to cherished myths, fears, and assumptions that the match uncovered. While each of us may have a private encounter that made a greater impact, there is no doubt that these events were catalysts for ripples of feminist consciousness and action that have spread across the entire range of sport in our society.

We have pinpointed 1975 as a critical year for us because it was on a cold, damp March afternoon of that year that almost 40 undergraduate women had gathered on a rocky field for their first meeting of the newly formed softball club at Seton Hall University. We had volunteered to coach the club and to prepare for its development as a varsity sport the following year. As we greeted these student-athletes, we brought with us at least two discernible goals. One was professional. Given access to the research role of participant-observer, we could use this opportunity to gather data, explore concepts, and develop suggestive interpretations about women and sport. Here was a chance to confront the study of this topic with an experiential directness usually denied to social scientists and to those like us whose sport background was informal, avocational, and lacking credentials.

Our second goal was more personal. As women, we were at the edge of "SportsWorld," that "amorphous infrastructure" identified by journalist Robert Lipsyte (1975, p. ix) that "helps contain our energies, shape our ethical values, and ultimately, socialize us for work, or war or depression." We did not want to prepare these women to enter Sports-World, nor to accept the status of the "truncated males" of philosopher Paul Weiss's (1969, p. 215) uninformed and condescending vision of women. But could we put into practice a feminist framework around softball, and if so, which one of the many emerging approaches to feminism were we to use?

How could we, in a single season, begin to experiment with new modes of sport participation that would avoid the limitations of SportsWorld and sexism; meet the divergent needs and interests of the softball club members; be true to our own, and often conflicting, understandings of what it meant to be feminist and athletes; and still establish a team that would be ready for varsity competition the following season? It was an outrageously impossible task and we embraced it with the freedom of knowing we had much to learn and only our "egos" to lose! The events of that club season forced us to experience once again many of the dilemmas that we had known as young girls, later as intramural participants, and now as "coaches." What was new about this venture was that we approached these dilemmas with an informed, critical, and more clearly differentiated vision of their origins. But dilemmas they remained. Indeed, they established some of the prominent themes of this book. We would like to share a few of these with you.

Institutional Accommodation vs. Institutional Transformation

Because sport had always been a male domain, it had developed male-centered games, styles, values, jargon, rituals, and interpersonal relations that can be summed up briefly by references to "locker-room" culture and "jock" roles. Most of the softball club players, especially the more skilled ones, had thoroughly absorbed these elements of sport as played by men. For example, they called each other "guys," teased those who threw and ran "like girls," derided the opposition, and planned tactics to intimidate umpires and "psych out" competitors. We discussed with them the limits and dangers of mimicking male sports models. We suggested that we could take our games and infuse them with different styles, postures, goals—ones that reflected a more humanistic approach and a feminist consciousness that would help us define ourselves and alter our sporting experience.

But what do these lofty ideas mean at the concrete level? After years of socialization that prepare both sexes to accommodate themselves to existing institutions that "were created by men without regard for the experience of women" (Christ & Plaskow, 1979, p. 7), we stood at a social frontier that required self-examination, critical evaluation, and repeated experimentation. By the end of the season the club was developing a style and tone that differed substantially from many of the teams we played, a fact that was devious to all club members, but not always welcomed by them. At least half of the time we called each other women—not girls, ladies, or guys. We cheered well-executed plays by competing teams; we encouraged aggressive play but did not tolerate verbal and physical intimidation. The players themselves took control over the flow and strategy of the game-in-progress. We tried to avoid mediating or arbitrating personality clashes and encouraged direct discussion by parties to any problem. In these and more subtle ways we began to learn how difficult and how liberating was the choice to alter our sporting experience.

Hierarchical vs. Participatory Sport

By assuming the role of coaches we were immediately confronted with the realization that inequities in power can lead to corruption of social relations and an estrangement of the less powerful from the meanings and enjoyment of the activities they pursue. Efforts were made to democratize the running of the club. Players were asked to participate in the decision to choose practice times, playing positions, batting orders, game strategies, and the like. We also asked the women to determine what, if any, negative sanctions should follow violations of agreed-upon rules, such as attending practice, late arrivals for games, or improper social conduct on the field.

The results were mixed, producing the usual complexities that accompany democratic efforts. Many members expressed little desire to make choices, preferring to yield to their coaches or to their more vocal peers. Other members were highly opinionated and unwilling to compromise their strong preferences. For our part, we were pleased by the sharing of suggestions but bristled at, and resisted, those that did not conform to our "more informed" opinions! We resented the enormous consumption of time required for democratic decision making. Dictates, orders, and pronouncements seemed ever so more efficient. Nor were we clear ourselves about how to balance the wishes of the majority and the minority. The cohesion of the club often paled by comparison to the highly disciplined, well oiled teams coached by field generals whose command was never in doubt. We tempered our occasional envy by recalling that democratic conflict is as important as hierarchically achieved unity.

Winning vs. Everyone Plays

The edge of this dilemma was made very sharp by the wide range of talent and motives on the club. There were women who could play every position and there were others who literally had never played the game. For example, as part of our "coaching" strategy, we once attempted to discover which players would be our "speed on the basepaths." Each player was told to start on the word "go" and we would clock them as they ran around and touched each base. Little did we suspect that one woman would take us so literally and be so unaware of the jargon as to circle the bases and *touch* each one with her *hand*.

The interest in winning as contrasted with "just" learning, was always there. How could it not be? Even the novices placed a great value on winning. We also wondered if the club's success would be judged not by the fact that 40 women came out for the sport, remained with the team, and improved their skills, but by whether we had a "respectable" won-loss record. Without that record the varsity status for the next year might be jeopardized.

We remained loyal to the club ideal of "everyone plays," however. We spent more time during practice with less talented and knowledgeable players. We avoided the structure of first-string lineups and deliberately gave more playing time to those whose showed greater interest and effort during practice sessions. We lost our first game 28-0! The "star players" were frustrated and confused but eager for the next contest. Those of more modest talent were ambivalent, enjoying the chance to play but aware that their participation contributed to the "Charlie Brown" defeat.

The temptations to abandon the "everybody plays" approach for that important first victory mounted as loss followed loss, but we remained loyal to our desire to avoid a first string structure. We were aware that the team's status as a club sport, and our temporary positions as volunteer coaches made this decision an easier and less costly one for us. But even at this level of sport, playing everyone resulted in the dropping out of some of the better players. The irony of this situation did not escape us. If the better players "cut" themselves this season, then the next season the "real coach" of the "real" varsity team would "cut" the majority of the players who had remained loyal to the club and its commitment that all should play. Although we continued to lose each successive game, albeit by closer scores, most of the players had managed by the end of the season to place an equal value on the process of the games themselves as well as on the end product. Victories came to be measured not simply by the final score but by how much improvement was made by the individuals and the team, by how much fun they had, by how much they learned, and by how hard they tried.

On the personal level, the end of the softball experience left us brimming with ambitious goals to initiate a series of research projects and scholarly analyses of women and sport. During the fall of 1975 we conducted a survey of women's sport participation and began preliminary analysis. However, as is often the case in academe, by the following semester we became absorbed by other scholarly demands. We developed and revised our courses on the Sociology of Sport, the Sociology of Women, and Women and Politics. We each wrote a book on selected aspects of role change that focused on women and that used a feminst context as a frame of reference (Kelly & Boutilier, 1978; SanGiovanni, 1978). We continued to play sports and monitor the new research and writing on women in sport. Our ideas about women and about sport progressively evolved as new approaches to the study of sport and of women's place in society were emerging. In the pages that follow, we wish to highlight the major themes of these new developments and to indicate how they can advance our understanding of the sporting woman.

PART 1/
Women and Sport:
Theoretical Issues

As we noted in the preface, this book is divided into two major parts. In Part 1 we focus on the central theoretical, methodological, and disciplinary issues involved in the study of women and sport.

We begin our exploration of women's place in sport in chapter 1 which consists of a rejection of mainstream social science and outlines our call for a humanist approach to social science. In addition, chapter 1 contains an overview of the four major approaches to feminism and examines the potential ability of each feminist framework for understanding the present and future shape of women's involvement in sport. The stress on humanist social science and the multifaceted nature of feminism provides the central framework for the entire book.

The historical journey traversed in chapter 2 applies an interpretative vision to a recounting of the development of modern sport and the American woman's role in it during different eras of our history. The chapter concludes with a brief recounting of the female athletic explosion of the 60s and 70s and applies various feminist models for interpreting the potential impact of this change on both women and sport.

Susan Birrell, in chapter 3, provides a critical review of the efforts by the psychological community to explain the sources of female athletic participation and the possible psychosocial consequences of their involvement in sport. After presenting the strengths and weaknesses of varied psychological approaches to understanding the sporting woman, Birrell concludes that a satisfactory grasp of relevant questions requires a radical revamping of existing assumptions, concepts, and methods presently employed by sport psychologists.

Chapter 4, The Social Context of Women and Sport, fills a pivotal role in this book by drawing the theoretical discussion to a close and laying the foundation for the institutional analyses in Part 2. In this chapter, we employ a humanist sociology to uncover the problematic nature of the relationship between sport and woman. We examine sport as a masculine domain, evaluate the barriers to women's participation, and generate questions about the nature of women's experience in sport.

Chapter 1/
Alternative Approaches to Sport Sociology and Feminism

Within the past decade, the study of sport has become an emerging part of scholarship in the social sciences, especially in psychology and sociology.[1] Research and theory about sport, health, and recreation, which had stressed its biological and technical dimensions, has begun to systematically incorporate the psychological and social qualities of sport into its scholarship. Today, a complex network of research institutes, centers, journals, and academic organizations[2] attests to the explosion of interdisciplinary work aimed at gaining better insight into what traditionally has been considered the "toy department of life."

Why the recent interest in sport by social scientists? The concerns of physical educators, journalists and reporters, sport buffs, and biographers seems self-evident, but what are serious social scientists doing here? A better question to ask why it took so long for social scientists to turn their attention to one of the most pervasive and powerful of social institutions! In his important essay, Charles H. Page (1973, pp. 1-39) explores this "striking case of scholarly astigmatism." It should serve as a reminder that academic interests and viewpoints are often dependent on extraneous factors, such as the "prestige" of a subject matter, the absence of "star" scholars working in the area, or uncontested assumptions about what is the proper subject of serious scholarship. This initial bias against entering the domain of sport fortunately has been overcome. The scholarly community has begun to accumulate a body of data and explanations about sport; it has witnessed an increased sophistication in the use of research strategies, a greater sensitivity to the complexities of sport as a psychosocial and physical phenomena, and the emergence of alternative opinions about how sport is, and should be, investigated. It is this last issue that we wish to develop in some detail, because we believe that at this juncture in the study of sport, and more especially in the study of women's involvement in sport, different perspectives on both sport and women bring with them competing assumptions, values, research aims, interpretations of data, and implications for public policy (Loy & Segrave, 1974).

Two general approaches to sport sociology[3] have been identified (Eitzen & Sage, 1978, pp. 12-13; Loy & Segrave, 1974, pp. 290-292). The first is a *normative* orientation that originates by making value assumptions about what sport should be, then accumulating evidence to determine the extent to which sport reflects these assumptions. Included here are such subtypes as: (a) the politically motivated study of sport done to enhance the service of sport for the goals of the state, (b) the morally motivated study of sport by physical educators to prove that sport develops moral virtues and builds character, and (c) the muckraking approach to sport which is oriented toward documenting the existence of what the sociologist believes are undesirable elements in sport (e.g., racism, nationalism, commercialism).

The second approach to sport sociology is *non-normative*. The goal of this orientation is the empirical description and explanation of what *is* in contrast with what *ought* to be. This approach is characterized by the objective, value-neutral stance of the researcher, who does not take sides but merely "reports the facts." However, it is generally accepted in sociology[4] that while objectivity is a basic tenet of science and a goal to strive for, value-neutrality is extremely difficult, if not impossible, to achieve. Scientists are people with consciously and unconsciously held beliefs, values, and feelings that affect every stage of the scholarly process. Our best hope is to recognize and admit to ourselves and to our readers these subjective influences and to struggle with the tension between them and the call to be as truthful as humanly possible. Our worst predicament is to pretend to be value-free, deluding ourselves and others that theory and method are immune to our subjective orientations. As

Gouldner (1963) observed so poignantly, "there is and can be no value-free sociology. The only choice is between an expression of one's values. . .and a vain ritual of moral neutrality" (p. 51).

In a significant and courageous article, Melnick (1975) has critically evaluated the state of sport sociology and offered some emerging paradigms that could guide the future of this embryonic field. He begins by observing that, influenced by the historical development of sociology as a scientific discipline, most sport sociologists have espoused the notion of value-neutrality, contending that this orientation would serve to gain credibility within the academic and professional community, would generate scientific truths, and would yield more powerful explanations about sport as a social phenomenon. Major examples of this value-free stance can be found in the works of such prime contributors to the development of sport sociology as Kenyon and Loy (1965) and Loy (1972). While not disputing the value of the scientific method of inquiry, Melnick's passionate concern, which we share, is

> our need to distinguish between the indispensable canons of scientific inquiry and *moral indifference*. It is when the value-free ideology, motivated principally by a concern for professional respectability, becomes a cloak for moral indifference or is used to rationalize scientific nonaccountability, that sport sociologists must stand up and take notice of their discipline's future. (1979, p. 22, original italics)

Writing with a similar concern, Eitzen and Sage (1978, p. 13) declare that "a very serious problem with the value-neutral approach is that it does not take sides. It takes the way things are as a given entity (not good or evil). Thus, research in the name of value-neutrality supports the status quo" (p. 13). This accepted value-neutral stance of the sociologist who seeks to discover and explain what is, not what ought to be, has given rise to the dominant orientation in sport sociology—what has been called the "functional-systemic" paradigm (Lee, 1973, p. 124). Using this paradigm, the sport sociologist's aim is to show how and why sport maintains existing cultural and social life. The conventional arrangements, policies, ideologies, and actions that comprise sport as a social institution are rarely questioned; the connections between sport and other institutions—the family, school, government, the economy, the mass media—are treated as unproblematic; the issues of power, control, conflict, and self-actualization are ignored. The prime concern is how persons and groups function in sporting roles and processes and how sports contribute toward maintaining society's stability and integration. Melnick, while granting that this approach has contributed to our knowledge of sport, nevertheless believes that the serious limits to this approach should encourage us to develop alternative paradigms with complementary methodologies that stress conflict as well as accommodation, change as well as stability, autonomy as well as conformity, and what ought to be, not just what is.

Melnick offers two alternatives that can liberate those sport sociologists who are dissatisfied with the arid, detached, and conservative aspects of the functional-systemic orientation. The first alternative is the "muckraking" or " 'dirty' sociology of sport" paradigm (Melnick, 1975, p. 30). Oriented toward social change, researchers seek to challenge myths about sport, to expose covert problems as endemic to the essence of sport as presently structured, and to motivate groups and individuals to social action based on these insights. While we recognize the value of this paradigm, an often-observed limitation is its failure to offer solutions for the problems it uncovers.

Aware that there are aspects of SportsWorld that must be changed, this paradigm lacks a fully developed philosophy of what it should be. To criticize the evils of sport is no small task. One risks the counterattacks of those who hold sport as a sacred institution, of those who would defend the values that sports are "intended" to produce, and of those anti-intellectuals who would insist there must be at least one arena of life that need not be examined, dissected, criticized, and analyzed. But criticism alone is not sufficient. Muckraking produces valuable findings and agitates to action, but too often it leaves unexamined the philosophical bases of the critique. To know what one does not like is often easier to identify than that which should replace it. A revolution in the sporting paradigm requires clarification of the vision of the end result of that revolution. How will people and sport differ as a result of the new dialectic between them? On what philosophical grounds does one assume that sports, as now constructed, do an injustice to both participants and society alike? How will people and society benefit from the transformations of sport? It is the second paradigm identified by Melnick that holds the hope for the answers to some of these more basic and philosophical questions. It is to this paradigm that we direct our work.

This second paradigm, still barely elaborated, has been termed "humanist-existential" (Lee, 1973, p. 128). It has as its focus a "man-centered (sic) sociology" that serves human goals and needs, one that is sensitive to forces that impinge on self-actualization for those involved in sport. Founded in a humanist social/psychological tradition of what people are and can be, this paradigm affords the greatest opportunity for people to restructure and to re-orient their own institutions.[5] This is a vitally important paradigmatic attribute in any consideration of women in sport. Because the vast majority of the history of this institution has deliberately excluded women, their entrance into the sporting world must be marked by a greater consciousness of its impact on them and sports itself. It is not enough to criticize male-oriented sport. One must have a set of values, structures, processes, and goals for sports which would incorporate those human qualities that until now have polarized women and men. Strength with grace, competition with compassion, rationality with intuition, product with process have yet to merge into the sport experience and fulfill its potential for both sexes and for sport itself.

While we recognize that these two competing approaches to the sociology of sport are not exhaustive nor mutually exclusive, we should heed the warning of Andrew Yiannakis (1979) who, in an editorial in the newsletter of the North American Society for the Sociology of Sport, insisted that:

> greater emphasis should be placed on creating a climate of intellectual discourse on matters theoretical, conceptual, and normative, and emphasize less the current obsession with 'piecemeal' quantitative research. Until the domain has been adequately excavated theoretically, statistically significant results are often theoretically meaningless in and of themselves. What is needed most at this point in sport sociology is a 'paradigm war' in which differing schools of thought and orientation battle it out in the academic arena, thus creating a climate of intellectual ferment, excitement, and of course, new knowledge. (p. 1)

He also calls for a greater concern on the part of sport sociologists with normative issues and their practical implications, noting that "very few of us actually write or speak about such matters. As a result, sport sociology's potential contributions to society still remain to be articulated and demonstrated" (1979, pp. 1-2). As social scientists, we prefer and will use in this book a humanist sociological perspective. Although the dimensions of this framework are far from fully developed, some of its fundamental principles are discernible.

A *humanist* orientation can best be outlined comparing it with other approaches to sociology. Traditional or mainstream sociology is characterized by value-neutrality, moral detachment, positivism, and the accumulation of knowledge only for its own sake. Humanist sociology, by contrast, stresses a value-committed science, one that recognizes the moral involvement that sociologists bring to their work. It is an activist approach to sociology that seeks to use knowledge about social life to enhance human freedom and dignity. In their search for explanations of social life, humanist sociologists reject the assumption that only positivism can produce "scientific" knowledge; rather, they insist that we can understand social existence by using such research alternatives as participant observation, unobstrusive measures, and emphathetic understanding *(verstehen)*.

Major proponents of the emerging humanist orientation in sociology include such prominent figures as Alfred McClung Lee (1973), Peter L. Berger (1963), and, most importantly, the germinative thinker C. Wright Mills (1959). Although they and other humanist sociologists may differ in their emphases and areas of scholarly interest, they share the humanist framework that guides their sociology. This framework recently has been summarized and extended by Scimecca (1981), who critically evaluates the humanist potential of the basic perspectives in sociology: functionalism, exchange theory, conflict theory, and symbolic interactionism.

According to Scimecca (1981), functionalism "condemns human freedom to irrelevance and so is of little use to humanist sociology" (p. 7). The functionalist assumptions about value consensus, social stability, the internalization of rules, and the legitimacy of authority, among other premises, have of course been widely criticized by proponents of other sociological perspectives. Exchange theory, espoused by such men as George Homans (1950) and Peter Blau (1964), also holds little promise for a humanist sociology. The major limitation of this school of thought rests on its failure to view social action as more than the result of responses to external stimuli; that is, its failure to define people as active creators of their social lives.

Scimecca (1981) has observed that a humanist sociology is most likely to emerge by combining the insights of conflict theory and symbolic interactionism. Each of these perspectives makes its unique contribution toward defining this new orientation. Conflict theory, especially as developed by Ralf Dahrendorf (1959), offers a realistic portrayal of the role of power and the structural control over rewards and punishments as the organizing principle of society. However, as Scimecca (1981) notes, "conflict theory still does not go far enough; it does not consider the possibility that individuals can choose to overcome the constraints imposed upon them" (p. 13).

What is lacking in conflict theory is provided by symbolic interactionism. This school of thought, established by George Herbert Mead (1956) and refined by Herbert Blumer (1962), insists on viewing people as active creators of their social world. The reflexive, assessing, and choosing human being, according to symbolic interactionists, is dynamically shaping and being shaped by society.

Sociologists who are forging a humanist approach to their discipline owe their greatest debt to C. Wright Mills, who, in *The Sociological Imagination* (1959), tried to combine the insights of conflict theory and symbolic interactionism. This synthesis recognizes the dual importance of the power of social structure and the promise of free human beings.

In the pages that follow, we will use this dual sensitivity as a guide as we explore women's involvement in sport. For the present, we wish to highlight some of the assumptions of our humanist sociology of sport. Specifically, we believe, as persons and as social scientists, that a humanist approach to sport contains the following principles and tenets:

1. There is no intrinsic benefit to the present values, beliefs, and ideas that comprise the dominant themes of American sport and shape this powerful institution. For example, we believe that the exaggerated emphasis on competition, material success, bureaucracy, hierarchy, professionalism, and conformity are but a few sporting attributes that serve those in power and prevent sport from enhancing the quality of our lives as individuals.

2. The "social problems" being uncovered in sport (moral and legal corruption, violence, racism, commercialism, elitism) are not minor failures in the ideal working of the sport institution that can be easily repaired with good data and good will; rather, we see these other problems as intentional, expected outgrowths of the very structure of sport as presently constituted. Radical change—that is, one that "goes to the root"—and not reform, is required to eliminate or at least alleviate these problems.

3. Sport, like other institutions, is conservative by nature and definition, serving to inculcate and celebrate select values, rules, and behaviors believed to be necessary for maintaining society. Like all institutions, sport channels our ideas and actions in culturally acceptable ways, limiting our vision and experience to only those approved by dominant cultural demands.

4. All institutions, including sport, are created and maintained by people and therefore can be changed by them. Sport has evolved, developed, and changed along with other alterations in social life. It is not a fixed, inviolate sphere of human activity; it can be reshaped if people want a different emphasis and a different promise for sport.

5. Sport and play are essential, universal, and enduring aspects of being human; whatever form they take in particular societies and historical eras, they should always be a source of joy, self-discovery, and freedom.

These assumptions about sport are not unique to us. We share them with others, both within and outside the academic community, whose devotion to humane values and sporting ideals carved the way toward a critical reexamination of sport. Some of their names are well known: Harry Edwards, D. Stanley Eitzen, Paul Hoch, Jean Marie Brohm, Robert Lipsyte, Dave Meggyesy, Andrew Yiannakis, Leonard Schecter, Jack Scott, and Thomas Tutko. Responses to their writings range from studied disdain through head-shaking bewilderment to joyful acclaim. Harry Edwards (1973, p. 90) and Merril J. Melnick (1975, p. 30) warn that a critical approach to sport will not be popular within the academic and sport establishments. Although we hope that our readers will give us a fair hearing, we cannot affort to ingratiate ourselves to anyone at the expense of our personal and scholarly convictions. In fact, if this book does not upset its co-authors and contributors, sport sociologists, athletes, physical educators, and feminists, we probably have not done as good and honest a piece of work as we should have.

Alternative Approaches to Feminism

Just as there exist different orientations toward sport, each with its selective preferences and interpretations, so too, there exist different models of feminism, each with a unique image of woman, a set of explanations for the source of her oppression as a personal and social being, and a vision of her participation in society that will enhance her potential for self-fulfillment and genuine equality.

The second wave of feminism, beginning in the mid-sixties, has today yielded an unprecedented frontal attack on the subjugation of women in all areas of society. Action (political, legal, economic, sexual) and insight (literary, scientific, theological, existential) have flowed back and forth from the pens and mouths of feminists as they discover, document, and denounce the tragically profound and simply irritating ways in which many women have been denied and denied themselves access to whatever it has meant to be full human participants in the worlds that men with power have created.

But feminism as an overarching ideological tree has many branches, each with a special origin, each leading in a different direction, each with divergent implications for the liberation of women and men. To better evaluate the present status of women's participation in sport and the scholarship being done in this area, we want to clarify these different branches of feminism, showing their implications for how we understand and study this issue.

Two philosophers, Jaggar and Struhl (1978), have offered a sound classification of the various models of feminism that have emerged over the last 15 years. In their excellent introduction to *Feminist Frameworks*, they argue that every framework or model has a dual function, offering both a *description* of women's oppression and a *prescription* for eliminating it. Thus, each framework carries within itself "different diagnoses of what is wrong with the present" which "necessarily generate different proposals for the future" (1978, p. xi).

Table 1 summarizes for each feminist framework (a) the cause or roots of women's oppression, (b) the implied solution to overcome this oppression, and (c) a major proponent of the framework.

Table 1
Alternative Feminist Frameworks

Framework	Roots of Oppression	Solution(s)	Major Proponents
Liberalism	Lack of equal civil rights and educational opportunities	Elimination of discrimination based on sex	Ann C. Scott Alix K. Shulman
Marxism	Systems of social organization that produce unequal classes; property and profit reside in the ruling class	Socialist revolution resulting in the means of production becoming the property of society as a whole	Evelyn Reed
Radicalism	A. Women's childbearing functions	Technological advances/control over means of reproduction	Shulamith Firestone
	B. Compulsory heterosexuality	Lesbianism as a personal and political preference	Charlotte Bunch
Socialism	Patriarchal forms of culture/social organization *and* economic class oppression	Elimination of both class society and the institution of gender	Gayle Rubin Juliet Mitchell

Note. Adapted from Jaggar and Struhl (1978, pp. xii; 82-85). An article by each of the major proponents is in Jaggar and Struhl (1978).

What all four frameworks have in common is a rejection of the conservative orientation. Conservatives deny the existence of women's oppression, arguing that women's place in society is determined by biological facts and that "for women, freedom is something like the knowledge and acceptance of biological necessity" (Jaggar & Struhl, 1978, p. xii). However, these four frameworks differ significantly in their basic philosophical assumptions about people, society, and culture (Jaggar & Struhl, 1978, pp. 80-85)—differences that will influence how one approaches the issues of women and sport.

Liberal Feminism

Espoused by Betty Friedan, Gloria Steinem, *Ms.* magazine, and the National Organization for Women (NOW), the framework of liberal feminism sees the root of women's oppression as caused by the lack of equal civil rights and educational opportunities for women. Liberals do not attack per se social inequities of wealth, power, and prestige; rather, they attack their distribution on the grounds of ascribed qualities such as sex, race, and age. They believe that when women are given equal opportunities they will actualize their potential and should be rewarded by the dictates of the market demands for their achievements. Liberals believe that the elimination of discrimination based on sex can be accomplished by *reform* within the present structure of American society. They believe that reform can be achieved by the extension of political, legal, and educational opportunities to women. They assume that once these rights and chances are mandated, *all* women—regardless of their race, ethnicity, age, sexual preference, social class, or marital status—will have equal access to these opportunities and will be equally rewarded for their talents.

These assumptions are strongly refuted by other feminists who argue that equality of opportunity cannot be introduced into a society that is structured to allow certain groups to retain their social and economic advantage over other groups. For example, even if women as a group are granted the right and opportunity to have an abortion, enter professional schools, or obtain a mortgage, the truth of the matter is that many women who are poor, rural, uneducated, members of minority groups, lesbians, or physically handicapped will still not have the same resources to take advantage of these opportunities and claim these rights. Others argue that just as civil rights legislation for minorities has not eradicated racism, neither will the Equal Rights Amendment or other laws eradicate sexism. These deeply rooted prejudices cannot be eliminated simply by changes in the law; they must be combated by other, more basic changes in people's consciousness and the very structure of cultural and social life.

Marxist Feminism

The framework of Marxist feminism in particular rejects the possibility of any real equality of opportunity existing in a society where wealth and power rest in the hands of an elite ruling class. These feminists assume that the daughters (and sons) of the rich and privileged families will always have the advantage of their inherited positions and that this class will never create and enforce laws, policies, and arrangements that threaten its vested interests. They view liberal reform as a cruel, deceptive, and ineffective strategy for eradicating what they believe is the root cause of women's oppression—the existence of a class system in society. Thus, Marxist feminists believe that oppression by sex is a derivation of the more primary oppression by social class. Once social classes are destroyed, private ownership and profit abolished, and the means of economic production redistributed to the society as a whole, the oppression of women will disappear.

This argument is challenged by other feminists. Liberals, for example, resist the assumption that all people can or should be socially equal; furthermore, they do not want a revolutionary restructuring of their political, economic, and social institutions and their cultural way of life. Other feminists refuse to treat economic inequities as more important than sexist oppression. They point to the socialist and communist nations, such as Sweden, Cuba, the USSR, and China, where class inequities are significantly reduced yet various forms of sexism remain embedded in the cultural and institutional life of these societies.

Radical Feminism

This viewpoint is "the least developed and systematic" of the feminist frameworks (Jaggar & Struhl, 1978, p. 83). Radicals differ considerably among themselves, but they agree that the oppression of women is historically the earliest, the most universal, and the most difficult form of oppression to eradicate. They do not believe, as do the Marxists, that the elimination of social classes will insure women's equality, nor do they accept the liberal position that equalization of legal and educational opportunities will insure all women an equal chance at self-actualization. What then will? The answers to this question are as varied as the range of radical feminist thought. Some, like Shulamith Firestone in *The Dialectic of Sex* (1970), see the root of women's oppression in biology itself, where enforced childbearing functions keep women physically dependent on men and limit their autonomy. Implied in this perspective is that women's freedom rests on their control over the means of reproduction—birth control, abortion, voluntary sterilization, artificial wombs, and other innovations that would give women real choices over the issues surrounding child-bearing.

Radicals who locate the source of women's oppression in compulsory heterosexuality call for a woman-identified existence in which a woman "commits herself to other women for political, emotional, physical, and economic support" (Bunch, 1978, p. 136). This extended vision of the woman-identified woman concentrates on women granting to other women the range of commitments that society demands be given only to men. Still other radical feminists, like Mary Daly in *Gyn/Ecology* (1978) and Robin Morgan in *Going Too Far* (1977), call for a total and continuing exploration of new forms of being-in-the-world. They ask for no less than a complete reevaluation of such taken-for-granted ideas as culture, society, and human nature. As Daly puts it (1978), "The radical being of women is very much an Otherworld Journey. It is both discovery and creation of a world other than patriarchy" (p. 1).

Every radical feminist insists that the major source of women's oppression is a deeply rooted sexism requiring radical transformation of both personal and social existence. For obvious reasons, radical feminists are accused of "going too far" (Morgan, 1977, p. 8); they are dismissed by many feminists as too exclusive, unrealistic, offensive, or simply crazy. Their radical vision, however, must not be swept aside simply because it challenges, threatens, or offends. Indeed, it is precisely because of these qualities that we should encourage it, along with other approaches to feminism, in order to harvest what truth may be embedded in it.

Socialist Feminism

The framework of socialist feminism attempts to bridge the gap between Marxist and radical approaches. Proponents argue that both economic inequities *and* sexism should be seen as fundamental and equally important forms of oppression, neither having clear predominance over the other. Unlike liberals, they stress the greater struggle by women from different races, ethnic groups, and economic classes in gaining equal opportunity; unlike Marxists, they do not assume that a classless society will eliminate male privilege; unlike radicals, they refuse to consider economic oppression as secondary in importance to women's oppression. Socialist feminists see the oppression of women as a dual problem that must be fought as such. Privilege based on class or sex is interrelated and must be eradicated together. The socialist approach recognizes that class inequities must be abolished if all women, not just the more advantaged, are to gain from any enhancement of women's rights. They also recognize the need to abolish patriarchal forms of cultural and social life, such as the nuclear family, enforced heterosexuality, polarized sex-roles, and other forces that maintain male privileges even in economically more egalitarian societies.

Thus, what distinguishes socialist feminism from the other three approaches is not the identification of still other sources of sexism. Rather, it is the socialist recognition and development of the *interactive nature of the sources of sexism*, patriarchal culture/social organization, and class oppression, that are found in radical and Marxist frameworks respectively. This dual sensitivity to the problems of oppression by economic class and the institutionalization of gender make socialist feminists more vulnerable to criticism by proponents of other perspectives. However, this model yields a more varied range of alternatives for alleviating the complex problems of sexism. By recognizing the interaction between sexism and other social forces—classism, racism, heterosexism, ageism—it affords greater flexibility in formulating the problems and potential solutions to overcoming the oppression of *all* women.

Since this book, from its original conception, was intended as a feminist treatment of women and sport, we have spent enormous time and energy reading, observing, discussing, and arguing over the merits of different approaches to feminism. We believe that the strength of the feminist movement has been and will continue to be different from other movements for human liberation to the extent that it encourages and nourishes the growth of different visions of feminism (Morgan, 1977). The demand for ideological conformity, so prominent in many male-dominated social movements, would surely signal the failure of feminism to go beyond the limits of patriarchy. At the same time, it would be naive, morally deficient, and intellectually dishonest to pretend that every vision of feminism is as good as the next in its power to transform the status of women, to transcend their problems in sport, and ultimately, to create the better society.

So, where do we stand? Forced to choose among the four frameworks presented, we would say that today we lean strongly toward socialist feminism. We have, as individuals, as women, and as social scientists found ourselves in the past supporting liberal, Marxist, and radical positions on both women and sport. We must honestly admit that we still wander across the boundaries of these four orientations, forcing ourselves to grapple with the complexities of feminism while often yearning for the emotional and intellectual serenity of a commitment to a single orientation. But serenity must not be purchased at the price of personal or intellectual integrity and rigor. Each of these frameworks has its benefits in describing, and prescribing for, certain aspects of sexism. The advantage of the socialist framework is precisely that it is the least unidimensional and clearest approximation of the complexities of sexism as a social phenomenon. But it, too, has its limitations, and in some areas new feminist perspectives may prove more useful.

We briefly have outlined our academic orientations to the institution and study of sport and to our ideological position of feminism. We now wish to be more specific about how these two forces converge in the case of women and sport. Below are listed a series of propositions, principles, and premises which form the foundation of our approach to women and sport:

1. *Sport is a patriarchal institution.* Sport has been created and shaped by men without regard to the existence and experience of women. It is clearly a patriarchal institution, celebrating masculine power, values, and behaviors. It is on an equal footing with political, military, and economic institutions in training, encouraging, and

rewarding the primary emphases on competition, discipline, rationality, control, product, and victory that reflect the major androcentric values of society and the profile of what is considered quintessentially masculine.

2. *Sexist ideology pervades sport.* A virulent, anti-woman and anti-feminine ideology pervades the structure and dynamics of sport. The historical and contemporary exclusion of women from this institution, now well documented,[6] rests in part on a presumption of woman's assumed biological inability to compete on an equal footing with men and the usually unexamined importance of this criterion. Second, the exclusion of women from sport rests on an appeal to culturally prescribed ideas of femininity. Sports are by definition activities that promulgate and proclaim power, strength, virility, endurance, courage, and virtually every characteristic which is solely attributed to the masculine gender. Is it any wonder that ipso facto any encouragement of female participation has always produced an outrage at the "masculinization" of women and the "feminization" of sport?

3. *If women change, men and sport don't have to.* The extraordinary increase in women's sport participation at the informal, organized, and corporate levels of involvement (Eitzen & Sage, 1978, pp. 16-19) has been a result of changing definitions of women, prompted by the feminist movement, which have expanded the meaning of being female to include qualities and skills previously thought to be the exclusive domain of males. However, there have been virtually no complementary challenges to the accepted definitions of either men or sport, both remaining the measure by which women should be evaluated. Left unchallenged, the dangers of this trend will be a hollow victory in which women are quickly absorbed into male-centered sporting structures, coopted by the sporting establishment, and stripped of their chance to bring a different ethic and enrichment to sport.

4. *There is a liberal bias in the study of women and sport.* The major orientation of those involved with women's sport participation is, if it is feminist at all, a liberal one. It emphasizes political and legal redress, civil rights and the recruitment of women into established sport structures. This has resulted in a dual neglect. First, there has been a general failure to extend the opportunities for women's sport participation to minority women, poor women, older women, lesbian women, fat women, working women, handicapped women—that is, to all those women who do not fit the model image of the promising athlete, who may not be a "good investment," who do not have easy accessibility to schools and elite athletic clubs, or who want something different from what SportsWorld has traditionally

offered. Second, there has been a failure to seriously consider the range of feminist analyses of sexism and to apply them systematically to a consideration of alternative pathways for encouraging women to play sports. This has led to uncritical embracement of male-structured sports, with minor alterations, and wishful statements that "we will be different."

5. *Sport sociology is dominated by sexist research.* Research on women and sports, while it has grown almost as fast as the pace of women's involvement in sports, generally reflects either a sexist bias, as does much scholarship, or at best a liberal feminism. Indeed, what is curious about the present status of research and theory on women and sport is the virtual neglect of the topic by feminist scholars well-known for their powerful and provocative treatments of sexism in all other areas of social life.[7] Ironically, it has been mainly male scholars, journalists, and athletes who have been most critical of established sports, who have been able to suggest different modes of playing sports, and who have pleaded for the women's movement to use its vigor and vision to reshape the nature of this institution! While we will speculate later as to the reasons for this situation, our point is that unless research and explanations are informed by nonsexist assumptions and guided by the conscious awareness of the limits of a particular feminist framework, there seems little reason to engage in the exercise at all.

6. *Women are not men.* In the fight to gain equality, women have, by their words and actions, spent yet another era attacking the principle of male superiority. We have affirmed and exhibited, in all social arenas, our ability to be, to have, and to do what historically has been denied to us because of our sex. Yet, whether due in part to biology, to segmental participation in society, to sex role socialization, or to personal preference, we are still people different from men. The descriptive terms for women come easily to mind: cooperative, nurturant, intuitive, aesthetic, process-oriented, emotional, yielding, compassionate. Lest we be misunderstood here, we want to make clear that: first, we believe these to be qualities potentially accessible to men as well as to women; second, these are not attributes intrinsic to "the nature of woman" in any biologically deterministic sense; and third, that these very same qualities have been used as an ideological weapon to keep women as an exploited class of inferior beings. But if we have these qualities, should we not affirm them as a good, should we not celebrate their capacity to inform and transform us, and should we not insist that we carry them into our sporting roles thereby transforming sport itself?

In a prophetic vein, Harry Edwards (1979) warns that by "settling for involvement in male-dominated sports as now structured, women run the risk of making the same mistake made by blacks in their liberation struggle. Upon close examination, the 'change' demanded by black liberation groups from the most militant to the most condescending is only superficial" (p. 196). By fighting for radical "change" rather than merely "the terms of exchange," Edwards (1979) believes that "women could very well succeed where the black civil rights movement has failed—and that is in developing an alternative social model in which the younger generation can be socialized with values stressing cooperation rather than antagonism, participation and self-actualization rather than confrontation and domination" (pp. 196-197). We know it is possible to bring these qualities to our games; what is less certain is if we have the will to do it.

A Special Note on the Biological Aspects of Women and Sport

Perhaps the most studied and most frequently written about topic is that of the biological dimension of women's sport participation. Rare indeed is the book on women and sports that does not deal with some of the following topics: endocrinology, pulmonary physiology, neuromuscular characteristics, menstruation and pregnancy, body composition, VO_2 max. capacity, etc. The question of biology has always been central to the issue of women's involvement in play and sport because, first, their assumed biological differences and limitations, relative to men, had been and still are used as rationalizations for excluding women from sport, and second, because very little has been known about the realities of women's biology as it relates to physical activity. Both proponents and opponents of women's sport participation have vested interests in the outcomes of this research and are eagerly awaiting the next set of research findings to use in forwarding their particular platform.

In order to examine the degree to which "biology is destiny," scientists have spent endless research hours establishing that there are very few significant physical inhibitions to women's general participation in play and sports. Physical educators, sports physicians, and exercise physiologists (Adrian & Brame, 1977; Harris, 1973; Hudson, 1978; Ryan, 1975; Wilmore, 1974) have dispelled most of the outlandish myths and realistic hesitations about the physical abilities of women. It would be a mistake, however, to conclude that this issue has been settled once and for all in favor of a "nurture" as opposed to "nature" explanation of women's degree and type of sport participation and achievement. It would be just as much a mistake, at this time, to draw any real conclusions on what the remaining and consistent biological differences will be. It is not our intention to address this issue in detail in this book, nor are we qualified to do so. We will leave it to the medical and biomechanical sciences to provide the answers to this recurrent question.

This exclusionary statement does not alter the fact, however, that as social scientists and students of the sociology of knowledge we realize that the asking of a question arises from an underlying philosophical position. Indeed, it is the very question posed, how and why it is asked, and the conclusions drawn from the answer that should be critically evaluated rather than treated as unproblematic or taken for granted. We do not wish to imply that investigations into the biological differences between the sexes and their consequences for women's sport are not important and warranted. However, much of this research, in our opinion, is grounded in unconscious and unexamined sexist assumptions. For example, studies of women's biological proficiency at tasks requiring strength, speed, and endurance (attributes that favor male biology) are not complemented by equally enthusiastic studies of male proficiency at tasks requiring balance, dexterity, and flexibility (attributes that favor female biology). That is to say, women's capacities are being measured against male standards in sports that are structured to favor precisely those characteristics grounded in men's biology. The implied assumption is that male performance is the benchmark against which females should be judged and encouraged to strive for, without a complementary attention to the deficiencies of male performance and efforts to encourage their improvement in these areas. A good example of this bias appeared in a recent study (Marlowe, Algozzine, Lerch & Welch, 1978) reporting the efforts of a motor development program to *reduce* "feminine game choices" among boys. The underlying sexism in this and other research is clear: Females can and should be encouraged to throw farther, run faster, jump higher, endure longer, but males should avoid the movement vocabulary and game choices associated with "feminine" play and sporting activity.

A related issue has to do with the implications of research findings on women's biological potential. It is one thing to establish the fact that with proper diet, training, facilities, and coaching, females can play baseball, football, or ice hockey; it is another thing to argue that they should be playing such sports given their attendant emphases on male-centered biological, psychological, and social preferences. Until recently, women were excluded from many spheres of social life (e.g., wars, certain jobs, sports) because of presumed biological limits that said "we couldn't do it." Now, as we approach the realization of our full biological potential, we should be especially thoughtful and value-conscious about accepting a dictum that we should be involved in an activity merely because "we can do it." In this regard, we would question the value of using the findings from biological research as the sole or primary criterion on which to base recommendations for a future vision of self-enhancing sport participation for women.

Notes

1. For a comprehensive set of references to the literature on sport, see: Loy, McPherson, and Kenyon (1978).
2. See Loy (1980) for a historical overview and present evaluation of the development and status of sport sociology.
3. It is difficult to collapse the varied theoretical approaches to sport sociology into just two categories but we have done so here for the purpose of analytical clarity. The sociological study of sport has employed multiple theoretical orientations, such as symbolic interactionism, ethnomethodology, role theory, functionalism, conflict theory, Marxist theory, and the like. The other social sciences, especially psychology, also exhibit a range of intellectual and value-orientations in their approach to sport. See Tutko and Burns (1976), Scott (1971), and Martens (1979) for discussions of these issues. Also see Theberge (Note 1) for a synthesis of radical and feminist critiques of sport.
4. For classic statements on this issue, see Becker (1967), Berger (1971), and Gouldner (1971).
5. See Craig (1976) for an anthology devoted to this humanistic approach to play and sport.
6. Readers, monographs, and popular works on women and sport are appearing with great frequency. For a good introduction to this range of material, see Harris (1972), Gerber, Felshin, Berlin, and Wyrick (1974), Adrian and Brame (1977), Oglesby (1978), Kaplan (1979a), and Twin (1979).
7. Most of the academic women writing and doing research on women and sport come, as might be expected, from the professional physical education community which posits a limited, liberal approach to feminism. Feminist scholars from the humanities and social sciences, such as Jessie Bernard (1971), Janet S. Chafetz (1978), Jo Freeman (1975), Eleanor Maccoby and Carol Jacklin (1974), Kate Millet (1970), Robin Morgan (1977), Constantina Safilios-Rothschild (1974), and Laurel Walum (1977), while they have produced definitive anthologies and monographs on virtually all other facets of sexism, have been curiously silent about the effect of sport in women's lives.

   Given the power of sport as a dominant institution in our society, with its blatant display of sexism, this neglect on the part of feminist scholars is especially intriguing and disturbing. In a significant observation, Hall (1977, p. 39) speculates that either they "feel unqualified to write about sport and leisure, or they dismiss it as unrelated and unimportant to the real issues underlying social differentiation and inequality." A discussion of some of the sources and consequences of this scholarly neglect will be treated briefly in chapter 4.

Chapter 2/
The American Woman's
Sporting History

There have been many efforts to understand the meaning and place of play and sport in the human community. Historians and philosophers have attempted to differentiate the common and universal characteristics of play from elements that are specific to a particular culture, time, and society. Indeed, are there universal, intrinsically human qualities to play, or do history and culture entirely shape how we play our games? What can we learn about a society by examining its patterns of play, games, and sport? Even within the same society are there intelligible and systematic ways in which play and sport have changed over time? By following the development and history of sport and play, we can begin to answer some of these questions.

These historical answers also may provide some means of assessing if and how women fit into the ludic world. Are the characteristics of *man* and sport repetitive of themes of *man* and politics, *man* and religion, *man* and all social institutions—that is, marked by a label bearing the words "for men only, women enter at your own risk"? Ultimately, we must ask if the historical developmental patterns of human play are facilitating or hindering female entrance into this male domain and whether, given the nature of SportsWorld, women want to gain access.

Johan Huizinga (1950) was among the first historian-philosophers to consider seriously the issue of human play and sport. In fact, Huizinga defined humans as *Homo Ludens,* that is, "man (sic) the player." Play is an activity which humans engage in for no other purpose or goal than the participation in the action itself. Unlike fishing, hunting, or planting in order to obtain food, sexual relations in order to reproduce the human species, or tool-making in order to ease one's work, play has no "in order to" attached to it. It is performed for its own sake; it is an area of free, nonutilitarian activity; it is processually complete and requires no end product; it is inherently human. To play is to be human, to be human is to play.

Though play is intrinsically human and universally found in all cultures and times, the forms that play and sport assume reflect the values and structures of the particular society. "An important indicator of the essence of a society is the type of sport it glorifies. The examination of the structure of a society's dominant sport provides important clues about that society and its culture" (Eitzen, 1979, p. 40). Sports, games, and play are societal artifacts which teach as much about the values, structures, and reward systems of a society and culture as unearthing its art forms, its literature, or any other remnants of its history and social life.

Sports and its values are a microcosm of the society itself. The values of the society are mirrored in its sporting rites and its rituals, habits, language, goals, and passions. Competitive, aggressive, individualistic societies structure their sports to emphasize the glories of winning and the disgrace of losing. Cooperative, serene, and group-centered societies play their games to enhance the communal, playful, and joyful traits of their social life. The aggressive, competitive, individualistic approach to sport is so well documented and experienced that it needs no elaboration at this point. However, the second of these two orientations almost violates the Western, "developed" world's very definition of sport. George Leonard provides an example with the game *taketak* played in New Guinea among the Tangu people. The object of the game is to tie, to end in a draw, not to defeat the "opposing team." The game ends when each side has scored exactly the same number of points. "*Taketak* expresses a prime value in Tangu culture, that is, the concept of moral equivalence, which is reflected in the precise sharing of foodstuffs among the people" (Leonard, 1973, p. 45).

Another fundamental orientation of every culture, of every society, is its attitude toward, acceptance, and evaluation of half the population—women. The institution of sport can serve as a microcosmic version of the entire society's orientation toward women. Indeed, the task of this chapter is to trace the history of sports in light of its contribution to our understanding of the status, role, and evaluation of females and the traits designated as "feminine." We propose to investigate the relationship between sports, women, and societal values in three distinct ways.

First, the development and modernization of sport itself will be outlined. The values, emphases, structures, and processes of modernized sport are those of the modern nation-state. The modern nation-state has offered a greater variety of roles. As a result, women also have been more fully exposed to the demands, opportunities, privileges, and limitations of modern sport. An investigation of the dimensions and characteristics of modern sport will afford a clearer vision of the new sporting roles contemporary women find available to them. Modernization affects all social life, and sports prove no exception. Modern sporting activity requires close scrutiny to ascertain whether women can or should accept the invitation to join the game.

Second, we will present a brief history of the sporting activity of women in the United States. As sports have changed, developed, "modernized," so too has the place of women in sports changed. The changing character of sport has had an impact on the feminine experience of the sporting world. As women engaged in sports, how were they affected? Were sports altered? Were women's experiences in sports during various periods the same? Did women approach sports with different goals, objectives, and energies as the expectations of society about women changed? Examining women's experience in sport during the various periods of US history is one way to chronicle women's shifting roles in the entire society.

The third objective of this chapter is to detail the most recent explosion of female athletic activity. The major historical thrust has been toward equalization of sporting opportunities for women, but the "revolution" of the 1960s and 1970s deserves special note and attention. Seemingly, in no other era have so many women participated in so many sports at so many levels of organization with such widespread societal acquiescence and approval. The sporting opportunities for women resulting from the second wave of feminism have increased enormously. Our task will be to record this revolution and to assess how feminist this athletic explosion has been.

Modern Society and Modern Sport

Rational, hierarchical, bureaucratic, objective, impersonal, standardized, specialized, complex, technocratic, authoritarian, emotionless, scientific, and goal-oriented are just a few terms which readily come to mind when describing modern society. The prominent sociologist Max Weber (1947) described both the blessings and the woes of societal modernization and national development. Management specialists like Frederick W. Taylor (1911) recognized very early in the century the implications of these new developments for the economic and business realms. But these trends were not confined to the business and work world. They have permeated all aspects of modern life. They *are* modern life. These are core values adhered to in every realm; sports, sporting organizations, and the world of play are affected as well.

The spontaneous, joyful, innovative, ruleless, flexible world of play has little or no resemblance to the organized, competitive, structured, rule-infested world of modern corporate sport. Modern sport has taken on the traits of modern society. It has mirrored the developments of the nation-state and has glorified and exalted the same values. Allen Guttman (1978) in his excellent work *From Ritual to Record* describes seven factors which differentiate the early forms of play from the current complexities of modern corporate sport.

Secularization

Religious meaning surrounded the first recorded sporting events—the Olympic Games. These were sacred festivals; they were celebrations of religious aspirations as well as physical and athletic prowess. The Olympic Games were held to honor Zeus. Other Greek games, such as the Pythian games and the Isthmian games, were held to worship other gods (Harris, 1972, p. 16). Ritualistic athletic events were often part of a religious plea for bountiful crops and fertility. The primitive equation of physical endeavors in games with religious rites is well documented and continues even today among some tribal, "less modern" peoples (Brasch, 1970).

Slowly in the Western, Christian, modernizing world the religious connotation of athletic feats and events diminished. Religious leaders, especially those of the Protestant Reformation, actively opposed and denounced sport as profane, sacrilegious, and an instrument of the devil. Sport was associated with pleasure, joy, gambling, drinking, dancing, and a general neglect of spiritual matters. Gradually, sport lost its religious meaning and significance.

The ultimate secularization of sport came with the near total secularization of society. Scholars (Redmond, 1973; Rogers, 1972; Rudin, 1972; Synder, 1972) have ironically noted that sport has replaced religion as the symbolic expression of the sacred. Now sporting heroes, teams, slogans, "Halls of Fame," and sports fanaticism, rather than saints, proverbs, shrines, beatitudes, and holy wars, gain the attention and religious fervor of the former churchgoer turned spectator/player. Sporting events are religious happenings; sport, according to some, has become the new "opiate of the people." Demystification and secularization reach their apex when the symbols of faith, hope, and love are no longer other-worldly gods but humans engaged in all-too-human physical, competitive sporting contests.

Specialization of Roles

The day of the "renaissance man," the person of many skills, talents, accomplishments, and assignments, is long gone. The generalist has faded with the advance of the total specialist. Modern society has witnessed the emergence of a division of labor unequaled in former times. Specialization, that is the total concentration on one skill, on one area of knowledge, on one realm of expertise, is the norm in nearly every social institution. We no longer go to the medical general practitioner with our ailment, we go to the specialist. Educational specialization has grown enormously, as has the fragmentation of the work world. Perhaps the ultimate in specialization is achieved on the assembly line of the factory. Modern mass production demands little of the worker except the routinized repetition of the same task.

An inevitable consequence of this extraordinary division of labor is the concomitant need for interdependence, hierarchical authority, coordination and the increase of personal alienation. Few see the entire product; few know the end results of all the unique, specialized acts performed by all the segregated, isolated, fragmented actors. The joys experienced with the initiation and the completion of an entire effort have been sacrificed to enhanced efficiency and proficiency, mass production, and the well-oiled machine.

Sport also has succumbed to the same forces of modernization. The field goal kicker in football, the designated hitter in baseball, the spiker in volleyball are but a few examples of the extreme degree of division of labor in modern team sports. Football has an extraordinary amount of sports specialization. It even has a special team just for kickoffs.

Individual sports have experienced a similar trend. For example, sprinters do not run in long distances; the expert in the butterfly does not compete in the breaststroke; and the high jumper does not attempt the broad jump. Ironically, one of the most significant specializations in modern sport has been the development of the spectator, the modern person whose sole participation in the game is to watch and cheer for the extreme specialists on the playing field. The era of the renaissance athletes, such as Babe Didriksen, an Olympic gold medalist in track and field, a professional golfer, and an outstanding basketball star, is no longer.

Rationalization

Weber (1947) stressed the extreme rationalization of modern life. Specifically, in sports, rationalization means that:

> there is a logical relationship between means and ends. In order to do this, we have to do that. The rules of the game are perceived by us as means to an end. More importantly, new rules are invented and old ones discarded whenever the participants decide that ludic convenience outweighs the inertia of convention. The rules are cultural artifacts and not divine instructions. (Guttman, 1978, p. 40)

By contrast, in "primitive" societies hunting skills may be attributed entirely to magic or divine intervention (Barton, 1938, p. 38). There is no attempt to train for spear throwing or to develop new techniques to increase accuracy because control is not seen as being in the hands of humans.

Modern rationalization is marked by standardization and regimentation of both ends and means to achieve those ends. Rigid adherence to universalistic rules designed to foster conformity would have been resisted by the Greeks, who were accustomed to altering the length of the stade race or the size of the discus in various contests. We still have our superstitions about sports and what brings "good luck," but good-luck charms or talismans are never substituted for training, practice, and regimentation.

Again, the work place affords the best example of the modern extreme of rationalization. The goal is always the same: production of the most goods and services at the lowest unit price with the highest profit margin. If to accomplish this, the assembly line routine alienates the workers, segments their relations with one another, and generally leads to discontent, this is not a concern until it begins to interfere with the goals of the business. Industrial psychologists will attempt to alleviate the conditions of the workers. For example, they may advise formation of workers' councils and democratization of the workplace, but the reasons for these recommendations remain the same—to foster greater production at less cost. The goal remains the same; the change in the means arises only to better attain this goal. The rationalization of means accomplish the same results; never questioned is the end or the goal itself.

We have already come to expect the same trends in modern sport as in society. The theme of rationalization confirms this pattern. The goal in sports is winning. All means and techniques that enhance the accomplishment of that one goal are exploited. The means may be legitimate, such as the acquisition of new knowledge about the kinesiology of the sport, technological advances in equipment design, and new techniques of training. However, chances of winning also may be enhanced by cheating, intimidating opponents and officials, or by utilizing violence to injure the opponent. For the sake of victory even these methods are construed as rational and are condoned.

In Germany and Eastern Europe the rationalization of sport has achieved such sophistication that it is called a science *(Sportwissenschaften)*. Athletes' physical, psychological, and training schedules are systematically studied and regulated to produce the optimum results. Techniques have been developed to isolate the "physical specimens" most likely to be outstanding in particular sports. For example, Kornelia Ender, the world-record East German swimmer, was selected for special training at a very early age as the results of a blood test (Gilbert, 1980, p. 116)!

With but one end—winning is not everything, it is the only thing—any means are "legitimate." Individual freedom is limited to achievement of the goal. Action, rewards, meanings, norms, social controls, sanctions, and group integration are all grounded in this one end. It allows little or no deviance in role performance (Coakley, 1978, p. 97). The obsessive nature of this end permeates the slogans and the "blood" of every successful athlete. "Winning is living. . . . Everytime you win, you're reborn; when you lose, you die a little. . . . No one ever learns anything by losing" (Snyder, 1972, pp. 89-102). With such slogans, is it any wonder that any means which achieves victory become rational?

Bureaucratization

Part and parcel of the Weberian analysis of the rationalized, modernized society is greater bureaucratization. Universalistic goals, efficiency, formal structures, organizational domination of the individual, unquestioned hierarchical authority—all accompany bureaucratization. Examples of the modern increase in bureaucratic formations are so well-known that it is unnecessary to chronicle them here.

Once again, sport follows the trends of society. Sports bureaucracies—and they are nearly endless in number (AAU, NCAA, AIAW, USOC, NBA, NHL, USLA, etc.)—control all aspects of corporate sport (Gilbert, 1972, p. 34). They set the rules and they change them. They establish schedules, eligibility, codes of conduct, entrance requirements, trade and exchange rights, and all the conditions of competition. Athletes who ignore the sports bureaucracies' mandates are declared ineligible, are ostracized, and often are literally prevented from competing in their sports. "You can't fight city hall" has its equivalent in sport—"You can't play the game if you buck the establishment." The cost of deviating is enormous; it amounts to athletes' very ability to define themselves as athletes and participants in the sports they play.

Modern life is complex, intricate, interrelated; it produces organizations that foster and reflect these same traits. The simple, spacious, leisurely game of baseball is replaced by the complex, regimented, time-limited game of football. The rules for football are more intricate, the regulations more profuse, and the control by the outsider more extreme. Bureaucracy thrives on, creates, and promotes the very complexities it then tries to regulate. The cries of "too big," "too much red tape," "endless regulations," "too much government," and "too many restrictions" fall necessarily on deaf ears. Bureaucracies are as much the product of secularization, specialization, and rationalization as their creator. Each is bound up with the other. Bureaucracies can be identified and located. They are easy targets of criticism. But bureaucracies are as much the symptoms of modern life as the producers of it.

Quantification

In modern society, numbers count and all aspects of life are viewed as quantifiable. Quantity is the ever-present and ever-pressing concern of modern society. How many and how much are questions far more important today than are questions of quality or of effectiveness. Numbering items standardizes them, makes them conform to a set pattern, and allows the comparison of units of behavior we would expect to be distinct and incomparable. Bureaucracy, rationalization, and quantification are all pieces of the same cloth.

Quantification has become an obsession in sport. Wins versus losses, batting averages, earned run averages, pass completion percentages, numbers of unforced errors, and racing times in thousandths of seconds are all examples of the extreme quantification that has infiltrated the modern corporate sport scene. Sophistication of measurement devices allow greater and greater exactness. Quantification spreads even to the most aesthetic of sporting events; for example, judges score gymnastic exercises, skating performances, and dives on the basis of a uniform

AMERICAN WOMAN'S SPORTING HISTORY / 31

numerical scoring system. Athletic events are transformed from acts of physical and mental prowess into numerical summations which quantify the seemingly unquantifiable.

Records

As the title of Guttman's book indicates, the sport record has replaced the sporting ritual. It is the new ritual. Records that are certified, quantified, retained, and maintained by the rationalized sporting bureaucracies are the counterpart of the modern passion with records and record keeping. Much of the computer revolution is the result of the bureaucratic need for complete, detailed, and constantly updated records and record keeping. The computer age fulfills the bureaucratic need for control over and supervision of its "product." Information can be retained and stored because the quality of the act has been reduced to a series of quantified, standardized digits.

Sport bureaucracies ratify records established within the guidelines of rationalized-universalistic rules and conditions. Records in sport have become so detailed that it is nearly impossible not to have set some record just by engaging in the activity. Triviality is quantified, recorded, broken, recorded again, and broken again. Victories that do not break a record are viewed as less important victories. Records become the "marvelous abstraction that permits competition not only among those gathered but among those distant in time and space" (Guttman, 1978, p. 51).

Equality

If asked to select the most sacred value enshrined in all the ideologies of the 20th century, we would choose the value of equality. At least in theory, privilege grounded in class of birth has become ideologically indefensible. Various nation-states may differ on whether the equality espoused is an equality of opportunity or an equality of condition, but there is no doubt that the honorific title of "democratic" has embedded in it a devotion to some concept of equality. Now of course action need not follow from words. More often than not, equal opportunity or condition is honored in the breach rather than in the practice. But equality remains a principle verbally adhered to and honored.

The devotion to equality in sport is most easily seen in the equalization of the conditions of competition. All competitors have an equal opportunity to win because none is given an advantage during the contest itself. However, equalization of access to the contest, game, or sport itself has been much slower. Exclusion from sports because of an ascriptive status, be it sex, class, age, or race, is as old as sport itself. Modern sport, however, has begun to foster sport accessibility to groups previously excluded. The "Special Olympics" for exceptional children is one dramatic example. However, our main concern is the history of the sporting opportunities for women. In prior ages women had restricted access to ludic activities. Often females were entirely excluded and at times even punished for merely watching men play their games (Franks, 1979, p. 96). As the remainder of this chapter will demonstrate, the sporting status of women in the modern world has changed. Women are now entering the modern sporting world.

It is particularly to the issue of equality, and specifically equality of access by sex, that we must now turn. The history of women's participation in sport reflects different themes, stresses different attributes, and raises different questions than the history of men's involvement in sport. In order to grasp the changing relationships between women, sport, and society, it is essential to review this history. We need to know the range of female sport participation, its social settings, its justifications, its changing patterns, and its philosophies. This historical overview can then provide a benchmark by which to assess the current changes in women's approach to sport, the feminist relevance of these changes, and their likely impact on society.

A Short History of Women's Participation in Sports: The American Case

It is obviously beyond the scope of our work to present a complete historical account of women's participation in sports. We will, however, utilize the history of the American woman's experiences as an abbreviated, typical, and representative case study of that history. Throughout US history different groups and classes of women have engaged in a vast array of sports, in a variety of social settings, with a wide range of motivations and apologetics to defend their participation. Table 2 briefly summarizes the major dimensions of the American woman's sporting history. Since our major concern is with where women fit into the sporting scene now and in the future, their sporting history provides merely a yardstick by which to measure the so-called female athletic "revolution" of the 60s and 70s. By knowing where the sporting woman has come from, we can better understand where she might be going.

Table 2
Historical Eras of Women's Sports

Era	Social Darwinism and Female Sports Activity[a] 1880-1917	First Female Athletic Era 1917-1936	The "Feminine" Reaction to the Athletic Era 1936-1960	The Female Athletic Revolution 1960 to the Present
Group	A. Leisured nouveau-riche upper class women B. Middle class women	Middle and working class women	All classes but fewer and fewer total numbers. Activity the exception not the norm	All classes and more and more participants. Encouragement of participation throughout life cycle.
Location	A. Social clubs and class-exclusive associations B. Women's colleges	Educational institutions, commercial establishments, communities, national and international arenas	Intramurals in educational settings and private clubs	Community, family, educational institutions, clubs, and commercial establishments
Activity	A. Fox hunting, golf, and tennis B. Basketball, tennis, field hockey, and bicycling	Tennis, swimming, diving, ice skating, golf, softball, basketball, roller derby, field hockey, track and field	Swimming, tennis, golf (primarily individual sports) Team efforts in the context of cooperation and play	All traditional sports and the development of new ones: swimming, tennis, golf, field hockey, basketball, softball, gymnastics, track and field, soccer, rugby, football, volleyball, etc.
Purpose/motivation	A. For enjoyment only and explicitly noncompetitive B. Play for fun and health but team concept adds a sociability factor. Still explicitly noncompetitive	Highly competitive, elitist, exploitative professional and amateur sports	Less competitive and fewer levels of competition with only a skeletal professional range	Full range of motivations—for fun, play, competition, sociability, sense of accomplishment, to win, for money, for professional titles, etc.

Table 2, continued

Apologetic[b]				
	A. Sports became a form of conspicuous consumption, hailed as an art form in which those of lesser "breeding" had neither the time nor the wealth for participation. B. The medical profession began to advocate mild activity, physical well-being, and *proper eugenics.* White Anglo-Saxon Protestants feared the influx of new immigrant "breeds" and healthy women would be the best guard against the "dilution of blood lines by the 'hordes.' "	Women entered the labor force during WWI which led to a concern for their physical fitness to perform these jobs. Requirements of the roles of worker, citizen, and athlete began to rival those of "womanhood" and motherhood. Commercialization and professionalization increased. Advocates of women's sports employed the competitive norms of American culture to legitimate amateur and professional sports. Athletes encouraged higher levels of competition and insisted on better facilities and more sports.	The "back to the home" philosophy forced the apologetic to focus on the value of sport only for health reasons and to actively denigrate the competitive, "masculine" facets. Most women avoided sports, questioned the femininity of the participants, and perceived no deprivation for the lack of this social experience.	Feminist apologetic which insists that there is nothing intrinsically alien to the female of the species, including sports.

Note. This table has been constructed using the fine historical summary provided by Stephanie Twin in her introduction to *Out of the Bleachers* (1979). The sporting eras are historical approximations, not rigid periods. Their titles attempt to convey the major thrust of women's sporting activities during the period.

a. This period produced two distinct groups of women engaged in sporting activity. Since they existed in different social locations, they have been designated as A and B here.

b. An apologetic (see Del Rey, 1978, pp. 107-112) is an explanation of why "it's OK" for women to be where they are not expected to be, in this case in sports. Apologetics are constructed and promulgated in an effort to reinforce the socially acceptable aspect of the action and to minimize the perceived violation of the current social norm. Thus, the apologetics themselves are indicators of the status of women at a given historical moment.

From an examination of Table 2 a few generalizations about the history of US women in sport emerge:

1. The pattern of participation has been a fluctuating rather than a linear one. There have been times of high activity, such as in the First Female Athletic Era, followed by periods of very low activity. Onward and upward "progress" has not been the norm.

2. Classism pervades the history of sport as it does every institution. "We are all equal," but some of us are more equal than others. Sports were first socially acceptable and defended for upper class women. Only gradually did middle class and working class women acquire more equal access to sports.

3. It is during the periods when women have emerged most completely from the private spheres of home and family that their numbers and their opportunities to engage in sport have increased most dramatically.

4. There is a hierarchy of sport acceptability. There are sports, especially individual sports such as golf, tennis, riding, and swimming, that have a much longer history of societal approval than team sports such as basketball, softball, volleyball, and so on.

5. The social acceptability of sport is predicated on an ideal image of what a woman "should be." Sporting activities which stressed restricted motion, minimal energy, and exercise and sociability found acceptance earlier than did sports which stressed the opposite traits.

6. The motivations of the participants were also legitimate only if they were "feminine." Play, enjoyment, social contact, cooperation, physical fitness, weight control—all were acceptable. Competition, aggressiveness, physical mastery, and "character-building" were defined as masculine and therefore unacceptable.

Women adopted as their own these socially created motives for pursuing sport. Since their private motives were forged according to the terms of a social apologetic, few women experienced stress, conflict, or a sense of contradiction.

The apologetics for women's participation in sport always have been formed in terms which virtually ignore the women themselves and their wishes. If society needs healthy "breeders," medical opinion will determine the appropriate physical activity levels for healthy "breeders." If men, for example, after wartime, need to reassert their masculinity, then women must abandon the male domain of sports. If there is need of symbols of social arrival and mobility, women assume sporting postures that make their social class conspicuous.

It is critical to note that women's greatest access to sport has come precisely during the period of modernization of sport and the nation-state. In large part modern sport has eliminated those structural aspects of sport which most closely would have resembled and approximated the "feminine" experience of the world. Thus, most women entered sport at the very time when the character of the activity itself was more alien to their experiential world as *women*. Equality of opportunity to participate in games that increasingly exclude the traits traditionally accepted as feminine, such as spiritual, general, emotional, nonhierarchical, qualitative, and unrecorded, produces a unique problem for the sporting woman. She seeks entrance into an institution which increasingly negates many characteristics associated with her gender identity. But the "keeper of the keys" expects accommodation on her part. Never questioned is the value of "modernized sport."

In each historical era the apologetic works to assuage the males and the masculine SportsWorld. The explanation of female "nonconformity" is framed in terms that appeal to men's concerns and respond to their needs and interests. Any apology assumes that there is "something wrong" with the action. The history of women's apologetics in sport demonstrates that these apologies are formulated to gain the approval of both sexes. Up until the second wave of feminism, all apologetics were devised and adapted to the social expectations about the status of women. It is only with the "feminist revolution" of the 1960s and 1970s that the role of apologetics has been questioned. It is only within the past generation that female sports participation has been justified by an appeal to *woman's* interests, *her* concerns, *her* values, and *her* self-edification. Representing such a major shift, the specifics of the female athletic revolution of the 60s and 70s now will be outlined.

The Female Athletic Revolution

One of the major attributes of the modernization of sports is the equalization of access to sporting activity. Our brief history of female participation has demonstrated that starting with the 1960s, more women were participating in sports with less need for apologies. Our next task is to recount some of the facts that have solicited the label "revolution" to describe these developments.

It is our dilemma and, we believe the essential dilemma of the women playing sports, to evaluate critically the modernization of sports and to create a feminist approach to them. Creativity, innovation, and consciousness must pervade this revolution or it will be just another aborted revolution. We quote Robert J. Beuter, (1972) who echoes the sentiments of some of the most vocal critics of sports, such as Jack Scott (1971) and Dave Meggysey (1970):

> The *goal* of the new values is not success—accumulation of goods and all that this entails—but rather the development and cultivation of the person,

his (sic) growth in awareness and inner peace. The *means* is not individual striving but group participation and cooperation, communal sharing and mutual engagement with experimental culture forms—all of which lead not to class consciousness but to increasing openness and acceptance of others. The *manner* is not puritanical but sensual: gratification is immediate, suppression and discipline give way to free expression, and optimistic pragmatism is replaced by a utopianism, that, to be sure is somewhat pessimistic and nihilistic. Thus the new values repudiate authority and tradition in favor of protest and social change, and they reject technology with its props of elitism and class consciousness (Beuter, 1972, p. 390, emphasis added).

As women we may ask why women, who have just begun to knock at the door of the sporting world, should be asked to transform the institution. Isn't it asking too much to both gain entrance and to transform the arenas? We believe the vital question is whether entry is worthwhile if there is no transformation. We believe that as "outsiders" women can enter and mimic the SportsWorld constructed by men for men or they can revolutionize it. SportsWorld now stands ready to accept women and to engulf them in the rituals of the modern secular religion. The events of the sixties and seventies prove this. The transforming feminist impetus has yet to be articulated or to be acted on. There may be little time before the "outsider" becomes just another insider, another adamant defender of modern sports. There are many facts of the female sporting explosion which suggest that the outsider status is being lost and very few indications that a feminist perspective has illuminated the changing status of women in sport.

Trends in Female Sport Participation

The current movement by women into sport can be marked symbolically by the running of Kathy Switzer in the Boston Marathon of 1967, by the King vs. Riggs tennis match in 1973, or by the passage of the Higher Education Act of 1972 with its controversial Title IX provision. The decades of the sixties and seventies have witnessed a virtual flood of new sporting opportunities and an enormous growth in the number of women willing to seize them.

In the Educational Setting

- The number of girls in interscholastic sports programs increased by 600% between 1970 and 1979 (Hammer, 1979, p. 6). By 1980 girls represented 33% of all high school athletes (*Women's Sports*, 1980, p. 44).

- A similar pattern emerges from the data on female intercollegiate activity. At the beginning of 1980 women represented 30% of all intercollegiate athletes (Wood, 1980, p. 31).
- Monies spent by educational institutions on female athletic programs are another barometer of changing times. In 1978 an estimated 10,000 women received athletic scholarships from approximately 460 different universities and colleges representing an expenditure of seven million dollars (*Time*, 1978, p. 54). By 1980 over 700 colleges and universities had some form of athletic scholarship for women (*Women's Sports*, 1980, p. 47).
- As late as 1974 only 2% of college/university athletic budgets were allocated to women's sports. By 1977 in seven of the "Big-Ten" schools the average had increased to 7% and monies averaged $259,000 compared to $3,759,714 for men (Hogan, 1977, p. 421).

The Community, Amateur Athletic Setting

Figures on the female athletic boom outside the educational setting are more difficult to acquire. And yet, even a casual observation of community recreational sports indicates that girls and women now are competing for resources and facilities. Tennis courts, golf clubs, ball fields, racket ball courts, and so on are frequented more and more by females. Demands for quality equipment, adequate officiating, longer schedules, more practice times, and better groomed fields and courts, are coming increasingly from women. Let us look at a few facts in this setting:

- One of the most dramatic growth sports is running. Six and a half million women jog (*Women's Sports*, 1980, p. 44). The first all-women's "minimarathon" in New York City in 1972 had 78 entrants. In 1979 the number of official entrants was 5,289 women from 38 states and 5 countries. In the race that day with 5,288 other females, including mother-daughter teams, females ranging in age from 7 to 65, and women in wheelchairs, Grete Waitz of Norway set a world's record for the 10,000 meter event (Moran, 1979, p. 59).
- After nearly a decade of resistance, the Amateur Athletic Union (AAU) in 1972 sanctioned the entrance of women into marathons, the grueling 26 mile 385 yard race.
- In 1975 the AAU approved powerlifting competition for women. Comprised of the squat, the bench press, and the deadlift, the International Women's Powerlifting Championship had 68 women entered in 1978 (Bennett, 1978, p. 1) and in 1979 received national television coverage by NBC (Drexler, 1979, p. 39).
- Writing of the Women's International Bowling Congress, Kurt

Anderson notes that in 1979 4.2 million women belonged to the organization, "which means it's the largest women's sports organization on the planet. If it were a religion, the WIBC would be the fourth largest domination in the country" (K. Anderson, 1979, p. 35).

- Women of all ages have begun seriously to take up the sport of fishing. Ronnie DeLuca currently holds five world fishing records (Dullea, 1978, p. A15).
- By 1974 there were 75 women's crew and rowing associations in the United States with over 2,000 women participating (Peterson, 1974, pp. 54-58).
- Rugby and football teams have been initiated in community sponsored leagues (Hammer, 1979, p. 6).
- The emergence of soccer on the American sporting scene did not leave women untouched. By 1977 there were 88,000 players, 25% of whom were girls (Drezner, 1977, p. 52). By 1980 more than 1 million girls were playing soccer.
- Devotees of speed skating have grown in number since its inclusion in the Olympic Games. Sheila Young, herself an Olympic medalist in speed skating, along with numerous other women have taken up the sport of cycling. They have succeeded in getting women's cycling events included in the 1984 Olympics, and a similar explosion of interest in this sport is likely to follow.
- Thus far we have cited the less traditional developments at the amateur community setting. However, there also has been an enormous growth in the traditional community and religiously sponsored leagues for basketball, softball, and volleyball. In addition the number of girls and women taking up unorganized, individual sports cannot even be estimated. In tennis alone, 6.5 million of the 14 million tennis players in the US are girls and women (*Women's Sports*, 1980, p. 44).

In the Professional Setting

The multitude of developments at the amateur level has been matched, particularly in the seventies, by the expansion of professional sports for women. There are now sports in which women, like their male counterparts, can earn a living, in some cases a very lucrative one.

- Tennis! Who could possibly write about the female sporting revolution without mentioning tennis? Although professional tennis for women has a long history, it was only in 1970 that Gladys Heldman encouraged eight women tennis players to boycott Jack Kramer's

Pacific South West Tournament when he refused to allot any more than 1/12th of the entire prize money for the women participants. Instead, those eight women played a tournament in Houston sponsored by the Philip P. Morris tobacco company, manufacturers of Virginia Slims. Thus began the now well-known Virginia Slims Tour for women, later sponsored by Avon (Struller, 1979, pp. 29-32).

The new women's tour initiated a whole series of changes. By 1975 the women were demanding and receiving prize monies equal to the men at the United States Open. The prize money for the Virginia Slims Circuit amounted to 1.25 million dollars for 12 tournaments in 1978. As late as 1970 Margaret Court captured the Grand Slam of tennis and still earned less than $15,000. By 1979 there were individual tournaments in which the prize money amounted to more than $100,000 (Leavy, 1978, pp. 20-47).

- The other lucrative and popular professional sport for women is golf. As with tennis, the financial successes of the women's golf tour are of relatively recent origins. For years the life of the female pro golfer was far from glamorous. Shuttled from city to city on a weekly basis, most women had to pay to play their game. As late as 1963 Carol Mann, one of the more frequent tournament winners, was contemplating giving up the game because of the financial burden it imposed on her (Weber, 1979, p. 35). Many believe that the LPGA turned the corner when Ray Volpe became the commissioner in 1975; Volpe sold the market potential of the LPGA to big-name commercial sponsors (White, 1979, p. 9).

With more tournaments and greater purses the LPGA began to capture greater public attention. In 1978 four women earned over $100,000 playing golf, and the newest sports phenomenon, Nancy Lopez, led the women with earnings of $189,913 (*Women's Sports*, 1979, p. 23).

- There is a pro women's bowling tour; however, tournaments are sporadic, infrequent, and unorganized, with little money to be made. It is estimated that weekly expenses range around $500 and yet in 1978 no woman won as much as $30,000. By contrast, in that year the top male bowler, Mark Roth, earned $134,500 in winnings and endorsements. It simply is too expensive to be a pro bowler for most women (K. Anderson, 1979, pp. 35-56).

- An abortive attempt to start up a professional basketball league was followed by a successful beginning in 1979. William Byrne, the first president of the Women's Professional Basketball league, promoted an increase in the number of teams and games during the 1980-81 seasons. The US boycott of the Olympics meant that a number of top amateur athletes, such as Carol Blazejowski and Ann Meyers, turned professional and added to the prestige and publicity of the league (O'Connor, 1979, p. 45). Nonetheless, the average salaries for the women were in the $5,000 to $15,000 range while those for the men of the NBA were $143,000 (Williamson, 1979, p. 64).

- In 1977 Judge Helman ruled that Cathy (Cat) Davis could be licensed to box in the state of New York. As of 1978, 13 jurisdictions licensed female bouts (Haitch, 1978, p. L31).
- Robyn Smith, Mary Bacon, Jennifer Rowland, Kathy Kusner, and Karen Rogers are not exactly household names. They along with about 100 other women have entered into another all-male sporting bastion, thoroughbred horse racing. It is only recently that a few female jockeys have begun to receive public recognition as good jockeys and not just as curiosities. The result is that they are receiving better horses to ride (Deford, 1972, pp. 102-106).
- In 1977 the women's professional racketball tour was composed of 16 women including the singles champion Peggy Ateding. The National Racquetball Club sponsored eight tournaments and the national championships between September and June. Once again, the themes of the "lesser sports" are repeated. Prize money does not cover expenses; and there is a vast disparity between the prize money for women and men (Smolkin, 1977, pp. 22-24).
- An event with strong male resistance to women entrants is car racing. Combining the speed and power traditionally associated with men and the vehicle that may be the personification of masculine virility—the car—is it any wonder that resistance to the "girls" has been so adamant? However, women have joined every phase of car racing. In 1977 Shirley Muldowney was the top fuel drag racer, male or female, in the world. Marie-Claude Beaumont was the first woman since World War II to enter the European Le Mans race. Perhaps the most well known woman racer is Janet Guthrie who, in May 1977, was the first woman to qualify and to race in the Indianapolis 500-mile Memorial Day race (Dowling, 1978, pp. 34-63).
- In 1975 a professional circuit for women surfers was initiated. Margo Oberg won the first Hang-Ten Invitational surfing meet and captured $1,500 in prize money (Gleasner, 1977, pp. 11-12).
- Professional volleyball has had a great deal of controversy associated with it. Much of the conflict arises because of a dispute between star Mary Jo Peppler and coach Chuck Erbe. Mary Jo Peppler coached teams to US championships in 1972 and 1973. Although Peppler was widely acclaimed as player and coach, the United States Volleyball Association (USVBA) insisted that she and her team tour Japan and accept Charles Erbe as their coach. Their

record on tour was one win and twenty-four losses. Erbe subsequently informed Peppler that she would not be wanted for the 1976 Olympic volleyball team. Peppler turned professional and joined the International Volleyball Association as one of the two women playing on men's teams. Subsequently, the Association has since gone co-ed, with women playing professional volleyball on mixed teams since 1975 (Lapin, 1976, pp. 20-23).

- In August 1975 a Women's Professional Softball League was formed. The income inequities between professional baseball and women's professional softball are extreme. Salaries for softball players normally ranged form $1,000 to $3,000 per season. For their "high salaries" the women were contractually bound to attend "Meet the Fans" ceremonies, to perform at promotional exhibitions, and to run softball clinics (Hogan, 1976, pp. 39-41). The women played an average of 140 games per year with countless double-headers and traveled by bus from small town to small town. Spectator interest, media coverage, and playing facilities were all poor. As a result, in 1979 the Women's Professional Softball League suspended the season. Efforts currently are underway to achieve corporate sponsorship so that the League can resume play. Prospects, however, do not look promising.

The Female Athletic Revolution—Feminist Dilemmas

This short enumeration of the developments in women's sports in the 60s and 70s demonstrates the veritable explosion that the American sporting scene has witnessed. The Women's Sports Foundation estimates that 36 million women engage in some form of exercise three or more times each week (Sloan, 1978, p. 4). Surveys conducted by Gallup confirm the changing attitudes and habits of the American public. In a survey conducted in May 1975, 59% of those polled agreed that girls should be permitted to participate in noncontact sports on the same teams as boys, and 88% agreed that "girls should have equal financial support for their athletic activities as boys." Other indications of participatory expansion are provided in an October 1977 survey in which respondents were asked if they did anything regularly to keep themselves physically fit: 47% of the national sample (50% of the men and 45% of the women) answered yes, representing a two-fold increase over the 1961 figure of 24%. We suspect that a greater proportion of this twofold increase was due to the heightened participation of women (Gallup, 1978, p. 76).

Our previous discussion has detailed some changes in the status, number, settings, sporting events, and levels of participation by women. What is yet to be established is how radical these changes are. More specifically, have the 60s and 70s seen the establishment of a feminist approach to sport, and if so, into which feminist rubric (liberal, Marxist, socialist, radical) do the changes fit?

We believe the answer to this question is that the changes most closely approximate the liberal feminist model. For the most part the liberal position has simply sought the inclusion of women—the equal opportunity approach. However, there are even severe limits to the success of this minimal feminist demand. The continued inequities in budgets, resources, salaries, status, etc. attest to this evaluation. Furthermore, several general trends cast doubt on the transforming potential that the inclusion of women has had or can have on the institution of sport. Indeed, most developments seem to portend the co-option of the female outsider into the "one of the boys syndrome" so frequently associated with sports. Let us briefly look at some reasons why this judgment of liberal feminism and co-option is the most appropriate label for the female athletic revolution.

In the educational setting, the changes are minimal and conducive to the maintenance of the status quo. Almost without exception, Title IX has been viewed only as an attempt to get equality of opportunity. Equal monies, equal facilities, equal schedules, equal salaries, and equal programs are sought—and equal abuses are accepted. Increased monies go into traditionally accepted sports. Emphasis on elite varsity athletics overshadows intramural, nonelite, high-participatory efforts. The few outstanding female athletes at each educational level achieve "equal opportunity" while the remainder of the girls/women still await equality. Chapter 6 will elaborate more fully on how the inclusion of females at all educational levels has done little to change either the institution of sport or the participants themselves.

Girls and women continue to receive social acceptance for individual sports more readily than for team contests. Social approval for sports such as tennis, golf, and gymnastics is high. As noncontact individual sports, they offer the dual "benefits" of continued segregration of the female athlete from teammates and the continued confirmation of the participant's "femininity."

The value and advantages of team sport for human bonding (Tiger, 1970, p. 98) are easy to extrapolate. Men who participate in team sports are more likely to learn through sports, as they do from their other important positions such as worker and citizen, the skills, attitudes, and abilities necessary for teamwork, cooperation, and group activity. By contrast, women engage in individual, nonteam, noncontact sports. As with the most accepted female roles of wife and mother, cooperation, adult contact with members of her own sex, cohesion, teamwork and the resulting skills are not developed, encouraged, or socially approved. Sport is another segment of life which pits women against women and certifies that the female-to-male bond overrides and outweighs any bond between women. The joy men experience in a team victory or the anguish they share in a team defeat, is unknown to the female who plays only individual sports (Hennig and Jardim, 1977, pp. 45-47).

Individual, noncontact sports such as gymnastics, tennis, ice skating, golf, etc. have the added "advantage" of remaining a vehicle which fulfills a traditional feminine function—the glamor function (Bernard, 1971, p. 81). The concern for attire and appearance often becomes more significant to the athlete and the audience than what she does. How do I look? Does my designer tennis dress enhance my sex appeal? Do the accessories to my golf outfit match? Men, without this glamor function to perform, can arrange their appearance and clothing mainly in terms of what is functional for the sporting activity itself. The popularity of noncontact sports is due in part to the demand for women to retain their "need to primp" and their fear of "masculinizing" their appearance. Women can play golf and tennis and still be attractively dressed, neatly groomed, and sexually available. In short, women can play these sports and still be considered "feminine."

Almost without exception women wish to emulate men's professional sports activity. Comparisons are made in terms of salaries and monies received. Equality is sought. Little attention is paid to how the game might be altered to emphasize values other than those associated with SportsWorld. The masculine approach and emphases are accepted. Women professionals fall into the same questionable practices as their male counterparts. The short experience of professional softball afforded some of the best examples of the imitation of the negative features of men's baseball. There were frequent franchise changes; players were bound by reserve clauses; players began to form unions to battle management (DeCosta, 1977, pp. 38-58); major contract violations occurred (Tyson, 1977, pp. 48-52). The US government even sent the World Champion Connecticut Falcons as goodwill ambassadors to the People's Republic of China.

Athletic women are often more likely to gain both public acclaim and monetary rewards as a result of nonathletic features. Promotional endorsements, which may constitute the greater portion of a professional athlete's earnings, are garnered for nonathletic reasons. It is a "public relations man's delight" to have a genuine winner like Chris Evert Lloyd, but that does not prevent promoters from touting "good looking" women like Laura Baugh even before they have established themselves as consistent winners. The media focus on women athletes for non-athletic reasons. As jockeys, Robyn Smith's attractiveness and mystery and Mary Bacon's "red-neck" anti-feminist views appeal to the media more than their ability to handle a horse coming down the stretch (McCabe, 1977, p. 15). Janet Guthrie receives attention because a male driver—Unser—

says no woman should be allowed to drive (Dowling, 1978, pp. 34-63). Mary Jo Peppler gained more fame from winning the Women's Superstar Competition, the media-initiated promotional gimmick, and for her ongoing dispute with Chuck Erbe than for her ability as a volleyball player (Jordan, 1975, pp. 49-57). Further examples could be provided but the thrust remains the same. Women gain attention for being good looking, feminine, well-dressed, ladylike, petite, and controversial rather than for their athletic achievements.

Societal inequities are repeated in the realm of women's sport. Poor women, minority women, fat women, handicapped women, and lesbian women never have the same chances to compete or to excel as do the white "all-American middle class" female superstars, such as Chris Evert Lloyd, Peggy Fleming, Dorothy Hammil, Mickey King, Cathy Rigby, and Laura Baugh.

What makes these women marketable is too often not their ability in sport but a femininity, a "softness," a "ladylikeness" that says "yes, you can compete seriously in sports and still be a lady or be sexy." Marketability in these cases has meant that sponsorship comes from cosmetic firms (Avon, Helene Curtis), from makers of products specifically aimed at women (Colgate-Palmolive household goods), from cigarette firms that deliberately utilize a feminist theme (Virginia Slims—"You've come a long way, baby"), and from companies producing sports equipment used by these athletes. It is precisely when men like Ray Volpe and women like Gladys Heldman could prove that the general public would watch women play these sports, then buy the products being endorsed, that female athletes' incomes began to more closely approximate men's.

Certain sports are stigmatized by the people participating in them. Social suspicion of the female athlete is increased when the female is black, from a lower class, lesbian, or necessarily must develop characteristics that are defined as "masculine," such as strength. Thus, black women in track events; strong, muscular women in field events; lesbian women in team sports like softball and basketball, all face multiple problems of acceptance.

Social approval is retained for sports in which the participants are all white, from higher social classes, and for whom there are no doubts about their sexual preference. Of all the stigmas noted, that of sexual preference has a special significance for sporting women. The issue of lesbianism remains a dormant but ever-present and undiscussed topic. Even the disclosure of Billy Jean King's relationship with Carolyn Barnett has not produced an open and candid look at this issue. The myth of masculinization of athletic women has always been a societal concern. Mere participation in sport can cast a woman's sexual preference into question, just as participation in ballet can for men. What makes this issue particularly problematic is that the lesbian athlete is rarely a feminist. Thus, she is taught and encouraged to accept the social definition of her preference as deviant. She seeks merely to hide it, to keep it private, and to avoid the sanctions that would be forthcoming if her sexual orientation were uncovered. No greater testimony to this strategy and attitude toward lesbianism among athletes need be cited than that of Billy Jean King.

Seemingly, the lesbian issue must be addressed by every female athlete—even those in sports that are now socially accepted. In fact, there have been deliberate efforts made by the touring tennis and golf professionals to diminish and keep low-keyed any rumor of lesbianism among their ranks. Indeed, Betty Hicks (1979, p. 42) contends that professional golf was slower to capture popularity than tennis because it was tinged with the "stigma" of lesbianism. Undoubtedly, team sports will encounter even greater resistance.

Attempts to sexually integrate sports are far more successful precisely when women *cannot* compete on a par with men. For example, female auto racers and jockies have a more difficult time receiving backing because their ability to "win" is often more a function of the instrument (the car or horse) than the human participant. Bowling is another instance of a sport where integration of the tours has been resisted because there *are* women like Barbara Thorberg whose 217 average in 1978 would have ranked her third among all pro bowlers, male or female (K. Anderson, 1979, pp. 35-56). By contrast, volleyball was relatively easy to sexually integrate because the structure of the co-ed game always kept women at a disadvantage. Professional volleyball rules require that one women be on the court at all times, but women are only on the back line, do not spike (the power aspect of the sport), and play with nets set at the men's internationally established height which is six inches higher than the women's (Lapin, 1976, pp. 20-23). There are also male bastions of sport which will resist the inclusion of women merely for historical and symbolic reasons. Women today can run marathons in times that would have won medals in the 1948 Olympics, but due to the connection of this distance with purely male symbols—sports, the Olympics, war, and even citizenship—attempts to include this distance in internationally sanctioned meets continually failed (Kuscik, 1976, pp. 28-31). Not until 1984 will the event be added to the women's Olympic roster.

Major bureaucratic positions within women's sports are assumed by men. Commissioners of leagues, presidents of franchises, executives, managers, and even coaches of teams are frequently men. They get the acclaim for the success of the sport. The credit for the monetary gains of the LPGA goes to Ray Volpe; successful volleyball programs are turned over to men like Chuck Erbe. Thus, opportunities for women to assume positions of authority and power even within women's athletics are curtailed.

Women at all levels of sports, and especially in professional sports, now answer to the demands of bureaucracies. Spectators, corporate sponsors, media promoters, and technology dictate the shape of their games. The athlete's own personal desires for enjoyment and self-actualization are too often eliminated.

There is a noticeable absence of a feminist perspective among sporting women as well as an overwhelming silence among most feminists regarding sports. The exceptions to this pattern are the athlete who wants equal rights in sports and the liberal feminists who include sport as an afterthought in their pursuit of social equality. Thus, the developments of the 60s and 70s have confirmed a liberal feminist approach to sports. This framework will have minimal impact on both sports and women. Questions of class, race, age, economic status, sexual preference, and other factors which inform Marxist, socialist and radical feminist frameworks are neither addressed nor pursued.

The liberal aim is to be "one of the boys" and to gain equal access to an institution which we believe is in need of radical change. Unless we extend our critical analysis beyond this liberal perspective, women's sports will fall victim to the same "modernizing" trends that characterize men's sporting institutions within the modern nation-state.

Chapter 3/
The Psychological Dimensions of Female Athletic Participation
by Susan Birrell

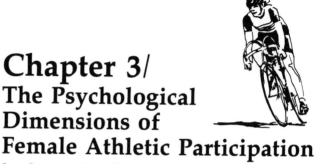

Sport remains highly associated with the so-called "masculine" element of our culture, and the female in sport is still considered a woman in a man's territory. Thus the female athlete is a special case in two senses. Because of her sport interests, she is considered a special kind of female; because she is female she is considered a special kind of athlete. Awareness of her exceptional status surely colors the female athlete's approach to sport and makes her sport experience qualitatively different from that of the male athlete. The female athlete's special status raises significant questions about the psychological dimensions of her sport involvement. In this chapter these psychological dimensions are explored with reference to research in the fields of psychology, psychology of women, and psychology of sport.

The review is structured in terms of two major questions:

Appreciation is extended to Linda Yanney and Pat Krug for their help in the preparation of this manuscript.

1. What are the psychological *determinants* of sport involvement for females?
2. What are the psychological *consequences* of sport involvement for females?

Unfortunately, the research related to these two general questions is fragmentary, uneven, and only mildly encouraging. Although much energy has been directed to both topics, particularly the first, little creative research has been attempted or accomplished. In terms of their potential significance, some issues have received too much attention, while others are only beginning to be explored. In short, the area remains descriptively rich but theoretically barren. Nevertheless, the research that does exist furnishes some preliminary understanding of the psychological dimensions of the female athlete.

Generally, psychologists seek to explain behavior by focusing on the development and display of those general characteristics—personality traits, motives, styles of interaction—that make each individual unique. In order to understand patterns of sport involvement, psychologists attempt to isolate those particular characteristics suspected of influencing behavior in sport. Psychological factors are, of course, tempered by an awareness of cultural forces, and nowhere is this more clearly seen than in the case of the female athlete. While the bulk of this book stresses cultural or sociological concerns, this chapter searches for explanations of sex differences in rates and styles of sport involvement by using psychological reference points.

Psychological Determinants of Female Sport Participation

Women's rates of involvement in sport have always lagged behind men's.[1] A partial explanation of this difference can be found in cultural constraints on female sport involvement. Specifically, such constraints center around the notion that the two roles the female athlete seeks to fill—female and athlete—are incongruous. The result of this cultural bias can take many forms, from actively discouraging a girl or woman from becoming involved in sport to subtly socializing her to the point where she feels guilty or embarrassed about wanting to play. Although cultural factors can never be ignored, in this discussion attention is directed to the psychological factors which may influence a female in her decision to become involved in sport.

Psychobiological Sex Differences

The tendency to view males and females as vastly different creatures is grounded in the undeniable fact that the two sexes differ biologically. But the existence of *biological* differences between the sexes by no means proves that *inherent psychological* differences also exist, although that false assumption has profoundly affected the way we deal with women and men in our society.

It is undeniable that at some point in their lives males and females in most societies come to behave differently from one another. Differences in behavior patterns are noted at an early age, and these differences tend to become more pronounced and more stable as the individual grows older. The essential question, however, is this: are the different behavioral patterns of males and females due to inherent sex-linked psychological differences, or are they due to differences in social learning experiences, i.e., social pressures to conform to preconceived ideas about how males and females should act? Evidence supports the latter explanation.

A child is assigned to a biological sex category at the moment of birth by reference to her or his external genitalia. In a few exceptional cases where biological sex has been improperly interpreted, individuals have been incorrectly assigned to a sex category, i.e., biological males are falsely categorized as females and thus raised as girls (or vice versa).[2] When these individuals reach adolescence, they discover their biological sex is inconsistent with their sex assignment and thus the sex–based social treatment they have received. Ongoing research at Johns Hopkins University (Money & Erhardt, 1972) deals directly with the social consequences of such mistaken sex identity. In most cases they have found that the social treatment individuals have received based on their presumed sex identity is a more important factor in determining psychological development than is their real sex identity.

Based on those and similar findings my position is that while biological or physiological sex differences represent raw materials which may influence behavior, the most important determinant of psychological differences between the sexes is the social learning that takes place in the hundreds of interactions in which individuals participate every day. The cumulative experience of these social situations has a major effect upon the development of individual behavior and attitudes. However, some intriguing research has brought the issue of psychobiological origins of sex differences into sharper focus in recent years, and this issue deserves our attention.

The logical place to begin our investigation is with the landmark review of research on the psychology of sex differences published by Eleanor Maccoby and Carol Jacklin in 1974. Their book is the cornerstone on which most subsequent research reviews are founded. It remains a highly respected though not infallible source.

Probably the most notable conclusion reached by Maccoby and Jacklin is that most psychological sex differences are assumed or perceived and not real. In other words, many commonly held beliefs pertaining to sex differences in anxiety, competitiveness, dominance, and compliance, among others, are unsubstantiated in controlled studies. They are cultural myths which continue to be perpetuated, without basis, merely because we assume they are true.

Maccoby and Jacklin, however, do cite four sex differences which they feel have been well substantiated by research. Those four sex differences are:

1. Females have greater verbal ability than males.
2. Males have greater visual spatial ability than females.
3. Males have greater mathematical ability than females.
4. Males are more aggressive than females.

Maccoby and Jacklin's conclusion that these four differences exist from birth should arouse our theoretical curiosity. What is the source of these allegedly inherent sex differences?

According to dramatic and controversial research undertaken in the last few years, sex differences in verbal, visual spatial, and mathematical ability may all be attributable to sex differences in the structure of the brain.[3]

Sex differences in aggression are sometimes explained with reference to sex hormones which are differentially distributed between the sexes before birth; indeed, to some extent Maccoby and Jacklin themselves subscribe to this explanation (1974, p. 243).

Thus, the current theories used to explain the four sex differences considered to be innate by Maccoby and Jacklin offer *psychobiological* explanations of sex differences in behavior. Two of the sex differences under consideration may influence involvement in sport, i.e., sex differences in visual spatial ability and sex differences in aggression; so we turn now to a review of the theories which seek to account for those differences.

Brain structure and perception. Even though the question of sex differences in brain structure is basically a biological one, theoretical assumptions about and pragmatic interpretations of the research serve as a clear reminder that scientific research does not exist in a cultural vacuum. For example, for many years a debate raged over whether males or females had larger brains. The argument was centered on the assumption that the sex which had the larger brain could be considered intellectually superior. The debate was never resolved. But the significance of the debate is not rooted in its ultimate scientific resolution but in the decidedly unscientific interpretation of the data. Whichever part of the brain was thought at the time to be the intellectual center was invariably found by scientists to be larger in males than females. Later, when research indicated that another part of the brain was the intellectual center, it was common for researchers to reverse their previous "findings" (Shields, 1975). Obviously, the relative sizes of portions of male and female brains did not change; rather, the acceptable interpretation of the data did. Clearly, unconscious stereotypes about the sexes can color even "scientific" research.

Although debates about the size of the brain no longer are common, recent developments in understanding the structure and functions of the brain have again made this area of research and its implications a matter of great controversy. Many proponents of gender equality are afraid that acknowledging a sex difference in brain structure will destroy any hope for equal treatment of the sexes (see e.g., Gornick, 1982). Unfortunately, this sort of fear is justified; undoubtedly some will use the research as a simplistic and sexist justification for excluding girls or boys from participation in certain activities (like sport) because "everyone knows that women (or men) are no good at that sort of thing."

The fear that acknowledging biological differences between social categories will result in a legitimation for discrimination has a precedent in the debate created by Jensen's (1969) assertion that blacks are inherently lower in IQ than whites. Many proponents of racial equality feared that Jensen's conclusions would be used as "proof" that blacks are genetically inferior to whites and thus do not deserve the efforts made to grant them equal social and economic opportunities.

Frightening as this scenario is, our reaction to it need not be defensive in nature. Rather than ignoring or attempting to suppress or dismiss unpopular research findings, we must examine them with professional care. Actually, the case for the existence of psychobiological sex differences is quite weak. Even if we should find that psychobiological sex differences do exist, we should realize that those differences are merely differences in the assignment of raw materials. The shape these materials come to have is the result of social processes which rest in the hands of the individual and those with whom she or he interacts. Once again we return to the thesis that *social factors*, not biological factors, are the most important influences on human behavior. With this in mind, perhaps we can review the research on brain differences more dispassionately.

The human brain is composed of two assymetric hemispheres which tend to be specialized, with certain skills more developed in one side than the other. Generally speaking, the left cerebral hemisphere handles *verbal skills* while the right cerebral hemisphere handles *spatial functions*, including complex visual spatial functions (Kimura & Durnford, 1974), tactile spatial ability (Flanery & Balling, 1979), depth perception (Levy, 1974), holistic cognitive processing (Witelson, 1976), pattern recognition (Levy, 1974), musical tasks (Geschwind, 1974), and emotional responses (Geschwind, 1974). It has long been believed that the left hemisphere of females generally is more developed than that of most males, a fact which explains the greater verbal ability of most females. Many males, on the other hand, appear to possess a more developed right hemisphere, explaining their relatively better performances on spatial and mathematical problems.

However, recent research elaborates this pattern. Jeannette McGlone (cited in Goleman, 1978) has found that the brains of many women are less specialized than many men's, i.e., women appear to have verbal and spatial abilities present in both hemispheres.[4] According to Sandra Witelson (1976), these differences may have an effect upon the performance of skills calling for the coordination of complex tasks. She proposes that it may be easier for individuals with less hemispheric dominance (often women) to perform tasks which combine verbal skills with spatial skills (such as reading). Those individuals who demonstrate more hemispheric specialization (often men) may excel in tasks which require doing two separate and parallel cognitive tasks at the same time (such as talking while running a machine).

While current research strongly suggests that sex differences in brain structure do exist, our understanding of that phenomenon is far from complete. Moreover, we need to remember several things. First, the sex differences that seem to exist are gross differences. Even at this biological level, apparent differences between the sexes are better categorized as general tendencies rather than absolute differences. For example, boys *tend* to be better at spatial tasks, while girls *tend* to be better at verbal tasks. Second, we remain uncertain about the causes of the differences in these skills that are manifested in later life (i.e., the sex differences in SAT scores) that is, how much is due to psychobiological predispositions and how much is due to differential social reinforcement. It is quite likely that sensitive parents and teachers recognize their childrens' innate talents and cater to the further development of those talents through differential opportunities, training, expectations, and rewards. Finally, because research in this area is rapidly growing and changing, current theories are not thoroughly tested and remain at the hypothetical stage.

Thus if we were to ask how these sex differences might affect sport involvement, we must remember the difficulties and implications of separating biological differences from their social context, and we must be fully aware of the speculative nature of that exercise. For instance, if we were to predict that girls are at a disadvantage in sport situations which require skills in analyzing spatial information (basketball, softball, tennis, and field hockey are a few examples) we must remind ourselves that in fact girls do excel in such sports.

In a related vein, the skills required of sport announcers typically feature the ability to analyze complex spatial patterns while keeping up an intelligible line of verbal commentary. Witelson's (1976) research indicates that this role would most likely be filled by those whose brain hemispheres are more specialized (most males), and that is the case. On the other hand, women's supposed superior ability in verbal skills should give them an advantage in sportswriting. The fact that this "innate" advantage is not reflected by the presence of a larger number of female sportswriters indicates once again that regardless of psychobiological "advantages," many important social patterns are determined by access to opportunities.

Sex differences in aggression. Because sport is often thought of as an aggressive activity, an understanding of the phenomenon of aggressive behavior is of particular concern to those interested in understanding behavior in sport settings. Specifically the question is whether aggressive behavior in sport is sex–linked. The popular belief appears to follow this pattern: sport is an inherently aggressive activity; boys are inherently more aggressive than girls; therefore, it is only natural that boys are drawn to sport because it suits their temperament. But a closer look at the situation reveals that this facile argument is not as sensible as it first appears. The argument rests upon two assumptions: the natural aggressiveness of sport and sex differences in aggression.

By nature, sport is a physical, competitive activity, often involving physical contact and the application of physical force to an object or opponent. Thus sport contains several qualities or components of behavior often mistakenly labeled as aggression. Researchers distinguish between aggression and related behaviors such as competitiveness, assertiveness, dominance, and activity level. Aggression is defined as behavior with intent to harm another (Berkowicz, 1964; Dollard, Miller, Doob, Mower, & Sears, 1939). By definition, then, sport that is properly played is not aggressive because the participants do not intend to harm their opponents.

However, common sense, argues that some sort of "controlled aggression" is an inherent and legal part of sport. To handle this dilemma, sport psychologists distinguish between reactive aggression and instrumental aggression (Martens, 1975a). *Reactive aggression* is aggression in the classic sense: behavior with intent to harm; and there is no place for reactive aggression in sport. *Instrumental aggression* is a byproduct of working toward non-aggressive goals; examples include the incidental contact involved in defending a goal line or scoring a basket.

While drawing this distinction solves the definitional dilemma on a theoretical level, it creates a new problem at the empirical or operational level: how do we distinguish between the two? A hard check to drive an opponent away from the hockey puck may constitute legal, instrumental aggression; throwing down hockey gloves and squaring off for a fist fight is clearly an act of reactive aggression. Thus, instrumental aggression, if it is not kept in control by players and referees, can escalate to reactive aggression, and it is this potential for the display of reactive aggression that probably earns sport its reputation as an aggressive activity. For the injured player, the distinction between reactive and instrumental aggression may seem truly academic, but for the sport psychologist the inability to assess intent and thus draw such distinctions poses a serious methodological problem for observational research on interpersonal aggression in sport. For the purposes of this discussion, the aggression in sport is not "true," that is, intentionally harmful aggression, but instrumental aggression, a competitive and assertive behavior style.

In contrast to women's sports, sports for men seem structured to allow for more physical contact, interpersonal injury, fighting, and other behaviors related to aggressive behavior. In the minds of many, sport merely encapsulates behavior typical of society in general. The sex differences in aggression in sport, therefore, would seem to mirror our assumptions about sex differences in aggression in other social situations as well. Before making this assumption, however, one important distinction should be emphasized. Aggression in sport is not truly comparable to aggression in other social settings, because it is both legal and normative behavior, that is, it is an acceptable and expected feature of that particular social situation. In this instance, then, it is unwise to generalize *from* sport; a more productive strategy is to examine patterns of differences between the sexes and relate those general patterns to the specific situation of sport.

Sex differences in aggression appear to be well documented in the real world, although the magnitude of those differences is probably greatly exaggerated. For example, cross-cultural studies consistently reveal that males in most cultures are more aggressive than females (Maccoby & Jacklin, 1974), but considerable variability exists in the extent of these differences (Montagu, 1974; Tieger, 1980). Moreover, although crime statistics consistently demonstrate that most violent crimes are committed by men (e.g., Adler, 1981), American women are more violent than the common stereotype suggests.[5]

With some qualifications, then, it does appear that sex differences in aggression do exist in the real world. But researchers often prefer to rely on the results of controlled experimental studies to inform them of the dynamics of such behaviors. So a brief review of the empirical evidence pertaining to sex differences in aggressive behavior is in order.

Maccoby and Jacklin's (1974) conclusion that sex differences not only exist but are perhaps biologically based has recently been challenged by some provocative reviews (Frodi, Macauley, & Thome, 1977; Tieger, 1980; see also the rejoinder by Maccoby & Jacklin, 1980). In their review of the experimental research on aggressive behavior in adults, Ann Frodi and her colleagues (1977) drew some interesting and surprising conclusions. Males were more aggressive only under certain circumstances.[6] In general, the review indicates that the tendency to display aggressive behavior is related to the individuals' interpretation of the situation and her or his judgment regarding the appropriateness of aggression as a response. These interpretational patterns generally differ by sex.

This pattern is confirmed in several interesting ways in the research and is consistent with the observation that aggression is more likely to be considered gender-appropriate behavior for boys than for girls. For example, Bandura's (1965) work has shown that although females *learn* aggressive responses to the same extent as males, they do not *display* such responses as readily as males. Females will act aggressively "only if they see the situation as permitting females to behave aggressively, or if they are in some way acting anonymously" (Frodi et al., 1977, p. 647).

Another example of this pattern is the finding that although males demonstrate more aggression than females in *unprovoked* situations, there are no sex differences in aggressive behavior in *provoked* situations. This finding strongly suggests that while females choose not to act aggressively in neutral situations, they interpret aggression as an appropriate and justifiable response to provocation.

Other factors that apparently mediate a female's decision to act aggressively include her tendency not to perceive aggression in ambiguous situations, her greater anxiety after aggression, and her greater susceptibility to feelings of guilt over aggressive behavior. Frodi et al. (1977) conclude that

> women's aggressive behavior must often be moderated by arousal of aggression anxiety over the propriety of such behavior. It seems likely that a significant proportion of variation in aggression between (and probably within) the sexes can be accounted for by guilt or anxiety avoidance or arousal. . .sex differences seldom appear when aggression is allowable behavior for women. This suggests that women's proneness to aggression anxiety or guilt may, in fact, be inhibiting aggressive tendencies in many situations in which sex differences are found. (p. 645)

Frodi et al. (1977) also reveal that sex differences in modes of aggressive response are not as pronounced as originally believed: little support could be found for the conclusion that men demonstrate more overt physical aggression while women demonstrate more indirect or displaced aggression. Finally, they report that sex differences in aggressive behavior are most pronounced in studies which utilize self-report measures. In such studies men are more likely than women to acknowledge overt physical aggressive behavior (Frodi et al., 1977). Once again, the pattern suggests the existence of a social desirability effect probably attributable to gender role prescriptions. In summary, a thorough review of empirical research on sex differences in aggression among adults shows a much less marked difference than social stereotypes would lead us to expect.

Since the review by Frodi et al. (1977) focuses upon adult samples, one should wonder what research reveals about sex differences in aggression among samples of children. A review of the research by Shaklee (1982) leads to the conclusion that sex differences do exist in aggressive behavior among children. Maccoby and Jacklin's (1974) earlier review also reached this conclusion. However, the research on aggression in children is compromised by some methodological problems (cf., Tieger, 1980). The operationalization of aggression, for example, is not consistent with the theoretical definition of aggression as intentionally harmful behavior. For example, in one study cited by Shaklee, aggression is equated with a competitive move in a game situation.[7] Studies that rely on observational methods introduce the possibility of observer bias: ambiguous behaviors may be labeled as aggressive if displayed by boys but not so labeled if displayed by girls. Moreover, some sex differentiated behaviors are often mislabeled as aggression, for instance, rough and tumble play, activity level, and playing with toys like guns and soldiers, that imply aggression (Shaklee, 1982; Tieger, 1980).

In conclusion, some doubt exists concerning the hardiness of reported sex differences in aggression among children. This is a topic of pivotal importance, for as Tieger (1980) points out, the case for a biological basis for sex differences in aggression rests upon the ability of researchers to demonstrate that these differences exist from birth and cannot be accounted for by social learning experiences.

Theoretical bases of aggression: hormones vs. social learning. Although many theories of the causes of aggressive behavior exist, they can be divided roughly into two categories: those theories which stress biological factors and those which stress social factors. Examples of the former include Freud's Thanatos principle of aggression as self-destructive behavior; ethological theories of Ardry (1966), Lorenz (1966), and Storr (1968);[8] and differences in sex-related hormones.[9] Examples of social theories include Dollard's (1939) frustration–aggression hypothesis and social learning theory (Bandura, 1973). Of these various theories, two are most appropriate to this discussion of sex differences in aggression: sex-related hormones and social learning theory.

All males and females produce both "male" hormones (androgens, including testosterone) and "female" hormones (estrogen and progesterone), but the ratios between these hormones differ by sex: males normally secrete more androgens than estrogens. Some research has linked levels of aggression to hormones. Specifically, it has been demonstrated that when laboratory animals are injected with testosterone, an androgen or "male" hormone, aggressive behavior can be produced. This occurs in both male and female animals. This link between testosterone and the display of aggressive behavior in animals has been taken as evidence that the human male's tendency toward more aggressive behavior may be related to his relatively higher ratio of androgens to estrogens.

However, the credibility of the hormonal explanation of sex differences in aggression relies upon our willingness to generalize about human behavior from the research on rats and monkeys. Tieger (1980) voices strong and cogent reservations about the acceptability of such generalizations. Unfortunately, little research on human subjects is available for analysis because ethical considerations forbid the manipulation of hormonal balances in human subjects. But one major exception to this void is the research of Money and his colleagues (cf., Money & Erhardt, 1972) on individuals with hermaphroditic syndromes induced by hormonal imbalance. According to Money and Erhardt, girls with these hormonal anomalies, i.e., girls who have such an excessively high level of male hormones that their genitals were male appearing, were not more aggressive than hormonally normal girls. According to Money and Erhardt, "This lack of predisposition to aggressive attack suggests that aggressiveness, per se, is the wrong variable on which to expect gender-dimorphic behavior, despite popular stereotypes to the contrary" (1972, p. 99).

Thus, theories of hormonal differences are not supported by the research on human subjects. A more convincing array of studies can be found in support of the social learning theory. Social learning theory focuses on aggression as a learned behavior and attends to the processes through which aggressive responses are learned. These include socialization through primary and secondary agents (such as parents and the media), modeling and imitative behavior, and differential reinforcement.

Social learning theory would predict that any individual who is exposed to aggressive models and who is positively reinforced for demonstrating those aggressive behaviors will probably act aggressively (cf., Bandura, 1965). Therefore, if boys as a group are exposed to more aggressive models and reinforced for aggressive behaviors to a greater extent than are girls, more boys than girls would be expected to act aggressively. This explanation certainly fits the patterns of behavior reported in the reviews cited above, specifically, the tendency for females to display aggression only in situations which make aggressive behavior an acceptable and legitimate situational response for females. Moreover, females are inhibited from aggressive behavior by guilt and anxiety. The evidence seems clearly to demonstrate that differences in aggressive behavior are attributable to differences in gender role socialization practices, which differentially reinforce aggressive behavior for females and males. Females have learned their lessons well: not only do they manifest less aggressive behaviors than males in neutral or unprovoked settings, they have internalized the proper emotions of social control—guilt and anxiety. At present, then, it would seem most productive to continue research informed by the social learning theory of aggression.

The implications of this research have direct relevance to sport, whose researchers and theorists should continue to investigate the elements of social learning that either introduce or perpetuate aggressive behavior in sport. Coaches and elite or star athletes have the potential to become models of particular types of behaviors; and coaches, parents, fans, and teammates have the potential to reinforce certain behaviors, thereby increasing the chances that particular behaviors will be learned and displayed.

In conclusion, although males and females *may* differ on inherent levels of aggression, the more important area for study is the investigation of the social conditions under which "appropriate" responses to aggressive feelings are learned. How much overt aggressive behavior is "good" is a philosophical question best debated elsewhere. However, if women decide that overt aggression is good whether in social life or in sport, then there is no reason why women cannot learn to express their aggressive tendencies in more overt ways, i.e., by imitating the traditionally male model of aggressive behavior. On the other hand, if women decide that overt aggression is bad and that the male-dominated model of sport puts too much emphasis on it, they can reject the male model, arguing that traditionally female ways of dealing with aggression are superior to traditionally male responses. I feel that it is important to stress the point that blind imitation of the male model will not necessarily promote equality. Instead, the desire to beat men at their own game, to prove that women can be just like (i.e., as "good" as) men reflects an admission of fundamental inferiority. It implies that women have not yet grasped the possibility that female ways may be superior to male ways, not only for girls and women but for all human beings.[10] With careful reflection, an enlightened approach to understanding psychobiological sex differences can be achieved.

Personality Traits of Female Athletes

Whenever the topic of psychological dimensions of sport involvement is raised, most people anticipate that the discussion will focus upon personality traits of athletes. Are the personalities of athletes different from those of non-athletes? Are there specific sport "types"? These are the same questions many sport psychologists have tried to answer through research using personality trait inventories. Unfortunately, as fascinating as the questions are, they remain unanswered, for the massive amounts of research attention spent in collecting and analyzing data of this nature have failed to establish any consistent patterns. My review of the research leads to one of two conclusions: either no differences in personality traits exist between groups (i.e., between athletes and non-athletes; between gymnasts and football players), or sport psychologists have failed to discover the differences which do exist because their approach to this topic has been either theoretically or methodologically inappropriate. Before any conclusions can be reached regarding the personality traits of female athletes, a critical review of the research tradition seems in order.

Personality research. The term "personality" refers to the notion that every individual has a unique set of characteristics which differentiates her or him from every other individual. The study of personality traditionally has focused upon personality *traits*, which are conceived as enduring and stable predispositions that account for the consistent patterns of individual behavior. Such traits might include autonomy, extroversion, dominance, intelligence, nurturance, and deference. The trait approach to the study of personality is based upon several premises: that there are a number of discrete traits that can be isolated and labeled, that the amount or level of each trait *differs* by individual, and that these levels can be measured.

After many years in which personality inventories have been used extensively by sport psychologists, a major debate has emerged over the validity of this line of research. Some researchers remain staunch supporters of the trait approach (e.g., Kane, 1978; Morgan, 1978, 1980; Ogilvie, 1967, 1970; Ogilvie & Tutko, 1966; Williams, 1978), but others have persuasively argued that trait research is too seriously flawed to be acceptable (e.g., Carron, 1975; Kroll, 1976a, 1976b; Martens, 1975a, 1975b; Rushall, 1968a; Singer, Harris, Knoll, Martens, & Sechrese, 1977; Smith, 1970). In light of the evidence against personality trait research, it must be concluded that this approach to understanding the behavior of athletes is probably a dead end.

The most obvious problem with the trait approach is that findings are generally inconsistent; a study done by one researcher often reports data inconsistent with those collected on similar groups by another researcher. Thus, dependable conclusions are impossible to draw. This disheartening inconsistency is probably due to the reluctance of trait theorists to consider the significance of *situational* factors in predicting human behavior. Trait theory assumes that traits exist as predispositions to act in a predictable way regardless of the social situation. A more common stance taken by psychologists today is the *interactional approach*, which posits an interrelationship between individual personality and situational factors. As will be seen later, this theoretical position underlies motivational research and is a major difference between trait and motivation research.

Studies on personality traits of athletes are generally atheoretical in nature. Most research is undertaken in a theoretical vacuum, without benefit of a strong guiding framework that might furnish insight, interpretive power, and stability. However, most of the problems with these studies are methodological ones. They include the poor operationalization of variables; inadequate sampling techniques; use of a variety of instruments, which produces inconsistent results and causes erroneous attempts to compare findings; unreflective choice of instruments, resulting in the use of inappropriate inventories; uninformed or nonexistent statistical analysis; failure to distinguish between raw scores and normal scores; generalizing beyond the data; and inferring causal relationships from correlational evidence (see also Martens, 1975a; Rushall, 1968a).

A final criticism, raised by Rainer Martens (1975a) and others (Scott, 1972), warns of the questionable ethics involved in using such unsubstantiated results to predict success, to select athletes, and to "handle" problem athletes. Indeed, as more and more psychologists–turned–entrepreneurs set up consulting services with trait analysis as their stock-in-trade, this ethical concern becomes one of the most significant ones in the field of sport.

Personality research and the female athlete. When followed to its logical conclusion, trait theory raises serious issues in the explanation of behavioral sex differences. We know that women and men behave differently, but we do not yet fully understand why this is so. A trait approach attributes sex differences in behavior to the possession of different traits, arguing that males normally possess certain traits, such as dominance, and females certain others, such as nurturance. If we assume that observed sex differences in behavior are due to *inherent* psychological differences, such as traits, it follows that behavioral differences between the sexes must always exist. However, assuming that behavior is *learned* because socialization situations for girls and boys emphasize and reward different behaviors, then one can conclude that observed sex differences in behavior are due to social learning and are not immutable. Thus, the model of behavior that is adopted will significantly alter conclusions about the extent or inevitability of sex differences in behavior, such as sport involvement. On theoretical grounds, then, acceptance of the trait paradigm has significant ramifications for the study of women in sport. With this in mind, we turn to research designed to evaluate female involvement in sport from a trait perspective.

Because the docket of evidence indicates the unreliability and invalidity of personality research, one can only be disappointed to find that research on female athletes has not managed to avoid these theoretical and methodological pitfalls. Indeed, those doing research on female athletes generally appear to be ignorant of the debate over the appropriateness of this line of research. Nevertheless, it is encouraging that of the seventeen studies reviewed, all but one were published before 1973, and the exception (Balazs, 1975) did not rely solely on trait analysis but reported supplementary data gathered from intensive interviews. No doubt this indicates a welcomed trend away from the one–dimensional trait studies of the past.

Most of the studies reviewed used either Cattell's Sixteen Personality Factor Questionnaire (16PF) or the Edwards Personal Preference Schedule (EPPS) to assess personality traits.[11] This uniformity of instruments allows us to make comparisons across studies. The review that follows focuses upon five hypotheses which have interested sport psychologists for years and have formed the basis of many studies. It must be stressed that while these five hypotheses have been addressed, *none has been proved.*

1. *Female athletes differ significantly from female non-athletes.* Since the 16PF and EPPS are tests for which population norms are available, all the studies reviewed here speak to this hypothesis. Every study found some statistically significant difference between athletes and the test norms.[12] However, the differences are inconsistent across studies. Of the two commonly used inventories, the EPPS appears to provide consistent results on some traits[13] but not on others. Great inconsistency is found in studies using the 16PF. Thus, when the evidence is examined, little support can be found for the hypothesis.

2. *Team sport participants differ from individual sport participants.* The second hypothesis is based on the theoretical assumption that because team sports are considered less appropriate for females, they attract a different type of female. In the two studies which address this issue (Malumphy, 1968; Peterson, Weber, Trousdale, 1967), no consistent differences were found between the groups. Thus, no support can be found for the second hypothesis.

3. *Different sports attract individuals with different personality traits.* The third hypothesis is also based on the assumption that different sorts of activities appeal to individuals with different personality structures. But when profiles of athletes in different sports are compared, again we see how both theoretical and methodological failures in the literature itself have produced "results" which are virtually meaningless. For example, while one study reports consistent

profiles for female fencers regardless of level (Mushier, 1972) another reports significant differences among swimmers and among track athletes (Kane, 1972). Even more telling is Bird's (1968) study of Canadian ice hockey players. She used three inventories and appeared to be oblivious to the startlingly inconsistent evidence she uncovered. The same trait for the same women measured by three different inventories demonstrated great range. For example, the trait dominance measured high on two inventories but low on a third. Thus, little evidence exists to support the third hypothesis.

4. *Successful female athletes differ from average or unsuccessful female athletes.* Three studies tested this hypothesis. Kane (1968) found significant differences between the superior and average athlete, but he does not specify further. Williams et al. (1970) found that high–level fencers differed from low–level fencers by possessing more dominance, but Mushier (1972) found no difference by level in the fencers she studied. There is too little evidence regarding this hypothesis to warrant any conclusions.

5. *Female athletes differ significantly from male athletes.* Only two studies addressing the fifth hypothesis could be found. Kane (1968) reports no differences between superior male and female athletes. Ogilvie (1967) concludes that males are more extroverted and that females are probably more stable and tough-minded. As is his custom, however, Ogilvie presents no data. Hypothesis five remains unsubstantiated.

In conclusion, this brief review has pointed out the enormous methodological and theoretical shortcomings of this research tradition. Due to these failings, the personality studies of female athletes are disappointingly inconsistent and inconclusive. Many thoughtful researchers have abandoned trait research. Those concentrating on female athletes would be well advised to do likewise and explore new avenues for research.

Personality and Gender: Masculinity, Femininity, Androgyny

No one can deny that individuals can be biologically classified and that the terms female and male have meaning in reference to that fact. However, many people balk at the use of the terms feminine and masculine to denote behaviors most appropriate for females and males, because these terms carry hidden political messages within them. They imply that females must develop their feminine qualities and males their masculine ones or risk the consequences of being labeled deviants. Since sport is considered a masculine, i.e., male-appropriate, activity, girls who are interested in sport and boys who are not are often treated with some suspicion. They have not learned their lessons well enough. Their femininity or masculinity, reifications of femaleness and maleness, are in question.

There are several serious problems involved in research on masculinity and femininity. Many of the problems are the result of sex biases in conceptualization, methodology, and theory. A major conceptual problem concerns the very notion of categorizing traits by sex. When one says that a certain trait or behavioral pattern is "masculine," one is saying that the characteristic is more appropriate to those born into the male sex category. With few exceptions, such statements are based on cultural prerogatives rather than biological ones. This practice results in the perpetuation of severe limitations on the potential growth of all individuals, both male and female.

Another limitation of assigning traits by sex is the arrogant tendency of males to co-opt the "best" traits, or for traits or behaviors possessed by males to be more highly valued than those possessed by females. This state of affairs is reflected in our very way of thinking of sport: sport is considered a masculine activity in our society because it has come to emphasize behaviors traditionally thought of as masculine, such as aggression and achievement.

These conceptual problems infect and debase the research on masculinity and femininity. They are matched by equally serious problems of methodology. The inventories used to assess masculinity and femininity are valid only to the extent that they adhere to cultural prescriptions of masculinity and femininity. They have the power to discriminate between males and females only because they accept as unproblematic these cultural definitions which are incorporated into the inventories themselves. This conceptual problem of "cultural bound" tests is widely acknowledged in debates over race and IQ; it is the very same type of criticism that is emerging over gender inventories (Deaux, 1976).

The most damaging critique of research on masculinity and femininity attacks the deep-seated belief that the concepts are bipolar. Bipolarity assumes that if males are high in a particular trait, e.g., independence, then females are low in that trait, i.e., they are dependent. Janet Spence (Foushee, Helmreich, & Spence, 1979; Spence & Helmreich, 1979b) and Sandra Bem (1975) have argued that men and women are not polar opposites. They do not differ in kind but in degree. Thus if men are independent, women may not necessarily be dependent, but merely less independent. To assume that males and females exhibit totally opposite behavioral patterns is to oversimplify and misunderstand sex-based tendencies in behavior.

Both Spence and Bem have demonstrated the need for new categories to understand the distribution of characteristics by sex. Traditionally, sex-role inventories have been scored on a bipolar scale so that a high masculine score automatically means a low feminine score and vice versa. Spence and Bem independently found that a more accurate assessment could be gained by the use of two scales, one measuring masculine traits and the other feminine. They found no correlation between scores on the scales, confirming their belief that masculinity and femininity are independent patterns, not polar opposites. On the basis of their research, Spence and Bem both advocate adding a new concept to our understanding of sex role behavior: *androgyny* refers to the combination in an individual of both feminine and masculine behavioral characteristics.[14]

The articulation of this new conceptualization of sex–based characteristics has had considerable impact in both social science research and the popular literature, and androgyny has been accepted as "a good thing." Many, including sport psychologists, have adopted the concept uncritically. But regardless of how attractive the concept of androgyny appears to be, great care should be taken to evaluate its strengths and weaknesses before it is uncritically accepted as a useful concept.

In her writings, Bem (1975) intentionally laid the groundwork for interpreting androgyny as good. She clearly stated that androgyny represents a new standard of mental health in which masculinity and femininity are tempered with one another to produce a more flexible human being. Bem argued that such an individual, free from the fetters of responding to situations in a gender–stereotypic manner, has the capability of responding to situations from a greater repertoire of behaviors. Most followers accept this rationale. Only a few, such as A. Kaplan (1979), raise the point that androgynous individuals might be prone to conflict over appropriate responses to a given situation (i.e., a girl comes home crying from a neighborhood skirmish: Should she be comforted, counseled in the arts of self-defense, or both?)

Moreover, Bem and her followers assume that androgyny means that only the "best" traits of both sexes will be adopted. This leaves open the political question of who is to decide which traits are good and which are bad.

Spence and her colleagues (Spence & Helmreich, 1978) appear to have a more professional orientation toward the concept of androgyny, and their research generally appears freer from the theoretical and methodological problems that have plagued Bem's more popularized work. However, regardless of the methodological debate which currently rages over the use of the Bem Sex-Role Inventory (BSRI) and, to a lesser extent, Spence's Personality Attribution Questionnaire (PAQ),[15] the very introduction of the concept of androgyny has had a positive effect upon research on sex differences. The concept of androgyny has had a sensitizing effect by strongly undermining the traditional bipolar conceptualizations of masculinity and femininity and by broadening the range of behaviors considered appropriate for males and females. Perhaps one day individuals will no longer be derided for displaying cross–sex behavior patterns but applauded for the breadth of their interests and capabilities.

The obvious application of androgyny research to sport will be the embracing of androgyny as one more useful *trait* by which to describe female athletes. This trait approach must be resisted if the full import of this conceptual breakthrough is to be realized. Nevertheless, some researchers will use the terms descriptively, asking whether male and female athletes are high masculine, high feminine, androgynous (high feminine and high masculine) or undifferentiated (low feminine and low masculine). Some research already has begun to move in this direction (Colker & Widom, 1980; Duquin, 1978; Myers & Lips, 1978; Spence & Helmreich, 1978).

Perhaps a more promising use of the concept is ideological rather than empirical. Carole Oglesby (1978) and Mary Duquin (1978) convincingly argue for the reconceptualization of sport as an androgynous activity. Sport, they argue, contains both traditionally masculine characteristics and traditionally feminine ones, but the male traits have been emphasized to the neglect of equally important female contributions. Indeed, those feminine characteristics that are valued, such as the artistry of a graceful move or the aesthetic quality of movement, tend to be valued only when they produce the desired outcome, winning. Next to the male value of productivity, they are second-class values; the most graceful wide receiver in the world will never earn a place on the team if his statistics do not reflect some offensive output. Moreover, those sports which feature aesthetics as their primary focus, those which focus on the beauty of human movement, such as synchronized swimming, gymnastics, and ice skating, are categorized as "female" sports and enjoy less status than more "male" sports. The male gymnast or skater, for example, may perform moves which are more acrobatic or which demonstrate the strength component of the activity perhaps to emphasize the male interpretation of the "female" sport.

Sport need not be narrowly viewed only as an arena for the display of power and dominance behaviors; it also could serve as a showcase for other valuable traits associated more with females than males. For example, nurturance and sensitivity are valued attributes which should be welcomed in sport. Furthermore, studies with the Webb Scale (Loy, Birrell, & Rose, 1976; Webb, 1969) suggest the ethic of fair play is more frequently endorsed by females than males; it is not inconceivable that females can contribute a renewed emphasis on fairness and integrity to sporting activity.

While still a new avenue of development, perceptions of gender roles have begun to move from traditional bipolar conceptualizations of masculinity/femininity to the acknowledgement that other possibilities, i.e., androgyny, exist. This is a significant advance, but the final stage may not be androgyny, as so many suggest, but gender role transcendence, a state of affairs in which the fraudulent terms masculine and feminine are finally abandoned altogether. When this occurs, discussing activities as "masculine" or "feminine" will finally become an anachronistic practice.

Motives of Female Athletes

Trying to understand the behavior of athletes by referring to their motives is similar in some ways to trying to understand such behaviors through a trait approach. Both efforts rest on the assumption that general predispositions toward behavior exist as stable personality dimensions in individuals. They differ, however, in the *complexity* with which they conceive of the dynamics of human behavior. Unlike the simple deterministic stimulus-response (trait-behavior) model of behavior adopted by trait theory, motivational theory conceptualizes behavior as the product of *interacting forces.* These forces include not only relatively stable *motives* (trait-like predispositions to act in a certain way) but the activation of these motives due to specific *situational factors.* According to motivational theory, mere possession of a motive (trait) is not enough to enable one to predict behavior. Motives must be evoked by a specific situation or they remain dormant and, consequently, have no effect on behavior. Thus, motivational theory offers a more sophisticated analysis of the sources of human behavior by attending not only to individual predispositions but to the social situations as well.

Of the many motives which have been explored by psychologists, three motives are particularly relevant to expanding our understanding of what draws females to sport and what accounts for the experiences they have in that setting. This review concentrates on the research tradition surrounding these three motives: the need for stimulation, the need for achievement, and the need for power.[16]

The need for stimulation.[17] Several researchers have hypothesized that the need for stimulation is a significant motive in sport involvement for both males and females (Berger, 1970; Donnelly, 1976; Hymbaugh & Garrett, 1974; Ryan & Foster, 1967). According to Peter Donnelly, the need for stimulation "is concerned with the way in which individuals react to their sensory environment and particularly with the arousal-producing properties of varying degrees of environmental stimulation" (1978, p. 23). Since sport is an activity which offers many dimensions of stimulation—novelty, complexity, uncertainty, physical contact—it is logical to expect an individual's choice and style of sport involvement to reflect her or his response to demands for a need for stimulation.

In his review of sport-related research on the need for stimulation,

Donnelly (1978) concluded that, because of its potential for presenting the participant with a complex physical environment, sport does appear to be used as a means for satisfying individual needs for stimulation. Among male athletes the results are highly suggestive: those with a high need for stimulation are most apt to be drawn to sports (Ryan & Foster, 1967; Ryan & Kovacic, 1966), to be involved in contact sports, to participate in high-risk or high-harm sports (Berger, 1970; Hymbaugh & Garrett, 1974), and to enjoy sports with a high degree of temporal and spatial uncertainty (Berger, 1970; Donnelly, 1976).

In research that includes women, the results reveal the same tendencies but are not always statistically significant. For example, Nealon (1973) found that female athletes are higher than female nonathletes in need for stimulation, and Walker (1971) found that female athletes had greater pain tolerance than did female nonathletes. Donnelly (1976) discovered that the need for stimulation was significantly related to a number of environmental dimensions of sport, including temporal/spatial uncertainty.

A few studies have demonstrated a lower need for stimulation among females as compared to males (Donnelly, 1976; Petrie, 1967). Moreover, Donnelly notes "fewer women participate in the team and contact sports which seem to tap need for stimulation most directly" (1978, p. 2). Indeed, it seems that conditions which satisfy need for stimulation, such as those that involve physical contact, are often judged unacceptable for female involvement (cf., Metheny, 1972). Whether women's low participation in such sports is the result of a relatively lower need for stimulation or merely discriminatory exclusion from highly stimulating environments remains an important and debatable issue.

Achievement–related motives: Need to achieve, fear of failure, fear of success.[18] Since sport so clearly offers an opportunity for participants to display competence in comparison with fixed standards of excellence, motives which relate to such a need should be expected to be significant elements in understanding and explaining behavior in sport. Three *achievement–related motives*—the need to achieve, the fear of failure, and the fear of success—have been explored by social scientists.

The first motive to be explored was the *need to achieve*, "a relatively stable disposition to strive for achievement or success" (Atkinson, 1966, p. 13). The need to achieve is conceptualized as a positive motive which, when activated by situational forces, impels individuals who possess it to display certain patterns of behavior. Among these patterns are the tendency to seek out and engage in achievement situations[19] (Atkinson & Feather, 1966) and the tendency to succeed (French, 1958; McClelland, Atkinson, Clark, & Lowell, 1953; Warner & Abegglin, 1955). Both these tendencies might be expected to manifest themselves in sport settings.

The need to achieve is often in conflict with a separate, negative motive, the *fear of failure*. Individuals characterized by a high fear of failure are so threatened by the possibility of failure that they go to all lengths to avoid it. The need to achieve and fear of failure are not polar opposites but two separate motives which interact to influence behavior in achievement situations. Since the discovery of fear of failure as a separate dimension in achievement motivation, virtually all the significant research undertaken has taken both achievement–related motives into account. Today when one refers to the achievement motive, it is taken for granted that the need to achieve and the fear of failure are both being measured.

In the early years of research on the need to achieve, researchers found that, in contrast to men, women's achievement motives did not predict their achievement behavior. Soon women were eliminated as subjects in most studies. However, some interested researchers began to seek explanations for this unexpected pattern. They found that while women possessed achievement motives comparable to those of men in *relaxed* testing situations (Alper & Greenberger, 1967; Maccoby & Jackin, 1974) the introduction of arousal situations brought about a sex-linked response. Arousal situations in which intellectual or leadership qualities were emphasized led to an increase in achievement behavior for males but a decrease for females (Veroff, Wilcox, & Atkinson, 1953), while arousal situations in which social approval (Field, cited in McClelland et al., 1953; Sears, cited in Hoffman, 1975) or affiliative factors (Crandall, 1963; Crandall, Dewey, Kotkovsky, & Preston, 1964; Garai & Schein-field, 1968) were emphasized led to an increase in achievement behavior for women but no change for men. These findings point to the major criticism of this research tradition: it has been sex-biased. By featuring situations in which leadership and intellectual qualities were stressed, experimental settings used to test achievement–related motives traditionally have been more conducive to the display of motives by men than by women. Moreover, cue pictures used to elicit achievement–related imagery traditionally have depicted men rather than women, and the men in the pictures have engaged in traditionally male–dominated activities. Thus, the very concept of achievement has been defined in male terms, and it is not surprising that most women have failed to demonstrate achievement motives or behaviors in such a situation.

Confusion over sex differences in the achievement motive still persists. One of the most exciting and interesting contributions to a solution was Matina Horner's (1968) suggestion of a third achievement-related motive which she labeled *fear of success.*

As part of a study of sex differences in achievement motivation, Horner presented college students with a sentence cue about a successful male or female and asked them to write short stories about the key character.[20] Although less than 10% of the men wrote negative stories about the successful male, as many as 62% of the women wrote stories about the female which contained images of negative consequences resulting from her success (Horner, 1968, p. 108). This negative imagery fell into three categories: her social rejection and loss of marriageability; her guilt, despair, or self-doubt about her femininity; and denial of the possibility that she could really have done so well (Horner, 1968, pp. 105-106).

Horner identified this response pattern as a manifestation of a fear of success: a motive activated in situations in which it is expected that "success . . . will be followed by negative consequences" (Horner, 1971, pp. 98-99). On the basis of her data, Horner concluded that fear of success was a motive more prevalent in women than in men.

Taken at face value, the concept has great appeal as an explanation of sex differences in achievement situations. For example, it suggests a plausible explanation for the differential appeal of sport as an achievement situation for girls and boys. Girls have traditionally been negatively rewarded for their involvement in sport, and a successful woman athlete used to be prone to all three negative consequences of achievement: social rejection, questioning of her femininity, and disbelief that a girl could perform such athletic feats.

The research, however, has some serious flaws which must be recognized before the findings are embraced wholeheartedly. Critiques have concentrated on two major problems. First, fear of success is not found predominantly in women, and therefore is not significantly related to sex (Brown, Jennings, & Vanek, 1974; Feather & Simon, 1973; Heilburn, Kleemeier, & Piccola, 1974; Hoffman, 1975; Levine & Cumrine, 1975; Romer, 1977; see also the reviews by Condry & Dyer, 1976; Tresemer, 1974; Zuckerman & Wheeler, 1975). Second, when both sexes write stories about both the male and female cue, men as well as women write more negative stories in response to the female cue (Feather & Raphaelson, 1974; Monahan, Kuhn, & Shaver, 1974; Robbins & Robbins, 1973). Thus, replications of the research have failed to confirm Horner's original findings, and it is now generally acknowledged that the test does not measure a stable and enduring personality disposition, but responses to "inappropriate sex role behavior" (Tresemer, 1974).

Major reservations about methodological problems in the research must temper our evaluation of this research tradition. Despite condemnations of this research tradition, two contributions of Horner's work deserve mention. First, Horner's research has been responsible for channeling research energy into the study of achievement-related motives and behaviors of women, long a neglected area. Second, the possibility that a fear of success exists in individuals as one component of their general achievement-motive pattern is worthy of further exploration. However, in order for the notion of fear of success to make a permanent contribution to the literature on achievement motivation and our understanding of behavior in sport, the present conceptualization must be abandoned.

Fear of success is not a motive of the same scope and permanence as need to achieve or fear of failure. All the evidence indicates that it is a *situationally defined* rather than *stable* element of behavior. As such it might be logically incorporated within Atkinson and Feather's (1966) model of achievement motivation, which posits achievement behavior as a result of the interacting factors of motive, expectancy of success, and value of success. What has been labeled by Horner as fear of success is a behavior pattern attributable not to a stable motive but to the situational factor of value of success. This value, or situational incentive, of success depends upon the individual's perception of the appropriateness of success in a given situation. As the research by Horner and others clearly shows, those perceptions are constrained by gender role expectancies. Thus, more attention should be directed to the study of the dynamics of achievement situations that evoke or repress positive achievement behaviors.

Achievement related motives and sport. Sport offers an obvious arena in which to explore the relationship between achievement–related motives and achievement behaviors. One might expect achievement motives to explain both involvement in sport and success in sport. However, research efforts have been few, and results generally have been inconclusive.

Several studies have reported higher levels of achievement motivation for female athletes than the general female population (Dayries & Grimm, 1970; Neal, 1963; Plummer, 1969). However, while the tendencies are clear, the results are not always statistically significant.

Other studies have measured the relationship between level of achievement motivation and success in sports. Best results have been reported when sport-specific measures are used to test achievement motives (Daugert, 1966) and when both need to achieve and fear of failure are assessed (Roberts, 1975; Yeary, 1971). In these cases, results are in the predicted direction: level of achievement motives is positively related to success.

Studies designed to explore fear of success in sport settings have been disappointing. Before Horner's research popularized her interpretation of fear of success, Bruce Ogilvie and Thomas Tutko (1966) used a different conceptualization of fear of success to explain the underachievement patterns of certain athletes. Because of their orientation to case studies and to psychoanalysis, Ogilvie and Tutko's work remains at the descriptive level, yet the conceptualization of fear of success as a non-sex-linked motive is theoretically more appropriate than Horner's.

Birrell (Note 2) and Wittig (1975) have experimented with sport-specific fear of success measures. Both administered their own tests to samples of males and females, and both concluded that measures based upon Horner's conceptualization and methodology are more apt to tap sex stereotyping than any deep-seated motive to avoid success. Clearly, if fear of success is to be a useful concept in understanding behavior in sport, a major reconceptualization and further testing and validation are necessary.

Research on achievement-related motives in sport is hardly convincing, and much of the blame can be laid to problems of methodology. Much of the sport research has conceptualized the need to achieve as if it were a unidimensional personality trait. This simplistic view disregards the fact that most theories of motivation conceive of behavior as the result of a complex interaction of motives with situational cues. Need to achieve and fear of failure are *motives* which must be situationally aroused before they become *motivations* capable of inducing behavior. Individuals with a high need to achieve (a motive) have a general tendency to want to do well in challenging situations, yet the decision to pursue excellence in any particular situation depends upon situational factors and the individual's general assessment of them. For example, individuals who decide to pursue an achievement goal, such as trying out for the tennis team, do so because some elements in the situation arouse a latent motive to achieve, changing it into a motivation. Clearly, research in sport will not advance until the complexities of motivation are fully understood and inappropriate or incomplete measures of motivation are abandoned.

Such a strategy might also enhance a fuller understanding of the sport experience of women. A significant aspect of sport involvement concerns the positive or negative feedback an individual receives relative to her or his efforts and achievements. When a girl with a high need to achieve is negatively sanctioned for her involvement or success in sport, she is likely to consider abandoning that activity in favor of finding a more socially appropriate and rewarding situation in which to display her achievement–related needs. Until sport represents an opportunity for females as well as males to demonstrate their ability and to share pride in their accomplishments, the world of sport will continue to lose highly achievement–motivated girls and women to other areas of social life.

The need for power. A nagging problem in achievement motivation research has been the inability of the achievement motive to predict performance in competitive test situations (Atkinson, 1974; Entin, 1974; Horner, 1974). The problem stems from an inability to differentiate between achievement and competition. Achievement-related motives should predict *achievement* behavior, i.e., behavior in situations in which an individual's performance is assessed in terms of some standard of excellence. Sport is clearly an example of such an achievement situation. However, sport is just as clearly an example of a *competitive* situation, i.e., a specific sort of achievement situation in which an individual's performance is assessed in relation to the performance of other individuals.

Virtually all sport situations are both achievement situations and competitive situations, yet the two elements may be weighted differently. In sports in which competition is *indirect*, such as golf, gymnastics, track and field, swimming, or mountain climbing, individuals measure their accomplishments against an inanimate standard of excellence—par, the clock, the environment. Individual performances will have relatively little effect upon the performances of opponents: participants cannot hinder one another's performances.[21] In such situations, achievement may be more salient to the participant than is competition.

In sports featuring *direct* competition, such as tennis, boxing, football, hockey, and basketball, the individual is contending directly against another. One's skill will have a direct impact on the skill that opponents can display and in some ways, might "steal" their performance, as in a blocked shot, a strikeout, or an ace. In such situations, competition may be more important to the participant than achievement. Therefore, achievement-related motives may be more successful in predicting behavior in some sport settings than in others.

In situations that stress competing against and overpowering an opponent, it is quite likely that another motive is at work. This motive has some commonality with other motives variously labeled "social comparison motivation" (Veroff, McClelland, & Ruhland, 1975), "competitiveness" (Martens, 1975b, 1976), and "need for power" (McClelland, 1975; Winter, 1973). In this discussion I will use the latter terminology.

If power is "the capacity to produce effects (consciously or unconsciously intended) on the behavior or feelings of another person" (Winter, 1973, p. 10), then a person with a high need for power is one who is "concerned about establishing, maintaining, or restoring his (sic) power that is, his (sic) impact, control, or influence over another person, groups of persons, or the world at large" (Winter, 1973, p. 250).

Research on the power motive lends itself to ready application in a sport context, and some psychologists have explored the notion that sport involvement may represent a manifestation of the need for power. David McClelland (1975) defined four stages of power motivation which he believes are arranged in hierarchial order and correspond to Freud's and Erikson's theory of psychosocial development:

Stage 1: *Dependence*, drawing strength from others or serving powerful others;

Stage 2: *Autonomy*, the desire for self-control;

Stage 3: *Competitiveness*, the need to assert oneself;

Stage 4: *Altruism*, dedicating oneself as an instrument of higher authority, such as God, Art, or Science.

According to McClelland, people in different stages manifest their power needs in different ways. Stage 1 individuals, for example, are prone to power-oriented reading (McClelland suggest *Sports Illustrated* as an example), with Stage 3 individuals more likely to satisfy their need for power by participating in competitive sports.

McClelland contends that women generally manifest power needs typical of the first two stages and usually do not move beyond them. Others might suggest that McClelland's choice of stages and the order in which he ranks them represent a severe sex-bias and virtually guarantees that women will be found in the first two (inferior) stages. Although McClelland's assertion lacks the empirical proof that would connect the individual's need for power with the specific situation that would answer that need, his model does represent an accurate depiction of social stereotypes.

McClelland's observations are borne out in sport situations as well, where traditional roles for women fall into Stages 1 and 2. Roles representative of Stage 1 include cheerleaders, twirlers, groupies, and admiring fans. Active participation in sports can be related to Stages 2 and 3, and male/female contrasts are interesting here as well. Sports which would satisfy Stage 2 needs include indirectly competitive sports such as gymnastics, diving, swimming, track, and golf, as well as noncompetitive outdoor sports such as hiking and skiing—most activities considered acceptable for female participants. Stage 3 sports include the directly competitive sports more characteristic of and more acceptable as male sports: boxing, wrestling, football, hockey, basketball. Stage 3 also includes roles generally delegated to males: coach, referee, owner. Stage 4 is reserved for very special athletes and would comprise a tiny sample; Muhammed Ali and Billie Jean King are examples. Though this line of inquiry is unscientific, it does provide much food for thought.

Psychological Consequences of Female Sport Participation

The previous pages have examined some of the factors that might contribute to a woman's decision to participate in sport. Whatever the reasons that originally impel them to participate, girls and women will remain involved only as long as the positive effects outweigh the negative. Aside from the enjoyment that females derive from sport, other consequences which are often more difficult to delineate or anticipate may also occur. This section, then, addresses the potential consequences of sport involvement for females, with the thought being that the consequences of sport involvement often become the determinants of future involvement.

Less is known about the consequences of sport involvement for females than about the determinants because less research has been directed to the topic. In fact, far less is known about the psychological consequences of sport involvement for males or females than people realize. The review of research that follows attempts to discriminate between consequences alleged to result from sport involvement and those which have been demonstrated through research findings.

Fitness, Body Image, and Self Concept

Recent efforts by women's rights groups have encouraged women to become more comfortable with and take more control over their own bodies (see *Our Bodies, Ourselves,* 1971). If sport involvement can aid in reaching that goal, it would be a significant accomplishment.

One of the acknowledged consequences of regular involvement in sport or physical activity is increased fitness level and a feeling of physical well-being. Fitness may have psychological consequences, because enhanced fitness level often has a positive effect on one's body image. Since a positive relationship generally exists between body image and self-concept, one could hypothesize that improving a woman's fitness through sport would increase her positive feelings about her body and enhance her self-concept. Although there is considerable research on body image and sport involvement (Allen, 1972; Mathes, 1978), few studies have addressed this specific hypothesis. Snyder and Kivlin (1975) report that female athletes have a more positive body image than do female nonathletes, and Allen (1972), on the basis of her review of the literature, goes one step further by suggesting "If we can create a more stable, positive body concept through positive experiences in body oriented activities, then indirectly we change the person (self)" (p. 41). If this assertion is borne out by further research, sport involvement indeed has significant psychological consequences for females.

Role Learning and Trait Acquisition

The fact that sport is legitimated by so many social institutions—the family, the schools, the government—is direct proof that sport is deemed socially beneficial. The list of promised benefits is extensive and includes the development of such characteristics as perseverence, competitiveness, drive, industriousness, and character, as well as a sense of fair play, the ability to deal with people from different social backgrounds, and the ability to win and lose graciously. Many observers have noted that these benefits are extended to boys with more frequency and sincerity than they are to girls; although it is common to claim that boys develop character through sport, one seldom hears the same boast for girls.

The development of these valued attributes is assumed by many to be among the consequences of sport participation, and one of the most commonly believed social functions of sport is socialization. Generally, however, research has not substantiated this belief. There is some evidence that roles specific to sport situations, i.e., competitiveness, sportsmanship, or team play displayed *during* the game, are learned in sport settings. However, no evidence supports the hypothesis that roles learned in one social setting, such as sport, are transferred to another, such as work (Kenyon, 1968; Loy et al., 1978, p. 244). Thus, one of the cherished beliefs of our society, that sport builds character, is unsubstantiated.

Several recent descriptive studies, however, have presented persuasive arguments that early play patterns do affect experiences in later life. Studies of women who reach executive levels in male–dominated fields suggest that one factor these achieving women tend to have in common is a love of sports as children (Fischer, cited in Sutton-Smith, 1979; Harragan, 1977; Hennig & Jardim, 1977). It is quite possible, of course, that involvement in sport is not the *cause* of these women's achievement. It is more likely that these women possessed some special qualities, such as a high need to achieve, which sought expression in many different settings throughout their lives and manifested itself on the playing field, in the business world, and in various other achievement settings. After all, a significant number of girl athletes never go on to achieve such success. Nevertheless, more research should explore this interesting hypothesis.

Female athletes as socializing agents. As the above review indicates, little empirical evidence can be found to support the hypothesis of *socialization through sport*. However, another side to this topic is the notion that due to their own sport experiences, many female athletes act as agents of *socialization into sport* for other women and girls.

Individuals' early experiences color their interpretation of future events. Thus, females who have positive experiences in sport are more likely to continue their involvement and to recommend involvement to others. An interesting consequence of sport involvement, therefore, is the process which occurs when female athletes become agents of socialization. This can happen in a number of ways; two of them will be discussed here.

The first is the process of *role modeling*. The more females are perceived to be enjoying themselves and to be valued in their roles as athletes, the more likely it is that younger females will follow in their footsteps. When we do not see women in certain roles, the exclusion of women from those roles is perpetuated. Until pioneers take the personal risks to break into new territory—as did Janet Guthrie in auto-racing, Robyn Smith in horse racing, Bernice Gera in baseball umpiring—many will not even realize that certain possibilities exist. In this sense, the contribution to female athletes made by Billie Jean King cannot be overemphasized. Particularly in her defeat of Bobby Riggs, but also in her spearheading of the campaign to equalize men's and women's purses in tennis, she symbolized a new consciousness of women's rights in sport. Many have followed her lead.

A second process is the *social learning* effect that female athletes will have on their children. Although studies suggest that women involved in sport are more influenced by males, particularly fathers and particularly in early years of their lives (Greendorfer, 1978; Greendorfer & Lewko, 1978; for a fuller discussion see Chapter 5), later generations of women will be more apt to have mothers who are or have been active in sport. Whether mothers serve as active role models in sport for their daughters or only to encourage them to participate, the result is likely to be an increase in respect for and participation in athletics for girls.

Role Conflict

Enhanced self-esteem through positive body image and the development of socially desirable traits, if proved, would certainly be considered positive psychological consequences of sport involvement. This section will focus on an element of role behavior which is considered by many to be a negative but common consequence of sport participation for females: role conflict.

Role prescriptions for the female and the athlete. In 1970, Inge Broverman and her colleagues asked psychiatrists to construct ideal images of a psychologically healthy male, a healthy female, and a healthy adult (Broverman, Broverman, Clarkson, Rosencrantz, & Vogel, 1970). The startling results of this study revealed that trained psychiatrists—those very people entrusted with the responsibility of helping us to maintain our mental health—harbor severe gender role prejudices. While they consider the healthy man and the healthy adult to be virtually identical, they view the healthy woman and the healthy adult as contradictory roles. The implication is clear: in order to be considered a healthy adult, a person must be a man. Psychologically sound as they are, women are not considered healthy adults.

More recent research has shown some modifications in these trends. In a replication of the Broverman et al. (1970) study, Brooks-Gunn and Fisch (1979) found no change in college males' assessment that healthy women were not healthy adults; however, college females perceived the healthy woman as androgynous. The study reveals a lessening of negative stereotypes about women, but only in the eyes of women. Encouraging as this change is, strong predispositions about gender role prescriptions continue to limit in subtle ways the potentials of women.

The same general paradox binds female athletes. The societal pictures of the healthy female and the healthy athlete differ considerably. Research indicates that males are perceived as independent, active, competitive, adventurous, self-confident, ambitious, and rough, among other traits[22] (Bem, 1974; Rosenkrantz, Vogel, Bee, Broverman & Broverman, 1968). Females, on the other hand, are perceived as dependent, passive, noncompetitive, nonadventurous, unambitious, gentle, and not self-confident (Bem, 1974; Rosenkrantz et al., 1968). Moreover, these traits are attributed even by segments of the population which would be expected to be more liberal in their attitudes toward women, i.e., the educated and women themselves. The traits attributed to women are hardly those expected on the playing field, where the valued assets are competence, self-confidence, persistence, assertiveness, and action— qualities more in keeping with perceptions of males. Again, conclusions are quite clear. To be a proper athlete, an individual must be a male.

Because female sport involvement traditionally has been regarded as a departure from socially acceptable definitions of female behavior, negative reactions to women in sport are merely exemplary of reactions to women in any social situation that demands self-confidence, assertiveness, and competence. Before the female athlete is discussed specifically, it might be instructive to consider societal reactions to competent women in general.

Reactions to competent women. A major theme that runs through research on perceived differences between males and females is competence. Males are often perceived as more competent than females, even by other females. Moreover, in a startling experiment, Philip Goldberg (1968) discovered that women are just as prejudiced against women as men are. Given articles to evaluate, women rated those allegedly written by men as superior to those allegedly written by women, revealing their unconscious belief in the intellectual superiority of men. More recent replications of Goldberg's study (Levenson, Burford, Bouno, & Davis, 1975; Peck, 1978) have shown an encouraging reversal in Goldberg's original finding. Hopefully this positive trend will continue in the future.

If women are expected to be less competent, perhaps even incompetent, how does society respond to a competent woman? Apparently, she may be competent as long as she remains "feminine." In a study designed to assess reactions to competent and incompetent males and females, Spence et al. (1975) had college men and women react to a taped interview in which a male or female revealed himself or herself as either competent or incompetent and as having either traditionally feminine or traditionally masculine interests.[23] The researchers found the subjects valued competence more than incompetence, regardless of sex. However, when characteristics were combined, they found that subjects preferred competent-feminine women more than competent-masculine women. The exception to this pattern was found in the sample of women subjects whose attitudes towards women was liberal; in this case, competent-masculine women were preferred.[24]

Feldman-Summers and Kiesler (1974) found that men and women attribute the success of others to different factors according to the sex of the individual. When told of a man who had become a successful doctor, men and women agreed that he succeeded *due to ability*. However, when told of a successful woman doctor, men and women attributed her success to the fact that she *tried* harder. Moreover, men thought the female doctor probably had easier tasks, while women felt that female doctors probably had tougher tasks.

Although designed to test another construct (the fear of success), the research conducted by Horner (1968) is generally acknowledged to measure reactions to female success in a male–dominated field. Horner found her subjects responded to female competence in three general ways: they perceived the competent woman as a social reject; they imagined that she felt guilt, despair, and doubts about her femininity; and they denied the possibility that she achieved the success legitimately, if at all.

It is quite clear from these studies that competent women are viewed with misgivings, apprehension, and skepticism. In order to receive positive feedback about their competence, females must choose with care those areas in which to excel. Some women choose to excel in sport and the next section investigates social reactions to women in sport.

Reactions to Female Athletes

Social reactions to female athletes vary according to the sport in which they are involved, for some sports are perceived as less offensive to standards of approved female behavior than others. The classic work in the area is Eleanor Metheny's (1972) essay exploring the apparent criteria which serve to determine the relative social acceptability of various sports. Empirical research generally substantiates Metheny's observations.

Generally, the more acceptable sports include gymnastics, swimming, and tennis: sports which emphasize aesthetic qualities or which are individual in nature. Team sports and sports which are more directly competitive, such as basketball, hockey, and softball, are generally judged to be less acceptable (Genovese, 1975; Kingsley, Foster, & Siebert, 1977; Malumphy, 1968; Snyder, Kivlin, & Spreitzer, 1975; Wittig, 1975).

Aside from the type of sport a female athlete chooses, she might be judged by her involvement style or level of ambition. However, research is sparse and inconclusive. Kingsley et al. (1977) studied reactions to ambitious female athletes. Subjects responded to autobiographical sketches of women athletes who described themselves as having high or low aspirations. No difference was found in reactions to the profiles in relation to ambition. However, another study (Birrell, Note 2) tested reactions to extremely ambitious female athletes, i.e., those competing successfully against males, and found that such athletes were judged negatively.

Others have investigated how women athletes are perceived in relation to the image of the ideal or typical woman. Pat Griffin (1973) found that female athletes and female professors were furthest from undergraduates' image of an ideal woman; closer to the ideal were "girlfriend" and "mother." Ann Hall (1972) reported less difference in profiles when the image of the female athlete was compared with that of a "feminine woman." Both images were judged positively; however, athletes were judged significantly more potent than the feminine woman, who was seen as impotent or helpless.

Selby and Lewko (1976) explored the roots of early stereotypes by surveying the attitudes of children toward women in sport. They found that girls had more positive reactions to women athletes than did boys. Moreover, they discovered that while girls who participated in sports had a more positive attitude toward female athletes than did nonparticipating girls, boys who participated had more negative attitudes toward female athletes than did nonparticipating boys.

Role conflict and self concept. The role of female and the role of athlete make different, sometimes conflicting, demands on the individual who fills both roles. According to long held beliefs, such an individual must deal not only with the force of public opinion that discourages her from serious sport involvement, but with her own self doubts: she must possess some inner strength or confidence to help her deal successfully with her dual role. However, while many assume that role conflict necessarily leads to lower self-esteem among female athletes, that relationship has yet to be demonstrated.

Perhaps the most intriguing research tradition dealing with the self-concept of female athletes is that begun by Dorothy Harris (Note 3), who compared an athlete's perception of her social self with her competitive self. Harris (Note 3) and others (Kennicke, 1972; Tyler, 1973; cf., Harris, 1977) have demonstrated that women clearly see their athletic role as separate from and to some degree inconsistent with their general social self. For example, Harris (Note 3) reported that compared to the social self, the competitive self emphasized achievement, dominance, aggression, and endurance, and was less affiliative, change oriented, deferent, abased, and feminine. The difference appears to be restricted to the female athlete's perception of herself in her competitive role. Tyler (1973) compared social and competitive self-perceptions of varsity athletes to those of students enrolled in sport classes. She found that while the social self-concepts were similar, the competitive self-concept differed.

Women athletes measure up fairly well when they compare themselves to their own ideal selves. Sullivan (1973) found that although their self-concepts did not measure up to their ideal selves, athletes generally saw themselves more favorably than did nonathletes. Athletes were particularly apt to describe themselves as more active and more potent. Tyler (1973) also discovered that the athlete's social self was different from her ideal self.

Two points must be made with regard to this line of research. First, in the absence of comparable studies on men, researchers do not know whether men experience role conflict between their social self and their competitive self. Instead, we assume that the two roles are essentially congruent.

Second, despite such seeming ambiguity about her role, the female athlete apparently suffers no deep injury to her self-esteem. Indeed, results of several studies suggest that sport involvement serves to enhance an individual's self-esteem (Snyder et al., 1975; Snyder & Kivlin, 1975; Snyder & Spreitzer, 1976). This is interesting information when viewed in the larger context of studies on women's self–esteem. Maccoby and Jacklin (1974) found no evidence of a sex difference in self-esteem, but Stake (1979) found that when an ability/performance component of self-esteem is tested specifically, females are lower than males. Since sport appears to be a situation in which an ability/performance component would have strong input into feelings of self-esteem, and since research indicates *increased* self-esteem among female athletes, more discriminating research is necessary.

Another approach to the female athlete's self-concept is taken by Jan Felshin (1981) who has discerned an "apologetic" operating for women in sport. As the term implies, the apologetic refers to the tendency of many female athletes to approach their involvement with a degree of shame. Rather than assert the positive aspects of her athletic role, she seeks to "document the validity of her womanhood within the cultural connotations of femininity" (1981, p. 488). In other words, she has accepted the subtle judgment that involvement in sport for women carries with it a stigma. Instead of working to undermine such an interpretation, she attempts to demonstrate that she is an exception—she is feminine—and she should not be stigmatized like the others.

Attributions for success. Another area which shows great promise for providing understanding of the psychology of the female athlete is attribution theory. Attribution theory attempts to assess the causal explanations given by individuals concerning certain outcomes, in this case why one was successful or unsuccessful in sport. Thus, causal attribution could index a female's reaction to herself as a competent person.

Causal attribution is defined in terms of two internal factors, *ability* and *effort*, and two external factors, *luck* and *task difficulty*. Generally, females tend to attribute outcomes to *external* factors while males make more *internal* attributions (cf., McHugh, Duquin, & Frieze, 1978). More specifically, Kay Deaux and her colleagues (Deaux & Emswiller, 1974; Deaux, White, & Farris, 1975; cf., Deaux, 1976) have discovered that women tend to attribute their success to luck and their failure to lack of skill, while men attribute success to skill and failure to bad luck. This defeatist attitude prevailed regardless of whether or not females outperformed the males.

Few studies have tested the causal attribution patterns of female athletes (McHugh et al., 1978). In a study of high caliber athletes, Lefebvre (1979) found no sex differences in attribution. Both females and males attributed their success to ability and effort, and their failures to bad luck. Research in this area is just beginning, but in the future, research joining causal attribution theory to achievement motivation theory may uncover new ways to understand the female athlete.

The consequences of sport involvement for females traditionally have been somewhat negative, as the above review implies. As the result of their athletic participation, female athletes have not always been viewed in positive terms by others, and to some extent that view has been internalized. While female athletes do not seem to suffer negative consequences related to their total self-concept, when they reflect upon their specific role in sport, they are aware that they deviate from the ideal or typical female role model. Bowing to social pressure in many cases, female athletes have felt it necessary to offer an apologetic for their involvement in sport. Yet the future is by no means bleak when one considers the fact that new generations of female athletes are growing up in a more positive atmosphere.

Conclusion and Prospectus

Involvement in sport for women is increasing, and so is the amount of research aimed at understanding the psychological dimensions of their involvement. On both accounts, therefore, there is reason for optimism regarding the future. However, some critique of the status quo might aid in guiding effort and attention away from certain dead ends and toward areas where much of importance remains to be done.

Future Research on the Female Athlete

Since interest in sport as an area for study is only a recent phenomenon, it is not surprising to find that research on women in sport remains in the preliminary stages of descriptive analysis. Little of profound theoretical significance has emerged. Nevertheless the growth of knowledge in any field is always constrained by the sorts of questions one asks and how one looks for answers. If researchers are to discover more about the psychological dimensions of female sport involvement, they must redress certain problems in substantive, methodological, and theoretical areas.

The review in this chapter was based around two general substantive questions:

1. What are the psychological determinants of sport involvement for females?
2. What are the psychological consequences of sport involvement for females?

Certain ways of answering these generic questions have received more attention than others. I want to suggest ways of readjusting the focus on these substantive areas that I believe will yield more insight into the topic of women in sport.

In the study of *psychological determinants*, attention might safely be diverted away from studies of personality traits and toward areas of more promise. Certainly a more sophisticated conceptualization of motivation in sport is called for, so that motives for involvement are placed within their proper situational framework. Another area where research would be of considerable benefit is the exploration of psychobiological sex differences. The latest research on such topics as hemispheric specialization and hormonal differentiation must be monitored, and studies designed to assess the significance of such findings for behavior in sport must be undertaken.

In order to understand *psychological consequences*, research should focus on more sophisticated ways to assess role conflict among female athletes. This is a significant area and past studies have touched only the surface. Since studies on female entrepreneurs suggest a link between early play patterns and later achievement, that lead should be followed up with specific research procedures, such as longitudinal studies which attempt to assess the possibility of a causal relationship. Finally, until a more promising future is predicted for studies of the impact of socialization through sport, that area should be approached with caution.

Undoubtedly the questions asked in any field are closely related to the ease with which the answers may be gathered, i.e., the available *methodology* (cf., Coser, 1975). In the case of research on psychological dimensions of sport involvement, this tendency has manifested itself in the pro-liferation of certain research traditions, such as personality trait studies, at the expense of more profound topics. No doubt part of the reason for this is expediency; studies utilizing standard trait instruments are relatively easy to design, administer, and analyze. But our understanding of the female in sport could surely be enhanced if other methods were employed. For example, the role conflict experienced by female athletes has usually been studied by means of paper-and-pencil tests. Yet the pro-cess of role conflict might be more completely understood if interac-tionist methodology were employed to study it. Intensive structured in-terviews are likely to uncover common elements of that experience un-tapped by paper-and-pencil tests. Although sample size may be drasti-cally reduced by using such a time-consuming procedure, the richness of the responses would surely compensate.

Another methodological issue of significance is sample selection. As in many other fields, those interested in studying women in sport have drawn their samples from available populations—almost always the white, middle-class college student. The dangers of generalizing results beyond this very elite population are obvious. Moreover, in much of the research that is being conducted relevant to sport, researchers have restricted their samples by excluding women as subjects. Because of that deliberate sex bias, certain relevant areas of research (i.e., achievement motivation and need for power) are not yet applicable to women.

Finally, we must consider the limitations to our understanding of women in sport imposed by the theoretical perspectives which underlie research strategies. In some cases, as we noted above, there is ample evidence that research is done with no guiding theoretical framework at all. In most cases, however, the quantitative research methods that are employed reflect an alliance with the theoretical schools that Ritzer (1975) associates with the social facts paradigm.[25] Very few studies in sport emanate from the social definitions paradigm, where qualitative methods are employed. Yet much could be gained from adopting such an approach, and, specifically, from becoming more familar with the tenets of symbolic interactionism.

In brief, symbolic interactionism's view of the nature of social reality and the nature of the individual's relation to it represent a significant departure from the theoretical stance which generally underlies studies in sport. Interactionists believe that objects, actions, and individuals are devoid of meaning until meaning is attributed to them through the social processes of communication and negotiation. Thus individuals are *active creators* of the definition of the situation: They have power over the events in which they participate and can best be understood as dynamic forces in their own lives.

For researchers, this view holds a significant message: If we are to understand the meaning of social situations, we must be privy to their construction, i.e., we must become part of the situation through interaction and communication. For women, this view has an equally significant message: We all have power to define ourselves and the world in which we live. The potential of the definitionist paradigm in guiding researchers to new ways of understanding behavior in sport and in enlightening women about their potential power of definition in sport and everyday life has been greatly overlooked. For a fuller understanding of the range of psychological dimensions of sport involvement, future studies must be generated from this paradigm.

The Future of the Female Athlete

Sport involvement for females has progressed significantly in the past decades. Data indicate that the numbers of girls and women participating in sport are increasing, and that a greater acceptability of women in sport exists today than ever before.[26] Hopefully, this will result in a more positive social evaluation of women athletes and more positive psychological consequences of sport involvement for females. Already there are encouraging signs that by the time the next generation matures, the female athlete will finally be allowed full opportunity to grow through sport and will receive full recognition of her achievements. There is no doubt that this change will benefit the individual and society as they move toward an important goal—encouraging all individuals to develop their potential to the fullest.

As I have suggested in this review, the key issue in the future of the female athlete focuses upon two related questions: Are males and females significantly different people? If so, what are the implications of that difference? *Physiologically*, males and females differ in ways that most would consider to have a significant effect upon some elements of sport (see e.g., Klafs & Lyon, 1978). In terms of their *social experiences*, males and females in our society clearly are raised with different sets of expectations, rewards, and restrictions. The role conflict felt to be inescapable for the female athlete attests to this. But this chapter has focused upon the *psychological* differences which might affect sport involvement, and from that framework I make some suggestions about the future of the female athlete.

Contrary to popular belief, very few innate psychological differences exist between the sexes. Of the four possible psychobiological differences (Maccoby & Jacklin, 1974), two may affect sport involvement. The implications of those research traditions were discussed, and it was concluded that cautious and open-minded use of that research is imperative. In summary, we can conclude that innate psychological differences between the sexes are minimal. Males and females seem to possess more innate similarities than differences.

But what are the implications of the differences that do exist, including the physiological and cultural differences? If true equality is ever to be accomplished, much of the progress must come by changing the value climate and the social context in which sport takes place, and by wise attention to ideological matters. But what is the "proper" ideological response to the existence of sex differences in sport-related areas? It appears to me that women have three choices. We can ignore the differences; we can seek to overcome the differences; or we can accept the differences for what they are. Each alternative has a positive and a negative aspect.

The first alternative, ignoring the differences, could be generated from two very different positions. Dismissing the differences because they are considered insignificant emanates from a position of confidence. But dismissing them in the hopes that they will disappear or be forgotten reflects an endorsement of the notion that the existence of sex differences necessarily implies that one sex is better than the other. Of course, sex differences do *not* mean that one sex is superior to another, only that they are different. Perhaps it will be a sign of true equality when women no longer feel it is necessary to condemn any study or policy that suggests that males and females may differ.

The second alternative, attempting to overcome the differences, also has its positive and negative aspects. On the positive side, many of the elements that are considered psychological sex differences are really culturally generated stereotypes. These can be changed and should be if they restrict individuals from realizing their full potential. Combating erroneous, uncomplimentary, and restricting stereotypes about female athletes is a valuable, often heroic, enterprise. But on the negative side, attempting to overcome differences often means trying to be more like men. Usually this is a self–defeating process which reflects poorly on women's self–confidence as women. One dramatic example of this is the increased use by female athletes of *steroids*, a class of hormone related to androgens, the male hormone. Steroids stimulate the increase in muscle bulk that is normally associated with males, and they are believed to enhance strength. To that end, men and women and an alarming number of adolescent boys and girls have begun to use steroids. However, steroids have several disturbing side effects on females, including the appearance of facial hair, decreased breast size, lowering of the voice, and delay of menstruation. Their use is condemned in many quarters for all users, male or female. Former UCLA women's track coach Pat Connolly spoke about the specific tragedy of women opting for taking steroids before they fully understand and appreciate their own naturally developed talents:

Women. . .can do a lot of things tremendously well. We don't even have any idea of how well we can do some things because we haven't been trying very long. But by taking male hormones, a woman is really changing what she is all about. (quoted in Kirshenbaum, 1979)

Connolly's point is extremely well taken. The use of steroids can be read as a sad commentary on the self-image of the female athlete.

The final alternative, accepting the differences, could result in two dramatically different results. On the one hand, it could mean accepting our lot in life as women defined by a traditionally male culture. This is a conservative stance which features a defense of stereotypic feminine qualities. The Phyllis Schlafly crusade represents one example of this position. As the Marxists would remind us, that position is basically one of false consciousness. It is clearly unacceptable. Matters are at their worst and individuals are reduced to objects when sex differences are invoked as a justification for a blanket restriction to freedom of choice. A case in point is the exclusion of women from sport activities deemed "inappropriate for women," such as auto racing, marathons, and boxing.

On the other hand, acceptance of the differences may denote a celebration of the uniqueness of the female experience. This position would reflect the deep confidence women have in the essential femaleness they share with one another. While the most ideologically enlightened alternative, in my opinion, this position is not without its problems. Women have had so little time to explore their unique experience of the world that there exists no consensus about what comprises that uniqueness. As Mary Daly (1974) and other radical feminists would argue, women's experience has been subverted by male interpretations of the world for so long that it is a painstaking, time-consuming process to attempt to recover it. Nevertheless, it is a noble effort.

Applied to sport, this position suggests that girls and women should question the structure and values of sport in our society to see if it does reflect significant elements of the female experience. If not, it may be necessary to reconstruct sport from a female perspective. This is the very issue at stake in the AIAW versus NCAA battle for control of women's collegiate sport. With a women-controlled AIAW in charge, the possibility of new models for women's collegiate sport existed; and the vision of some of its leaders was a revolutionary one. With the male-controlled NCAA in power, women have little chance of becoming anything more than second-class citizens in another man's town.

In summary, though the future looks bright for significant changes in rates and styles of sport involvement for girls and women, this is a time when significant decisions about the future of sport for women are being made. The ideological stances taken by sport leaders will have tremendous impact on decades of female athletes. Ten years from now the psychological dimensions of female sport involvement may reflect some dramatic social changes.

Notes

1. Virtually every study of rates of involvement in sport documents the same trend: males traditionally have been and continue to be more involved in sport than females. This relationship holds true for all forms and levels of their involvement, both as producers (e.g., as athletes, coaches, trainers, managers, announcers, owners, agents, and the like) and as consumers (e.g., fans who attend sporting events, watch sport on television, listen to it on the radio, read about it in the newspaper, or talk about it to their friends) (cf., Loy, 1968; Loy, McPherson, & Kenyon, 1978; McPherson, 1975).

2. In any case, even when genitalia are ambiguous, correct biological sex can be determined by chromosome tests.

3. Other researchers favor the theses that sex differences in spatial ability are attributable to a recessive gene (Stafford, cited in Brooks-Gunn & Matthews, 1979) and hormones (Bock & Kolakowski, cited in Brooks-Gunn & Matthews, 1979).

4. McGlone's (cited in Goleman, 1978) evidence is based on observations of patients with structurally equivalent brain damage in one hemisphere. Compared to males, females appear to have less severe losses. McGlone argues that this is so because the female brain tends to reproduce both functions in both hemispheres to a greater degree. Thus damage to the left hemisphere, which controls verbal ability, may result in more serious loss of that capacity to males whose right hemispheres are too specialized in terms of spatial tasks to compensate.

5. Within the family, women are as likely as men to resort to nonlethal violence (Straus et al., and Maurer, cited in Frodi et al., 1977) and are more likely than men to be child abusers (Gelles; Gil, cited in Frodi et al., 1977) and child murderers (Pollock, 1950). It is an interesting comment on our societal perceptions of gender roles to note that when a woman kills a child, she is charged with infanticide; a man committing the same act is charged with murder. In addition to crimes of violence within the family, recent trends show an alarming increase in crimes perpetrated by women over the past two decades (Adler, 1981; Smith & Visher, 1980; Steffenmeir, 1978), with a significant though less dramatic increase in violent crimes (Steffenmeir et al., cited in Steffenmeir, 1978).

6. In these studies aggression is often operationalized as the intensity of an electric shock administered to another individual.

7. The game called for children to fill their own chutes with as many balls as possible. Pressing a button to release balls from an opponent's chutes was considered an aggressive behavior (Hoving, Laforme & Wallace, 1974, cited in Shaklee, 1982).

8. See *The Descent of Women* (Morgan, 1972) for an amusing view of ethological arguments from a woman's perspective.

9. Also classified here would be theories focused upon chromosomal disorders (the XXY chromosome) and improper functioning of the amygdala. However, these attempt to explain anomalies; we concern ourselves here with those theories purporting to explain normal variations in aggressive behavior.

10. This argument represents one example of the conflicting prescriptions suggested by the liberal and radical feminist frameworks discussed in Chapter 1. The liberal view would advocate beating the men at their own game, while the radical view questions the very structure and values of that game.

11. Inventories most often used to measure traits in sport–related research include Cattell's Sixteen Personality Factor Questionnaire (16PFQ, the Edward's Personal Preference Schedule (EPPS), the California Personality Inventory (CPI), the Minnesota Multiphasic Personality Inventory (MMPI), and the Maudsley Psychological Inventory (MPI).

12. Rushall (1968) argues persuasively that statistical significance between groups may be a less accurate means of reporting actual differences than reporting the normed scores. When the sten scores of the sample groups are examined, for example, one finds many scores reported as statistically significant which are within the "normal" range of the population distribution. Rushall argues that only scores below 2 or above 7 can safely be indicative of significant variation. Even using Cattell's more liberal recommendation of accepting as significant those scores below 4.5 and above 6.5, one finds researchers reporting relatively modest differences either as significant or with no reference at all to population norms (cf., Bird, 1968; Malumphy, 1968; Peterson et al., 1967).

13. For example, Balazs (1977), Neal (1963), and Williams, Hoepher, Moody, and Ogilvie (1970) report scores for the athletes in their samples that indicate a low need to affiliate and high needs for achievement and autonomy.

14. Bem developed an inventory by means of which individuals were classified into one of three categories: high masculine-low feminine, high feminine-low masculine, and androgynous (either high masculine-high feminine or low masculine-low feminine). Later, Spence, Helmreich, & Stapp (1975) argued that a fourth category was necessary in order to discriminate more clearly. They suggested that the androgynous category should include only those who scored high masculine and high feminine, and they argued that those who scored low masculine and low feminine were not the same as androgynous individuals but should comprise a fourth category, labeled undifferentiated. Bem soon adopted this conceptualization.

15. For critiques and rejoinders of this research, see Locksley and Colten (1979), Pedhazur and Tetenbaum (1979), Yonge (1978), Gaa, Liberman, and Edwards (1979), Spence and Helmreich (1979a) and Bem (1979).

16. Some mention should be made, however, of other motives that might be of considerable assistance in understanding the athlete yet have received little research attention. For example, the need for approval, which might furnish insight into the player-coach relationship, has been completely ignored. And the need to affiliate, which Alderman (1974) has suggested as a factor of sport involvement, has received only slight attention, though results have

been suggestive (Balazs, 1975; Neal, 1963; Williams et al, 1970). Those two motives are clearly areas which call for further research.

17. For an extensive review of this research tradition, see Donnelly (1978).

18. For a more detailed review of this research tradition, see Birrell (1978a; 1978b).

19. An achievement situation is one in which (a) the outcome is challenging and uncertain; (b) behavior is evaluated by a definite standard of excellence; and (c) the individual perceives that the outcome is determined by her/his own skill (McClelland, 1961).

20. The now classic sentence cues were "After first term finals, Anne (John) finds herself (himself) at the top of her (his) med school class" (Horner, 1968, p. 138).

21. I do not wish to discount totally either psyching out an opponent or social facilitation effects, merely to minimize them. They are a constant in both indirect and direct competition.

22. It should not be forgotten that these differences are *perceived* differences. Maccoby and Jacklin (1974) found no evidence that these sex differences are based on any real behavioral differences.

23. Feminine interests included a major in interior and fashion design and interests in playing bridge, gourmet cooking, art, and singing in the college glee club. Masculine interests included a major in physics and interests in reading history and biographies, sports cars, and Red Cross lifesaving.

24. Spence et al. (1975) found that results differed depending on how the question was asked.

25. Ritzer (1975) discerns three paradigms, or disciplinary overviews, within sociology: social facts, social definitions, and social behavior. The social facts paradigm treats social phenomena such as institutions and groups as if they were real and focuses on them as the basic subject matter of sociology. In this perspective, human behavior is viewed as determined by social structure: The individual is constrained by the system and must learn to adjust to it. In contrast, the social definitions paradigm is more concerned with the process through which individuals define their social system. Human behavior is a creative process because individuals are continually renegotiating the meanings of social actions. The social behavior paradigm is not discussed here.

26. Figures from various sources show a dramatic increase in sport participation for women in the past decade. Data from the National Federation of State High School Associations (1981) show that girls' participation in interscholastic athletics increased 531% from 1971 to 1981. On the intercollegiate level, participation of women doubled between 1973 and 1978, to the point where women now represent 30% of all collegiate student athletes (AIAW, no date).

Chapter 4/
The Social Context
of Women in Sport

Woman. Sport. These two words rest curiously next to each other, like unrelated, detached strangers. Each carries with it a special sociological meaning and the connections between these two words—these two worlds—yield a set of intriguing and complex questions. It is our aim in this chapter to examine some of these questions, to explore the assumptions behind them, the methods used to study them, and the tentative answers given to them. Before we get to the questions, however, we want to use broad brush strokes to paint a sociological picture of the meaning of woman and then of sport.

Woman as Sex Role Player

An individual's sex as female or male is assigned by others at birth and is understood to be an ascribed characteristic, generally thought to be beyond the person's ability or desire to change over the course of her or his life. While sex refers to one's biological attributes, a person's sex role refers to the set of psychological traits and social expectations considered appropriate for how females and males should behave.[1] Thus, the roles of woman and man, and the gender definitions of their behavior as feminine and masculine, are social constructions rather than biological facts. These sex roles and definitions are established by society and taught to individuals, starting at birth. Each society, guided by its dominant cultural orientations, and each historical era, influenced by the exigencies of that time period, has generated varied and changing meanings of what women and men are or should be. Taking into account all the variations and alterations of these meanings, one fact looms large: in most societies, greater power, privilege, and value has gone to men and to what has been defined as masculine.

Whenever one group is dominant over another there exists an ideology to justify this inequality; that is, a set of beliefs that legitimates the existing system of inequality as one that is natural, moral, and inevitable. Sexism refers to the ideology that justifies the inequality between women and men. In a Western society like ours, sexism includes uncritically accepted beliefs rooted in biology, religion, psychology, philosophy, history, art, folk wisdom, and the like. These beliefs explain and justify the "natural superiority" of men and masculinity. As such, sexism pervades the entire culture. It is promulgated by family, church, school, government, business, and other social institutions. It is taught to us from infancy and incorporated into our consciousness; it shapes our self-images and affects the way we relate to others and how we experience the world.

An important fact should be stressed here, one that was brilliantly developed by Karl Marx in his analysis of social class inequities. In any system of socially structured inequality *both* the dominant and subordinate groups tend to accept the ideology that justifies the existing system. Slaveowners and slaves, capitalists and workers, parents and children, men and women come to believe in the ideological justification of inequality. Marx labeled as false consciousness the subjective acceptance by subordinate groups of the dominant group's ideology. Women, socialized to believe and encouraged to accept their assigned place in society, live in this state of false consciousness. This means that any effort by women to eradicate sexism must be directed initially at two goals: first, they must throw off the veil of this false consciousness so that they can see clearly the reality of their objective situation; second, they must identify the various forms that sexism takes in society. These tasks are, of course, intimately related, each dependent on and enhancing the other. Every time a woman feels guilty about being raped, every time she is offered and accepts a lower salary, every time she is embarrassed by her body, every time she automatically plans tonight's dinner, she has a chance to question these and countless other feelings and behaviors and to see their connection to her oppression by sexist arrangements and processes in the society.

This task of simultaneously being able to recognize sexism in both the public realm of society and the private world of one's consciousness has been the joy and burden of the second wave of women's liberation that reemerged in the late sixties in the US. Espousing a feminist ideology, which as we stated earlier takes different forms, the contemporary women's movement is historically unique in a number of ways.

First, it has identified the sweeping range and profound depths of sexism that pervade the entire culture and structure of our society. This movement is not satisfied with equal pay for equal work, mandated quotas for women in professional schools, laws without enforcement, husbands who "help" around the house, token women on TV, lesbian bars that won't get raided, or easier access to birth control devices. We do not mean to imply that these are trivial advances that are easily won and now are available to all women. They are not. Even if they become so, however, they are now not enough. The present feminist movement is expanding its criticism to include our language, history, fashion, medicine, music, science, and religion; every aspect of social existence is under suspicion, no aspect is left unexamined. Unlike the first wave of feminism, symbolically bounded by the 1848 Seneca Falls Convention[2] and the passage of the Nineteenth Amendment in 1920 which gave women the right to vote, this later movement with the benefit of hindsight has not stopped at token gestures, segmental legislation, or piecemeal reforms.

Second, it developed and modified "consciousness-raising" strategies to help women understand that their personal experience is tied to power relations in the public sphere. Out of these passages between the personal and the political, women have begun to see that their individual problems are collectively shared by other women. They have begun to see that the origin of their problems rest in sexist society and not in any intrinsic inferiority.

Third, guided by the force and direction of Simone de Beauvior's *The Second Sex* (1953), the analysis and development of strategies to overthrow patriarchy has been elaborated into a worldwide movement that cuts across the boundaries of male-created divisions of race, religion, nation, territory. Women in Israel, Ghana, Iran, Mexico, Italy, Cuba, and India are giving shape to a feminist consciousness that resonates with their unique social and cultural contexts, sensitive to what is similar and what is different in the forms that sexism takes under various systems of patriarchy.

Fourth, aided by the advances made by women over the last century, feminist consciousness is no longer restricted to politically active, elite, intellectual, and privileged women. In retirement villages, on farms, in factories and offices, in lesbian communities, on welfare lines, in supermarkets, at church socials, and on golf courses the word is out: women are on the move, women are resisting, women are challenging, women are changing. Emerging, too, especially in the US, is a loosely connected network of service organizations, magazines, referral groups, bookstores, restaurants, research centers, hotlines, music festivals, and vacation retreats that provide space and support for the women's movement. Feminists across this nation are creating a culture that either modifies or opposes the present patriarchal forms.

Due to these and other differences, this second wave of feminism has and should continue to have greater force in changing not only the roles of women but the very arrangements and activities that shape and support them. One of these is sport and it is the subject of our next painting.

Sport as a Social Institution

Sociologists use the term institution to refer to a cluster of interrelated values, norms, and expectations that are developed by people to meet a particular societal necessity. Every society must be able to solve certain problems if it is to endure and prosper. Sexual behavior must be regulated, someone must care for and teach the young, power needs to be regulated and allocated, goods and services must be produced and distributed, physical and emotional health must be provided, and meaning must be given to existence. Out of the attempts to solve these problems and meet these needs, people develop relatively stable institutions such as the family, education, government, the economy, medicine, and religion. The values, norms, and expectations that make up the basic elements of each institution function to regulate human behavior and to channel it in socially acceptable ways. To the extent that institutions serve to make social life orderly and predictable they are conservative; they function to unify, conserve, and maintain the existing society (Berger, 1963, pp. 87-90).

Sport is such an institution. There exist many definitions (Caillois, 1961; Huizinga, 1950; Loy, 1968) and conceptualizations of sport as a social institution (Edwards, 1973; Loy et al., 1978). We prefer to use the one offered by Eitzen and Sage (1978, pp. 16-19), who define sport as "any competitive physical activity that is guided by established rules." They clarify and specify this definition by differentiating three levels of sport. *Informal sport* consists of physical activity carried out in a playful manner and mainly for the participants' enjoyment, with rules devised by the players themselves to regulate the competition. Examples of this level of sport include a casual game of paddleball, a game of touch football, or a pickup softball game. *Organized sport* involves the elaboration of some elemental organization to order the sport, such as official rules, formal teams, schedules, leagues, tournaments, and the like. These elements of organization are intended to benefit primarily the participants in their pursuit of sporting experience. This level of sport includes city recreational leagues, interscholastic and some intercollegiate sports, club-sponsored tournaments, and the little league, PAL, and YMCA programs. The third level of sport, *corporate sport*, retains some of the dimensions of informal and organized sport. It differs from these two levels, however, in that it is dominated by the demands of profit and power and is controlled by large bureaucracies. These organizations, such as the AAU, NCAA, IOC, and professional sports organizations use their economic and political power to enhance their own survival and growth. They devote themselves less to the desires and needs of the participants and more to the demands of owners, alumni, sponsors, fans, and other vested interest groups. Big-time college athletics, most major amateur sports, and professional sports are organized along these corporate lines. As Eitzen and Sage note (1978), "these three levels of sport can be placed on a continuum from play to work. As one moves from 'informal sport' to 'corporate sport', the activities become more organized with a subsequent loss of autonomy and pleasure by athletes" (p. 19).

Just as there are different levels of sport organization, each with its unique structures and processes, there are also differences in the type and degree of people's involvement in sport as an institution. Harry Edwards (1973, p. 86) devised a categorization of these differences which sensitizes us to the fact that one's type and degree of involvement affects one's motives, goals, priorities, and rewards vis-a-vis the sporting experience. These characteristics differ, for example, depending on whether one is a player, coach, trainer, umpire, cheerleader, owner, equipment retailer, or fan.

Both of these general factors—the level of organization and the type and degree of involvement—influence the meanings one brings to her or his sport participation and consequences of that participation. Although these brief comments should underscore at least some of the complexity of this institution, we want to explore in more detail the perceived functions of sport as an institution embedded in the larger society.

As an institution, the structures and processes of sport are said to serve a variety of societal needs. Some see sports as providing a safety valve for people, helping to channel their hostility, tension and energies in culturally prescribed ways. Sport is said to offer role models in the form of athletes who possess the desired mental and physical attributes that people should strive for. Others observe that sport disseminates and reinforces accepted cultural values and lifestyles (Eitzen & Sage, 1978, p. 11). Considerable theoretical debate continues over the extent to which sport serves as a ladder for upward mobility, a vehicle for racial and ethnic assimilation, a hedge against delinquency, an opportunity for moral development, and a source of national unity and international goodwill.[3]

There is greater consensus over the fact that sport, as an institution, has accumulated over time elements that complement those of other institutions and help it to buttress the foundation of society. It is in this sense that sport is often called a microcosm of society, reflecting the basic values, beliefs, rules, and ideas of the larger system. In addition to the major trends that characterize contemporary American sport (discussed in chapter 2), Eitzen and Sage (1978, pp. 66-74) identify a core set of American values that pervade the institution of sport. In both the larger society and in sport, primary importance is placed on the following values:

Competition and success. Virtually nothing can shake the American belief that competition, not cooperation, motivates people to excel and to win. In sport, as in society, the means is heightened competition, the goal is victory. Winning becomes equated with success and losing with failure, resulting in an exaggerated emphasis on final outcomes as a measure of one's personal and social worth.

Hard work, striving, and deferred gratification. The Puritan work ethic is extolled as one of the three means to achieve success in both sport and other social endeavors. Effort, perspiration, practice, and preparation are the keys to winning; losing is a result of not giving 100%. For both winners and losers, continued striving—the second means to success—is essential. Quitters and those who "rest on their laurels" will jeopardize their chance to get to the top or to remain there. The third means to achieve, deferred gratification, demands a future orientation, a willingness to postpone pleasure and reward to a later time when one can harvest the fruits of present labors.

Progress. Just as Americans are encouraged never to be satisfied with present attainments, so too, in sport, one should never fail to strive for more victories, new records, larger scores, superior skills. Constant progress is the measure of the true champion, both on and off the field.

Materialism. The rewards for one's efforts and accomplishments are expected, in our society, to be extrinsic, especially in the form of financial and material acquisitions. How much money one makes, particularly in professional spectator sports, is the yardstick used to determine the value of success for both athletes and owners. Indeed, the conspicuous consumption of leisure and sporting activities (Veblen, 1953, pp. 170-182), in the form of expensive equipment, plush club membership, sportswear, and season tickets, is expected and encouraged by citizens with even the most rudimentary involvement in sport.

External conformity. The American belief in and acceptance of "the system," with its structure of authority, rules, procedures, and sanctions, is also mirrored in sport. The coach, manager, and front office are to be respected and obeyed just as are the police officer, teacher, judge, physician, and employer. There exists a belief in the "hierarchy of credibility" (Becker, 1967, pp. 240-241), which holds that one's superiors have legitimate claim to be in authority and therefore to command obedience and respect.

Along similar lines, in his analysis of the institution of sport, Harry Edwards (1973, pp. 103-130) examines the dominant American sports creed—a set of beliefs about the benefits of sport for the individual and the society. According to Edwards, the assumed benefits of sport include character development, discipline, competitiveness, physical and mental fitness, religiosity, and nationalism. These professed benefits are espoused to varying degrees by citizens with the most remote to the most intense involvement in sport.[4] The composite picture of the individual who participates in sport is the red-blooded, wholesome, virile man, one sound in body and mind, whose belief in religion and patriotism, guided by self-discipline and the competitive spirit, will make him successful in sport and in other social endeavors.

As a socializing agency, sport allegedly instills these qualities in young boys so that they will be able to successfully assume not only sport roles but also their roles as breadwinners, workers, soldiers, and citizens. The basic sociological axiom that institutions are interrelated and interdependent is quite evident here. Sport, like the family, education, the mass media, and religion, socializes its members to maintain existing cultural patterns. It does this by instilling in people the requisite motives and skills to assume socially valued roles in other institutions and to desire the rewards offered by these institutions. It is no wonder, then, that sport participation is encouraged by religious leaders, school administrators, business and labor representatives, and officials of the military and the government. Nor is it surprising that those who have been critical of sport continue to be viewed with suspicion and hostility and defined as traitors and heretics who must be exorcised from the body social. As Edwards (1973) explains it, "any attack upon the institution of sport in a particular society would be widely interpreted . . . as an attack upon the fundamental way of life of that society as manifest in the value orientations it emphasizes through sport. Hence, an attack upon sport constitutes an attack upon the society itself" (p. 90).

With this warning in mind, we are ready to begin an examination of the connections between woman and sport. Several questions stated in simple terms are, in our opinion, at the heart of the public and scholarly debate over the relation between these two social realities.

- Why is sport, of all the social institutions, the most exclusively masculine domain? Why have men established and maintained an institution in which women's participation has been vigorously resisted or simply ignored?
- Why have the majority of women resisted becoming involved with sport except at the informal level or in socially accepted sports (e.g. tennis and gymnastics) and sporting roles (e.g. cheerleaders, boosters, or casual spectators)?
- What factors account for the present upsurge of interest by women in extending their type and level of sport participation?
- Why is there conflicting opinion within the feminist and academic communities over the benefits and costs of the contemporary revolution in women's sport?

For analytical purposes, the sections that follow will treat each of these questions separately, although it is obvious that they are connected by many threads which will be elaborated further in the second part of the book.

Sport as a Masculine Domain

The traditional polarization of sex roles has produced in our society two different kinds of human beings—women and men—who are expected to play different roles, hold different attitudes, espouse different values, and express different feelings. Women are to assume roles in the private sphere as wife, mother, and homemaker; men are expected to assume roles in the public sphere as worker, citizen, and active creator of social and cultural life. In these restricted roles, women are expected to be expressive, men to be instrumental. Among other traits, femininity has come to mean nurturance, dependence, cooperation, intuition, and passivity; masculinity has come to mean aggression, independence, rationality, activity, and competition.[5] Although this artificial, socially constructed polarization is presently being challenged by many women and some men, the men who have created and maintained contemporary institutions and culture have done so in accordance with these understandings of being women and men. In particular, they have shaped institutions to generate, strengthen and celebrate the role of men and the values of masculinity which simultaneously devalues the role of women and the values of femininity.

It is in this sense that many scholars have reflected on the isomorphism between sport and masculinity (Beisser, 1973; Duquin, 1978; Franks, 1979; Oglesby, 1978; Scott, 1975). Each social reality supports, informs, and reinforces the other so that being athletic and being masculine calls forth and rewards similar values, attitudes and skills. If we explore this connection between sport and masculinity, we can begin to understand some of the reasons why men resist women's participation in this institution.

One of them has to do with the task of socializing infant males so that they can grow up to assume the conventional role of men with its appropriate masculine orientation. In a society where the meanings and models of masculinity are more and more remote from the everyday lives of little boys, games and sports become crucial vehicles for teaching the virtues of masculinity and the principle of male dominance and privilege. In a review of the literature, Duquin (1978, pp. 93-96) identifies the myriad ways in which parents, siblings, books, language, schooling, and other agents of socialization forge in the minds of both girls and boys the idea that sport is a masculine domain to be entered by boys and avoided by girls. In "Sport and the Masculine Obsession," Jack Scott (1975) states: "It has been my experience that American men who grew up actively participating in competitive athletics intuitively understand the role sports played in forging their manhood. Sport is our 'civilized' society's most prominent masculinity rite" (p. 2). It is on the fields, courts, rinks, and playgrounds of America that boys learn to be men and to value masculinity. It is in their games that they assert their difference from girls and their superiority over them. It is in sport that they learn to compete, to control, to take risks, to be strong, and to achieve mastery over self and others. It is in sport that they begin to understand why and how they are to become men.

The function of sport as a socialization agency for men has assumed even greater significance when one considers the social and cultural changes that have marked the past century. The closing of the frontier, the shift from rural to urban lifestyles, the growth of bureaucracy and technology, and changes in the nature of work have led to a frustration of the masculine impulse. Work requires less brawn and more brains. Almost half of the labor force consists of women who help put food on the table. Police and fire departments, social service agencies, and insurance programs protect the lives and future of family members. The dictates of bureaucracy and government reduce the opportunity for innovation, risk-taking, and personal ingenuity. The complex problems of urban life are beyond the grasp of individual men with private resources and personal solutions. Men now find fewer opportunities to display courage, initiative, independence, and strength than they used to. Their world has changed without a complementary alteration in the traditional conception of their sex role. The impact of these changes on the increased involvement by men in sports has been forcefully presented by a number of scholars (Beisser, 1973; Chorbajian, 1978). According to Leon Chorbajian (1978), "Jobs are often boring; men must take orders and comprise their image as rugged individualists in order to survive. The resulting frustration of these traditional values is often worked out in vicarious forms of involvement. One such area is spectator sports which is heavily governed by traditional male values" (p. 165). Thus, not only does sport function to socialize males to traditional sex roles, it also is one of the few remaining institutions (the military being another one) that still permits the enactment of traditional masculinity. In this light, sport serves as a safety valve mechanism for the expression of anachronistic ideas about masculinity that have lagged behind those social and cultural forces that demand new conceptions of men as human beings.

In a thoughtful observation, the psychiatrist Arnold R. Beisser (1973) identifies the connection between sport and gender roles:

> Within the roles of everyday life there is diminishingly small space for the expression of some of man's physical characteristics. The male animal is physically stronger than the female; he is the primitive defender and aggressor. Modern technology has made physical strength partially obsolete. Yet in a contradictory way we still expect expression of strength and aggression from men. . . . The marvels of electronic gadgetry may equalize the sexes during the week, but on the Saturday athletic field, strength still prevails; that is, maleness prevails, . . . As the functional differences between male and female diminish, sports interest rises in a nostalgic return to premechanized days when physical strength was all important. (p. 90)

In the absence of alternative understandings of their place in society, men cling ever more strongly to an institution that confirms their identity and social dominance. To allow women into sport would be an ultimate threat to one of the last strongholds of male security and supremacy. To put it another way, if women can play sports then "men aren't really men."

A second reason for men's resistance to changes in women's sport participation is embedded in the hierarchical ranking of sex roles. Cultural definitions have not merely differentiated men from women; they have attached to them evaluations that rank men higher than women in social value. In a review of the research on sex role stereotypes, which conceives of femininity and masculinity as opposing poles, Chafetz (1978, pp. 37-44) contrasts the positive imagery used in describing masculine traits with the negative connotations associated with femininity. The masculine role is described by words bearing positive connotations: brave, logical, confident, strong, trustworthy, and the like; the feminine role is described in negatively charged words: petty, weak, coy, frivolous, vain, and so on. Although Chafetz cautions us to remember that we do not know the extent to which Americans who are not white or middle class subscribe to these stereotypes, she notes that these images of women and men are those most commonly held in the dominant American culture. Other research (Lockheed & Hall, 1976) reveals that *both* sexes, including children as young as 5 or 6, rate masculine characteristics higher than feminine ones, thus demonstrating the power of socialization to inculcate this sex role hierarchy in the consciousness of both the dominant and subordinate group.

Thus, part of the complex of a masculine self-image is a conscious and unconscious denigration and distrust of women and of femininity (Daly, 1978). What secures and enhances the activities prescribed for men is, in large measure, due to women's exclusion from them. The absence of women and of attributes defined as feminine are two of the elements that clarify men's roles. Men are what women are not; men do what women cannot. In a crucial insight about sport, Franks (1979) notes that "the mere presence of women is enough to devalue these sacred male ceremonies" (p. 102). The social stigma attached to being feminine and to including women in their activities has led men to forcefully insure a sexual division of labor in most areas of social life. In every institution, the roles of women and men are clearly delineated. Furthermore, it is now well documented (Bullough, 1974) that as women have entered particular fields of activity (e.g. elementary school teaching, nursing, clerical work) men abandoned them or insured themselves the more dominant position within these fields (e.g. principal, physician, employer). Similar trends appear in sport. Women have their "proper place" in this institution. They can be involved in tennis, golf, gymnastics, and swimming but should avoid the more manly contact team sports. Even when women play basketball, softball, football, tennis, and golf, men are quick to point out the difference between "the woman's game" and "the real game" that they play! By so doing, they confirm their difference from women and maintain their distance from them as well.

From an ideological point of view, men have resisted the intrusion of women into their games by conjuring up fears that changes in women's level and type of sport participation will "masculinize" women, stripping them of their unique female qualities. While this point will be discussed in more detail later, we believe that this argument can be read differently. That is, it could be understood as a rationalization of men's deeper fear of what could be called "the feminization of sport." This appeal to the alleged masculinization of women can be interpreted as an ideological justification for keeping sport as a masculine domain. As long as sport remains a protected sphere of male sexual identity, men will resist intruders that could confuse and threaten this valued imagery.

A third source of men's resistance to women's athleticism is grounded in the specific cluster of elements that define masculinity. While we are

well aware of the benefits that accrue to being men, there are real emotional and social costs that they must pay to play this role. Men are not
allowed, as women often are, to display attributes assigned to the other
sex. Severe social penalties are given to men who express fear,
dependence, need, physical intimacy, and other socially defined feminine
traits.

Sport is an exception in this regard. It is in sporting activity that men
are allowed the rare opportunity to express those feelings forbidden in
most of their other roles. They can embrace each other unself-con-
sciously, holding and hugging, touching and kissing without threat of
ridicule and suspicion. They can express fear, hesitancy, pain and doubt
and be nurtured by other men. They can grieve together and be comforted. They can be irrational, cooperative, sentimental, and supersti-
tious in the accepting presence of male camaraderie. In sum, in the
absence of women, they can allow themselves to express what sexist
ideology insists must be suppressed if they are to lay valid claim to being
"real men."

An extension of this idea is hinted at by Franks (1979) who believes
that competing against other men must, in and of itself, offer some
special significance. She speculates that "Perhaps sports offer men a vital
and coveted medium through which they can express to each other indirectly what society has forbidden them to express outright and perhaps
they fear the consequences of letting the 'outside' into their club" (Franks,
1979, p. 103). It is the expression of physical and emotional intimacy between males that is the issue here. We believe that this is an important
factor in explaining the special joy and intensity with which boys and
men pursue sports and a major determinant of their reluctance to include
women in their games. According to Beisser (1973), physical contact
among men, beyond the brief handshake, remains a strong social taboo.
His words bear emphasizing as they relate to sport:

> The one place that allows and encourages close physical contact between
> males, and paradoxically this is in the service of the most masculine of ac-
> tivities, is sports. Far from being considered 'queer', male physical contact on
> the athletic field is sanctioned. The team goes into a huddle, the linebacker
> pats his linemen on their buttocks, scantily dressed men collide, bump into,
> and hit each other in basketball, boxing, and wrestling. Home run! Touch-
> down! Victory!—and the players embrace! The thousands who watch roar
> their approval. Such actions outside the stadium, on the street, for instance,
> would be viewed with suspicion, a knowing glance, and perhaps even the
> summoning of the vice squad. Sports provide a culturally acceptable, useful,
> and vital place for such expressions. (pp. 91-92)

Two distinct but related issues are relevant here. One is the fact that
sport allows for the expression of assumed feminine qualities, albeit in

the safety of exclusively male groups. In the clubhouse, the locker room, the dugout and on the field men can display a side of themselves that is held in check by the demands of their sex role. That this expressive emotionality enhances men's self-actualization and existential gratification has been empirically documented. Recent research (Bem, 1975b; Bem, Martyna, & Watson, 1976) has shown that androgynous persons, that is, persons who are both instrumental *and* expressive in self-image, possess greater behavioral flexibility and exhibit greater social and psychological well-being. We believe that part of the attraction of sport lies in this opportunity for men to be expressive insofar as sport allows a more humanistic outlet for these emotions. The burden of unrestrained instrumentality that pervades the rest of men's lives can be lightened by the protected cover of sport. It is a source of release and relief that they would be hesitant to abandon.

The other issue has to do with the rampant homophobia[6]—the intense fear and hatred of sexual intimacy between persons of the same sex—that characterizes much of patriarchal culture. To a degree, women are able to express to other women feelings of intimacy, tenderness, love, and caring. Men do so only at the risk of being labeled feminine or homosexual. Even lesbians do not meet with the same degree of intense hatred as homosexuals. According to Erich Goode (1978), the reaction that a lesbian receives "does not have quite the savagery that the male homosexual faces. But notice: it is primarily because of *sexism* that this is the case. It is only because the dominant heterosexual male does not take lesbianism seriously that it is not condemned to the same degree as male homosexuality" (p. 392, original italics). Except under extreme situations, such as combat or death, men's relations to other men are expected to be distant, rational, competitive, joking, and the like. Whatever expressiveness they are allowed must be channeled toward women, thus depriving them of the rich emotional ties that they also could have with other men.

Despite the frequent analysis of sport as an arena of repressed homosexuality, we doubt whether it is necessary or important, except to psychoanalysts, to delve into some of the unconscious motives behind men's involvement in sport. Nor do we believe that one's sexual preference need be a salient issue at this stage in the discussion. What seems more significant to us is that, regardless of one's sexual orientation, sport allows men the freedom to cultivate and express more emotional bonds with other men. In the rituals, rigors, and rhythms of the sporting experience, men can enjoy these intimate exchanges prohibited off the field. Thus, not only does sport allow men a chance to display the repressed side of their humanity, it also allows them to display these feelings to other men.

In sum, we believe that each of these three functions of sport—socialization to the male role, denigration of women and femininity, masculine expressivity and male intimacy—rests at the core of men's resistance to women's movement into sport. Doubtless there are other sources of their resistance, such as the increased competition for scarce sport resources and rewards, machismo, the fear of being beaten by a woman, hesitancy about the unknown future consequences of women's participation, the need to reorder established routines, rules, and customs within sport, etc. We feel, however, that these are more superficial factors that camouflage the roots of men's anxiety about women and sport. Unless we address ourselves to these and other core issues neither men nor women will be able to accommodate themselves to the changing role of women and sport with the humanism, intelligence and sensitivity that should accompany institutional transformation.

Barriers to Women's Sport Participation

In this section we shall explore some of the reasons why most women have been reluctant to participate in sport with the same intensity, range, and depth of involvement that characterizes men's participation. This issue has been at the center of virtually all discussions of women in sport. Scholarly essays, empirical research studies, feminist analyses, and position papers by physical educators identify a wide range of factors that deter women from sport participation. We cannot give equal time to all of them, but we believe that the following factors contribute most significantly to reducing women's desire and ability to engage in sports: (a) the potential for role conflict that exists when women engage in sport, (b) the failure of sport to reflect values and interests that resonate with women's world view and life experiences, (c) the inadequate socialization of women to assume roles in sport, and (d) the institutional sexism that blocks women's sport activity. We will stress the first two factors in our discussion because we believe that they are more fundamental barriers to women's involvement in sport and they have yet to receive much critical analysis. The other two issues are only mentioned at this point because Part 2 of the book is devoted to them in detail.

The Role Conflict Controversy

As we suggested in our discussion of sport as a masculine domain, the roles of woman and of sport participant contain conflicting and incompatible expectations that make it virtually impossible for women to fulfill both sets of demands. Given the cultural configurations of these two roles, many scientists have hypothesized that women who become involved in sport may experience the interpersonal and psychological strain that results from conflicting role expectations. As Sage and Loudermilk (1979) put it:

> One of the oldest and most persistent folk myths, and one of the main deterrents to female sports participation, has been the notion that vigorous physical activity tends to masculinize girls and women. Women of physical competence have been stigmatized as masculine by a tradition that taught that women who have excellent physical competence must be unfeminine. The stereotype of the female athlete as aggressive, frustrated, and unfeminine is well described. . . . Thus, consciously or unconsciously, athletic achievement has been equated with loss of femininity. (p. 89)

Women who take sports seriously and who invest considerable amounts of time, energy, and emotional commitment to physical pursuits are, with some exceptions, felt to be jeopardizing their claim to being feminine and being accepted as "normal" women. The stigma attached to serious sport involvement is said to frequently produce much personal and social strain for women. Words such as tomboy, mannish, unladylike, and lesbian serve the function of keeping women's participation at socially acceptable levels and types of involvement.

Scholarly evidence suggests that because of the intimate relationship between sport and masculinity and the negative sanctions applied to women who cross this sex-segregated role boundary, it is likely that sportswomen may perceive and/or experience role conflict (Felshin, 1974b; Harris, 1975; M. Hart, 1976; Malumphy, 1971; Snyder & Kivlin, 1977). This concern over role conflict pervades the popular literature as well. The discussion of the tension between femininity and athleticism is revealed in the titles of such articles as:"Why do women want to be jocks?" (Koslow, 1975); "It was as if all girls in phys ed . . . were less than a she" (Harris, 1975); "An 'Unfeminine' Stigma" (Scannel & Barnes, 1974); "Women Athletes With Femininity: Why Not?" (Liscio, 1977); "Women Athletes Are Women, Too" (Kaplan, 1979b). In both the scholarly and popular literature the issue of role conflict tends to be discussed within the framework of traditional definitions of both sport and sex roles. The aim of these inquiries is to determine the extent to which women experience conflict when they play sports and how they devise strategies for reducing or resolving this conflict. Later we will discuss the limits of this approach to the question of role conflict.

In an effort to specify the conditions under which sportswomen may experience role conflict, some researchers have argued that the amount of conflict is related to the *type of sport* women pursue. It has already been noted that greater social approval is given to playing sports that demand grace, balance, flexibility, skill, and dexterity, while sports that require speed, strength, endurance and physical contact are severely stigmatized for women. According to numerous scholars (Eitzen & Sage, 1978; Malumphy, 1968; Metheney, 1965; Snyder et al., 1975), this variation in social acceptability accounts for some of the reasons why women are more likely to be found in gymnastics, golf, and tennis rather than in track and field, auto racing, or softball. In addition, research shows that women receive greater social approval for participating in individual or dyadic sports than in team sports (Debacy, Spaeth & Busch, 1970; Snyder & Kivlin, 1975).

Empirically, the question of the degree and type of alleged role conflict for sportswomen is far from settled. The research being done in this area, like other areas of new exploration, is producing conflicting findings and should be generating much debate over its assumptions, methods, and interpretations. In one of the latest empirical studies, Sage and Loudermilk (1979) investigated the amount of perceived and experienced role conflict among 268 female varsity college athletes from 9 sports and 13 different colleges. They found that female college athletes did perceive and experience conflict between the roles of woman and athlete, but that "the extent of role conflict did not reach the level that was anticipated by the investigators" (Sage & Loudermilk, 1979, p. 94). While the amount of general role conflict was not found to be as high as might be expected, the researchers did find that women athletes who participated "in traditionally not socially approved sports experienced greater role conflict than those participating in more socially approved sports" (Sage & Loudermilk, 1979, p. 95).

Citing previous research that reported similar findings, the researchers offer several explanations for their data. With respect to their primary finding, that the overall level of reported role conflict was not as high as they anticipated, the investigators suggest two possible interpretations. First, they speculate that women who either perceive or experience role conflict may withdraw from sport participation before college and thus are not likely to be found in samples of female college athletes. Second, they point to other research which shows that female athletes (compared with their nonathletic peers) report higher self-esteem and more positive self-imagery, suggesting that the benefits of sport give women athletes a sense of competency and self-determination that serves to resolve potential role conflict. Regarding their other finding, that role conflict is related to the type of sport played, the researchers speculate that women who play less socially acceptable sports are, in fact, treated negatively by those who feel that only certain sports are acceptable for women to play.

In reviewing the literature, we found a considerable amount of theorizing about how sportswomen could reduce or resolve the dissonance (Festinger, 1957) and role conflict they experience. In fact, there were more theoretical discussions of this issue than there were actual research investigations of the conflict experience itself. In her treatment of female adolescence as a time of crisis for girls who engage in sports, Tyler (1973, pp. 30-31) identifies a variety of ways that teenage girls resolve this conflict. Some girls, as stated above, drop out of sports altogether. Other girls choose to remove themselves from social situations and activities that demand feminine role behavior, while remaining active in their sport roles. Another strategy is for girls to bring to their social roles the attitudes, postures, and orientations of the athletic role. This strategy is exemplified by the "typical jock" stereotypes of the mannish, tomboy, or lesbian athlete. Other girls are not willing to abandon either role and manage to be both athletic and feminine according to the appropriate demands of different social situations. As Tyler notes (1973), "They are as secure of their femininity whether dressed in an evening gown or a sweatsuit. There is no dissonance or conflict, for these women are cognizant of and proficient in both roles" (p. 30). Other ways of resolving role conflict have been suggested by Layman (Note 4), who feels that participation in individual sports rather than team sports may reduce conflict. She also notes that conflict may be minimized by perceiving sports as not in conflict with one's self-image.

Finally, the most well-known strategies for reducing the cognitive dissonance and role conflict that is experienced by women in sport is suggested by Jan Felshin (1974a, 1974b) and are known as "the apologetic." According to Felshin (1974b):

> Each woman in sport is a social anomaly when sport is seen as the idealized socialization of masculine traits and the ideals of femininity preclude these qualities. Because women cannot be excluded from sport and have chosen not to reject sport, apologetics develop to account for this sport involvement in the face of its social unacceptability. (p. 432)

These apologetics may take on a variety of forms and include: (a) the exaggerated use of feminine accouterments (makeup, ribbons, jewelry, style of uniform) by sportswomen; (b) the denial by women that they take their sports seriously as personal achievements rather than as casual forms of sociability; (c) the pursuit of the more socially acceptable individual sports; (d) the affirmation of feminine values such as beauty, grace, muscle tone, and so on as justifications for playing sports; and (e) the adherence to and espousement of a more traditional, conservative view of women's role in society, one which excuses sport participation. These apologetics function to legitimate women's involvement in sport and to resolve or reduce the role conflict women might perceive or experience. The apologetic implies that women in sport can look feminine, are feminine, and want to be feminine (Felshin, 1974a, p. 204), thus serving to reassure the participants *and others* that sport does not invalidate their claim to being "real" women.

At this point in our discussion we want to share with the reader our uneasiness about the methodological, conceptual, and philosophical difficulties that are at the core of the treatment of this topic. Reflecting on the contradictory findings that have emerged regarding this issue, Mathes (1978) argues that: "When large numbers of athletes and nonathletes indicate that sport 'detracts from being feminine' and that a 'stigma' is associated with sport participation and yet indicate they feel positive about their bodies and social role, then further analysis is demanded" (p. 69). We feel that before any further theorizing and research is done on this topic we need to critically assess the usefulness, validity and clarity of how role conflict is conceptualized and researched.

Conceptual Problems of Role Conflict

The way in which an issue is conceptualized is grounded in certain personal and intellectual assumptions that shape both the questions that will be asked and the research strategies employed to investigate them. We feel strongly that the present status of discourse on role conflict for women in sport suffers from a number of poorly conceived, vaguely understood, and inadequately articulated conceptual problems.

First, most of the theoretical discussion of role conflict treats both the roles of women and sport participant in very vague, amorphous, and general terms. Roles involve the enactment of clusters of expectations that link the role player to many others in a complex network of interaction. The role of athlete, for example, links the person to other role partners, such as coaches, referees, competitors, teammates, fans, and so on. Each of these relationships carries with it different, specific sets of rights and obligations and therefore different potentials for conflict. The same is true for the role of woman, which, although a more diffuse role, nevertheless requires different expectations depending on with whom the woman is interacting. Thus, any treatment of role conflict should specify the particular axes along which the conflict is being investigated. For example, the potential for role conflict may differ if we focus on the female athlete's relationship to her coach as opposed to her competitors; it may take different forms if the referee is a woman or a man; it may differ in intensity if we consider her relationship to the press as contrasted with the relationship she has to spectators. Investigations into role conflict presently suffer from a failure to specify these particular relational contexts in which conflict may emerge. This inadequate specification, then, prevents the possibility of generating suggestive hypotheses that can identify more precisely those factors that influence the nature, content, degree, and range of conflict.

Second, roles not only govern the on-going relations people have with different others; they also contain attitudes, behaviors, and norms that role occupants are expected to adhere to as general characteristics of their role. The present research on role conflict also fails to distinguish among these general role orientations. Exactly what dimension of either role is in conflict with what aspect of the other role for the sportswoman? By glossing over detailed specifications of both roles, we are seldom able to generate research that can begin to answer this question. Is the woman athlete a "poor loser"? Is she unwilling to intimidate officials? Is she worried about her muscular appearance? Does she not train hard enough? Is she too friendly with the opposition? Is she concerned about behaving too aggressively? These kinds of questions cannot be answered when investigators do not specify the many normative, attitudinal, and behavioral expectations that go into defining both roles.

Third, roles take shape and are activated in specific social contexts, and as the contexts change so do the role demands and the potential for conflict. Here again, insufficient attention to contextual influences obscures the nature of the conflict. A sportswoman may perceive her body as acceptable in athletic contexts but not in social settings (Mathes, 1978, p. 68). She may experience different conflicts during training or practice as opposed to actual competition. Her dilemmas may take differing forms in the clubhouse, in the locker room, in the trainer's office, or at postgame socials. She may encounter different conflicts in the privacy of her home as contrasted with the demands of being on tour. Each context may generate unique configurations of possible conflict and require particular strategies for resolution of the conflict. In order to grasp the complexity and differential impact of these contextual influences, greater attention must be paid to them in devising conceptual models for our theory and research.

Fourth, the type and level of sport involvement by women will influence the particular profile of conflicting demands. Although previously identified research occasionally has taken into account type of sport involvement (e.g. individual vs. team sports), other dimensions remained undeveloped. For example, the potential for conflict may differ depending on whether one is a novice athlete or a veteran, a "star" player or a benchwarmer, an amateur or a professional, a high school participant or a college athlete with a full-ride scholarship. In addition, a dimension discussed earlier, the level of involvement of sport—informal, organized, or corporate—will certainly alter the type and range of conflict that may be perceived or experienced by women engaged in sport.

Fifth, women bring to their sports not only their sex roles but other social memberships as well, such as age, race and ethnicity, social class, marital status, and the like. Each of these other roles cannot be ignored when discussing conflict for the sportswoman, because each influences how she is oriented toward sport *and* how she defines herself as a woman. For example, some research data show that team sport participants are more likely to come from the lower social classes while participants of individual sports are more likely to come from the upper classes (Greendorfer, 1978, pp. 129-130). Other research (Yorburg, 1974) indicates that traditional, conservative images of women's role are more likely to be held by lower class women, rural women, and white women, while higher class women, urban women, and black women espouse a more liberal view of women's role. With respect to age, research shows that persons in adolescence and young adulthood are more likely than mature adults to emphasize and exhibit sex role differences (Birrell, 1978; Maccoby & Jacklin, 1974).

Thus, if a woman is rich or poor, black or white, young or old, or resides in an urban or rural environment this will affect the type and amount of conflict she may encounter. The same may hold true for other differences among women, such as their marital status, sexual orientation, ethnic and religious affiliation, and the like. What is needed, then, is a recognition of the social heterogeneity of women, their locations in different parts of the social structure, their participation in different subcultures, and their enactment of different roles—all of which affect the multiple ways in which role conflict may be perceived and experienced. Furthermore, these differences among women will influence their *resolution* of role conflict, a factor which is also neglected in most treatments of this topic. For example, the decision to retire from professional athletic competition, and the timing of that exit, may depend partly on whether or not the sportswoman has children. In sum, the heterogeneity of women will shape the resources available for resolving conflicting pressures, the strategies used for the resolution and the definition of successful accommodation to role conflict.

While these five suggestions for improving the conceptualization of role conflict are not exhaustive,[7] we believe that they are major issues that must be grappled with in order to give clarity and validity to present investigations into this problem. Much of the dissatisfaction that we feel about the status of scholarship in this area is due to simplistic approaches to the issues. More attention must be given to the multidimensional nature of both sport and sex roles and their complex ties in different spheres of social action. We must develop conceptual maps of this topic that take into account the contextual and structural determinants of role definition and role playing. We also need to devise theoretical paradigms that will do justice to the richly complicated differences of meaning that women bring to their roles. All efforts that treat role conflict as a homogeneous, unidimensional phenomenon will inevitably result in the confusions, contradictions, and omissions that characterize much of the theory and research to date.

Methodological Problems

Given the intimate relation between theory and research, we should expect that limited conceptual models of role conflict would yield limited research designs and data. Some major deficiencies of present research include: (a) the use of small, unrepresentative, and non-comparable samples of women college athletes; (b) the questionable reliability and validity of the measurement of such concepts as athletic participation, sex role orientation, role conflict, and the like; (c) the absence of theoretically based control variables that would specify findings and make possible meaningful comparisons between subgroups; and, (d) the virtually exclusive use of structured survey instruments and packaged tests of statistical significance as the means of collecting and analyzing data. The typical research investigation[8] is usually carried out on a nonrepresentative sample of approximately 200 students who are varsity college athletes or students in physical education courses and, at times, their nonathletic college peers. They are asked to fill out questionnaires containing some measure of their athletic involvement and sex–role orientation. Their responses to selected measures of conflict are solicited. Data are then subjected to standard group comparisons and ANOVA tests of significance. Most of the interpretation of data is descriptive, cryptic, and ex post facto.

We understand that limited resources are often the reason behind these types of research strategies, but we also believe that certain biases and professional pressures serve, consciously or unknowingly, to encourage this type of research. One of these is the unwillingness or inability to question our conceptualizations of problems and to engage in the arduous and lonely task of reworking conceptual models. It is far easier to use existing theoretical models, standardized scales and measures, and conventional modes of analysis rather than to devise ones that better meet the needs of the topic and the present research problem. It is easier to accept someone else's definition of the problem rather than rethink the usefulness and significance of the problem as presently stated. In his critical assessment of the state of sport psychology, Rainer Martens (1979) raises some soul-searching questions that get to the core of our own concerns:

> I suspect more than a few sport psychologists have dared to risk some introspective analysis, flirting dangerously with such thoughts as: Am I participating in a big intellectual and academic game in which, in the 'name of the

game', problems are being manufactured rather than formulated, methodological tools are being used because they have the 'good scientific stamp of approval' rather than because they have been logically and theoretically derived from a problem, and that quantification is to be achieved at any cost, even at the understanding of a problem? (p. 95)

Martens bravely and accurately identifies another source of what we believe to be a present methodological deficiency in studies of role conflict—the pressure to do research that mimics the positivism of the natural sciences, with their emphases on laboratory experiments and quantification of data. In the desire to gain professional respectability, and under the pressure to publish articles whose acceptability is too often evaluated by their degree of quantification, we have ignored other techniques for both data collection and analysis. Field research, participant observation, intensive interviews, and content analysis are just a few of the techniques that are more appropriate to emerging areas of inquiry than are laboratory experiments of surveys. The former techniques are best suited to investigations of uncharted areas of inquiry, such as role conflict among sportswomen, because they facilitate the development of conceptual models, insights, sensitizing concepts, and hypotheses (SanGiovanni, 1978, p. 16). Taking his own advice, Martens has decided to change his research site from the laboratory to field settings in order to observe and describe sport behavior, noting that:

We have been so enamored with our operational definitions, clever manipulations, and high-powered statistics that we are in danger of losing sight of the phenomenon these instruments were designed to illuminate. We clearly need to spend more time observing behavior in sport and building our own theories unique to sport. Then we can test them! (Martens, 1979, p. 97)

Two examples of the dangers of present methodological strategies for researching role conflict can be briefly cited here to illustrate our point. The easy accessibility of college students as research subjects has produced a host of research done on a very select sample of young women, aged 18-22. These women are at a stage in the life cycle when their gender behavior and gender identity are critical issues to be negotiated as they experiment with establishing stable emotional and sexual relations with others. Persons in this age group are more likely to define themselves in terms of masculinity and femininity and are more likely to exhibit greater sex-role differences than are persons at younger or older ages (Maccoby & Jacklin, 1974). However, these are exactly the young women who are being asked about the potential conflict between being women and being athletic! Clearly, one would expect that respondents at different ages and stages in the life cycle may hold different attitudes and perceptions regarding this issue, yet few researchers seem sensitive to this problem. One who is, Susan Birrell (1978a), notes that:

> an unanticipated age factor may have contaminated the results. Conclusions based on data restricted to the age group 18 to 22 must be strengthened by a sampling from other age groups. It is a further irony that the easily accessible college population may have been distorting research conclusions regarding sex differences for years. (p. 151)

For example, if studies of role conflict investigated the experiences of prepubescent girls or women in their thirties, the dynamics of role conflict for these sportswomen would surely be different from that of 18-21 year old participants. In addition to the age bias that stems from sampling college students, we would add the biases of other factors, such as social class, race, ethnicity, and religion, which also are not randomly distributed among college populations and would also limit the generalizability of such findings.

Another instance of the limits of research that is uninformed by sound theory can be seen in the treatment of apologetics. Felshin (1974a), Del Rey (1977), and others have hypothesized that women who play socially acceptable sports such as tennis and golf have less need to apologize for their participation than do women engaged in unacceptable sports such as contact team sports. However, the social class backgrounds of women who select themselves into different types of sport are ignored both in conceptualizing and researching the relationship between these variables. We already know that women from higher classes hold more liberal views of their role in society and that tennis and golf are more likely to be played by members of these classes. Thus, if we consider the social class origins of respondents, we could just as easily hypothesize that women who play individual sports may have less need to apologize for their sport participation not because they play socially acceptable sports but because they come from class backgrounds where women are viewed as competent, autonomous, and achieving persons whose athleticism does not violate their definition of women's proper role. Conversely, lower class women, who are more likely to pursue team sports, adhere to more conservative views of sex roles and for this reason may feel more pressure to justify their participation in sports.

We would suggest the following as a tentative model to facilitate thinking about the perception of role conflict and the offering of apologetics: social class is one factor that influences both attitudes toward women's role and the type of sport pursued; apologetics are a function of the extent to which one views what one is doing as being in conflict with one's views of being a woman (see Figure 1).

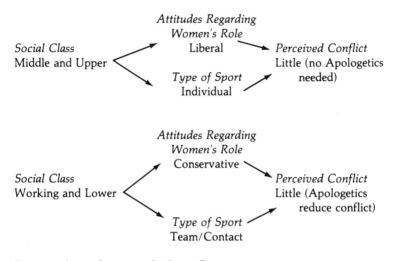

Figure 1. An explanation of role conflict.

This model might explain why less perceived role conflict is reported in the literature than might be expected and how apologetics may work differentially to reduce whatever conflict might exist. Women from higher classes may not need to apologize for their involvement in sport and perceive little conflict between their roles. Women from lower classes may use apologetics to reduce conflict because they adhere to more traditional views of women which do not include active involvement in sport. While this model would need to be elaborated to include other factors affecting role conflict, we believe it illustrates the usefulness of grappling with the real complexities of such an issue rather than settling for simple models that are more easily researched and statistically manipulated. In fact, this model raises questions about the very interpretation of attitudes and behavior as apologetics in the first place. We should be very cautious as social scientists not to *impose* meanings on the behaviors or research respondents. Merely because some women choose to play socially acceptable sports, espouse traditional views of women's role, or choose to wear jewelry and makeup does not necessarily mean that these behaviors are being used as apologetics. Rather than applying these meanings to actions, we should design research to elicit from respondents the meanings they give to their own behavior. In this way, we can generate theory that is grounded more firmly in the reality we are trying to explain.

In sum, we must not rush into the labs with structured instruments and packaged statistical programs; rather, we should first do the more difficult but more exciting work of enriching our conceptual maps of the terrain to be explored. To do any less is a disservice both to social science and to women in sport.

Philosophical Problems

In chapter 1 we discussed the different philosophical orientations of social scientists and feminists and stressed how these differences lead us to raise certain theoretical questions, to choose particular research designs, and to derive specific interpretations of data. We also stated that much of the research on women in sport, if it is nonsexist, is based on a liberal view of feminism with its unique values, assumptions, and intellectual orientations. A perfect instance of this liberal bias appears in the writing and research on role conflict for sportswomen. It is no coincidence that this topic, along with Title IX, has received the most attention in scholarly and lay discussions of women and sport. Every text, reader, journal article, symposium, and magazine story raises The Big Question: Can a woman be feminine and still play sports? Behind this question are unstated, perhaps unconscious biases and value judgments that must be identified if we are to encourage the whole range of critical approaches that will nourish an open and intellectually rich discussion of women and sport.

We feel that underlying most analyses of role conflict is an uncritical acceptance of the traditional role of woman *and* the conventional arrangements of sport. To ask if women can remain women and still play sports means that one has in mind a view of women and of sport that accepts the socially constructed definitions of these two realities as contradictory and conflicting. To ask this question means that one accepts the white, male, heterosexual, middle class definitions of women and of sport. This, indeed, is the liberal feminist's main preoccupation and the abiding concern of liberal social scientists. Given the existing definitions of woman and sport as constructed by those in power, by "insiders," and by those who wish to gain acceptance into the inner circle of privilege and influence, we continue to raise this question without bothering to look behind to its value assumptions. Indeed, the intense preoccupation with this question and the speculation and research marshaled to investigate it gives the issue even greater import than it might otherwise have. It implies that if scientists and other experts are raising the question then it must be an important issue and a significant problem! This particular issue is, of course, a single instance of the more general bias in most studies of women. Over and over again, as women move into nontraditional spheres of work, great concern arises about how they will grapple with their femininity as they become politicians, fire fighters, engineers, and truck drivers. We ask if a woman can still be a woman and be assertive, power-oriented, rational, achieving. We ponder the dilemmas women may encounter if they decide to remain single or childless, have an abortion, get a divorce, live alone, return to school, or start a business. What is hidden in these questions are the assumptions that women should and want to adhere to a very constricted definition of their personal and social existence, and that all women, by virtue of their biological qualities, should and want to embrace a single standard of being women.

But what does it mean to be a woman or to be feminine? Who will define these existences, and for whom? Is it even necessary to delineate sex roles at all and to label orientations as feminine or masculine? Liberals seem clear in their response to these questions. They have taken the definitions that men have imposed on women and reformed them in light of variations on the theme of what is acceptable and important to white, heterosexual, middle class women. Thus, we have our anxieties assuaged by research that assures us that, yes, we can lift weights but will not develop mannish builds and macho muscles; that we can be fiercely competitive on the field and yet still be sexually attractive after the contest; that sports will enhance, rather than detract from, our femininity; that we can win first place and a husband, too!

This liberal perspective that pervades the debate over role conflict needs to be balanced by equally important orientations that carry with them different assumptions, values, and preferences. Scientists and feminists who adhere to conflict or Marxist models of social life would begin by pointing out the class bias that favors certain definitions of women over other definitions. Women who are members of oppressed racial and ethnic groups, women who are poor, women who are powerless, rural women, older women, fat women do not necessarily adhere to or value the dominant image of the acceptable woman in our society. By choice or force, they have devised their own understandings of being women that are at variance with that of the dominant stereotype. The question of role conflict might take quite a different shape if we were to consider these women and their understandings of being women. Certainly we know that being strong, resourceful, assertive, independent, courageous, and tough—some of the aspects of the sport role—are no stranger to the woman on a farm, the Black or Hispanic woman, the woman who works in a factory, the woman on welfare, or the woman raising a family by herself. So when we ask if a woman can be a "real woman" and be involved in sports, who are we talking about? Whose ideas about femininity are we using as a measure? Whose definitions of being women are we referring to? The liberal bias becomes immediately obvious just by posing these questions.

In addition to ignoring the existence of competing political definitions of femininity and of women, radical feminism would involve a criticism of other aspects of the role conflict controversy. At the extreme, a radical perspective might oppose the existence of the question itself. It can be viewed as just another instance of the male-centered preoccupation with differentiating the sexes and then relegating "role conflict problems" to those women who dare assume attributes and activities that are the "proper domain" of men and masculinity. The question itself takes on an absurd quality if one refuses to separate people according to biology or to invest any significant meaning in biological attributes. The question of role conflict would be irrelevant in a radical paradigm that rejects heterosexuality as the only viable expression of emotional and sexual commitment. Indeed, many of the dilemmas allegedly faced by women who pursue sports are thinly veiled ones that center on a woman's heterosexual potential for attracting and keeping men's interest, for gaining men's approval, and for being able to assume the acceptable heterosexual roles of dating partner, sexual mate, spouse, and mother.

More specifically, the emphasis in virtually all treatments of role conflict and its resolution, at least by implication, reaffirm the social stigma and penalties attached to being lesbian or woman-identified women. Indeed, there is so much fear about broaching this topic that euphemisms such as mannish, masculine, or jock, are used by writers to gloss over the issue of the lesbian woman in sport. While there are occasional references to the fact that many women fear being labeled as lesbians, particularly if they pursue certain types of sport or engage in them in socially suspect ways, the topic remains deeply hidden in the academic closet, almost as if both researchers and respondents fear that they will open a can of worms. Rather than letting the issue surface so that it can be dealt with in a free and honest manner, it is brushed aside with vague allusions and coy euphemisms that have dangerous intellectual and social consequences.

A major intellectual danger concerns the fact that by failing to come to terms with the lesbian presence in sport we cannot understand a considerable range of issues that are part of the reality of women and sport: the prevalence of homophobia in the athletic community, the fear of being stigmatized, the need or desire "to pass," the process of "coming out," or the place of sport in the lesbian community. Other theoretically important topics, if investigated openly, would alter what we know about such important topics as the socialization and recruitment of women into sport, role conflict for the sportswoman, the elaboration of different sport subcultures, the organization of information control and passing, the distribution of sanctions, and so on. Just as social scientists enriched their understanding of the origins, structures, and effects of crime once they admitted to the existence of "white-collar crime,"[9] so, too, we can better grasp some of the dynamics of women and sport by addressing the issue of lesbian involvement in sport. The tendency to sweep the discussion of lesbian participation in sport under the academic rug is probably not so much a result of conscious choice as much as it is a consequence of ignoring or avoiding the philosophical assumptions that guide our theory and research. A self-conscious examination of our values and preferences should lead to a more enlightened and more humanistic approach to understanding this reality.

A second danger of ignoring the topic of lesbianism, and one that we believe is more important, is that it reinforces the fear, ignorance, and negation that characterize many people's views of this sexual orientation. Ignoring the topic also denies lesbians an opportunity to build bridges of support, understanding, and mutual respect with their heterosexual sisters. At a time when feminists, regardless of their specific location on the political continuum, have begun to address themselves to the ways in which sexual preferences have kept them divided and afraid of one other, it is vitally important that this issue be raised in the context of sport, just as it has been raised in analyses of sexual relations, civil rights, health care, motherhood, and so on.[10]

The topic of lesbianism and sport has barely begun to be systematically investigated in the sociological, feminist, and lesbian communities.[11] We wish to encourage the free and honest investigation of this issue by making the following points based on our impressions and observations:

1. Lesbians are engaged in every type, level, and degree of sport participation. While this point may appear to be laughingly obvious to some, it is apparently vigorously denied by others. Our point is that both extreme positions—that all women who play sports are lesbians and that no women in sport are lesbians—are incorrect and absurd postures held by persons who have vested interests in maintaining an unrealistic vision of the lesbian presence in sport.

2. The fear of being labeled a lesbian serves to keep heterosexual women out of sports or to assure that they will play sports in socially acceptable ways. We believe these and more clearly homophobic reactions exist because very few women in sports are feminist in any ideological sense of the term (Kaplan, 1979a, p. 52)—an intriguing issue in and of itself! These sportswomen have yet to define the personal as political. They prefer, instead, the safety of their private games and will leave to feminists ("Yes, I play sports but I'm not a feminist.") the more difficult task of articulating the existence of lesbianism in sport.

3. The tremendous stigma attached to being lesbian and the severe penalities that may be meted out to them have kept many lesbian sportswomen from being able to act as role models, to develop support systems, and to enact educational and legal programs that would enhance the rights of lesbians in sport and develop empathic ties to heterosexual women involved in sport. This situation is

slowly changing as both more women and more feminists become involved in sport. For example, the recently formed North American Network of Women Runners[12] is one of a few groups making an effort to embrace the needs of all women, including lesbians, in the formation and direction of the running movement. We expect these kinds of groups to increase in number and influence as the connection between feminism and sport is clarified and strengthened.

In summary, we have argued that the discussion of role conflict suffers from a limited vision of the definition of woman and her role as a social being. It also suffers from an acceptance of the structures and dynamics of sport as a masculine domain, with its emphasis on instrumentality, control, power, product, and other attributes of the male sex role. Embedded in the treatment of role conflict is the assumption that sporting roles, rules, and relationships will not and should not change. Thus, the question posed is how women will adjust to the potential conflict that sport activities may engender. The feeling seems to be that since they are the ones who want to enter SportsWorld it is they, not sport, that will have to change.

However, there are different ways of addressing this issue, ways that suggest the possibility of alternative orientations to sport, ways that suggest the idea that women may experience sport differently from men, ways that suggest that women may change how sport itself is experienced and constructed. We are now ready to examine the second barrier to women's sport participation—the fact that sport, as presently constructed, fails to reflect those interests and values that are central to women's world-view and life experiences.

Sport and Women's Experience

One of the dominant tensions in much of the recent feminists literature centers on the question of how women experience themselves and their world. Is their experience the same as men's and, if not, in what ways is it different? While it would be absurd to deny that there is a common structure of experience for both women and men as members of the human species, it is equally absurd to reject outright the idea that, for many reasons, women's experience in the world is not the same as men's. But how can we come to know women's experience and world view? How can we come to know if our cultural and institutional life reflects these experiences? Two feminist theologians, Christ and Plaskow (1979), suggest an answer:

Because women have often shaped and understood their lives according to norms or preferences for female behavior expressed by men, there is a sense in which women have not shaped or even known their own experience. (p. 6)

Out of the consciousness-raising groups and other vehicles for recognizing, naming, and sharing their experiences, "women begin to realize how fully the world has been defined by men. As they begin to question woman's place in man's world, they also begin to question the world that men have constructed" (Christ & Plaskow, 1979, p. 6).

However, since women always live in patriarchal society, how are they to know the degree to which their experiences are authentic or merely a product of sexism? Which experiences can be trusted to be both self-actualizing and socially transformative? Which experiences are self-negating and socially destructive? Christ and Plaskow (1979) identify two emerging positions regarding the feminist understanding of experience: "(1) women's *feminist* experience and (2) women's *traditional* experience, which includes, but is not limited to, women's body experience" (p. 8, original italics). The first model states that the experience of *liberation* itself is what is authentic and valuable in women's experience. Women's essential experience is centered on the recognition of their oppression, the identification of sexist culture and institutions, and a critical confrontation with these structures and processes. Using new feminist understandings, women can join with other oppressed groups to liberate their personal and social existence. The second model of women's experience focuses on the *traditional* experiences of women, such as marriage and motherhood, which:

although they have been distorted in patriarchy, can provide important clues for transforming patriarchal culture. Thinkers who focus on traditional experience believe that whatever sexist culture has rejected or denigrated must be revalued in a holistic feminist vision. Whatever is considered 'feminine'—intuition, expression of feeling, concern for the personal dimensions of relationships—may be reappropriated from a feminist perspective. (Christ & Plaskow, 1979, p. 8)

While social scientists are often content to leave to philosophers and theologians questions regarding the ultimate nature of human experience, we believe that we are on firm ground in stating that the dominant cultural and institutional life of a society is shaped according to men's values, men's understanding of the world, and men's experience in the world. This is as true for the institution of sport as it is for all other aspects of social life. Furthermore, we believe that women's alienation from sport, their indifference to it or reluctance to enter it, stems in large measure from the fact that, as presently constituted, what sport celebrates, what sport offers, what sport demands, and what sport rewards does not reflect much of women's experience in the world.

Readers may say that surely we overstate the case, particularly in light of the recent explosion of women's interest in sport! But let us look more carefully at some alternative ways in which sport can be understood and arranged and their implications for the quality and degree of women's sport participation. Mary Duquin (1978, pp. 89-106) identifies three models of sport, each of them having different implications for women's participation. According to her, sport can be perceived and conducted: (a) as an agent of masculine orientation, (b) as an instrumental activity suitable for both sexes, and (c) as an androgynous activity.

As we suggested earlier in this chapter, sport is arranged as an agent of masculine orientation and socialization. Its stress on instrumentality, power, product, rationality, and control, according to Duquin, will have different consequences for women, depending on their perception of sex roles. Using the Bem's Sex Role Inventory[13], Duquin (1978, p. 96) states that this model of sport will be *moderately* attractive to women who score masculine or androgynous on the BSRI while women who score feminine will have *low* rates of attraction to sport. Thus, if the majority of women are to become highly attracted to sport, sport itself must be arranged differently, since even androgynous women are expected to be only moderately attracted to sport when it is arranged as a masculine, instrumental activity.

What if sport is perceived and conducted as an instrumental activity suitable for both sexes? Would this second model of sport better reflect women's experience and enlarge the pool of women who would be highly attracted to sport? This model, in fact, is the dominant one arising over the last decade, as women have come to assert the importance of their instrumentality, which was so long denied to them under the traditional definitions of their sex role. Some feminists have pointed to sport as a vehicle for providing to women what has been prohibited until now. Sport can give women a sense of their physicality and an appreciation of their ability to excel in sporting endeavors. It can become a celebration of their body's strength and competence. It can be a source of self-esteem, personal autonomy, and social influence. The liberal pole of feminism has also begun to demand equal opportunity for women in sport, mainly under the legislation of Title IX, which argues that whatever benefits men may derive from sport should be made available to women as well. Thus, sport is being redefined as an instrumental activity suitable for both sexes.

However, while these changes in the definition of sport and of women account for much of the increasing interest by women in sport, Duquin carefully points out the limits to this approach. Under this model of sport:

Males are still expected to be solely instrumental, while females are expected to be both instrumental and expressive. The perception that instrumentality is important for both sexes has the effect of elevating the status of instrumental traits and behaviors over expressive traits and behaviors. One further step results in the subtle assumption that instrumentality is the only 'orientation for a healthy adult to possess.' (Duquin, 1978, pp. 97-98)

Duquin speculates that this model of sport would result in *high* attraction to sport by women with masculine or androgynous orientations but, again, only *low to moderate* attraction by women who adhere to traditionally more feminine orientations. The implication is clear: as long as sport is perceived and conducted in light of men's values and experiences it is primarily nontraditional women who will be attracted to and excel in sport. Women who embrace the more expressive dimensions of human experience will still find sport an alien territory.

It is the third model of sport—perceived and conducted as an androgynous activity—that seems to have the potential for appealing to the widest range of women. Sport is androgynous when it incorporates elements of both instrumentality and expressivity.[14] It is sport that allows for play as well as work, that celebrates beauty as well as technique, that stresses the process as well as the end product. It is sport that encourages introspection, sensitivity to others, ethics, and friendship. These emphases can be found in Eastern approaches to sport, in the Western adaptation of expressive themes found in the Esalen Sport Institute, in the New Games Foundation,[15] and in the early 20th Century philosophy of sport promulgated by the women physical educators in this country. Androgynous sport is expected to attract moderate levels of interest even from women scoring high in femininity, suggesting that women may not have to relinquish their expressivity in order to participate in androgynous sport.

It is this model of sport which comes closest to reflecting women's traditional experience of themselves in the world. It incorporates into sport those attributes and values that have been usually allocated to the feminine or expressive side of human existence. Rather than the one-sided focus on women's right to be instrumental, which presently characterizes a considerable amount of feminist ideology, this model encourages the equal importance of expressive and instrumental activity. It allows women to reassert those ways of being in the world, ways that are often derided or devalued in patriarchy, while simultaneously activating the instrumental part of their experience that is stunted under patriarchy. It is an approach that demands more than institutional accommodation on the part of men to women's entry into sport. Rather, it requires that the nature of sport be transformed from solely instrumental activity to one that recognizes the value of expressivity as part of human experience. It is also a model of sport which will ask that men become more attuned to their expressive qualities and that will give them the chance to have experiences that nourish these qualities. This model of sport will also make it an attractive activity for many men who are also presently alienated from instrumental sport, who find their need and desire for expressive experience severely limited by sport as traditionally conducted.

Indeed, we feel that the astonishing success of the running movement in the 1970s was due in large part to its androgynous qualities. Here is a sporting activity that encourages playfulness, intimate contact with nature, spiritual and bodily awareness, cooperation, sociability, solitude, and beauty. Running is inclusive of the human community, calling for participation by *all* people rather than excluding all but those endowed with extraordinary physical, psychological, and socioeconomic attributes. Running does possess many of the instrumental elements of sport, but its attractiveness is due in large measure to its ability to incorporate expressive elements as well, blending them into a physical activity that people can adapt to suit their unique sporting preferences and needs.

As we noted in chapter 2, changes in a society will be reflected in its sports. Although the US today is still dominated by the contact, team sports promoted by the mass media and business corporations, there are clear signs that many Americans are becoming dissatisfied with the standardized, instrumental, and rationalized themes exhibited in the sports of football, baseball, ice hockey, and basketball. We believe that the growing popularity of the martial arts, the more naturalistic sports, such as mountain climbing, canoeing, and cross-country skiing, and the aesthetic sports, such as ice and roller skating, freestyle skiing, and gymnastics, are a response to a call for more androgynous physical activity that better reflects the wide range of human needs that a sport can fulfill. Women are part of this larger population of citizens who are thoughtfully evaluating their relationship to sport. However, since women have not been active creators of sport, their present situation differs from that of men.

In choosing to engage in sport, women stand at the edge of a dilemma. As persons denied the opportunity to express our instrumentality, except if done in the service of our family and country or out of practical necessity, we may be tempted to enter SportsWorld unthinkingly, eager to merge with our male counterparts in the rationalized, highly organized, competitive, aggressive world of sports as presently constructed. We may be tempted to accept male definitions of competition, striving, victory, and recognition. We may try to emulate men in training, technique, officiating, equipment, and style of play, believing that these are the best or only ways to proceed with our games. Our games? We are even at the threshold of having to ask if the sports presently being played are ours in the sense that they emerge from, develop, and reflect our experience as women. Perhaps women must begin to reshape sports in their own image, giving birth to new sports as blacks did with jazz in music.

There is some empirical evidence to support the view that women's experience in sport is different from that of men. In a study of children's play activity, Lever (1976) found the following differences in play between the sexes: boys played outdoors more often and in larger groups than girls; girls were more likely to play in age-homogeneous groups than boys; boys played more competitive games than did girls; boys' games tended to last longer than those of girls; and boys were more efficient than girls at resolving conflicts during play. In a subsequent report, Lever (1978) extended her analysis of the data to focus on sex differences in the complexity of children's play and games. Her conception of complexity is one that reflects many of the attributes of modern industrial society and includes the following six dimensions: (a) the division of labor based on role specialization, (b) interdependence between members, (c) size of membership, (d) explicitness of group goals, (e) number and specificity of impersonal rules, and (f) action of members as a unified collectivity (Lever, 1978, p. 472).

Lever applied these dimensions of complexity to the structure of play and games and hypothesized that boys' play and game activities are more complex than those of girls. In a well executed study that used a variety of data collection techniques, Lever's findings clearly support her thesis. On each of the six measures of complexity the data show that the experiences of girls and boys is significantly different; the structure of boys' games and play is considerably more complex than those of girls. In comparison to boys' play and games, girls' activity is:

> mostly spontaneous, imaginative, and free of structure or rules. [It is played] without setting explicit goals. Girls have far less experience with interpersonal competition. The style of their competition is indirect, rather than face to face, individual rather than team affiliated. Leadership roles are either missing or randomly filled. Perhaps more important, girls' play occurs in small groups. (Lever, 1978, p. 481)

The significance of these differences in the structure of play for how children are socialized to their sex roles, to their acquisition of world views and values, and to their behavior as adults would be purely speculative at this time. In fact, it is only recently that social scientists have begun to study play, games, and sport as agencies of socialization, and virtually none of the work has focused on how these socialization experiences may differentially affect the sexes. What is important, however, is the recognition that due to cultural and historical factors sport has not been structured in the same way for women and men. Thus, over their life course, both sexes are primarily involved in different spheres of sporting activity, with different emphases, styles, skills, and goals embedded in the structure and dynamics of their sex-segregated games.

That these differences may carry over from childhood and become incorporated into more organized forms of sport competition is suggested in a recent study by Moseley (1979) of female collegiate athletes. In her admittedly exploratory and theoretically based study, she reported a number of differences between how young men and women athletes participate in sport, lending support to our contention that the meanings and modes of participation are not the same for both sexes. Moseley found that female athletes enjoyed playing just as much when their team had a losing as opposed to a winning season, while male athletes' enjoyment was more directly related to their having a winning season. In addition, the women were more likely than the men to say that their personal performance in competition was more important than the final outcome of the contest. In terms of motivation to play, the data show that the most frequently chosen reason for women's participation was to "enjoy exercise" while for men it was to "enjoy competition." These and other findings lead Moseley to suggest that "sports participation means different things to each sex" and that women have incorporated into their sex role a "female athletic role" that differs qualitatively from the "male athletic role" (Moseley, 1979, p. 16). Her findings also refute the assertion of role conflict and, therefore, the existence of apologetics to resolve the conflict. According to Moseley (1979), women athletes do not encounter role conflict "because the role of the female athlete is perceived as different from that of males. Therefore, it is possible . . . for the athletic and sex roles to be compatible" (p. 24).

Although the findings from these studies are exploratory and limited in their generalizability, they do provide additional support for our belief that women's experience in sport—their goals, motives, assessments, priorities, and the like—should not be assumed to be the same as men's.

By making women's sport experience problematic, that is, something to be examined rather than uncritically accepted, we can derive at least two benefits. As humanist social scientists we can continue to do research that investigates the ways in which women experience and express their involvement in sport so that we can generate theories that better fit the reality we are attempting to explain. Our concepts, hypotheses, and theoretical models should be grounded in and derived from women's actual sporting experiences. We should not superimpose onto these experiences our preexisting ideas that stem from an understanding of men's sport participation. As the studies by Lever and Moseley indicate, by making women's sport experience problematic we can uncover social facts that enhance our insights into the dynamics of sport and the role of women in this institution. If this is our theoretical task, then it also requires that we select research techniques that best elicit from women the quality and meanings of their involvement in sport. This means that we must be willing to use the more qualitative techniques for data collection—those descriptive, observational, and exploratory methods that allow us direct access to sportswomen in their natural settings. It also means that we must use methods that go beyond simplistic tests of the effects of one isolated variable on another or that reduce the richness of sport experience to verbally expressed attitudes or behaviors that can be quantified. The state of our present knowledge about women in sport is simply too negligible to do other than the intensive, varied, long-term investigations that are demanded whenever we begin to explore a new and complex intellectual issue.

A second benefit of making women's sport experience problematic is that, as feminists, we have the opportunity to identify our experiences in sport, to name them, to understand them, and to share them with one another so that our sports become authentic reflections of who we are and how we wish to be in the world. We have a responsibility to all women, regardless of the extent, degree, or nature of their commitment to feminism, to submit sport to the same rigorous analysis as feminists are doing to the other institutions of modern society. But we must do more than merely document the past and present ways in which women have been excluded from the mainstream of sport. We must do more than celebrate each time a particular roadblock to women's participation has been successfully challenged. We must go further than the boundaries of any legislation, any institutional framework, any ideology, any efforts that would make us believe that we have the right, best, only, or final answers. The process of becoming people who transcend the limits of present sex–role categories and the process of participating in sport that surpasses the limits of present institutional arrangements requires that we remain receptive to criticism, suspicious of ultimate solutions, willing to be unpopular, and optimistic about our abilities to effect social change.

Notes

1. Some social scientists make a distinction between the terms "sex role" and "gender role" while many others use the terms interchangeably. We shall follow the latter course as a matter of literary preference. The important point to keep in mind is that while biological characteristics define one's sex as male or female, cultural meanings determine the expected psychological and social attributes deemed appropriate for women and men. In addition, we should note the interactive nature of biological factors and cultural meanings; unfortunately, our language presently does not provide us with words that stress this interdependence.

2. In 1848 the first women's rights convention was held at Seneca Falls, New York. Its goal was to discuss and evaluate the social, civil, and religious liberties of women.

3. For a collection of readings that consider these and other functions of sport, see Yiannakis, McIntyre, Melnick, and Hart (1976).

4. As a sporting ideology, these beliefs are embraced and promulgated by many persons without regard to their validity. Social scientists and physical educators have not, to date, provided conclusive evidence that participation in sport does in fact generate or reinforce these qualities.

5. We have made a stylistic decision not to put quotation marks around the terms feminine/femininity and masculine/masculinity. However, we want to remind the reader that whenever these terms are used, they refer to socially constructed definitions of sex roles and not to any natural, intrinsic or ultimate understandings of what it means to be a female or male person.

6. For a discussion of the various dimensions of homophobia, see Weinberg (1973).

7. See Hall (Note 5) for an analysis of alternative conceptualizations of theoretical issues involved in studying women and sport.

8. For examples of this type of research, see the many articles on women and sport that have appeared over the past few years in *Research Quarterly.*

9. The concept of white-collar crime refers to crimes "committed by persons in upper white-collar positions such as managerial, ownership, executive, and professional vocations, as well as those committed by corporations" (Shoemaker & South, 1974, p. 193).

10. See *Our Right To Love: A Lesbian Resource Book* (Vida, 1978) for a discussion of lesbianism and its relation to women's issues.

11. Most discussions of lesbians and sport appear in the few paragraphs and pages of larger works on lesbianism or women and sport. Journalists and lesbian-feminists are more likely than academicians to discuss the topic in any detail, and the treatment remains largely anecdotal, rhetorical, or atheoretical. For a recent and promising essay on lesbian athletes, see Hicks (1979).

12. This organization's address is: P.O. Box 924, Shaker Heights, Ohio 44120.

13. In a famous series of studies Bem (1974, 1975, 1976) developed a Sex Role Inventory (BSRI) which allows individuals to score masculine, feminine, or androgynous. These scores measure respondents' perceptions of their sex role expectations.

14. Many feminists have noted that the concept of androgyny is inadequate because it presumes that masculinity (instrumentality) and femininity (expressivity) have distinct content. As a concept, it refers to the combination of both sets of gender traits in a manner that gives legitimacy to the dichotomous principles of feminine and masculine. As Duquin (1978) notes, "the step beyond androgyny is epicenism, the quality of being held in common by both sexes. When society reaches the perceptual point of epicenism, behavior, including sport behavior, will have no gender. Sport will then be perceived as human activity" (p. 103).

15. The New Games Foundation, created in 1974, is dedicated to the goal of

pursuing play and games with a focus on participation, creativity, and community. It holds workshops across the nation to encourage and teach this perspective on play. Its address is: P.O. Box 7901, San Francisco, CA 94120.

PART 2/
Women and Sport:
Institutional Analyses

In the second part of this book we want to use the insights gained from the previous discussions to explore how the social institutions of the family, the school, the mass media, and the government generate, shape, and give meaning to the problems and prospects facing the sporting woman. In short, we wish to examine the interplay of social ideas and social structures, the interaction between theory and fact, the link between the public world and personal experience.

In chapter 5 Susan Greendorfer focuses on the institution of primary responsibility for all socialization, including the socialization to sport—the family. After reviewing the dominant role played by the family as a socializing agency, Greendorfer examines the specific dynamics of gender role learning, especially as it involves the sex-typing of children's toy and play patterns. The chapter continues with an examination of the differences that boys and girls encounter in their socialization into sport, and the part played by parents in this differential exposure to sport. The implications of early socialization experiences of girls for their later sport participation is also critically developed.

A second arena in which girls learn lessons about sport and their place in it is our educational institutions, the topic of chapter 6. Sex-typing begun at home continues in the schools. After examining the existence of sex discrimination in athletic programs at all levels of education, we probe the intents, the implementation, the enforcement, and the consequences of the one piece of legislation aimed at altering this sex-typing in the schools—Title IX of the Higher Education Act of 1972.

The mass media's contribution to women's prescribed place in sport is the focus of chapter 7. Through a theoretical and empirical investigation of the nature and extent of the coverage of women in sport by newspapers, magazines, and television, we demonstrate the power of these symbolic institutions to consign women to limited places in the World of Sport. The chapter also evaluates the feminist implications of emerging changes in the media's treatment of the sporting woman.

Our final chapter serves three purposes. First, examining governmental policies at the international level of competition, specifically the Olympics, we address the issues of how deliberate policies can foster or inhibit international sporting success for women as well as men. Secondly, we look at US sports policies in order to establish the precedents and benchmarks which women's sports will encounter to the degree that they follow the paths already taken in men's sport. Finally, we look at the policy implications of the various models of feminism. For each model, we flesh out some possible changes in present policy decisions that would affect women's sport involvement in the family, the school, the mass media, and the government. Finally, our epilogue concludes this work with a call for re-examining the goals and strategies for intellectual work in the social scientific community.

Chapter 5/
Shaping the Female Athlete: The Impact of the Family
by Susan Greendorfer

One of the most heated debates in recent years involves the reasons why more women do not participate in sport. Defenders of the status quo frequently cite lack of interest and lack of ability as explanations, but most feminists believe the major reason is discrimination. Unfortunately, people usually think of discrimination only when it takes the form of overt social barriers or clearly identifiable obstacles; they fail to recognize the rather covert and subtle forms of discrimination embedded in cultural ideology. These inconspicuous forms merge into our socialization practices, and their results often appear as "quite natural." What needs to be understood is that these potent social forces are primarily responsible for determining who participates and who does not participate in many of life's experiences—including sport. Although some increases have occurred in opportunities for women to take part in sport, one very important social fact remains:

despite the presence of Title IX and despite increasing numbers of women participating in sport there are disproportionately fewer females than males who engage in sport. It is no accident that male sport participants number in the millions but female participants only in the lower thousands.

Female interest and involvement in sport is not a chance occurrence that depends mainly on innate skill or motor talent. Rather, it is a consequence of social learning which directs women away from sport instead of predisposing them toward sport. This chapter focuses on how such social learning is accomplished and the role that the family plays in this process. Particular attention is directed toward one undesirable form of discrimination—sex typing—and a good deal of the discussion is concerned with how the family transmits to children a sex-typed ideology of play, physical activity, and sport.

The Family and Socialization

The family is the foundation of the socialization process, representing one of the most fundamental institutions in human society. All other institutions depend on contributions and learning which are initiated in and through this basic social unit. The family conveys from one generation to another those traditions, perspectives, norms, and values that are vital for cultural maintenance. For these reasons, one cannot underestimate the role of the family. This and the following section will discuss what the family specifically does to accomplish the socialization process which links cultural patterns with individual learning. More importantly, however, it will be shown that toys and play are important aspects of this socialization process and that the family uses toys and play to incorporate sex-typed notions into the upbringing of young children.

In a general sense, the family teaches roles and appropriate guidelines for behavior. Therefore, much that is learned within the family context serves as a basis for an individual's behavior in other segments of life. The family provides a valuable social inheritance—the concept of what is and what is not appropriate. Although other social institutions, such as the school, peer group, and the mass media, shape individual development, these institutions merely reinforce what has been initiated within the family. This is especially true when it comes to beliefs and behavior in sport. The significance of this point will be discussed in a later section, and several of the following chapters will consider in detail how cultural ideology is perpetuated.

As previously mentioned, role learning is a major outcome of the general process of socialization. Individuals learn several diverse roles during their lifetimes, one of the earliest and most salient being sex role.[1] No other role directs behavior, emotional reactions, and cognitive functioning more than this role. Through the mechanisms of socialization—observation, imitation, discrimination, and generalization—people learn to adopt those behaviors which are important components of gender role. They also learn which behaviors are inappropriate and avoid either learning or behaving in those inappropriate ways. This entire process is facilitated by the family. Family members, usually parents, insure that children are exposed to activities more consonant with their gender role and reward them for behaving appropriately. These rewards may take many forms—additional toys, praise and encouragement, playing with the child, or actually offering instructions. For example, a father may show a son how to hold a ball and, as the son grows older, how to throw and catch. Meanwhile, a daughter may learn appropriate female activities because her mother serves as a role model. Girls play at what mothers "normally" do—setting tables, cleaning house, washing dishes, dressing dolls.

Quite often, however, young children gravitate toward an activity deemed inappropriate for their sex. When this happens family members administer some form of punishment. Although the nature of negative reinforcement and punishment differs for boys and girls, the effect is the same and may be no less severe, regardless of sex. A particularly potent form of negative reinforcement comes in the form of labeling activities as appropriate or inappropriate. For males the form is typically negative proscription—how not be be. Phrases like "don't be a sissy" and "only girls cry" are some examples. Boys also receive more physical punishment and threats when they choose "girls' " activities. As a result boys learn to avoid anything feminine at a very early age (Hartley, 1959). This is particularly true when it comes to toys and play.

For girls, the system of rewards and punishment is more diffuse, gentle, and subtle. Young girls are rarely allowed to venture far from their mothers—particularly in play activities. As a result, females are encouraged to be dependent and to seek affection. Their play activities are constrained; they rarely are allowed to run, climb trees, get dirty, or explore their environment. As a result, they have few chances to engage in punishable behavior (Hartley, 1964). If they do, however, negative reinforcement usually takes the form of psychological punishment. While boys may be spanked, girls who are physically active are made to feel deviant, unworthy, or guilty for choosing the "wrong" activity (Weitzman, 1979). Also, it is difficult to measure the long–term effect of a daughter seeing her brother praised, encouraged, and overtly taught physical skills while she receives no feedback whatsoever for demonstrating motor skill. This also could be a potent form of negative reinforcement which teaches girls that physical activity is only for boys and that practicing or developing motor skill is not worthy of respect, let alone attention.

Thus, two forms of sex-typed socialization become evident in early childhood: (a) lack of exposure to a variety of activities or experiences, and (b) self-selection away from activities labeled as inappropriate. Exposure (or lack of exposure) to experiences is mediated through the family, and this limitation or option to play in diverse activities is based solely on the biological sex of the child. Unfortunately, this lack of exposure has social learning consequences, the most insidious of which is self-selection or avoidance. The result is a limitation of the full range of social skills and developmental options (Huston, in press). Whereas boys are given a wide range of toys and are allowed to play in vast spacious areas away from the house and parents, girls are often limited in the range and variety of their play activities. Choices for girls are between dolls, stuffed animals, and tea sets. Girls are gently pushed into "feminine" activities and are rewarded for choosing such appropriate toys. After a while, they learn what not to choose because such toys are not compatible with "being a good girl" and playing with these toys does not bring them rewards or acknowledgment.

It is the contention of this chapter that such sex-typing of activities, which the family initiates, takes on greater importance as females grow older because it affects female interest and later involvement in sport. Thus, instead of accepting the pervasive viewpoint that low female participation in sport is part of the *natural order*, I propose that these low rates of participation are products of socialization practices and are the result of a chain of events which begins during early infancy and has life-long consequences. In addition, there are important links between early exploratory behavior, toy and infant play behavior, and physical activity/sport participation in adolescence and adulthood. Atchley (1977) supported this notion by stressing continuity. Continuity theory maintains that there is an integration between phases of the life cycle, and the habits, preferences, and dispositions that individuals develop become a part of life's activities through the process of socialization. In essence, the argument is simple: Continuity theory provides a framework which supports the hypothesis that constraint of female activity and exploration during early infancy predisposes girls toward quiet, sedentary forms of childhood play. This quiet style of play is reinforced by parents who provide their daughters with toys which promote expressive and sedentary activity. Parents do not encourage girls to be physically active or to learn gross motor skills. As a result, habits and values toward inactivity become incorporated into the lifestyle of most females. This deficiency results in low interest and low inclination to participate in sport. Thus, females are not likely to become involved in sport because there is no reward, little encouragement or instruction, and an orientation away from play styles that incorporate physical activity. This insidious form of discrimination is predicated by the fact that an infant was born female instead of male. It is not difficult to verify these differences in socialization practices. Literature and research on differential treatment during child rearing offer overwhelming support.

Gender Role Socialization as Sex Typing

Although there is a vast literature explaining how children learn their gender role (Goslin, 1969; Maccoby, 1966; Mussen & Hetherington, in press), the theoretical perspective emphasized here is that of social learning. According to this explanation, two forms of interaction influence gender role socialization: (a) parental reward of sex-appropriate behavior and punishment of sex-inappropriate behaviors, and (b) imitation of role models (Katz et al., 1977). Both forms of interaction have sparked heated debates. The first issue focuses on whether or not parents treat children differently on the basis of the child's sex, and if so, why (Block, 1976b; Maccoby & Jacklin, 1974). The second issue concerns whether same-sex or opposite-sex parents are the more influential role models (Perry & Bussey, 1979; Weitzman, 1975). Both debates have stimulated extensive research, and the implications/applications to sport are tremendous.

Social development is an outcome produced from both parents; however, it is not known exactly under what circumstances imitation of one parent, rather than of the other, takes place, nor when the behavior of one parent becomes more important than that of the other. Therefore, one cannot ignore the role of either the mother or the father when considering gender–role or sport–role socialization. Moreover, more attention is needed as to the quality and type of interactions parents have with their children, because these factors may shape social learning more than previously believed. For example, mothers tend to hold infants in order to perform caretaking functions, while fathers hold them more often to play. Yet, the manner or style in which the father plays with infants depends on the infant's sex (Lamb, 1975; Power & Parke, Note 6). Also, there is evidence that male and female infants are treated differently almost from birth (Goldberg & Lewis, 1969). Several studies indicate that baby girls are touched, handled, and talked to more until, by 13 months of age, they reciprocate by touching and talking to their mothers more than baby boys (Goldberg & Lewis, 1969; Kagan & Lewis, 1965). Results from such research suggest that this differential treatment created distinctive play behavior for the two sexes. Girls were more dependent and showed less exploratory behavior, and their play reflected a quieter style. In contrast, male infants were more vigorous, played with toys requiring gross motor activity, and tended to bang their toys (Lewis, 1972a). Although we cannot be absolutely certain whether differential treatment is a product of sex typing, these findings make such a hypothesis appealing.

Some of these findings have direct implication for physical activity. For example, a mother is more likely to pick up an infant daughter and restrict the range over which she may explore. Both parents allow boys a greater freedom to explore their play environment, and both seem to believe female infants are more fragile and in need of assistance (Lewis, 1972b). Because mothers believe that boys rather than girls should be independent and encouraged to explore and master their world, they are more likely to pick their daughters up when daughters cannot pass a laboratory imposed obstacle (Lewis, 1972c). Such parental behaviors are "natural," but they stem from a deeply embedded cultural ideology which nonconsciously assumes that females are *unable* or *incapable* of performing certain activities without help. This belief dictates parental behavior and triggers a sequence of parent-infant handling which indirectly dissuades females from most forms of physical activity.

Typically, a female is rewarded very early in life for being quiet and still, for not being active, and for not climbing or exploring her environment. The reward takes the form of parental touching and handling as well as verbal praise for "being a good girl." As a result, females learn to become dependent on powerful figures, to be sedentary, and most important of all, to view physical activity as behavior reserved especially for males. Female styles of play reflect this social learning; activities are expressive and not instrumental, are close to mothers in the house or covering small space in the nursery area, and are almost devoid of gross motor skill patterns (climbing, running, jumping, throwing). Unfortunately, females do not learn (are not taught) many motor skills at an early age; therefore, during childhood they do not have opportunities or experiences to practice and perfect movement patterns because there is a void in their learning. Not only does this delay motor development, but it also retards performance. As a result, girls do not have at their disposal the vast repertoire of movement experiences that boys have. Because motor skill learning is predicated on a series of progressive stages of development, failure to learn rudimentary skills interferes with subsequent learning and places a limit on future performance. If girls do not learn and practice basic motor skill patterns, the potential for performance at later stages is hindered. Anyone who does not learn basic or fundamental elements of motor skills cannot competently engage in sport and is thus disadvantaged. Unfortunately, this deprivation of movement experiences for females continues to be as systematic in the 1980s as it was in pre-Title IX days.

Of course, all females are not condemned to a childhood devoid of physical activity. Many young girls play in some games and sports. However, what generally happens? First, most girls can see for themselves that their skill level is not comparable to that of their male peers. Second, girls are not usually chosen to play on a team, or, if so, are typically chosen last. Third and most important, their peers tell them that they are not good—but then they don't need to be, because sports are for boys anyway. Two negative outcomes of these early socialization experiences occur: (a) lack of experience and hence no interest, and (b) lower skill levels or lack of success. In the second instance girls evaluate their performance as poor, have no expectation for doing well (or for success), receive few reinforcements for engaging in physical activity, and do not hold a high value for motor competence. As a result, a belief system evolves, one which does have some validity: boys are good in sport, while girls are not. Unfortunately, the underlying assumption behind this belief system—girls do not have the innate capacity to execute motor skills very well—is not valid. There is an element of circular reasoning in this profile, one which unfortunately, further reinforces our cultural ideology. Two important facts are forgotten in this cycle of reasoning: (a) motor skills are learned, and (b) subsequent motor performance is a product of both motor development and motor learning. If females are not exposed to motor experiences they will not learn motor skills. If they expect to fail and if they have limited experiences at success or even at practice, then they will fail. As a result, females will not be motivated or interested in physical activity. These are simple learning principles that have been overlooked in society's perpetuation of the sport ideology. Of course, one reason the ideology persists is because sport role learning is intricately interwoven in male gender role socialization (Kleiber, Note 7; Kleiber, Barnett, & Wade, Note 8).

Sex Typing in Toys and Play

Differential treatment by parents is not the only domain of behavior in which there is evidence of sex typing. Toys are potent socializing factors, and it is in this domain that sex typing has a pronounced effect on social development of children. In the past there was some debate as to whether boys and girls received identical toys. More recently, however, evidence of sex typing in toy selection has been convincing. Toy availability not only influences play experiences but also results in preferences and predispositions toward specific activities. Rheingold and Cook (1975) found that certain classes of toys were not found in girls' rooms, and that at almost every age boys had more toys than girls. These differences may not appear to be great; however, they have tremendous implications for sport. Boys were provided with objects that directed their activities away from home, toward sports and cars, while girls were given toys that encouraged activities toward the home, keeping house, and caring for children (Rheingold & Cook, 1975). In essence, the initial presence or absence of toys, as well as toys representative of specific categories, shapes play behavior of early childhood and influences preferences of later childhood. The result is obvious sex differences in play styles and preferences. Boys ask for trucks, guns, tractors, building blocks, and manipulative toys; they learn to move freely in their environment and to build objects (e.g., instrumental play). In contrast, girls ask for dolls and dress-up and housekeeping toys; their play is quiet, indoors, and expressive (Fagot, 1974; Maccoby & Jacklin, 1974; Sears, Rau, & Alpert, 1965).

Another form of sex typing is found in the labeling of toys, particularly those labeled as "masculine." Such toys are more complex, active, and social than "feminine" toys which are more simple, passive, and solitary (Goodman & Lever, 1974; Weitzman, 1975). Adults spend more time in choosing toys for boys. Cost is another indicator of sex typing, and boys' toys are more expensive. Of 860 toy boxes in a large toy store, 50% which were less than $2 were aimed at girls, while 31% were aimed exclusively at boys. In the $5 and over category, 18% were girl oriented and 34% were boy oriented (Katz et. al., 1977). An interesting chain of events occurs in toy behavior: boys spend more time with novel toys; boys receive more toys; and boys prefer "boy" toys. Once set in motion, sex typing is self-perpetuating. That is, "girl toys" acquire more and more reinforcement value for girls (and vice versa). Part of this reinforcement value stems from emotional toning by parents. Part is due to familiarization, which evokes requests for more similar toys (Hartley, 1966).

We see evidence of sex typing in toy and play styles by the age of 4, at which early age boys are more sex typed than are girls. Boys receive early rigid gender-role socialization pressures, are more *actively* discouraged from playing with sex-inappropriate toys, and have learned to avoid such toys. Although evidence of sex typing of girls seems to suggest less rigidity and more flexibility in sex-inappropriate play at younger ages, recent research suggests that girls also receive negative responses from parents when they play with opposite-sex toys (Fagot, 1978). What these trends indicate is that sex typing is not only still rampant in the 1980s but that the family seems to be impervious to the feminist impetus in the domain of toys and play. This trend can also be generalized to physical activity and sport. Thirty years ago fathers taught sons different types of motor skills than they taught daughters (Tasch, 1952); twenty years ago parents promoted sport as achievement training for boys but not for girls (Stoll, Inbar, & Fennessey, 1968); and today we find that parents still encourage boys in active gross manipulative play while they teach girls social and expressive play (Langlois & Downs, 1980; Tauber, 1979).

The age of heightened consciousness has had little effect on what parents believe about male and female infants and how they respond to their infants on the basis of gender. Differential treatment is still common, and the nature and type of parent-infant interaction differ significantly when we examine play patterns. Fathers are more physically rough and play more bouncing and gross motor games with male infants than with female infants (Parke & Suomi, 1980; Power & Parke, 1979). In experimental settings, mothers and fathers offer dolls to children believed to be girls more often than they do to children believed to be boys. Parents continue to encourage more motor activity for boys, and they respond to the motor activity of boys differently than they do to that of girls (Frish, 1977). Adults encourage nurturance play with dolls and puppets for girls but not for boys. In addition, parents offer more negative responses to daughters who engage in active large motor activities or manipulate objects; parents also engage in physically active play with boys but not girls, and positively reinforce daughters when they engage in adult-oriented dependent behavior (Fagot, 1978). Despite today's raised consciousness, parents continue to encourage girls in dependent behavior and feminine sex-typed play while they encourage boys in physically active play.

Differential Role of Mother and Father as Socializing Agents

Although we have considered both parents as promoting sex-typed behaviors, several studies indicate that fathers emphasize sex-typed play more than mothers. For this reason, fathers may play a more important role in childhood socialization (and sport socialization) than previously believed. Not only do fathers react more positively to physical activity by boys than girls (Tauber, 1979), but they also show more positive reactions when their sons choose "boyish" activities than when their daughters choose "feminine" activities (Fling & Manosevitz, 1972; Lansky, 1967). In addition, highly playful children have fathers who roughhouse with them, while girls who are highly playful have fathers who practice physical skills with them (Kleiber, Barnett, & Wade, 1978).

Fathers also play a role in sex typing female activities, particularly in choice of sex-appropriate toys or nursery school activities. (Fling & Manosevitz, 1972; Sears, Rau, & Alpert, 1965). Fathers of highly feminine daughters encourage sex-appropriate activities more than do fathers of unfeminine girls (Mussen & Rutherford, 1963).

Parents may not be fully aware of how their practices undermine the principle of equal treatment. Perhaps they consider play activities mundane, unimportant, and totally unrelated to the principle of equality or full development. Regardless of intent, however, females are subjected to social prototypes in daily behavior similar to the types which existed 30 years ago. Although much of this social learning is accomplished through indirect, casual, daily interaction with parents, the consequences, unfortunately, are pervasive, devastating, and long lasting.

Self-selection of Games by Children

It is difficult to explain exactly how parents convey sex-stereotypic perceptions of sports and games to their children. As suggested earlier, this is systematic, though possibly inadvertent. Another difficult question is what or how children read messages when boys are rewarded while girls are not. Nevertheless, by the time they reach elementary-school age, children have determined for themselves that active sports are masculine and not feminine, and they perceive that masculine games have a higher prestige value (Lynn, 1959; Rosenberg & Sutton-Smith, 1960; Stein, Pohly, & Mueller, 1971). Further evidence of this social learning appears in children's ranking of activities. Boys indicate that sports are the most important attribute for popularity, while girls indicate that grades are (Buchanan, Blankenbaker, & Cotten, 1976). Also, girls identify "to be nice" as most important, while boys identify "to be good in sports" as most important (Caplan & Kinsbourne, 1974).

These orientations are results of early sex typing, not "natural selection." Preferences and orientations are consequences of two kinds of influence, that which emanates from significant others and that which stems from the process of labeling. In many respects, the effects of labeling activities have been underestimated; however, some recent research on children's choices and performance serves as a reminder that we can alter behavior by merely labeling things differently. When offered a novel game, males performed better when told that boys do well in that game. When the boys were told that girls do well, their performances decreased. The same game activity created similar results for girls: girls' performances improved when they were told that girls do well in the game (Montemayor, 1974). This study should clearly demonstrate that labels strongly influence performance and motivation to do well. One should also remember that labeling has a particularly powerful effect on children's choice of games and sports.

During childhood girls play "girls' " games while boys play "boys' " games. In addition to the labels that channel children's behaviors into activities which differ depending on their gender, the games themselves are organized differently, and the play styles which emerge create even greater differences between boys and girls. As children grow older games become segregated, until, at 8 or 9 years, children's games show a clear separation between males and females. By the age of puberty sport participation is predominantly a masculine phenomenon in our society. The sport ideology, which operates more subtly during childhood, prevails during adolescence, a period when it becomes absolutely clear that games and sports are positively associated with the male but not the female gender role (McPherson, 1978; Sutton-Smith, Rosenberg, & Morgan, 1963). Although the social stigma attached to females who participate in sport may not be as strong now as it was in the past, most females learn that if they are physically active they are not going to get many rewards from such activities. Girls learn this lesson by age 12, if not sooner. They also learn that what is worth competing for and demonstrating competence in is socially defined for both sexes—and that sport is still not an activity worth achieving (Sherif & Rattray, 1976).

Games and sports are effective vehicles through which individuals are socialized into social, economic, and political roles (Webb, 1969). Through games children learn about their society, its rules, its expectations, and its acceptable roles. Games and sport provide rich experiences which allow children to practice skills to be used in later life. In simple terms, there are social and political outcomes of play and sport, and such outcomes go far beyond a legalistic interpretation of equal opportunity. Some games offer more diversity, flexibility, and range for learning social skills. Those are the games that males play, and it is precisely for this reason that participation in games and sports has become an important issue to some feminists.

Boys' games are structurally organized so that teamwork, cooperation, goal setting, rule negotiation, and compromise are possible social learning outcomes. Girls' games do not have a similar structural organization and therefore do not offer similar social learning outcomes.

Differences in the Structure of Boys' and Girls' Games

There are some striking differences between boys' and girls' games, such that children's games contribute to totally different outcomes—depending on the child's sex. For example, boys play in larger groups and in games with multiple roles that are complementary or interdependent. Also, boys can adapt rules of their games to fit the size of the group without losing the spirit of the game. Another feature of boys' games is their progressive development to more complex forms as boys grow older (Lever, 1976, 1978). Boys can learn basic skills at a young age but can build upon these skills and "get better" as they grow older. After learning to bat, they can learn to bunt, to "pull" the ball, and to hit behind the runner. This progression offers males continuous challenge in their games, an opportunity to deal with increasing complexity as well as the use of various strategies. Boys learn to work toward a specific goal, to settle disputes over rule interpretation, and to abide by compromise and majority rule.

In contrast, girls' games do not provide them with similar experiences or opportunities. Girls play indoors more, have limited experiences in interacting with their environmental surroundings, and tend not to play team or competitive games. Instead of learning cooperation and inter-dependence, girls learn to wait their turn, take turns, and to perform solitary, repetitive tasks. Since rules are few, simple, and explicit, they offer little room for discussion or interpretation when disputes arise (Lever, 1976, 1978). In addition, girls' games require less strategy and do not provide increasing complexity or a progression of skills. As a result the games are less challenging and frequently end over loss of interest or an arbitrary stopping point rather than with a clearly accomplished goal.

This comparison suggests one obvious outcome. Males are provided with game experiences which can be adaptable to a variety of adult role requirements. In contrast, females do not learn to develop strategies for achieving goals, nor do they learn to cooperate in order to compete. As a result they are limited in the number of social outcomes they can derive from their game playing and they are not prepared for a variety of roles. Harragan (1977) has argued that most females are not adequately pre-pared for leadership or managerial positions because of the games they played as children.

Recently, it has been argued that society's subtle, yet consistent, message to females regarding physical activity has changed—particularly since the advent of Title IX. Today more high schools and colleges pro-vide sports programs and introduce new sporting possibilities to thousands of girls to whom such possibilities were not formerly available (Sutton-Smith, 1979). As a result more females than ever before are tak-ing part in active and competitive games. Still, has the message really changed or has it only been *slightly modified?* Female participation in sport is acceptable and perhaps even rewarded when the activity pro-motes a feminine image.

True, female participation has increased in team sports, especially revenue-producing sports such as basketball. But the majority of women continue to participate in sports which are expressive, aesthetic, graceful, and fluid. Little interest, visibility, or recognition are given to women's sports that project an image of vigorous activity, strength, speed, or face to face competition. The female sport choices approved by society are actually as narrow today as they were twenty years ago. In 1964 Eleanor Metheny (Note 9), a physical educator, identified specific sports as ap-propriate and inappropriate—based on how consonant they were with the feminine image and with the meaning of "being a woman" in the

United States. The similarity between her classification then and society's approval now is striking: gymnastics, tennis, skating, and dance. Those sports she identified as inappropriate were those involving body contact and direct competition. Although the increased number of female participants is refreshing and encouraging, the fact remains that the same sex-typed message is being conveyed.

Children's Socialization into Sport

As discussed earlier, family influences have tended to channel the majority of females into activities other than sport and thus perpetuate sexism in sport. Yet, many women do become interested and involved in sport. Several become world–class athletes and demonstrate superior levels of performance, achievement, and competence. Obviously, these women consider sport to be an appropriate activity despite the fact that such a choice runs counter to society's definition of what is appropriate. Somehow, these women have been socialized into sport, value mastery of skill, and incorporate sport into their lifestyle. How were their social learning experiences different from the majority of females? What was the nature of their early childhood experiences, and how did the family provide a social milieu which supported their sport involvement? The remainder of this chapter focuses on answers to these questions.

As Barry McPherson, a sport sociologist, so aptly stated, "regardless of motor talent, unless children are exposed to social systems in which they have the opportunity to engage in sport and receive positive sanctions, it is unlikely that sport will become a salient aspect of their lifestyle" (McPherson, 1978, p. 219). This is an extremely important aspect of female sport socialization, because sport participation is not a cultural expectation. Therefore, in order to overcome the traditional outcomes of sex typing, some powerful social influences must be provided early in childhood.

Existing research not only supports this notion, but strongly suggests that the family, specifically the parents, plays a significant role in socializing females into sport. However, the forms these supportive influences take may be as subtle and diffuse as the negative influences we discussed in previous sections. For example, several studies reveal that female intercollegiate athletes are raised in families in which one or both parents actively participate in sport. In addition, games and sport are typical "family" activities, and during the athletes' childhood, their parents frequently played with them in these games (Greendorfer, 1974, 1979a, 1979b, Note 10). Also, most athletes acknowledge that the family first initiated their early interest and participation in sport. Parents are instrumental in influencing daughters' sport participation, and positive relationships have been found between parental encouragement, parental interest, and female adolescent sport participation (Snyder & Spreitzer, 1976).

Such findings suggest that a strong positive family environment may provide the impetus for reversing traditional sex typing in child rearing. Some important social learning principles are operating in the early experiences of these female athletes: Sport is viewed as a "family" activity; parents are not presenting a sex-typed orientation of sport to their daughters. Indirectly and directly, parents are encouraging sport participation, and these women perceive sport activities as "normal." Because the parents are participants themselves, they also serve as role models and tend to reinforce their daughters' play and sport behaviors. Other characteristics of childhood patterns were that these athletes enjoyed sport when they were young; that they were good in sport and rated their ability above average; and that they placed some value and importance on being good in sport. Related to this point, they perceived their parents as placing some importance on their being good in sport (Greendorfer, 1979a; Greendorfer, Note 11). Thus, women who become athletes have a history of early sport participation, were rewarded for their participation, and interpret their sport experiences as having positive consequences. Critical to this situation, however, is the family's role in providing a supportive and positive social milieu for their daughters.

This pattern is quite similar to that obtained by Orlick (Note 12), who studied boys' participation in sports. Orlick found that the parents were sport participants themselves and thus served as role models. They expected and reinforced their sons' participation, and their sons had expectancies to be rewarded for participation. Thus, research findings on both males and females demonstrate the powerful impact parents have on children's sport involvement. This impact cannot be underestimated in the case of females, because it directly or indirectly reinforces personal expectations for continued sport participation. Also, if continuity theory holds, level of physical activity in childhood should directly affect level of physical activity in later life. Available research on both lower levels and higher levels of activity strongly supports continuity theory. Inactivity in youth leads to inactivity in adulthood (Sofranko & Nolan, 1972; Yoesting & Burkhead, 1973), and childhood participation during adolescence is a primary predictor of adult sport involvement—for both males and females (Greendorfer, 1979b; Snyder & Spreitzer, 1976; Greendorfer, Note 11; Kenyon & Knoop, Note 13).

In sum, greater parental encouragement of physical activity leads to higher levels of daughters' childhood sport participation, and greater childhood sport participation contributes to higher levels of participation during later stages of the life cycle. This has been a consistent research finding. It not only supports the "chain of events" notion suggested earlier in this chapter, but it targets a specific social system in which change may be possible. Family influence is potent, regardless of the direction of influence, and research in this area should provide further insight into which social learning practices need to be altered—that is, if we desire further change.

Gender Differences in Children's Socialization into Sport

Although the family provides a general atmosphere or social climate, we need to examine more closely what each family member may be contributing to the socialization experiences of young females, particularly with regard to sport, and to discuss whether gender differences exist in the nature of this influence. A few studies suggest that some interesting and very complex dynamics are operating in the case of female sport socialization. For example, Greendorfer and Lewko (1978a) found that fathers, peers, and teachers were significant predictors of boys' sport involvement, while only fathers and peers influenced female sport participation. These findings lead to several discussion points—one that is related to the absence of teacher influence on females; several are related to exactly who in the family is a significant influence on both males and females.

Relative to the second point, Greendorfer and Lewko (Note 14) found that parents rather than siblings were of greater importance for both boys and girls. Also, when family member influence was compared, the data showed that the father was the most influential, while mothers, brothers, and sisters were not significant influences at all (Greendorfer & Lewko, 1978). These findings are surprising for several reasons. First, strong father influence on female sport participation is not consistent with earlier findings which demonstrated that like-sexed parents had greater influence on female sport involvement than opposite-sexed parents (Snyder & Spreitzer, 1973). Second, strong father influence runs counter to theoretical notions which would predict that mothers and older sisters were sport role models for young girls (McPherson, 1978). Most interesting, however, was the finding that siblings do not influence sport socialization. Many sociologists and psychologists of sport strongly believe that siblings, particularly older brothers, influence female sport involvement (Landers, 1979; Portz, 1973; Ziegler, 1973). They base this belief on the fact that the first play group for all children consists of their siblings; therefore, brothers and sisters should logically influence future play/sport behavior. The findings from the Greendorfer and Lewko study shatter that belief.

A more in-depth analysis of children's sport socialization (Greendorfer & Lewko, Note 14) found substantial gender differences. The results showed that the process of socializing boys into sport was much more consistent than it was for girls. Regardless of social class or race, the strongest predictor of boys' sport involvement was the importance of being good in sport. When family influence was compared to that of teachers and peers, the family was the most important predictor of boys' sport involvement. And when individual family members' influences were compared, fathers provided the strongest influence on male sport participation. Greendorfer and Lewko concluded that there is an underlying regularity in the process by which boys are socialized into sport. Regardless of geographical background, race, or social class, sport socialization for males appears to be institutionalized in this society.

When the data for females were analyzed, no clear or consistent pattern of influence could be found (Greendorfer & Lewko, Note 14). The social system influences on female sport participation varied according to the race and social class of the girls in the study. For this reason they could not identify specific agents who promoted female sport participation. These findings contradicted the previous study which demonstrated that the father was a primary influence on female sport involvement. However, an interesting fact did emerge from the data in the two studies. The father was a strong influence on those females who came from a college community and whose family had a high level of education and occupational status. This finding suggests that social class background plays an important role in determining who exerts influence on female sport participation. This notion is further supported by the literature that suggests that fathers, particularly lower class fathers, are more rigid than mothers in sex-role stereotyping (Biller, 1976; Lamb, 1975). Therefore, it is possible that fathers perceive some responsibility in socializing sons into sport but perceive sport as an inappropriate activity for their daughters. Even if fathers feel neutral about sport as an activity for their daughters, reinforcement of daughters' sport interest may be variable, inconsistent, or nonexistent. Similar messages may be communicated to the mother, who may or may not feel strongly about their daughters' sport participation. Thus, the process of socializing females into sport may be problematic or volatile because no specific family member considers it a responsibility to initiate daughters' interest in sport. In the case of families from a higher socioeconomic background, fathers may less rigidly sex-type activities and may play a more positive role in socializing daughters into sport. The data from the two studies under discussion would certainly support such an interpretation. Although this hypothesis is plausible, the question still remains who socializes young girls into sport and under what circumstances?

This leads to some important implications. First, even those females who are socialized into sport experience differential treatment from their parents. Second, the inconsistency in socializing agents suggests that there is absolutely no assurance that females will become involved in sport. It seems that female sport socialization is a function of parental predisposition and experience in sport—as well as a function of race and social class. In essence, female sport involvement is an accident of birth. In contrast, males, regardless of background and parental experience are almost universally exposed to sport socializing experiences.

Additional gender differences in recent studies also support our notion that little change has taken place in sport patterns. Lewko and Ewing (1980) found that regardless of age, boys were more actively involved in sports than girls, and that sport involvement occurred at an earlier age for males. They concluded that some systematic influence provided greater support for boys than for girls in sport related activities. The date of the study and the age of their sample of children are noteworthy, as are some of their more in-depth findings and their interpretations. Lewko and Ewing found that children active by age 9 were also active through age 11, but those not highly involved by age 9 were not highly involved at age 11. Thus, whatever the nature of the sport experiences, those positive influences had been exerted by age 9 and the pattern had stabilized. The gender differences in involvement suggest differential treatment as well. The findings from this study suggest another barrier to remove if equality in sport participation is to occur—reversing early social learning. Lewko and Ewing suggest that attempts to get low-involved children more actively involved in sport may not meet with much success, particularly after age 9.

Lewko and Ewing (1980) also found some variation in the types of influences on boys and on girls. Boys who were highly involved in sport were influenced by their fathers and had a higher value toward sport than those not highly involved. For the girls, those who were highly involved in sport received more influence from each family member, held a higher value toward sport, and perceived themselves to be more skilled than those less actively involved. This is an interesting profile, because it seems that several sources of influence must be present in order for girls to overcome stereotypic socializing experiences.

The data so far indicate that gender differences in toy selection, play behavior, and structural organization of games are socially derived by products of sex typing. Although sex typing first occurs in the family, the process is reinforced through other social systems and institutions, such as the peer group and the school. For this reason, we must not assume that females who are socialized into sport are not subjected to sex typing or that sex typing has not been a factor in their sport participation. We suggest that females become involved in sport *despite the presence of sex typing, but only under some very special circumstances*—when there is a strong supportive social milieu which counteracts this form of discrimination.

Female Socialization into Sport

The empirical results discussed in the previous section force us to face some critical issues when we search for a more detailed or comprehensive explanation of female sport socialization. Sociology of sport textbooks do not adequately cover the topic, in spite of the increasing amount of information on female patterns. Unfortunately, more recent data on women have not been integrated into the mainstream body of knowledge, which continues to use as its foundation findings obtained on white, adult, *male*, elite athletes. In this respect, sociology of sport is as sexist as the institution of sport. Because it considers only one select group, it misrepresents knowledge and distorts theoretical conceptualization. For these reasons we need to compare male and female patterns of sport socialization. On the one hand, general findings indicate that family influences are similar. On the other hand, some differences are striking, particularly when influences from other social systems, such as the school, are examined.

Although only minimal attention has been given to male sport socialization, research demonstrates the importance of a strong family influence. Adding support to Orlick's (Note 12) findings on young boys, Pudelkiewicz (1970, Note 15) found that the initial stimulus for males to become interested comes from a home environment which considers sport an important facet of life. In addition, Snyder and Spreitzer (1973) found that parental interest in sports was positively related to present sport involvement. They also concluded that sport involvement begins in childhood and is reinforced by parental encouragement.

Strong family influence is also a determinant of female sport involvement. Malumphy (1968, 1970) found that female athletes start young, come from a supportive environment, have family approval for participation, and have a history of family sport participation. Other studies reflect similar results. In two studies of college athletes, over 40% of the women reported that the family was the initial agency responsible for their sport involvement. Also, approximately 80% were involved in sport by the age of 8 (Greendorfer, 1974, Note 10).

Early age of involvement and strong family support are major influences on professional women golfers. In her study of LPGA competitors, Nancy Theberge (Note 1) found that the women began to play at age 12, while the average age at which they entered their first tournament was 14. Their first playing partners were their parents, and introduction to golf took place within the family. Peers reinforced these early influences during later stages of the life cycle. However, family support also took other forms: (a) parents encouraged daughters to compete at the highest level, and (b) parents were willing to incur the expense of private lessons and club membership (Theberge, Note 1).

All of these studies characterize the female athlete as coming from a childhood environment which is strong and supportive. The reinforcement that these female athletes get from significant others seems to be overwhelmingly positive, with relatively little discouragement of sport participation. Sport was incorporated into child-rearing practices in such a way that these women considered participation as normal, neither different nor extraordinary. When they were children, these athletes had little difficulty learning sport skills, and family members were usually their first "teachers" (Greendorfer, 1979, Note 11; Greendorfer & Lewko, Note 14). Not only do these women view their sport participation as "feminine" and as an important aspect of self-identity, but they experience little role conflict, believe in the validity of their participation, and have a deep affective commitment to sport (Hall, Note 5).

School Influences

This profile of strong family support is in sharp contrast to that of nonathletes. When they were children, nonathletes received lower levels of family encouragement to participate in sport and, as a direct result, became minimally involved in sport as adults (Greendorfer, 1979a, 1981). The implication of this finding is clear—if one major social system does not provide sufficient influence, then another must have a strong positive impact if sport socialization is to occur. The school is a logical choice because it influences so much of our cognitive as well as social learning and provides a context within which children learn many social competencies. However, research indicates that, for athletes as well as nonathletes, the school plays a minor role in socializing females in sport (Greendorfer, 1977; Greendorfer & Lewko, 1978, Note 14). Although the next chapter considers the role of the school in detail, a few research findings are pertinent to the present discussion. First of all, despite the implementation of Title IX, the school merely reinforces sport roles learned elsewhere. It does not introduce females to sport, nor does it have a strong impact in teaching them sport skills (Greendorfer, 1977; Greendorfer & Lewko, 1978, Note 14). This relatively insignificant role of the school represents a major difference between male and female patterns.

The strong impact that the school provides for males is not the only dimension in which sport socialization differs between the sexes. Similar to findings on children, a study of childhood influences on male track athletes revealed that childhood participation, the school, and male family members, in that order, strongly influenced present participation (Greendorfer, 1979b). These three variables were the major contributors to their adult involvement. In contrast, present participation of female track athletes was most strongly influenced by childhood involvement *and several other influences of almost equal importance* (Greendorfer, 1979b). Thus, instead of receiving major social system influence, females receive a greater number of diffuse influences. Although childhood family influence is critical, reinforcement follows a more general or diffuse pattern. What first appeared to reflect similarities between males and females disappears when we closely examine the impact of several social learning influences. Two distinct patterns emerge—one for males and one for females.

Because of this finding, a point mentioned early in this section needs repeating. There is danger of misrepresentation and bias when generalizing from findings based only on males. Because gender differences exist, any attempt to theoretically conceptualize the process of sport socialization must include females if the framework is to be of any value. For these reasons, I vehemently disagree with those sociologists of sport who feel that theoretical models are ready to be trimmed (Kenyon & Knoop, Note 13). To do so would be premature and would exclude data pertaining to females. It would perpetuate the generation of knowledge from a male standard, and at this point in time such a proposition is unacceptable.

Conclusion and Implications

The process of socializing women into sport is more complex than originally believed. Unlike males, who receive strong, consistent influences from all major social systems, females seem to have a more general, diffuse, and subtle pattern of influence. Although the family plays a major role by providing a supportive social milieu during childhood, individual family members differ in their degree of encouragement and support. Thus, even females who do become involved in sport are subjected to sex typing and differential treatment. In general, however, adult female athletes come from families in which toy, play, and game experiences are provided at an early age and are typically incorporated into normal family activities. As a result, sport socialization for females may not be conscious or deliberate; some of the most effective socialization takes place in situations where no explicit effort is made to train or influence others.

Such considerations have tremendous implication for future research. Indirectly, they suggest that researchers should attempt to capture some of the more subtle and dynamic aspects of the sport socialization process.

Because traditional research methods, such as survey techniques, assume a consciousness and direction of the process, perhaps researchers should deemphasize the use of such methods and opt for more direct techniques. Rewards and punishments are "simple" consequences of social interaction; however, social interactions are "natural" experiences of everyday life. Therefore, to capture interaction patterns, more field studies in natural settings should be undertaken. Observation of parent-infant or parent-child, child-child, and group-child interactions in play settings is absolutely essential. Another fruitful approach would be to analyze the content of verbal feedback, reinforcement, and punishment in play settings. Future research should also seek to understand how females perceive their sport experiences and whether their perceptions are similar to or different from those of males. More in-depth interview techniques might be appropriate for gathering this information.

The nature of future research questions needs attention as well. What are the consequences of sport participation? Do children really learn social skills through games? Are females handicapped by not playing boys' games or by not participating in sport? What are parental values and expectations of their daughters' sport participation? How do these expectations affect daughters' interest and future sport involvement? These few questions hardly exhaust the possibilities, but they do suggest some future directions.

Of critical importance to our discussion is the issue of "nonsocialization" and whether or not sport sociologists will recognize the political as well as social implications of this topic. This issue has deeper meaning than the mere description of family influence or the role of peers and the school on sport socialization. It touches many of the basic premises and practices in our society—several of which are discriminatory. The fact that proportionally fewer women engage in sport, despite the opportunities provided by Title IX signifies that female participation in sport is as much a political process as a social one.

Notes

1. In recent years, researchers have given considerable attention to the distinction between the terms "sex role" and "gender role." These terms had been used interchangeably and inconsistently in the literature. However, there is a conceptual difference between them. "Sex role" refers to biologically based characteristics and the chromosomal composition of individuals. "Gender role" refers to behavior and nonphysiological components of sex which tend to be culturally regarded as appropriate for males or females. Unfortunately, I use both terms in this chapter. I did not feel it would be proper to replace "sex" with the word "gender" in the discussions or citations of other authors. I did make such a change when referring to my own work, even though the original research may have used the term "sex" instead of "gender."

Chapter 6/
From the Classroom
to the Locker Room:
The Educational Environment

One of the distinguishing features of sport in the United States is its intimate connection with schooling. Educational institutions provide the social environment within which many Americans experience sport as they move through the life cycle. This strong institutional connection between school and sport is not shared by most other nations. In European countries, for example, sporting activity is primarily organized within local athletic clubs that serve as links between the individuals and their residential communities. In communist nations, governmental and political organizations play a major role in organizing sport for their citizens.

The significance of the connection between sport and educational institutions in the US differs for various subgroups in the society. As children, Americans gain their first and often major experience as athletic participants within the framework of competitive school sports. For many adults, the formal organization of school sports acts as the major link between themselves and their community. School athletic programs are a vital source of adult community recreation and help to enhance the social cohesion of local communities. In addition to providing opportunities for its citizens to assume sporting roles as participants and spectators, school sports programs are important sources of employment for individuals as coaches, trainers, and administrators. These connections take on added significance when one recognizes that, in industrial societies, educational institutions are a major vehicle for the transmission of dominant cultural values, social arrangements, and personal skills and attributes. Inevitably, any discussion of female sporting participation must consider the role of education and school sports programs in shaping the nature and consequences of this participation.

Along with the family, the school remains a primary and essential preserver of the societal establishment. In answering the basic questions of any study of socialization, that is, *who* learns *what* from *whom* under *what circumstances* and with *what effects* (Greenstein, 1965, p. 4), one cannot help but be aware of the pervasive presence of sexism in the American educational system. The nature of "who," whether male or female, determines in large part the "what" that is learned, the circumstances under which it is learned, and the consequences of the social learning provided by educational institutions.

Our society remains committed to the proposition that valuable goals are fulfilled by sports. One of those "valued goals" is that girls and women learn to watch, to cheer for and to subjugate themselves and their interests to those of boys and men. As noted in chapter 4, sport is a vital institution for the promotion of this societal, sexual division of labor. Indeed, sport may be the institution most resistant to change because it remains a masculinity rite which definitionally excludes females.

Harder to penetrate than the political smoke filled rooms; than the marble walled office of high finance and the mellow wood paneled classrooms of higher education has been the locker room . . . . The arguments all sound strangely familiar. They center around economics (schools can't afford to duplicate existing programs), health (women and girls would be injured, especially our vital reproductive organs), and modesty (would you want your 12 year old daughter to be tackled by a 16 year old sex maniac?). Although these arguments are all those we hear in every area; employment, politics, religion, they carry a frightening hostility and viciousness when sports become involved. Finally we seem to be challenging the core . . . the masculine ego. (Neville, 1977, p. 4)

It has only been in the last decade, the decade of women, that the patriarchal lessons being taught and learned in school sports have come under serious criticism. This chapter is organized around the connection between the various levels of education and the gender-role socialization they promote.

In the last part of the chapter we examine the major new innovation in sports-school public policy—Title IX. Specifically, we will seek to answer the following questions: What were the factors behind the symbolic and actual rejection of school sports as an exclusively masculine domain? How was Title IX legislation passed? What were the forces opposed to it? What does it purport to do; how successful has it been up to this time; what does it mean for the future organization, goals, and purposes of female sport participation in educational settings? Most importantly, to what extent does it address feminist concerns about the place of women in our sporting institutions and the society as a whole?

The School System and Sports

Play and Games—Grammar School

"To date, there is little evidence to suggest that the elementary school plays a key role in the process of sport-role socialization. Rather, most of the socialization at this stage occurs in the family, neighborhood, peer groups and voluntary sports associations" (Loy, McPherson, & Kenyon, 1978, p. 228). As noted by Susan Greendorfer in chapter 5, preschool children have already learned sex-appropriate play activity from their parents, acquired toy preferences shaped by parental choices and rewards, and assumed a social-psychological disposition toward the world of motion based on expectations about "sex-appropriate behavior." The overwhelming evidence is that children, especially female children, who have not been encouraged to engage in sports at home will not see this pattern substantially challenged or changed by the first school environment, grammar school (Lewko & Ewing, 1980). Thus, at the very time when girls are most likely to be physiologically capable of competing with boys and of playing games with them (Bentzen, 1966; Espechschade & Eckert, 1967), the girls have already classified athletics as masculine (Duquin, 1974, p. 4).

Janet Lever (1976), in her earliest efforts to differentiate the skills being acquired by young girls and boys in their play, sat in her "car near a school-yard every lunch hour for a month" (1976, p. 479). She examined the sex patterns that emerged on the playgrounds. Her observations remain perhaps the most theoretically fruitful for our understanding of children and their playing habits in grammar school. Specifically she notes six differences between girls and boys in their play (1976, pp. 478-488):

(1) Boys play in the public outdoors more than girls, who prefer the indoors playing sites.

(2) Boys play in larger groups than girls, who, regardless of the site of play, had fewer members in their play group.

(3) Boys' play occurs in more age–heterogeneous groups, whereas girls play in more age–homogeneous groups.

(4) Girls play male games more often than boys play female games. There is less stigma for girls who wish to play with the boys and accept the label of "tomboy" than boys who *seriously* take part in girls' games. Lever uses Goffman's notion of "role distance" (1961) to suggest that boys who play girls' games can do so as long as they do not give the activity any serious tenor.

(5) Girls *play* more often than boys, who *compete.* Play has no explicit goal, rules, winners, or losers, whereas formal games, which are preferred by boys, do.

(6) Boys' games last longer than girls' games.

After considering the consequences of each of these sex differences, Lever concludes that "boys' games help prepare their players for successful performance in a wide range of work settings in modern society. In contrast, girls' games may help to prepare their players for the private sphere of the home and their future roles as wives and mothers" (1976, p. 484). In short, the games children play have profound implications for the roles the society wants and *expects* them to assume as adults. Obviously, if the sex–role scripts of men and women are to expand, there must be serious consideration given to changing these early play patterns.

The observed separation of girls and boys on the playground is well grounded in a sex-role ideology which perpetuates the family's influence. There may be a few girls—tomboys—playing with the boys. The few who play sex-inappropriate games are clearly expected to outgrow this tendency. "It appears that until puberty academically successful girls evolve a 'bisexual' or dual self-concept. Both sexes are rewarded for achievement, especially academic achievement. Girls, as well as boys, are permitted to compete in school or athletics without significant repercussions" (Bardwick & Douvan, 1972, p. 229). It is only when a girl's athletic activity continues for too long or she is too intense about it that people express concern and apply social sanctions. A girl is expected to outgrow her sport infatuation, and she will be sanctioned if she does not.

High School: Higher Stakes

It is at puberty that the educational system assumes a greater importance in sex-role socialization. Farther removed from the socializing influence of the family, the peers and school setting achieve an importance heretofore unknown. School policy as to appropriate sex-role behavior in grammar school often amounts to "benign neglect." In the high schools the policy becomes actively discriminatory. School officials, teachers, counselors, and parents consider proper gender-role identity at this age too important to leave the viscissitudes of chance learning. The sex-segregrated policies are consciously and actively promoted. Puberty is the time when both sexes must accept and embrace their proper sex and gender identity; boys must become men and girls women. Sport in the high schools is seen as a vital area for developing the awareness of masculinity and femininity.

Three strains of recent scholarly activity attest to the greater public concern with secondary school sports programs. We can label these: the student athlete, the social status of the athletic student, and the abuses resulting from the "Lombardian ethos." We will briefly consider the significant issues and research in each area.

Academic excellence and athleticism often have been considered mutually exclusive. The caricature of the "dumb jock" is so widely known it needs no elaboration; however, recent scholarship suggests that this viewpoint needs much more empirical validation. The earliest studies of the academic performance of the high school athlete were summarized by Davis and Cooper (1934) and their conclusion was that athletes did *not* perform as well academically as nonathletes. The research of the 1960s produced a total turnabout on this issue. Scholars from the United States and other nations (Edismore, 1961; Bend, 1968; Schafer & Armer, 1968; McIntosh, 1966; Start, 1967) discovered that athletes were better students and even implied that sports, rather than detracting from academic performance, actually encouraged scholarship and academic excellence. Currently, the best conclusion from these highly convoluted and methodologically questionable investigations is "that participation in institutionalized scholastic or collegiate sport does not have a serious detrimental effect on academic performance" (Loy, McPherson & Kenyon, 1978, p. 230).

It is important to consider why there have been such inconclusive and contradictory findings. Among the theoretical and methodological problems presented by these studies are the following: (a) almost without exception they include only male athletes and totally ignore females; (b) far too often correlational statements slip silently into causal ones; (c) there has been insufficient attempts to control intervening and antecedent explanatory variables which might explain correlations—for example, higher grade point averages (GPAs) among athletes may be the result of eligibility requirements that eliminate students from the athletic pool who cannot maintain the grade average; (d) almost every study is cross-sectional and lacks the necessary longitudinal element which could explain the effects of continued athletic participation on academic performance; (e) endowment sponsorship of some studies (for example, the publication by the National Football Foundation and Hall of Fame), as well as the ideologically "ripe" nature of a sports fanatic times, may have influenced the results the scholars were "willing to find"; (f) finally, and most significantly, these studies like so many others in the sociology of sport fall victim to the enshrinement of a quantitative, empirically grounded, but theoretically weak, investigative motif. Questionnaires, GPA comparisons, and "hard facts" are employed to test hypotheses for which theoretically grounded explanations do not exist. The acceptance and utilization of these research methods necessarily entails that contradictory findings will continue to be reported.

The student athlete also has been the focus of study relative to his (rarely her) educational and occupational aspirations. Generally, the conclusions of these studies are much more consistent than those on athlete's educational attainment. For a variety of reasons, student athletes do manifest a greater desire to continue their education at the college level. These higher aspirations also exist in the occupational realm. The student athlete was more likely to have a "higher" career goal, was more likely to achieve it, and consequently was more likely to attain a better income than his (sic) nonathletic peers (Otto & Alwin, 1977). In one of the few studies which controlled for the influence of socioeconomic class, Picou and Curry (1974) found that the sporting activity of lower class youth had the same positive effect on his (sic) aspirations as those reported for students of a higher social class.

In his classic study of The Adolescent Society (1961), James Coleman documented the prestige that sport carries in the secondary school system and in the adolescent subculture. The single most vital predictor of an adolescent boy's popularity was his status as an athlete. Fifteen years later Eitzen's (1976) replication of Coleman's study found that sports had retained its attraction and importance for males. Although competitive sports had lost some of its appeal in middle and upper class high schools (Gagnon, 1976), interscholastic sports remained the focal point of a majority of school activities, school spirit, and community identification. One clear measure of public acceptance of school sports is found in school budgets, where sports and the cost of interscholastic sports competition have become an integral and unquestioned line item (Saario, Jacklin, & Tittle, 1973).

A more disturbing indication of the excessive social importance attached to school sports, and particularly interscholastic competition, can be discovered at nearly every state scholastic championship. The Lombardian ethos reaches its apex at these annual events. The final contestants arrive after a season of far too much time spent practicing, far too many games, and far too much pressure from a coach; far too much authoritarianism, cheating, intimidation, physical brutality, and exhaustion; far too much elitism and "cutting" of the less talented, less regimented, and less fanatic; far too many demands to sacrifice all for the school, made by administrators, teachers, coaches, parents, and peers; and far too much commercialism (Eitzen & Sage, 1978, pp. 100-104). After such a season, can either team be a winner?

The prevalence of the Lombardian ethos in secondary schools has been well documented by John T. Talamini. His recommendations were intended to bring high school sports in line with the principles set forth by the Educational Policies Commission. Among his policy recommendations were: the abolition of postseason tournaments; increased opportunities for all students, not just the varsity athlete, to engage in extramurals contests; initiation of co-recreational activities to break down sex barriers to sport participation; creation of carryover intramural programs so that physical activity could be part of one's entire life cycle; demands that coaches be recruited and monitored to insure that they provide good role models for youth and that their educational mission be foremost; the subsumption of all athletic programs in the physical *education* program; and finally, that all athletics be financed through tax monies rather than by commercial ventures such as gate receipts or sales (Talamini, 1973, pp. 171-172).

Educational policy, formulated primarily at the local community level, reflects a willingness to appropriate large sums of money for sports facilities, sports equipment, coaches, trainers, travel, and even security guards for when the "games" between schools get out of hand. However, until the mid-seventies the monetary endorsement of interscholastic sports was virtually for boys only. After all, sports were important for making boys men but not girls women.

In the seventies the feminist movement fostered a reconsideration of the sex-stereotyping and the discriminatory consequences of the secondary school sports program. Vocal parental agitation, educator reconsideration of the consequences of sexism, and legislation (principally Title IX) required a reassessment of the sports programs in most high schools. That reassessment led to an enormous increase in the opportunity for interscholastic sports competition for girls. Table 3 presents the figures for the increasing female participants in interscholastic sport competition for ten sports between 1971-1977.

Table 3
Growth of Girl Athletes in Interscholastic Sport Competition

Sports	Number of Participants		
	1970-71	1972-73	1976-77
Track and Field	62,211	178,209	395,271
Basketball	132,299	203,207	387,507
Volleyball	17,952	108,298	245,032
Softball	9,813	81,379	133,458
Tennis	26,010	53,940	112,166
Swimming and Diving	17,229	41,820	85,013
Gymnastics	17,225	35,224	79,461
Field Hockey	4,260	45,252	59,944
Golf	1,118	10,106	32,190
Cross-Country	1,719	4,921	30,798
TOTAL	289,836	762,356	1,560,840

The seventies have witnessed a remarkable growth in sheer numbers of female participants. From 1970 to 1977 the number of participants in the ten sports had increased 540%. As noteworthy is the greater diversification of organized sporting activity in the high schools. In 1970-71 45.6% of all the girls engaged in interscholastic sports competition were playing one sport, basketball. The first big increase in middle–class female sports activity occurred in basketball. Even during the era of relative inactivity, 1936-1970, basketball remained the most popular, at times the only, interscholastic competitive sport for girls. However, by 1977 basketball accounted for only 24.8% of all participants, was no longer the most popular sport, and had shown the least percentage growth of any of the ten sports. The sports that showed the most rapid increases in numbers of participants were volleyball, softball, field hockey, golf, and cross-country. In spite of the emphasis put on the "more feminine" sports of tennis, swimming and diving, and gymnastics, their growth was less dramatic.

The increased number of female high school athletes means more tax dollars will be spent on girls' sports programs. Although still far from parity with the boys, most high schools have allocated a greater proportion of their athletic budgets for girls' interscholastic competition. In one survey of 166 public high schools in New York, 71% had made budget revisions for the girls' program with little or no negative effect on the boys' budget. Illustrative of the changes is that in 1972 46% of the schools had spent *9% or less* of their athletic budget for girls; by 1978 77% of the schools were allocating *30% or more* to the girls' programs (Staffo, 1978, p. 3). Athletics for girls in the high schools have been expanded throughout the country: more monies are being spent; more sports are being offered; more equity in practice time has been achieved; and generally, the extreme neglect of girls and their athletic endeavors is waning. The greatest handicap remains in the facilities, which must accommodate nearly twice the sporting activity. It is doubtful that this problem can be solved. In most school districts, where adding to the space is out of the question, the answer may be in rescheduling use of the limited facilities to accommodate the girls.

Although problems still exist at the junior and high school levels, there are more reports of innovative programs, creative solutions to the lack of resources, and an openness to the female presence in sport than many "hard-liners" ever expected. Particularly noteworthy has been the attempts to sex–integrate the physical education component of programs (Blaufarb, 1977). The negative consequences of isolating the sexes in physical education and athletics have been more fully demonstrated by secondary school educators, and there has been no well organized, vocal, and powerful lobbying effort to withstand the "incursion" of the girls. However, the same cannot be said of higher education.

Corporate Sports Invade the School System: Collegiate Athletics

Athletics is a small part of the higher education industry; it accounts for not more than 1 percent of the $55 billion currently spent by institutions of higher education. Athletic participation in intercollegiate athletics represent a very small proportion of the total enrollment in colleges and universities. Only about 60 percent of colleges and universities have intercollegiate athletics programs, although those institutions account for most of the enrollment in higher education. Yet the expenditures and participation rates do not begin to reflect the importance that intercollegiate athletics occupies on the national scene. Some highly distinguished universities are better known for their athletic accomplishments than their scholarship, and no other subject can stir the interests of the alumni or governing board any quicker or more intensely than athletics. In fact, a somewhat perverse but iron law of academic administration says that the more intense, the more visible, and the more costly the athletic program, the less influence the chief executive officer has over it. That law is partly a function of another law: the

> more important the athletics program is to the university, the less likely it is
> to be funded from unrestricted university income. (Atwell, 1979, p. 367)

This quote from Robert Atwell points to just one of the major difficulties that face intercollegiate athletics. It is part of yet another study,
investigation, call for reform, and seemingly endless string of exposés of
the link between higher education, sports, and corporate business interests. Beginning in 1905 with President Theodore Roosevelt's intervention in the college football controversy, the issue of the adverse effects of
corporate sports on institutions of higher education has been studied at
least three times. In 1929 a report funded by the Carnegie Corporation
and under the project direction of Howard J. Savage uncovered the professionalism of intercollegiate football. The results were ironic. Savage
had decried the recruitment violations and special treatment of athletes.
Subsequently, these same practices were codified, and the regulation of
collegiate sports became increasingly separated from the administration
of the college/university. In the 1950s another investigation was undertaken. The American Council on Education (ACE) came down with two
recommendations: to outlaw spring football practice and to abolish
postseason bowl games. Spring practices continued and the plethorea of
bowl games increased. Again in 1978 an ACE study funded by a grant
from the Ford Foundation was undertaken. Its focus was threefold: (a) to
look at the relationship between the educational mission of the institution and athletics; (b) to consider the financial difficulties that athletic
programs created; and (c) to recommend ways to cope with unethical
practices relative to the student athlete (Hanford, 1979, pp. 352-355).
These three issues and the impact of Title IX, with its mandate to include
women in collegiate athletic programs, dominate the current discussion
of sports in the colleges.

This last issue of women and sports in the colleges—the impact of Title
IX—is our major concern; however, since it is a "piece of the collegiate
athletic pie" which the women seek to achieve, we must also briefly consider faults and difficulties already known to be part of that pie.

The unethical conduct of athletic directors, coaches, and school officials are so well known and so well documented that in 1974 the ACE
investigative team decided to give only a *partial* list of the abuses:

- altering high school academic transcripts
- threatening to bomb the home of a high school principal who refused to alter transcripts
- changing admissions test scores
- having substitutes, including assistant coaches, take admissions tests
- offering jobs to parents or other relatives of a prospect

- promising one package of financial aid and delivering another
- firing from a state job the father of a prospect who enrolled at other than the state's university
- 'tipping' or otherwise paying athletes who perform particularly well on a given occasion—and then on subsequent ones
- providing a community college basketball star with a private apartment and a car
- providing a quarterback with a new car every year, his favorite end with a 'tip', and the interior lineman with nothing
- getting grades for athletes in courses they never attended
- enrolling university big-time athletes in junior colleges out-of-season and getting them grades there for courses they never attended
- using federal work study funds to pay athletes for questionable or nonexistent jobs
- getting a portion of work study funds paid to athletes 'kicked back' into the athletic department kitty
- forcing injured players to 'get back in the game.' (Hanford, 1979, p. 357)

The disclosure of such practices, the suspension of violating schools, and official reprimands have not substantially alleviated these problems. In 1980 the public still is surprised to hear of extension courses at junior colleges that athletes don't attend but receive credit for so they can remain eligible to play; an entire survey of sports scandals are reviewed in the most widely read public mass sports magazine, *Sports Illustrated* (May 19, 1980, pp. 36-72). The illegal and unethical activities of many collegiate sports officials goes unabated.

The second recurring issue, the educational mission of collegiate athletics, remains vague and ill-defined. The academic performance, occupational aspirations, and social status of college athletes are not as frequently studied by the scholarly community. More concern is expressed over the administrative autonomy of athletic directors and the resulting inability of the chief *academic* officer of an *academic* institution to control that institution's direction (Davis, 1979; Grant, 1979; Stokes, 1979). When the control of the athletic program is no longer in the hands of academicians but under the aegis of professional athletic administrators, there is little doubt about which role has precedence in the student-athlete dyad.

The third crisis of collegiate athletics, its financial woes, directly affects the place of women in these programs. Intercollegiate athletic programs are costly. Despite the huge sums of money received from gate receipts, the sale of television rights, alumni contributions and the like, "69 percent of all men's athletic programs are deficit producing" (Lopiano, 1979, p. 394). These deficits are expected to continue and even in-

crease over the next few years. Insofar as the presence of women's programs dramatize and increase the cost of college sports, the persons promoting corporate, "semi-professional," entertainment sports in our
universities and colleges cannot help be dismayed. Their resistance is expected and has developed.

Resisted though it may be, women are making athletic strides on our
college campuses. Between 1971 and 1976, the number of member
schools in the Association for Intercollegiate Athletics for Women
(AIAW) increased from 301 to 843, an increase of 280%. Table 4 reveals
the numbers of AIAW institutions offering intercollegiate competition in
ten sports.

Table 4
Growth of Women's Sports in Colleges, 1971-1977

Sport	1971-72	1972-73	1973-74	1974-75	1976-77
Basketball	215	346	466	600	640
Volleyball	181	285	396	467	594
Tennis	198	300	417	506	560
Softball	120	175	254	303	342
Swimming & Diving	135	213	265	298	327
Track & Field	76	138	180	226	283
Field Hockey	165	213	249	284	256
Gymnastics	123	182	238	263	246
Golf	77	132	145	155	165
Badminton	70	98	124	127	117

Only two sports (field hockey and badminton) recorded less than a
twofold advance in the number of schools offering intercollegiate competition in the sport. Over 60% of the member AIAW schools in 1971-72
had intercollegiate competition in basketball (71.4%), volleyball
(60.1%), and tennis (65.8%). In 1975-76 these three sports remained the
only ones for which over 60% (actually 75.9%, 70.5% and 66.4% respectively) of the members offered competition. The percentage of
schools offering swimming and diving, field hockey, gymnastics, golf,
and badminton had declined. New member institutions tended to mimic
already existing patterns in intercollegiate competition by adding basketball, volleyball and tennis.

The number of actual intercollegiate sports increased as a result of
Title IX as did the number of women participating. From 1973-1978 the
number of women competing in intercollegiate sports doubled so that
now women account for 30% of all college athletes (West, 1979, p. 1).
Not surprisingly, the monies spent on women's programs expanded as
well. However, the data in Table 5 demonstrate that the proportion of

Table 5
Expenditures for Women's and Men's Athletics
(in thousands of dollars)

Division	1973 Dollars	1977 Dollars
Men's Programs		
Division I		
With Football	$1,614	$2,213
Without Football	235	317
Division II		
With Football	339	460
Without Football	134	146
Division III		
With Football	136	171
Without Football	59	83

Women's Programs				
	1973 Dollars	% of Athletic Budget	1977 Dollars	% of Athletic Budget
Division I	$ 27	2	$ 276	14
Division II	47	13	120	22
Division III	24	23	45	30

From "Solving the financial crisis in intercollegiate athletics" by Donna A. Lopiano, *Educational Record*, **60**, 1979, 394-408. Copyright 1979 by American Council on Education. Reprinted with permission.

the athletic budget going to the female programs remains substantially less than their proportion in the athletic population.

There are some noteworthy facts that emerge from this data:

1. Although the most dollars are spent in Division I schools and the increase between 1973 and 1977 has been over 1,000%, the proportion of the entire athletic budget going to women's sports in the big-time sports schools remains the lowest at 14%.

2. Less disparity between men's and women's programs has been and continues to be in the least "athletic" schools, that is, schools in Division III. There has been a 100% increase in the dollars expended in this division, which, although the smallest increase of them all, is the percentage of the total athletic budget that comes closest to the "equality" mandated by Title IX. Thus, in colleges and universities where sports has not been highly valued, the inequality of the programs has been the least and the women have fared the best.

3. One sport, football, a sport in which women have not traditionally competed, incurs the greatest expense in the athletic budget of each of the divisions. Without football or its cost equivalent, women's programs will never be as expensive as men's.

In the controversy over scarce athletic dollars, the foregoing facts do not substantially alter the positions assumed by big-time sports universities. The greatest resistance to women's sports has come from the major supporters of athletics for the intercollegiate *male* student. Citing the revenue production of big-time football, these universities neglect to indicate that 81% of all football programs do not pay for themselves (Lopiano, 1979, p. 394). This fact alone exposes the falsity of big-time football's "carrying minor sports." A realistic evaluation of the impact of Title IX, should it be truly adhered to, does suggest an increasing financial deficit for athletic budgets. Mandated levels of compliance (now assumed to be approximately 30% of the athletic budget) will mean that expenditures will double by 1981. Additionally, since expenses are not offset by revenues from ticket sales and the like, 50% to 95% of the monies spent on women's athletics will have to come from institutional sources (Lopiano, 1979, pp. 396-397). As startling as these figures sound, Lopiano emphasizes one harsh fact:

> Women's athletics programs obviously are a significant and compounding factor in the current and projected financial crisis. However, analysis of the situation in men's athletics demonstrates that failure to control the deficit trend in these programs is a problem that overshadows the financial effects of providing equal opportunity for female athletes. In essence, *the financial crisis in intercollegiate athletics would exist even if women's athletics were not a factor.* (p. 397, emphasis added)

But women's programs do exist, are expanding, and will cost money. Each of these facts is predicated on the existence of legislation (Title IX) and law suits to enforce that legislation. The law required colleges and universities to begin to treat their female athletes as full-fledged student-athletes. It is to the battle over Title IX and its implications for women, schools, and feminism that we must now turn.

Title IX: The Liberal Limitations of Public Policy

The Higher Education Act of 1972 and its Title IX provision, which prohibited sex discrimination in educational institutions receiving federal funds, marks the first time that the issue of women's and girls' access to sports has achieved the status of a public agenda item (Johnson, 1978, p. 321). While the topic of sexual discrimination addressed by the Act is a "highly emotional one (and) the issues involved go to the root of societal sex roles, on which most of the male members of Congress remain extremely traditional in outlook", it was the topic of athletic provisions which brought to the surface "expressions of the personal value systems of the members of Congress" (Fishel & Pottker, 1977, p. 132) and produced the greatest controversy. Apparently, provisions for equal pay for equal work for male and female teachers, scrutiny of textbooks and curriculum for sexist tendencies, elimination of sex-biased career and achievement counseling, and acceptance of sex-blind admissions criteria could be easily endorsed by a majority of the members of Congress and the society. However, having adolescent girls and boys playing sports on the same field was another matter. It has been the provisions of Title IX, which sought equalization of sport opportunity and rewards, which have engendered the most extreme, organized, and concerted lobbying pro and con, generated the most impassioned pleas, and garnered the most extraordinary claims about the benefits or pending disasters that will befall society if these legislative mandates are implemented.

Some facts about the history of Title IX after its passage by Congress will demonstrate the degree to which the athletic portion of the Act created the most concern. First, unlike all other areas of sex discrimination which were to be immediately addressed and adjusted, schools were allowed a three year grace period to comply with the sports/athletic provisions. Second, the Department of Health, Education and Welfare's mandate to promulgate regulations and interpretations of how to implement Title IX were delayed. Only on June 18, 1974, two years after the passage of the Act, did HEW release the proposed regulations. At the press conference, Secretary Weinberger indicated that the Department would allow public response and comment on the regulations for four months rather than the normal 30 days and expressed consternation over the fact that questions on the sport regulations were repeatedly asked. Weinberger sarcastically quipped that concern for college sports must be "the most important subject in the United States today" (Weinberger quoted in Fishel & Pottker, 1977, p. 113). After four months and over 10,000 written comments to HEW, on February 28, 1975 Weinberger sent the final draft of the regulations to President Ford. This secret document was subsequently leaked to women's groups and brought another barrage of negative responses to what were perceived as weakened regulations. Additional meetings were convened, this time with the President's Domestic Council, to try to prevent some of the retrenchment. The regulations were finally published in the *Federal Register* on June 4, 1975 and were scheduled to go into effect on July 21, 1975, some three years after the Act was passed. Additional clarifications and modifications were still to follow. On December 6, 1978 the Department of Health, Education and Welfare issued final guidelines to take effect in September 1979. It was only with these regulations that teeth were put into Title IX and loss of funds was threatened (Lapin, 1979, p. 44).

The history of lobbying relative to the Act does not end with the promulgation of the regulations. Compliance with the diluted provisions of the Act had been placed in the Office of Civil Rights (OCR) of HEW. Already overburdened with a backlog of cases in the civil rights area, the OCR was ill equipped to handle this extra task. The situation was further complicated when President Ford, after a July meeting with several football coaches (including the coach of the University of Michigan, where Ford had been a varsity player) expressed publicly his reservations about the regulations of Title IX in the sports area (Fishel & Pottker, 1977, p. 127). He requested that the OCR publish yet another clarification of this provision of the Act. Thus, women's groups seeking to present their case directly to the President had been allowed to meet with the Domestic Council while football coaches gained direct access to and the attention of the President.

Subsequent bureaucratic implementation of the regulations has begun to allay any fears held by major SportsWorld schools that radical change was about to occur. Compliance with the diluted and reinterpreted provisions has been placed in the OCR, which has not been able to get to the cases that have arisen.

Approximately 20% of the Title IX complaints that are brought to the OCR arise over athletic issues. Up until 1979, 19 college athletic complaints have been backlogged; 38 were under investigation; 6 were in enforcement; and 6 had been closed. Legal suits to clean up the backlog of Title IX complaints resulted in court orders to increase the enforcement staff to handle the backlogged cases (Lapin, 1979, p. 43).

There are no reporting requirements that the educational institutions must meet; at least two educational institutions, Brigham Young University and Hillsdale College, have publicly announced that they will not comply with the law; the NCAA has filed a suit in the district court in Kansas City against HEW and asked for an injunction against the enforcement of the sports provisions; and to date no school has lost federal funds for noncompliance (Huckle, 1978, p. 384). Thus, although the athletic bureaucracies, especially the NCAA, had failed to prevent athletics for women from becoming a matter for the public agenda, they have been able to retain control of the scope of the conflict (Schattschneider, 1960) and to effectively limit the adverse impact the new law would have on their self-conceived interests.

Informative as this legislative and bureaucratic history may be, it is not to this debate or controversy that we direct our investigations. The major hypothesis espoused here is that even the most "extreme," rigorous, and literal interpretation, implementation, and enforcement of the athletic provisions of Title IX would not alter the relationship of women to sports. The debate over public policy relative to this area expresses at best a liberal feminism. This approach precludes any substantive transformation of sex-role definitions and the masculine ethos of the sporting institution itself. In short, we wish to pursue how Title IX will leave intact a socially acceptable, and essentially sexist, definition of sports and women's place in them.

Contrary to popular understanding, Title IX is not intended to transform the structures and processes of sport itself. It will merely "force" (and not too effectively) educational institutions to make room for girls and women and minimally to reallocate scarce athletic resources and rewards. In return for these minor alterations, females are expected to adapt to the sporting institution as it is presently structured and to conform to its policies and practices. This institutional accommodation by the female "outsider" has many important policy consequences both for women and sport.

First, the Act clearly legitimizes the present and continued institutional linkage of sports to educational institutions. It leaves unquestioned the educational value of athletics, the proper role of sports in schools, and the values behind the allocation of educational funds. The major political and value conflicts embedded in educational budgets—which programs and groups should be funded and which can be "cut"—are never examined. The same issue that arises every time the controversy over intercollegiate athletics has surfaced, that is, how do these programs enhance the *education* and the life-preparedness of the participants, is left unanswered or confined to the "silly squabbles among the girls of the AIAW."

Second, the emphasis in school sports itself is on revenue production by spectator sports rather than on the lifelong benefits of athletic participation. The vast majority of the budgetary disputes about collegiate athletic budgets have to do with allocation of resources to varsity, interscholastic, or intercollegiate competition, not to greater participation in intramural programs. Benefits accrue to the elite athletes, male and female, and not to the massive student body. Their role remains a passive one. Sports generate prestige for the educational institution, financial contributions from alumni, vicarious pleasure for the spectators, and athletic prowess and a privileged status for the few. Title IX does not purport to change this. In fact, one of the most disturbing and unexamined consequences of Title IX has been its failure to help eliminate another form of discrimination, racism. An act expected to enhance equality of opportunity by sex should not produce the unforeseen and unanticipated effects of racism, but that is what appears to be happening.

As to the issue of racism it is necessary to distinguish between what is occurring in the secondary schools and in the colleges. The initial outcry against the requirements of Title IX in sports at the high school level has subsided (Lapin, 1979, p. 45). Public tax revenues to comply with the law made the task one which could be met within the confines of already existent structural and organizational arrangements. These changes, given social class and racial arrangements, necessarily increased the sporting opportunities for young, black, and poor females. High school educations, unlike college opportunities, are far more egalitarian. Despite high dropout rates, blacks and the poor in this country have a far greater chance of completing high school than they do in entering college. Title IX's success at the secondary level has meant more athletic programs for girls who are less likely to have the advantage of college.

A comparison of the participatory trends in the high schools with the AIAW sponsored intercollegiate competition discloses a racist and social class bias. With the exception of golf in the sports included on Table 3, only *team* sports—volleyball, softball, and field hockey—have shown over a tenfold increase in the number of girls participating in high school. Despite the participatory explosion in these sports in high school, the colleges have not increased their intercollegiate competition in these sports as dramatically as the number of potential participants should lead one to expect. Although greater numbers of schools offer intercollegiate competition in volleyball, softball, and field hockey, the increases are not at the same rate as the increases in interscholastic programs in these sports. Why? One explanation is that members of the lower class are more likely to participate in team sports but less likely to attend college. If the girl softball player does not attend college, the student demands for intercollegiate competition, scholarships, budget increases, and facilities do not exist. Demonstrated interest and demand are conditions for activation of Title IX requirements. If these potential participants are not there, their demands are not felt, heard, or addressed. The prior question of why they are not there, especially when athletic scholarships are now available, remains unasked and unchanged.

Going to college is an advantage that not all people enjoy. One suspects that the unequal distribution of educational opportunities similarly reflect a social class and racial distinction associated with various sports. Bluntly put, "young ladies" who play tennis are more likely to go to college than girls who compete in track and field. Despite the 635% increase in the number of high school girls competing in track and field, only 33.6% of the member AIAW schools offer varsity programs in track and field. By comparison, although there was a smaller increase (493%) in girls playing tennis in high school, in 1975-76 66.4% of the AIAW colleges offered this sport.

In one of the few studies of minority women in collegiate sports, Alpha Anderson (1979) discovered from a survey of 218 AIAW affiliated institutions that 91.6% of the female athletes were white, while black (5.8%), Chicano (1.0%), Indian (.5%), Oriental (.91%) and Puerto Rican (.14%) women accounted for the remaining 8.4% of the female athletes. Only one out of every 17 female athletes could be classified as minority, and less than 6% of them were black women. By contrast, 14% of the college undergraduate female population is black. Thus, black and minority women are underrepresented in the female collegiate athletic ranks.

Anderson's survey obtained data on participation by sport. In no sport did the black female's percentage equal the 14% presence in the general collegiate population. Only two sports, basketball (12.5%) and track and field (10.9%), had a significant percentage of black women. These are traditional sports for black athletes. The black women attending college are following the path already established by their male racial predecessors. Although the increase of high school participants in track and field has been 635% since 1970, still only 34% of the AIAW schools offer track and field as an intercollegiate event. By way of contrast, the high school increase for female basketball was "only" 293% since 1970 and yet by 1977 76% of the AIAW–affiliated institutions offered basketball. For several reasons this last point is worthy of a closer look.

First, basketball for women has a long history and therefore does not represent a dramatic reorientation toward collegiate or scholastic sports. Second, for many years basketball possessed a feature which enhanced its acceptability. Women's basketball was not "real basketball." With special rules that restricted individual player's movements to half the court, with a limited dribble rule, and with a very strict interpretation of what constituted physical contact, women's basketball would never have been mistaken for the game men played; thus, it was a popular game that did not "confound" the sex-role identity of the players. Third and perhaps most importantly, of all the sports in which women engage, basketball appears to have the most corporate, commercial appeal. Although not yet revenue producing, the potential for this development exists. Women's basketball games have been staged at Madison Square Garden and the national media has televised the Division I AIAW championship in basketball. The potential of women's basketball to attract large audiences and media revenue puts this sport in a unique position in the female athletic budget. Just as men's football and basketball have had a privileged status and produced the greatest abuses, women's basketball may do the same. A "superstar" sport which makes all others "minor sports," women's basketball may become the albatross that football is for the men's program. It also holds out the same false hope for black women's acceptance and, unfortunately, lays the greatest foundation for their exploitation by colleges and universities.

Third, the effects of Title IX will be to reproduce in female sports the same structural inequities already found in male sports. The domination of certain educational institutions in male sports is well known. Schools like UCLA, Ohio State, Michigan, Notre Dame, etc.—in short, the "jock" colleges and universities—are already being mimicked by educational institutions with reputations for female sports. It perhaps comes as no surprise that the pre-Title IX powerhouse names in women's basketball (for example Immaculta, Queens, Delta State, Montclair State) are being replaced by the same big-name schools which dominate men's sports (UCLA, Maryland, etc.).

Along with the replication of the elite sporting schools for women's sport will come the same pressures to replicate the male standards of success for athletic programs. Female programs will be measured and evaluated by such factors as the number of scholarships given out, the size of the athletic budget, the active recruitment of elite athletes, the size of the gate receipts, the interest generated by the media, and the number of victories and other external criteria of achievement. The abuses that such standards have generated in male sports have already been noted. As one sports commentator has already noted "You've come a long way, baby" when a major women's national basketball team is under investigation for alleged recruiting violations. There is no reason to believe that the greater demands for female athletic administrators, larger coaching staffs, higher salaries, bigger travel budgets, and bureaucratic and organizational turf-building will not lead women's sports along the same path that men's sports has taken. In fact the evidence substantiating these trends has already begun accumulating (Hogan, 1977).

It is one of the ironies of Title IX that the newest figures available on job opportunities for women in coaching show a decline. Bonnie Parkhouse has completed a study showing that between 1974-1979 at the assistant coach level men's positions have risen by 368% and women's by 174%. In addition, "at the head-coach level the men's positions are up 137 percent, while women's have *decreased* 20 percent" *(Women's Sports Foundation*, 1980, p. 44, original italics). Anderson's (1979) study of minority representation among coaches illustrates the existence of racism here as well. Of the thirteen sports for which she had data on coach's race, only 5.4% of the coaches were black (Anderson, 1979, p. 54). In basketball (11.3%), cross-country (9.8%), and track and field (13.0%), the "more-black sports," the number of black coaches was the greatest but still the proportions were lower than should be expected. Anderson also studied athletic administrators including women's athletic directors, assistant directors, sports information directors, trainers, team managers, statisticians, secretaries, facilities managers, and business and equipment managers. Among these groups only 5.7% of the jobs were occupied by blacks (Anderson, 1979, p. 45). Although a completely comparable male–female breakdown is not available, in 1973 79% of the administrators of women's programs in AIAW schools were women and 21% men; by 1976 55.7% were women and 44.3% were men (Lapin, 1979, p. 43). In summary, the work by Parkhouse and Anderson suggests that the explosion of women's collegiate sports has meant more careers and job opportunities for *white males.*

The repetition of the male history of athletic bureaucracies' struggle for control over amateur athletes is also underway in women's sports. In 1970 the woman athletic directors formed the Association of Intercollegiate Athletics for Women (AIAW) to act as the regulating agency for intercollegiate athletics. One of the primary lobby groups advocating a strict interpretation of Title IX, the AIAW is presently debating whether it should integrate the women's programs with the NCAA-sponsored ones (Hogan, 1977). The debate surrounds the possibility of having "separate but equal" programs or using the power, money, and influence of the NCAA to promote women's athletics in a unified program. Either choice—retaining a separate organization or merging with the NCAA—prematurely closes the public agenda on the issue of women and sports because neither questions the male-defined and masculine approach to sports.

The organizational battle between the NCAA and the AIAW over control of women's collegiate athletics was a matter of discussion at the NCAA Round Table as early as January, 1979. William E. Davis, president of the University of New Mexico, noted his opinion that "separate governing organizations for men and women, with often conflicting sets of rules and disparate philosophies, is sheer nonsense if common measurements are to be applied" (Davis, 1979, p. 21). Apparently, the existence of a law, Title IX, requiring equality of opportunity for both sexes, is being used as a lever to demand a common governing body. Mr. Davis speaks of "disparate philosophies" but implies that it will be the male, NCAA philosophy that will be finally accepted as the norm.

The battle between the AIAW and the NCAA for control over women's collegiate athletics rages on. At its 1981 Detroit convention the NCAA passed a series of resolutions which many believe mean the death knell for the AIAW. Among the resolutions passed were: (a) an expansion of the NCAA executive council to include women; (b) a plan to allow schools to follow any organization's rules until 1985 when the NCAA expects merger talks with the AIAW to be completed to its satisfaction; (c) the continuation of NCAA-sponsored women's intercollegiate championships in competition with those conducted by the poorer AIAW, which cannot afford to subsidize the schools participating in the championships as well as the NCAA does; (d) the initiation of

Division I women's championships, which are clearly the most prestigious and had been, until this year, the exclusive domain of the AIAW; and (e) an increase in the number of Division II and III championships sponsored by the NCAA. For many women these moves were seen as similar to "having the wolf babysit Little Red Riding Hood" (Wheeler, 1981, p. 16). The merger discussions between the AIAW and NCAA will have an important impact on female athletes in the nation's colleges and universities.

The path of merger threatens to negate the fundamental educational philosophy which forms a part of the AIAW's history. The AIAW maintains an educational philosophy precisely because it had its genesis in the American Alliance for Health, Physical Education and Recreation, an organization founded in 1885 by physical educators (Hult, 1979, p. 14). The philosophical tenets of the AIAW are: "(1) fair competition for all; (2) concern for the health and safety of the participants; (3) institutional autonomy whenever viable; (4) protection of the human dignity of the college student who also happens to be an athlete; and (5) treatment of the student-athlete as much as possible like any other student" (Hult, 1979, p. 12). These tenets have produced rules and regulations which protect the student-athlete and place the welfare of the student above that of the institution or external interests such as alumni, commercial groups, and the like. On paper at least, the AIAW has retained a balance between its goal of promoting female athletics and its dedication to the educational value of sports participation. "Participants were to be students first and athletes second" (Grant, 1979, p. 414). AIAW regulations restrict recruitment of athletes in order to prevent the extremes of collegiate bidding for elite high school talent. Financial aid based on athletic ability is monitored by the women's governing body. However, any other financial aid that a woman may be entitled to because of her economic similarity to other students is considered a matter for the individual institution to regulate. Transfer rules allow the student-athlete to change schools and compete in her sport immediately. The athlete has no less right to participate in collegiate activities, in this case sports, than the woman who transfers and wishes to participate in any college activity ranging from cheerleading to competitive debating. As Dr. Hult's article so rightly suggests, the differences in eligibility rules between the NCAA and the AIAW reflect profound philosophical differences in their approach to intercollegiate sport.

For feminists, the history of the earlier organizing body of the AIAW, that is, the American Alliance for Health, Physical Education and Recreation, (AAHPER) and its predecessors like the Women's Division of the National Amateur Athletic Federation (NAAF), highlights a major dilemma for women in sport. Openly opposed to the abuses that the

Carnegie Report uncovered in men's sports, the NAAF Women's Division celebrated its different philosophy in a 1937 statement of athletic principles. Its motto was "A Game for Every Girl and a Girl for Every Game." It opposed professionalism, commercialism, and spectator-oriented sports programs in favor of highly participatory, less competitive, medically supervised "play days." Not opposed in principle to competition, the women physical educators of the post-World War I era insisted that "women desire the promotion of sport for recreation rather than for commercialism" and labeled fierce competitiveness in sport as "infantile characteristics" that women should transcend (Twin, 1979, p. xxxiii). As this first wave of female athleticism reveals, it was easier for women to *abandon* sports and intercollegiate sports competition than to implement a new philosophy of sport which was so antithetical to the masculine ethos that pervaded this institution. The women physical educators were to discover that "modified stakes in modified games did not inspire girls to participate, nor schools to provide facilities and funding. . . . Most female physical educators were hostile to competition itself, not just to its excesses. The play days they advocated were trivial and boring" (Twin, 1979, pp. xxxiii-xxxiv).

The philosophy espoused by physical educators of the 1920s and 1930s reflect many of the goals and concerns that current feminists and educators have expressed. Why, then, did it fail? Why did women's first major entrance into intercollegiate sports end so abruptly and silently? The answer to these questions may hold the hope for the future of the philosophy the AIAW now maintains. We believe that the early female physical educators accepted the basic principle that sports was indeed masculine and not for women. This belief meant that they would emphasize an altered version of competition that left the masculine definition of sports unquestioned and unchallenged. They accepted female physical inferiority and the idea that biology was destiny. Their new sporting philosophy was a compensatory device which served to legitimate the dichotomy between recreation and competition, between feminine play and masculine sport.

Have the female educators and administrators of the AIAW learned the harsh lessons that the history of intercollegiate male sports teaches? Have they managed to escape the pitfalls of the men's games? To these questions the answer is progressively becoming more negative. Although the officials of the AIAW continue to resist take-over by the NCAA, they have separated from their parent organization, the AAHPER, and consequently from membership with the closest ties to the educational wing of the organization (Fields, 1977, p. 4). "The AIAW wants to avoid the mistakes that men's organizations have made in developing costly programs that emphasize high-pressure recruiting, winning seasons, and the enforcement of complex rules; however, they are largely doomed to fail" (Nyquist, 1979, p. 387). Nyquist cites the increased and heightened level of female national and regional championships. Violations have already occurred in letters of intent and recruiting practices. Expenses are mounting at rates that belie a commitment to the educational value of the dollars. The best barometer of women's collegiate sports is basketball.

> Women's basketball teams now play for money—mounting scholarships and growing gate receipts—exactly as men's do. Money, as a reporter recently remarked, has propelled women's basketball out of its infancy and into a 'tumultuous adolescence.' Consciously or not, dependence on money will move women toward full replication of practices in male athletics. (Nyquist, 1979, p. 388).

The second major difficulty is that although the AIAW espouses an educational philosophy, it has a very meagerly developed feminist consciousness. Liberal feminism, with its promotion of "equal opportunity" and its devotion and adulation of Title IX, presently dominates the organization. However, Title IX legislation in no way speaks to the "publics" that have traditionally been ignored. Public policy in this case is for a public primarily composed of white, single, 18-22-year-old, middle-to upper-class women whose sexual orientation is expected to be heterosexual and whose contact with sports is expected to be channeled into a relatively elite educational setting. The benefits for nonelite minorities who do not normally attend college, for the old, for those who prefer participatory sports to elite spectator sports, for the handicapped—in short, for a whole series of "forgotten publics"—are nonexistent and entirely beyond the pale of present legislative intent.

At the broadest level the debate over Title IX and public policy has completely avoided questioning the sex-role polarization that sports creates and the subsequent determination that sports is a masculine domain. Although social scientists and public policy makers are content to leave any questions regarding the ultimate nature of the human experience to philosophers and radical theorists, they do so only at the expense of leaving a vacuum that is filled by the dominant cultural and institutional definitions that have been shaped by men's values, men's understandings of the world, and men's experiences. Women's alienation from sport, their indifference to it, and their reluctance to enter it stem in large measure from the facts that, as presently constituted, what sport celebrates, what sport offers, what sport demands, and what sport rewards do not reflect much of women's experience of the world.

It is apparent from the content of Title IX that women are being asked to embrace a masculine model of sport and are being led to believe that Title IX represents a significant victory in the battle against sexism. We would be naive to suggest that implementation of Title IX would be a minor victory against the forces of established sports and traditional conceptions of women's place in society. However, we wish to caution that in failing to consider the real policy limits of Title IX as identified above, we may find ourselves a decade from now having won the battle but lost the war. The challenge to us is to recognize both the benefits and the limits of such legislation and to use caution and intelligence to demand that the present policy serve the widest possible public in the most humanistic manner.

Chapter 7/
Sports, Inc.: The Influence of the Mass Media

The mass media have become, within the past few decades, one of the most powerful institutional forces in modern society. Individually and collectively, the effects of TV and radio, newspapers, magazines, books, and movies have been debated with intense passion, measured with facts and figures, and analyzed from myriad theoretical perspectives. The consensus emerging from this concentrated attention to the role of the mass media is that they have become the major vehicle for passing on the social heritage of our society from generation to generation (Lasswell, 1948). We receive our primary information about the world from the electronic and written media. They shape our values, attitudes, and knowledge of ourselves and of others. Virtually no institution, social process, group, or person is left unaffected by the images and words that emanate from these sources.

Given the dominant place of the mass media in a modern society, it is especially important to examine the treatment of women's sport by the various media. This is a critical issue because the fact remains that, regardless of what is actually happening to the relationship between women and sport, it is the media's *treatment* and *evaluation* of that relationship that will shape its direction and content.

At the time of this writing, we have many more questions than we have answers to the issue before us. Indeed, it is only during the past decade or so that social scientists and communications researchers have begun to include women in their theory and research. Before then, "psychology, sociology, economics, and history were mainly written by men, about men, and for men" (Tuchman, Daniels, & Benet, 1978, p. 4). Although this situation is changing rapidly, gaps still remain in our knowledge about women, one of the major ones being the portrayal of gender roles in the mass media. In one of the few book-length treatments of this topic, Tuchman et al. (1978) underscore the limited information we have about the media's depiction of women and they offer that volume "to delineate a national social problem—the mass media's treatment of woman" (Tuchman et al., 1978, p. 5). However, even though the past decade of vigorous research on women has supplied both a data base and theory to guide us, our knowledge of the media's portrayal of the sportswoman is still meager.[1] We hope that this chapter will add to our understanding of media influences on the sportswoman by bringing together some of the theory and research on this issue and by suggesting alternate ways of analyzing both the nature and the effects of the media's treatment of women in sport.

Of the various media available, we have selected TV, newspapers and magazines as the major units for our discussion. These were chosen because they are highly influential mediums of communications and because some information is available on their coverage of women in sport. For each of the media, we will examine the following issues:

1. *The extent of coverage:* the proportion of the medium's time or space devoted to women's sports, women athletes, or issues related to women's involvement in sport.
2. *The type of coverage:* the specific sports or sporting events that receive the major proportion of the medium's coverage.
3. *The style of coverage:* the nature or way in which the coverage is portrayed, both visually and linguistically.
4. *The production of the media:* the extent and nature of women's involvement in producing coverage of women in sport, such as in journalism, broadcasting, production, and ownership.

Prior to our examination of these four issues, we believe that a brief summary of some general findings regarding the nature and effects of the mass media's depiction of women are in order. These data and ideas can serve as useful guidelines for fleshing out our discussion of the media's image of the sportswoman.

One of the major findings of media research on women is the relative absence of women portrayed in the various media. Addressing the fact that women are grossly underrepresented in the media, George Gerbner (1978, p. 44) states that this "absence means symbolic annihilation." Extending this idea, Tuchman et al., (1978, p. 8) note that dominant American ideas and ideals are incorporated in the media "as *symbolic representations of American society. . . .*" (original italics). These symbolic representations in the mass media tell audiences who and what is valued and esteemed in our society. Tuchman et al. (1978) summarize the meaning of this pattern of media underrepresentation:

> Consider the symbolic representation of women in the mass media. Relatively few women are portrayed there, although women are fifty-one percent of the population and are well over forty percent of the labor force. Those working women who are portrayed are condemned. Others are trivialized: they are symbolized as childlike adornments who need to be protected or they are dismissed to the protective confines of the home. In sum, they are subject to *symbolic annihilation.* (p. 8, original italics)

A second consistent finding regarding women's portrayal is that when they do appear they are depicted in highly stereotyped ways (Courtney & Whipple, 1974; Culley & Bennett, 1976; O'Kelly & Bloomquist, 1976; Tuchman et al., 1978). These depictions support earlier, more traditional images of women's place in society. In commenting on the latest research, Chafetz (1978) remarks, "The media of mass communications do appear to be gradually changing their portrayal of women. . . . However, the rate at which the image of women is changed seems to be considerably slower than the rate at which the reality of women's lives has been changing" (p. 46).

The findings of symbolic annihilation and of stereotyping are now well-documented, but there is still considerable debate over the *impact* of the content of media on their audiences. Does the absence of women or their symbolic annihilation, condemnation, and trivialization affect women's self-images and social behavior? Do adults mold their understanding of sex roles according to the stereotyped portrayals they find in the media? Are children socialized to accept the sexist world views and social arrangements that confront them on TV, in books, and in movies? Research continues to be conducted on these questions, and some tentative answers are emerging. Reviewing the latest research, Davidson and Gordon (1979) note:

While the data on impact are less complete than the data on content, it is now undeniable that television as a conveyer of traditional gender-role ideology has an important socializing impact on its heavy users. Thus, children, especially females, do notice the distorted representation of females in numbers and in the kinds of options that television portrays as available to females. Further, children tend to accept the segregation portrayed on television as accurate. (pp. 168-169)

There appears to be a tentative consensus that, although the media's portrayal of the sexes may affect adult behavior and self-images, the impact of the media is greater on children, who do not possess the more refined capacity of adults to judge the validity of media content (Chafetz, 1978, p. 95).

Television

Of all the media, television is clearly the most dominant one. It reaches the largest, most diversified audience; it appeals to a variety of senses; it is consumed in greater amounts than any other medium; and its potential impact on viewers is the most powerful. George Gerbner (1978) speaks unequivocally about the role of television in modern life:

We have been misled by many of the social scientists and researchers into considering television just another medium. But all other media have been used selectively. Television is not used selectively. It is used by practically all the people and is used practically all the time. It collects the most heterogeneous public of groups, classes, races, sexes, and nationalities in history into a national audience that has nothing in common except television or shared messages. Television thereby becomes the common basis for social interaction among a very widely dispersed and diverse national community. *As such, it can only be compared, in terms of its functions, not to any other medium but to the preindustrial notion of religion.* (p. 47, emphasis added)

If television is, as Gerbner suggests, the new religion of modern times, its portrayal of women in sport will greatly affect the assumptions, attitudes, and evaluations of its audience regarding the proper relationship between these two realities. It is to this portrayal that we now turn our attention.

The Extent and Nature of Coverage

One of the most dramatic examples of symbolic annihilation is found in television coverage of women's sports. One merely has to watch televised sports for a given week in any year to realize what future research will confirm with cold facts—women's sports, with rare exceptions, are seldom seen on television. For example, between August 1972 and September 1973, NBC devoted one hour out of 366 hours of "live" sports coverage to women (Gerber et al., 1974, p. 210). In 1979, Grete Waitz, the now-famous Norwegian runner, won her second New York City Marathon in a row and in so doing set a new world record for women—2:27:33. Here, in the media capital of the world and as late as 1979, one would expect this event to receive considerable television attention, especially since the marathon was being covered live. Instead, this is what happened:

> Cover stories and profiles had made Grete Waitz into a heroine of the sporting world in the intervening 12 months [between Waitz' 1978 and 1979 New York City Marathon victories]. Everyone lining the streets, every writer, every photographer—everyone was waiting to see what Waitz would do. *Everyone, that is, except television people.* The live coverage, not quite two and a half hours worth, *ended without so much as a syllable about Waitz.* So they signed off—at 2:27:00 into the race. *Astute tube watchers were able to view a world record being set during the closing credits.* (Niederman, 1980, p. 54, emphasis added)

As Gerber et al. (1974) note, "The coverage and attention to women's sports by the television media has been widely decried. The analyses that have been done suggest that women do not receive even one percent of the sport coverage" (p. 255). Even though that percentage may have increased slightly over the past five years, it remains extremely insignificant in relation to the actual percentage increase in women's sport participation that we identified in chapter 2.

The now-historic tennis match between Billie Jean King and Bobby Riggs, televised on September 20, 1973, gave a national audience its first exposure to many of the issues swirling around the dramatic increase in women's sports. Were women athletes as good as the men? Should tournament purses be equal for both sexes? Would spectators support women athletes? Could advertisers be convinced of the commercial value in marketing the emerging sportswomen? The way in which television presented the King-Riggs match reflected the values and interests of those who control the medium and served as a prophetic signal for how television would handle future coverage of women's sports. The match was a 3 million dollar spectacle, embedded in a circus-like atmosphere, and hyped as a "battle of the sexes" in which the victor would be rewarded with a $100,000 winner-take-all prize. The fact that King was only 29 years old and still near her competitive peak as a player, while Riggs, at 55, was long past his athletic prime, was hardly an issue for the promoters of this media extravaganza. Each contestant was portrayed more as an entertainer and ideologue than as an athlete, and the contest itself was transformed into something other than sport.

Billie Jean King won the match and became the symbol of women's athleticism. Bobby Riggs won acclaim and commercial value. The actual "loser" was tennis player Rosemary Casals, who was helping to broadcast the event. In the broadcast booth, the audience heard a symbolic contest between Casals, who supported King and feminism, and the voices who proclaimed male superiority. Casals' comments were met with hostile outrage by many on both sides of the issue and, as Felshin (1974a) noted, "A kind of backlash effect was the fury directed toward Rosie Casals who assisted in reporting the event and adopted a fiercely partisan and feminist stance" (p. 219). The message to and from the medium was clear. Television can present women's sports in highly commercialized, entertaining, and condescending ways, and people will watch, advertisers will pay, and ratings will rise. Routine coverage of women's sports, treated as a normal, acceptable, and valued sphere of athletic activity—that is, in the manner of coverage of men's sports—will not be tolerated or encouraged.

Two years after the King–Riggs match, television again found a place for women. In 1975, ABC, flushed with the success of "The Superstars" program for male athletes, initiated a similar format for women. This made-for-TV, pseudo-sporting event offers attractive purses for athletes who compete in multiple sports, none of which is the sport they excel in as either amateurs or professionals. For many women athletes, with the exception of some tennis and golf players, the prize money for this event exceeded their yearly earnings in actual competition. Obviously, the sportswomen were grateful for the opportunity to reap financial gain or to acquire some media attention and audience recognition. However, one of the effects of "The Superstars" competition for women dramatically underlines the difference between television's coverage of men's and women's sport. In speaking of this difference, Claudia Dowling (1977) remarks:

> Sure, it's [The Superstars] all in fun, and the men superstars look silly too. But there's a difference: the home viewer can turn the TV on almost any weekend and see male athletes doing what they're good at. Superstars, though, is one of the few opportunities the great audience in TV land has to see what women can do. And when the show is aired, there is one shot of the athlete performing at her peak in her sport for every four shots of comic relief or Superstars flash. (p. 69)

Thus, the television audience is left with their stereotyped images and limited information of women athletes intact and unchallenged. Ironically, as often happens in social action, events sometimes have unintended, positive consequences. In the case of "The Women Superstars," the program unwittingly provided women athletes a chance to meet one another, to exchange ideas and feelings about being sportswomen, and to create a network of information and support. In fact, it was at the first "Women Superstars" competition in 1975 that Billie Jean King and pro golfer Jane Blalock met renowned softball pitcher Joan Joyce. Their meeting led to the formation of the Women's Professional Softball League (Gilman, 1978, p. 42).

Not to be outdone by ABC's success with "The Women Superstars," CBS devised another forum for covering women's sports. In 1975, this network initiated "Challenge of the Sexes" which famed sports journalist Red Smith (1977, p. 72) correctly identified as another of television's "counterfeit sports." The "challenge of the sexes" is structured to confirm the worst suspicions of its audience: the women athletes must play with the advantage of handicaps in order to compete with men (e.g., in tennis, the women can use the doubles alley while the men must play within the singles lines). As Red Smith (1977) notes, "Even when handicaps are assigned to equalize the opponents, most matches between men and women are mismatches" (p. 72). The lessons of television are clear: the important contest is the one between the sexes; even when women athletes are given special advantage, they cannot compete with men; if they should win, they still lose because their victory was gained by receiving special treatment.

Since programming for television is dictated not only by the values of those who control the media but also by the desire for profit that demands large audiences (Tuchman, 1978, pp. 7-9), program planners and advertisers must agree on the commercial value of legitimate women's sports if they are to be aired. In fact, in the mid-seventies it was the decision of such major corporations as Colgate-Palmolive, Phillip P. Morris, L'eggs, Avon, and others to use women's sports as a vehicle for advertising their products that enabled special women's tournaments to be covered on television. We shall discuss the relationship between the business community and women's sports throughout this chapter, but it is important to note here that women's sports, like their male counterparts, need corporate sponsorship to gain television coverage. The difference, however, rests in the greater difficulty of obtaining corporate funding for women's as opposed to men's sports.

For the most part, financial backing for women's sports is obtained mainly for major, highly specialized events, such as an international championship or a national tournament. Corporate sponsorship is seldom found for regular-season competition, routine contests, or regional tournaments. In addition, corporations are primarily willing to sponsor only the socially acceptable sports of tennis, golf, figure skating, and gymnastics, leaving team and contact sports in the financial backwaters.

Even with corporate sponsorship, television programming blatantly discriminates against women's events when they are jointly held with men's contests. For example, it is customary to tape the finals of the women's championship and to broadcast *segments* of it after the "live" and complete coverage of the men's championship. The message is once again evident to the viewing audience: what men do is more important than what women do.

Similar patterns of television coverage are found in the Olympic Games. Significantly fewer women's events are covered, and their coverage is often taped and aired in fragments before or after live coverage of men's events. It is rare that a women's event will be broadcast in its entirety; usually only women's finals or semifinals will be shown. The exceptions to this rule are those events that confirm the stereotyped images of the acceptable sportswoman. Loving and detailed attention is paid to pixie-like gymnasts; special and extended coverage is given to graceful and dazzling figure skaters; the camera painstakingly records the fluid movements of swimmers and divers. And then, in a blinding flash of fragmented images, viewers see a few minutes of volleyball, basketball, speed skating, track and field, and alpine skiing, as television gives its nod to the mere existence of these events.

The picture is equally bleak when we look at the portrayal of national amateur sports for women. On occasion, a major network will devote a small segment of its weekend coverage to a special event of the "man bites dog" variety. We can view women boxing, see an interview with a quarterback from a factory-sponsored team, watch little girls in judo class, or learn of the newly-formed rugby team at a college. The treatment is often a mixture of amazement and bemusement, forced seriousness and patronizing caution.

One amateur sport that seems on the verge of breaking through the silence, if not the stereotyping, of television coverage is women's intercollegiate basketball. In 1978, according to Green (1979), NBC and the Association for Intercollegiate Athletics for Women (AIAW) reached an agreement that allowed the network to tape the championship game between UCLA and Maryland. Segments of that final game were rebroadcast the next day on "Sportsworld," a popular network program. The network and AIAW then agreed on purchasing the rights for the next year's championship game in 1979 and Green's (1979) comments reflect both the hesitancy and the changing attitudes of television decision-makers:

NBC officials maintained, as of 48 hours before game time, they would broadcast the game in its entirety only if it were close and exciting, last year's final between U.C.L.A. and Maryland having been neither. But after being favorably impressed with the semifinal games Friday night, the network decided to go with the full game, even at the risk of running over their two-hour time allotment. (p. 49)

If the three major commercial networks are making small strides, George Gallup (no relation to the pollster), the president of the independent TVS network, has larger goals in mind. Early in 1979, TVS and AIAW reached an agreement for broadcasting four championship meets in track and field, swimming and diving, tennis, and golf (N.Y. Times, 1979, p. 2). Reported to be an agreement that involves a "six-figure" contract for two years, this arrangement has some drawbacks. According to the New York Times article, the contract was not made with one of the three major networks, each event was to be presented on tape anywhere from five days to a month after the actual contest, and the rebroadcasting scheduled for Sundays was to meet with strong competition from rival network sports programs. However, George Gallup was quoted as saying, "We're going to put women's sports on the map in the next couple of years. This is something long overdue. I don't know why someone didn't do it ages ago" (T.V. and She, 1979, p. 2).

The overall trend of television coverage, as reflected in the TVS-AIAW arrangement, reveals a cautious, carefully monitored policy to slowly weave special women's athletic events into television sports programming. The beneficiaries of this policy—mainly young, white, middle-class girls and women—will be in college or have access to financial, personal, social, and other avenues of support for pursuing their sports. They will be playing socially approved sports in socially approved ways and for socially approved reasons like fame, money, school, and country. They will be the first and major group of sportswomen to gain in the struggle for equal access to television, and that access, if it is attained, could enlarge the opportunities and reduce the obstacles for the rest.

Television Production

Behind the cameras that project sports programs onto the television screen are countless persons whose decisions shape the amount and nature of coverage given to women's sports. Most of these people are men, but a growing number of women are now moving into such positions as broadcast journalists, sports announcers, station managers, and even sports producers. In certain ways, these women are challenging gender stereotypes just as surely as the women playing sports. A brief examination of their recruitment into programming and their performance in these positions will add further insight into television's treatment of women in sport.

By the mid-seventies, American women had begun to occupy many positions in society that traditionally were held only by men. However, according to noted sports journalist, Curry Kirkpatrick (1975), "No aspect of this onslaught has encountered more vehement reactions than women in sportscasting" (p. 86). It may be difficult to imagine women playing sports well, but it seemed nearly unbelievable to listen to women broadcasting men's sports. Using humor to make his point, Kirkpatrick (1975), asks: "Is it really surprising that a member of the very sex that burns the toast can announce a hockey score as 'Detroit 2, Red Wings 0'?" (p. 4). Apparently, many fans, media viewers, and television personnel think so. But as more and more women are hired to do pre- and post-game coverage, to co-anchor sportscasts and to do "color" and "play-by-play" commentary, the barriers to women in sportscasting are crumbling ever so slowly.

Part of the resistance comes from strongly held beliefs that women could never bring to sportscasting the same intensity, skills, and knowledge that men do. Acting on those beliefs, women sportscasters face unwitting and deliberate sabotage on the job. Information and access is withheld from them, they are often given assignments beyond their capabilities, they are evaluated by more stringent standards than male announcers, and "they are continually bad-mouthed, subjected to chauvinistic ridicule and sexist innuendo" (Kirkpatrick, 1975, p. 86).

An examination of the development of television's first two women football sportscasters highlights these themes (Gilman, 1976). In 1974, Jane Chastain had 12 years of varied sportscasting experience behind her when she was hired by CBS Sports as the first woman football sportscaster. Her manner was perceived by viewers as too austere, wooden, and abrasive, and when she misread a score during her first telecast, the switchboard lit up and letters arrived from viewers demanding that she be removed from the broadcasting booth. According to Chastain,

> I didn't want to be in the booth right away. I would have preferred to start with features and work my way up gradually. I'm not a star type, I'm a sports reporter. But I was just put in there and never really given a job—just a list of things *not* to do—'Don't be cute, don't be funny, don't rely on statistics.' The director constantly talking in my earpiece made me sound like I was reading what I was saying at first. The crowd noise threw me off, too. All these new things really required a learning period. (Gilman, 1976, p. 37, original italics)

Bob Wussler, then vice-president of CBS Sports, removed Chastain after the season and, in 1975, he hired well-known Phyllis George. This time, however, Wussler did not hire an experienced, no-nonsense sports reporter and move her quickly into sportscasting. Instead, he chose a woman whose credentials were outside of sport—Phyllis George was

Miss America of 1971 and had been a co-host of "Candid Camera" and the Miss America Pageant. Beauty and personality, not sports and reportorial skills, were the new criteria employed to avoid the prior year's mistakes. Listen to Wussler's explanation of his decision to hire George:

> She conveyed to me when I met her that she liked sports but she didn't know a hell of a lot about them. That quality appealed to me and I thought it would appeal to other men as well. Phyllis doesn't get into areas where she doesn't belong, but she does know personalities, and—you can't avoid it—she's very attractive. (Gilman, 1976a, p. 37)

With candor, Wussler admits that women sportscasters have a proper place and function on television and, after nine months of training at CBS, Phyllis George became the first woman co-host of the "NFL Today" show. She did pregame, half-time, and post-game segments and, according to Gilman (1976a), "Unlike Jane Chastain, George wore bright colors and smiled a lot. Also, unlike Chastain, George had nothing to do with scores and statistics and stayed in the studio, away from the sidelines" (p. 37).

The patterns revealed in these two portraits underscore the consistency with which gender stereotypes become the basis for assigning women to their "proper sphere." As women, these sportscasters will be what women should be—attractive, pleasing, supporting, expressive; they will do what women should do—add color, report the personal, and fill in the spaces left by men. Thus, television's inclusion of women in sportscasting seems, at first, to be a radical break with tradition, but in many ways it is not. Television may have extended the traditional sphere of women's activity, but it has arranged for women to carry out their new positions in traditional ways.

Much the same can be said of the new breed of female athlete/broadcasters who, like their male counterparts, are recruited more for their box-office appeal than for their broadcasting skills. Just as television found safe, noncontroversial, white male athletes to sit in the broadcast booth, so, too, it finds women like Cathy Rigby, Julie Heldman, Anne Henning and Julie Anthony. As Leavy (1977a, p. 64) notes: "many athletes-turned-broadcasters have no news sense, and little interest in, and less knowledge of, any sport other than the one they have played." An exception to the often bland commentary of these athletes is that of former Olympic gold medalist Donna de Varona. She has consistently spoken out, on camera, for the rights of women athletes and has raised difficult questions regarding the status of amateur athletics in the US. Overall, however, the rise of the woman-athlete-turned-broadcaster represents one instance in which television personnel seem equally willing to co-opt both male and female athletes.

The female presence at the highest levels of sports production is numerically the smallest but perhaps the most significant in its potential for enhancing the coverage of women's sports. Because the majority of men in television production adhere to highly stereotyped images of women, it is vitally important that feminist women become involved at this level of television production. One woman who has is Ellie Riger, the first woman to serve as full producer in the history of sports television. Riger began her television career in 1957 as a production assistant on a local New York talk show (Gilman, 1976b). Her job led to a professional contact with Roone Arledge, whose own career in television sports would soon move him to the top of the industry. During the sixties, she worked in a variety of jobs at ABC Sports, culminating in the 1968 Olympics, when she was an associate producer doing live coverage from Grenoble and Mexico City. According to Riger, after the Olympics

> it was the same old story. I was shunted into editing and sales, things that for me were moving backwards, not ahead. It was hard for a lot of the people at ABC to accept the idea of a woman actually being in their midst so in 1969 I left again to free-lance in documentaries. (Gilman, 1976, p. 52)

In 1972, the National Organization for Women had begun a campaign to call attention to the media's discrimination against women, and ABC, particularly its sports department, was one of its targets. Roone Arledge responded by making Ellie Riger television's first sports producer. Riger herself comments on the changing attitudes towards women's sports coverage: "Television coverage of women's sports came about through pressure. Now there are sponsors like Colgate who are looking at the market" (Women in the sports media, 1974, p. 21).

In 1974 and 1975, Riger produced hour-long specials, including "Women in Sports," which depicted both the full range of women's participation in sport, an in-depth portrayal of Billie Jean King, and a special emphasis on amateur athletics. She then proceeded to co-produce the Colgate-Dinah Shore Winners Circle Golf Championship, produce the 1976 L'eggs Tennis Tournament and several Wide World of Sports shows, and both produce and direct the Olympic film unit at both the Winter and Summer Games of the 1976 Olympics.

Riger's productions have helped women's sports gain the television exposure it needs in order to generate an informed and enthusiastic base of audience support. In addition, the presence of women like Riger and others who are working as production assistants can serve as role models and sources of support for the many women that want to enter this field. As Riger puts it: "We have to help each other. . . . I feel that I have a responsibility. Women have to stick together; we have to form our own little club to get ahead" (Lapin, 1976a, p. 44).

In forming their "own little club," women in sports television must decide if they wish to do more than merely emulate the coverage of men's sports. Equal coverage of women's sports surely seems a utopian dream at this time. However, if the type and nature of that coverage only imitates that of men's sports, then women will have lost their chance to transform sport as a human activity and to celebrate what is now ignored on television. Once again, women involved in sport face the dilemma of using conventional avenues of social change to reach ends that challenge these very same conventional meanings and ways of being.

Newspapers

Newspapers, like other news media, can be viewed as an "Institutionalized means of answering people's collective question, 'What's new?' " (Molotch, 1978, p. 179). What is news, however, is a social product emerging out of the interplay of those who produce the news and, to a lesser extent, those who consume it. Looked at in this way, the social construction of the news is a highly selective process, forged by the values and interests of publishers, advertisers, editors and reporters. These producers of the news, themselves a select segment of the population, construct the news mainly for and in terms of the interests of other select members of the population—politicians, corporations, unions, and other powerful interest groups. In a critical analysis of the function of news production, Molotch and Lester (1974) have offered suggestive evidence that the news that is created serves to support and perpetuate the established social and economic structure of the US. In this light, the construction of news is a political activity; that is, forged by powerful individuals and groups to maintain the established distribution of societal resources and rewards. In his treatment of the coverage of women in newspapers, Harvey L. Molotch (1978) develops this conceptualization of the news:

> The formal news business is not only the powerful talking to the less powerful. It is essentially men talking to men. The women's pages are a deliberate exception: Here it is the case that women who work for men talk to women. But in terms of the important information, the news pages, women are not ordinarily present. *Women are not present either as news producers or as persons for whom news is intended.* Those who publish news perceive women as being in the kitchen, just as they have traditionally been whenever men have important things to discuss with one another. News is a man's world. (p. 180, emphasis added)

From the start of the second wave of feminism, women and women's issues have received greater and, to a degree, more egalitarian coverage than in the past. Newspapers reported the reemergence of the feminist movement, articles appeared on the challenges to traditional stereotypes of women, editorials addressed themselves to the complex issues of sex discrimination, and larger numbers of females were hired to cover and report the news. However, the research and analysis of newspaper coverage of women reveals that many of the gross inequities, sexist assumptions, and patterns of past discrimination are still evident in newspapers today.

The coverage given to the feminist movement has, and often still remains, explicitly sexist (Morris, 1974). Ridicule, humor and condescension characterized many of the news reports of this social movement. Under the banner of equal time, groups of women who disagreed with feminists (such as Total Woman, or the Pussycat League) were given substantial coverage, (Tuchman, 1972). Feminist leaders were often treated as irrational, strident "man-haters" through the careful editing of stories and the selection of news photos (Miller, 1975). The most radical, extravagant, and extremist women were presented as rank–and–file members of the women's movement. This presentation of the "news" is explained by Molotch (1978) as stemming from men's interests and needs as they construct their news: "Men have no need of information that may cause women to wish to abandon their traditional social roles altogether. Serious treatment of women's liberation has been difficult to come by in the media because of this lack of interest to men" (pp. 181-182).

Furthermore, many newspapers choose to place news about the women's movement and women in general on the women's pages (Domhoff, 1978; Epstein, 1978; Lang, 1978). There, amidst the food recipes, gossip columns, fashion features, and the society news, are articles covering rape laws, the ERA, credit and salary inequities, and battered wives. The placement of news about women adds to the trivialization of this information, since the women's pages (now often renamed the "Family" or "Lifestyle" sections) contain what newspeople consider the "soft" news. Given the considerable disagreement over the impact of such news placement, Epstein's (1978) interpretation of this strategy is noteworthy:

> For women, the positioning of news about women only reinforces other messages they receive from society: that if a woman demonstrates competence in some important sphere, it is an idiosyncratic event, not worthy of general notice and not to be judged by a universal standard—that is, a male standard. (p. 217)

This "ghettoization" of news about women has its occupational parallel in the tendency to assign women reporters to cover news about women. This strategy has clear advantages—it obviously provides a vehicle for the treatment of women and feminist issues in less stereotypical ways than newspapermen would handle them, but it depends on the extent to which the reporters are feminist and not just women reporters. However, this assignment by sex again suggests that such news is by and for women only, allowing male reporters to continue the construction and coverage of "real" news.

The overall picture of newspaper coverage is aptly summarized by Molotch (1978) and serves to introduce our discussion of newspaper coverage of women's sports:

> Seldom do women appear at all in the newspages. There is no affirmative action in the content of the news print media. When women do appear, it is from a man's perspective of what is interesting. . . . Sex stereotypes are reified in the news but it is worthwhile to understand how and why. All of these stories are about events that may have happened, but they are *news* primarily from a man's perspective. It is locker-room talk. (p. 185, original italics)

The Extent and Nature of Coverage

Locker-room talk. The sports page. The press box. Many would say that the words and pictures derived from these sources are the major reason why many newspapers stay in existence. Sporting news sells newspapers—the sport section of the daily paper is believed by many in the newspaper community to be one of the most important sources of a paper's circulation and subscription. How much of the sports page is devoted to covering women in sports? How are women's sports portrayed in the daily papers?

While research on the content of the sports page with respect to women's coverage is still in its infancy, a number of studies confirm the general findings regarding the media's portrayal of woman. Susan Miller (1975) analyzed the news photos appearing in the *Los Angeles Times* and the *Washington Post* for the period covering July 1973 through June 1974. If a picture is worth a thousand words, then Miller's analysis of 3,661 photos tells a substantial story of symbolic annihilation and stereotyping in newspaper coverage. The function of a newspaper photo is important for several reasons. The photo is one of the first items on a page that captures the readers' eye, and it also serves to establish the context for the story itself. In comparing the photos depicting the sexes, Miller (1975) found that the ratio of women to men was greatest for pictures of politicians and public officials (1:32), followed next by photos of sports figures where the ratio was 1 photo of a female sports figure for every 22 photos of sportsmen. Further, the findings indicate that the sports section of the newspaper contained the lowest percentage of photos of women—6% for the *Post* and 10% for the *Times*. Table 6 summarizes these general findings for both newspapers combined.

Table 6
Photo Coverage of Women & Men, by Location in Newspaper

| Location in Newspaper | Percentage of Photos Showing[a]: | | |
	Women	Men	Both
All Photos	30%	81%	11%
Front Page	28	90	18
Inside News Section	24	86	10
Business	13	94	7
Lifestyle	70	50	20
Entertainment	39	78	16
Sports	8	95	2

Source: *Media*, National Commission on the Observance of International Women's Year (1977, p. 4). US Government Printing Office.
[a]The percentages across the rows add up to more than 100% because photos containing both sexes were counted twice, once in the appropriate single-sex column and then again in the "Both" column.

The data from Table 6 clearly show that sports remains one of the last arenas to acknowledge and encourage women's changing role. Although we believe that coverage of women's sports has shown some slight increase over the past five years, this improvement seems to be truer of the newspapers with smaller circulation and a more local market. The large, cosmopolitan, and nationally renowned newspapers are, according to Miller (1975), trying to expand women's sports coverage, but "because they focus primarily on 'big money' professional sporting events . . . the sports sections of the *Post* and *Times* continue to be dominated by photos of men" (pp. 74-75). It would seem that coverage of women's sports is caught between a rock and a hard place. There is not a mass audience for women's sport, partly due to lack of media coverage; however, without media coverage, it is difficult to build a mass audience. Given the emphasis on "big money," mass–spectator, professional sports in this country, women's sports coverage apparently will increase only to the extent that it follows the pathway of the dominant men's sports.

When women's sports is covered in the newspaper, the placement and style of its coverage reveals the continuation of sexist themes that we noted in television portrayals. Most news of women's sports is relegated to the back pages of the sports section. There, in one or two paragraphs, one finds only the absolutely minimal information on the athletic event—no development, no analysis, no slices of detail to flesh out the final score.

This treatment is less true of major national or international events in which women compete in socially approved sports, but even then women take a back page to men's events. A perfect example of this occurred when Grete Waitz broke the world record for women in the 10,000 meter race held in Central Park, New York, June 2, 1979. This event was carried on page 9 of the Sunday *New York Times* Sports Section the next day; the first eight pages reported the news of men's sports, none of which came close to Waitz's athletic achievement. Just as the placement of the story was indicative of the lesser importance attached to women's accomplishment, the headline also captured the less-than-serious import given to the event: it read: "Grete Waitz Sets Record in Park Run" (Moran, 1979, p. 59). There is no mention of what record was broken, in what time, or at what level of competition. Had it been a male athlete, we could envision a front-page headline grabber, such as "John Doe shatters World Record in 10K Race." Even the use of the words "Park Run" in the Waitz headline suggests a casual, pastoral romp through the park rather than a serious and demanding athletic race.

In various ways, many sports reporters treat major professional sportswomen primarily in terms of their gender role rather than their sport role (J. Kaplan, 1979a, pp. 73-103). They devote a considerable part of their story to describing the physical appearance and attire of the athlete; they ask detailed questions about her marriage plans, her new baby, or her husband's opinion regarding her sports career. They seem almost as preoccupied with role conflict as are social scientists! Reporters frequently ignore the more talanted athletes in favor of those with more sex appeal (J. Kaplan, 1979a, p. 91). They also seem especially curious about the sexual orientation of sportswomen, asking pointed and incessant questions about the existence of lesbianism in a way that has been characterized as "so much ugly curiosity" (Sports woman like conduct, 1974, p. 52). As one women tennis pro observed, "Reporters don't ask Arthur Ashe who the gay men on the circuit are. But they ask the women players which women players are gay" (Hicks, 1979, p. 44). While questions regarding the personal and social dimensions of athletes' lives may be mandated by the standards of professional sports journalism, it is the sexist bias in the pattern of questioning that we wish to underscore.

The kinds of questions reporters pose to women athletes but not to the men (and vice versa) begin to structure the way in which we perceive and evaluate women in sport. The selection of "newsworthy" quotes, the angle taken on a story, and what we eventually read in the papers often serves to confirm both the reader's and the reporter's stereotypes of women. In fact, sociological wisdom would suggest that this type of coverage could affect the image sportswomen have of themselves, giving credence to some of their own, deeply held feelings regarding female inadequacy and inferiority.

We need to put these and other criticisms of newspaper coverage of women's sport in the larger context of newspaper journalism. As we noted earlier, what appears in newspapers is the end product of exchanges, mostly between men, about what they consider newsworthy. Publishers, editors, and journalists bring to their conception of the news those stereotypes and prejudices about women that are embedded in our culture. Any attempt to change newspaper coverage of women's sport must begin with attempts to change these stereotypical ideas and feelings. One study that hints at the source of the problem is noteworthy. Choosing college communications students as their respondents, Orwant and Cantor (1977) wanted to find out if sex role stereotypes influenced students' ratings of audience interest in different types of news. The findings show clearly that the perceived interests of women and men in different types of news was based on stereotyped images of the sexes. Students ranked sports news as *last* among nine items of potential interest to women readers (fashion, cooking, and national politics were ranked as the top three) and ranked sports *first* among perceived men's interest. It is among communications students that the pool of future media personnel will be drawn, so this study underscores the need for challenging gender stereotypes among future generations of reporters if women's sports coverage is to change substantially.

Newspaper Production

Another avenue to changing the coverage of women's and, perhaps, men's sports is through the recruitment of women sports journalists. Perhaps no other controversy has received greater media attention than the perceived intrusion of women into sports journalism, especially if that meant that women would "invade" the locker rooms of male athletes. Kay Gilman (1976a) tells us why:

> Grantland Rice would never have believed it. In his day the kinship between sports and journalists had a distinctive male flavor, a cigar-smoke-and-whiskey camaraderie that did not welcome female intrusion. Sportswriting was as much a rite of passage for journalists as sports was for men and, as such, was sanctified beyond the reach of women. (p. 37)

Of course, there had been a few women sports journalists before the second feminist movement. Mary Garber has spent 36 years as a sportswriter, having started her career in 1940 at the *Winston-Salem* (NC)

Journal. Recently, there has been an increase in the number of women who write sports for newspapers and magazines. Garber, who says she used to know all of them, estimates there may be about 75 such women in the country today (Garber, 1978, p. 44). Not only are the numbers difficult to obtain, but the presence and impact of these women sports journalists is also open to discussion. We wish to consider two issues here: (a) the reaction by the sports establishment and sports journalists to the presence of women reporters; (b) the potential impact these women may have on sports journalism.

Access to news sources is one of the major components of successful reporting. In the case of sports journalists, access to athletes is crucial for covering the sports beat, and that frequently means access to male athletes in the locker room after the game. Melissa Ludtke, who was a reporter for *Sports Illustrated*, and her employer, Time Inc., became the center of a legal controversy over the issue of whether or not women reporters belong in men's locker rooms. In an excellent discussion of this case, noted journalist Roger Angell (1979) examined the major actors and plots in this reportorial drama.

After the 1977 World Series ended, Melissa Ludtke was refused admittance to the Yankees' dressing room. Bowie Kuhn, Commissioner of Baseball, refused to overturn the Yankees' ruling. Ludtke and Time, Inc., then filed suit against the Commissioner's Office, the New York Yankees, the president of the American League, and the Mayor and other officials of the City of New York (which owns Yankee Stadium). Ludtke based her suit on her claims that she could not perform her job without access to immediate postgame interviews and that this exclusion was based solely on her sex, thus violating her rights under the equal-protection and due-process clauses of the Fourteenth Amendment of the US Constitution.

Bowie Kuhn "responded in an affadavit that he had ordered women reporters kept out of all major-league clubhouses in order to protect the 'sexual privacy' of players who were undressing and showering, to protect the image of baseball as a family sport, and to preserve traditional notions of decency and propriety" (Angell, 1979, p. 46).

In Federal District Court in New York, Judge Constance Baker Motley agreed with the plaintiffs, and ruled on September 27, 1978 that all reporters, regardless of sex, should have equal access to the athletes, including the locker room if necessary.[2] Kuhn then requested Judge Motley to stay her order but the request was denied. During the 1978 World Series, Kuhn made a motion to the Second Circuit Court of Appeals again requesting a stay. A three-judge panel swiftly denied the motion. "The presiding jurist, Judge Walter Mansfield, commenting on the 'baseball is a family game' argument said, 'The last I heard, the family includes women as well as men' " (Angell, 1979, p. 47).

Kuhn dropped his appeal on February 8, 1979 and on March 9th sent a memo to the 26 major-league clubs urging them to establish, at their discretion, ways to give equal access to athletes to all reporters, regardless of sex.

If the degree of resistance to change is some measure of the change's threat to deeply felt beliefs and meanings, then the presence of women in the locker room apparently taps very sensitive collective nerve-endings. Fans, male athletes and their wives, television and radio personnel, various sectors of the sports establishment, feminists and antifeminists joined the journalism community in vigorous and vehement debate over the issue.

The publicity generated by this controversy, essentially stemming from the media's coverage of it, confounded and complicated the matter even further. While many members of the athletic and journalism profession were trying to devise at least temporary solutions to a difficult and challenging situation, the rash of media publicity fueled the controversy and turned it into a public media event. In fact, the truth is that in professional basketball, hockey, and soccer, women and men reporters have had equal access to athletes for the past few years. According to Melissa Ludtke Lincoln (1979, p. 52) one of the major reasons why these sports assimilated women reporters more easily than baseball was due to the lack of media publicity given to the events. She argues that the intense media coverage by television and newspapers turned the Yankees' locker room into "a three-ring news circus" (p. 52) and she suggests that this may happen in cities across the nation:

> Newspapers and local television stations may be tempted to send one of their female reporters, most likely one who does not care in the least about access to any locker room and will not be reporting on the game, to determine the effect that a woman has in a baseball locker room. (p. 52)

Baseball clubs, faced with this media intrusion, may decide to adopt a more restrictive policy of access for all reporters. This would, as it has in the past, divide reporters and may cause the men to blame the women reporters for instigating the problem (Angell, 1979). In a very real sense, then, the final resolution of this problem rests largely in the hands of the media personnel, especially those who work as sports journalists.

Roger Angell (1979), in researching this issue, spent a significant amount of time discussing the question of access with prominent male and female reporters and his candid interviews are a testimony both to his and to the reporters' intelligence and integrity as they search for answers to this question. We offer the following quotations from sportswriters as illustrative of one of our major arguments; namely, that women's passage into sport represents a profound challenge to the bonds between men and between men and sport, bonds that make up part of the larger celebration of male supremacy:

Jerome Holtzman: Sports is getting to be just entertainment. I suppose the fact that this was an all-male world was what made it so exciting to me at first. And now that it's being invaded and eroded it's much less attractive. Maybe I am a chauvinist—I don't know. The press box used to be a male preserve—that was its charm. (Angell, 1979, p. 78)

Maury Allen: When I was ten years old, my father began taking me to ball-games, and this relationship was very significant to me. It was male. It was something that separated me from my mother. Baseball is our most traditional game, and on an emotional level I don't want to break away from those traditions. (Angell, 1979, p. 84)

Jane Gross: My presence [in the locker room] doesn't change the way the players act or talk. I've begun to see that the pleasure men take in being with each other—playing cards together, being in a bar together—isn't actively anti-female. It isn't against women; it just has nothing to do with them. It seems to come from some point in their lives before they were aware that there were women. They have so much fun together. (Angell, 1979, p. 86)

The themes highlighted in these quotes echo, on a personal level, some major theoretical issues we discussed in chapter 4: sport as a masculine domain, sport as an intimate bond between men, sport as a way of being male, sport as a place safe from the female presence. The often–quoted explanations for keeping women out of the locker rooms—invasion of privacy, the sexual excitement of nudity, the players' wives, the decline of team morale, the occupational fears of male reporters—may have some credibility and should be investigated. However, it is our feeling that these justifications obscure the more deeply held values, beliefs, and identities that bind men to each other and to sport. We believe that behind these constructed explanations are the principles of male superiority, the denigration of the female, and the frustrations of the instrumental male sex role. Perhaps Roger Angell's (1979) own words say it best:

It seems to me that the people who run sports and who claim to be most concerned about the 'sexual privacy' of their athletes in the clubhouse . . . are men who want to keep both sports and sex in some safe, special place where they first locked them up when they were adolescents. The new presence of capable, complicated women in the inner places of sports means that relations between the sexes cannot be relegated just to marriage, or just to hotel rooms, either. . . . If men discover that the company of men does not equal the company of men and women together, they may decide that sports can be a common property of us all, a great dream or pageant or drama to be shared among us all, and that its idealization as a male ritual and religion is part of a national neurosis—a form of infantilism that degrades its players and watchers and feeds childish anxieties and delusions, which we can all begin to outgrow now, at long last. (pp. 93-94)

Although the presence of women as sportswriters initially has met with considerable resistance, the trend seems to indicate that an increasing number of women will join their male colleagues in the sports department of our nation's newspapers. What are some of the implications of this trend? What differences, if any, will the changing sexual composition of sportswriters have on the coverage of sports? Although the empirical answers to these questions await future research, we believe that the questions themselves must be raised and evaluated with considerable care because they go to the heart of feminist and sociological concerns over the direction of social change.

At the most obvious level, the recruitment of women into sports journalism signals the erosion of occupational discrimination and selected aspects of gender stereotyping. Women who wish to pursue careers in sportswriting, like those breaking ground in other traditionally male occupations, may soon find easier access to entry-level jobs. The women that have paved the way may serve as role models and socializing agents to the novice reporters, perhaps even building a network of information and support to ease the transition to full acceptance in the sportswriter's community. Legislation and its enforcement may facilitate movement up the occupational ladder, minimizing the present inequities in hiring, salaries, promotion, and so forth. In fact, the slow but clear presence of some of these trends is already visible. Among the growing ranks of female sportswriters on the staffs of newspapers and magazines are a few who already have their own columns and by-lines. Others have risen even higher—Nancy Williamson of *Sports Illustrated* has become a nationally known and respected sports journalist, and Le Anne Schreiber, in 1978, was appointed sports editor of *The New York Times*.

From a liberal feminist perspective, this struggle for equal occupational opportunities and benefits remains a primary goal. The liberal stream of feminism has placed top priority on equal rights for reporters, along with equal responsibilities and rewards. Liberal feminists have warned of the dangers of tokenism—"Yes, we have one girl who covers sports for us"—and have begun to identify the more subtle forms of sexism that may remain after numerical equality is achieved.

Beyond the liberal feminist horizon loom questions voiced by radical, Marxist, and socialist feminists about the kinds of women who will be recruited into sportswriting and the nature of their sports reporting. First, it matters a great deal whether the sportswriter is a feminist or just a woman reporter—the "yes, I cover sports but I'm not a feminist" syndrome. For many feminists, merely increasing the number of women who share the same sexist orientations and assumptions of their male colleagues is less than a shallow victory. It is a dangerous instance of institutional co-optation whereby women become unwitting accomplices to the dissemination of sexist ideology in sport.

Other feminists also ask whether women can or will bring to their sports reporting anything different from that of male reporters. Will women be tempted to become "homers"—slanting their sports coverage to please the local team and local readers? Will they become shills of the franchise front office, selling their words for a steak and a few drinks? Will they be able to avoid the pitfalls of some of their male peers and report sports news as if it is something more than the point spread, the latest brawl, the newest hype, the biggest salary or the most trivial statistic?

Some people will argue that covering sports is not influenced by the sex of the reporter. They believe that the social context of sports reporting and the occupational demands of the sportswriter will override any differences between the sexes. This may turn out to be true, but there are certain forces or factors that suggest otherwise. One of them has to do with the tendency to assign female reporters to cover women's sports. While this decision is grounded in sexist assumptions, it does suggest that women's sports will receive greater coverage as more women are recruited into sportswriting.

A second reason for suggesting that women's coverage of the news will be different from that of men's is also rooted in gender stereotyping and has been noted by certain reporters. According to Jerome Holtzman, senior baseball writer for the *Chicago Sun-Times*, "Women reporters have certain advantages over men. I've seen it. Athletes open up to women more in a one-on-one situation. Most of the women also have the advantage of their age, and that applies to younger male reporters, of course" (Angell, 1979, p. 78). This theme—that women will, because they are women—enjoy an advantage over male reporters in gaining emotional and psychological access to male athletes is echoed by Jane Gross, a member of the sports staff of *Newsday*, who cites as an advantage "the players' natural chivalry" (Angell, 1979, p. 86).

A third source of differential sports reporting can be tied to our earlier observation that in the world of sports all women, including those who become sportswriters, are *outsiders*. This fact may influence women's coverage of sporting news in several ways. First, because they are outsiders, female reporters will have a special vantage point from which to observe sports. As is the condition of all outsiders, they may be able to bring an objectivity, a new sensitivity, or a different orientation to their beat. Commenting on her position as an outsider, Jane Gross, states:

As a rule, you're not invited to come along to dinner with a half-dozen of the players, or to go drinking with them. . . . This means a lot, because I believe that all reporters should keep a great distance between themselves and the players. It always ought to be an adversary relationship, basically. (Angell, 1979, p. 86)

To the degree that women remain outsiders to SportsWorld, their capacity to assume and maintain an adversary position should result in a qualitative difference in the nature of their sports coverage.

Second, since women reporters are less likely than men reporters to have been frustrated athletes themselves, their professional relationship to players, and the nature of the coverage that emerges from this relationship, is less likely to contain either the awe or envy that clouds male coverage of sports. In an insightful comment on this difference, Stephanie Salter, a member of the sports staff of the *San Francisco Examiner*, notes:

I'm always amazed at the amount of hostility among the male writers that is directed at the players. Obviously, not all the writers are failed athletes, but there are far too many of them. You hear them asking these smart-aleck questions that are meant to show up the players and prove that the writers know as much about the sport as the players do. It's as if they're fighting over who will be the leader of the pack: Which of us is more virile—me with my pen or you with your bat? At least, we women are free of that. (Angell, 1979, p. 89)

If women can approach players with questions that are meant not to flatter or to intimidate but to inquire, to interpret, or to analyze, then readers may begin to sense a difference when they turn to the sports pages.

A third consequence of being an outsider centers on our belief that women's experience *in* the world and *of* the world is, in fundamental ways, different from that of men. The effects of this difference on sportswriting is hinted at by Jane Gross:

We women are interested in different things from the men writers, so we ask different questions. When Bob McAdoo gets traded from the Knicks, my first thought is, How is his wife, Brenda, going to finish law school this year? And that may be what's most on *his* mind. (Angell, 1979, p. 86, original italics)

Ironically, while women in sport are always asked questions about their love life, spouses, and children, these issues are seldom posed to men in sport. Women reporters may begin to redress this imbalance and we, as readers, may come to see our male athletes as embodied persons, with real-life ties to family, spouse, lover, or children. If women "are interested in different things," then these differences should reveal themselves in the questions, emphases, slants, and observations that capture the attention of women covering sports. If women live primarily in the world of affect, cooperation, emotionality, process, and aesthetics, then perhaps we will read more about what it feels like to lose, how players help each other, how families adapt to shifts in careers, the beauty behind the technique, and the moral costs of violence and drugs and cheating. We believe there is another dimension to most sports stories—one that goes beyond and behind the final score, the high percentage shot, the size of the purse, the first draft choice, and the most recent court decision. We believe women who cover sports may help to tell that story.

Magazines

Unlike television or newspapers, magazines can be more readily channeled toward specific segments of the population and their content oriented toward highly specialized interests. Thus, there exist magazines for members of various social classes and religions, age cohorts, occupational subcultures, regional populations, and so forth. If one is interested in news, fashion, economics, cars, food, or travel, there is a magazine devoted to that special interest. In this section we will examine the portrayal of sportswomen in magazines devoted to sport, in so-called women's magazines, and in magazines geared to the women's movement. Before we examine how women's sport is covered by these magazines, a brief comment on magazine portrayal of gender roles is in order.

Research devoted to analyses of how gender roles are portrayed in magazines lags behind studies of television and newspaper coverage. The preliminary findings on women's magazines suggest that women's role is still defined in primarily traditional ways (Franzwa, 1974; Rubin, 1976). However, this pattern is less true for magazines aimed at working-class rather than middle-class women; and, by the mid-1970s, middle-class magazines had begun to soften their hostility toward women who work outside the home (Tuchman, 1978, pp. 18-19). The overall thrust of magazine coverage seems to be a cautious and limited concern over the changing roles of women in the past decade and the impact that these changes may have on traditional understandings of women as wives, mothers, and homemakers.

One of the most important features of a magazine is its cover photograph. Given the fact that covers are of importance both to producers of magazines and to researchers as sources of data, we wish to examine cover photographs as a prelude to our subsequent discussion of magazine portrayals.

In a provocative essay, Marjorie Ferguson (1978) offers a conceptual framework within which data on cover photographs can be described and integrated. The cover of a magazine serves a variety of functions, according to Ferguson (1978, pp. 99-102). The most basic functions of the cover are to differentiate a magazine from its competitors and to sell that magazine to its appropriate audience. "The cover photograph, then, insofar as it represents an editorial stance or identity, also reflects the ideological implications of content that in turn reflect the producers' perceptions of culturally agreed-upon roles, goals, and values" (Ferguson, 1978, p. 99). It follows that covers represent magazine producers' conceptions and understandings of their readers' interests and needs.

Another and related function of the cover is to serve as a source of reader identification. From the producers' viewpoint, the cover should display a visual image that captures the readers' interest and the cover photographic model should be someone they wish to emulate. With specific reference to the models used on the covers of women's magazines, Ferguson (1978, p. 101) underscores the connection between producers' interests and readers' images: "The covergirl projects her possession of, and pleasure in possessing, culturally desirable attributes such as physical beauty and social importance. Her personal importance is stressed by her symbolic dualism in representing both a magazine's identity and its reader idealizations." Thus, the cover provides in a visual form the magazine's ideology, its identity and its understanding of its audience.

Based on her content analysis of the cover photos of the three largest circulation British women's magazines, sampled over 25 years (between 1949 and 1974), Ferguson (1978, p. 107) offers a typology of such covers. Each type represents a variation on the idealized, stereotyped imagery of women: (a) "Chocolate Box" projects women as blandly pleasing and devoid of individuality, (b) the "Invitational" suggests women's mischief or mystery, (c) the "Super-smiler" represents the aggressive, demanding "big come-on" approach, and (d) the "Romantic or Sexual" cover depicts women as overtly sensual.

In a basic sense, Ferguson (1978, p. 113) views the cover of a magazine as a source of social control. In its subtely, the cover informs, corrects, directs, and displays what are considered to be the appropriate identities, and attributes that readers should possess.

The Extent and Nature of Coverage: *Sports Illustrated*

We have chosen *Sports Illustrated* for our discussion of how sports magazines portray women's participation. It is America's largest, national weekly sports magazine; its coverage of sports is perceived by many to be the most professional, from both photographic and journalistic viewpoints; and its coverage is the source of several empirical studies of women in sport.

If cover photographs reflect producers' ideology and perceived reader interests, then the symbolic message from the cover of the nation's leading sports magazine, *Sports Illustrated*, is clear: women do not belong in sports.

To celebrate its 25th year of publication, *Sports Illustrated*, with a weekly circulation of several million readers, published a 26-page reproduction of every magazine cover it produced from August, 1954 through 1978. A content analysis of the 1,250 covers (*Women's Sports*, 1979, p. 12) dramatically illustrates both the symbolic annihilation and trivialization of women in sport. Women appeared on only 115 of the 1,250 covers and only 55 of these women were female athletes. Thus, sportswomen accounted for less than 5% of the covers. Women athletes appeared most frequently in 1955, when they made the cover eight times and again in 1976, when six women achieved the same recognition. In both years all the women were drawn from individual, socially acceptable sports. The year 1967 was significant as the first time that not even one sportswoman graced the cover. Billie Jean King became SI's first Sportswoman of the Year in 1972, sharing the annual honor with UCLA basketball coach John Wooden. In 1973, a benchmark cover did appear, entitled "Women Are Getting a Raw Deal," which was the first and only time women's sports was given sole cover attention. Nancy Lopez and Chris Evert were the only sportswomen on the cover in 1977 and 1978, although women appeared on the annual swimsuit covers during these two years as did two cheerleaders and one film actress.

The symbolic visual message of these covers is one that reinforces the traditional association of sport with men while occasionally giving minimal approval to the least threatening deviations by women from this cultural value. In a revealing interpretation of the now-classic cover of Chris Evert, named *Sports Illustrated's* Athlete of the Year in 1977, Kaplan (1979a) observes:

> For the cover picture, this sports champion was in a replica of an 1884 tennis costume—a long white dress complete with bustle. The underlying message to male readers was that if they were dismayed at a woman's getting the magazine's highest honor, they could console themselves by looking at the picture of prim and proper Chris, standing straight–backed in an Edwardian setting of bentwood furniture and potted palms. Holding an outmoded tennis racket, she was hardly the image of an athlete to be reckoned with. *The photograph suggested to male readers that while it was fashionable to recognize women as athletes, they could regard the whole thing as a joke.* (p. 82, emphasis added)

Sports Illustrated also published, in its Silver Anniversary Issue (August 13, 1979) a collection of pictures that served as a photo essay of the past quarter-century of sport history. Our own content analysis of these photographs reveals the following:

1. Of the 119 photographs of athletes, 105 were of men only, 12 were of women only, and 2 pictures were of both sexes.
2. There were no photographs of sportswomen for 14 of the 25 years covered in this historical survey of athletic achievement.
3. This symbolic annihilation of women cannot be accounted for by reference to women's fairly recent involvement in sport. There were no photographs of women athletes for the following years: 1956, 1959, 1961, 1962, 1965-1970, 1972, 1974, 1975, and as recently as 1979!
4. The range of sports depicted in the photographs was almost twice as large for men (15 different sports) as it was for women (8 sports).
5. All eight sports depicting women's achievements were individual rather than team sports, and all but two (horse racing and cycling) were of socially acceptable sports.
6. Of the 12 sportswomen pictured, 3 were minority women—Althea Gibson (in 1957), Wilma Rudolph (in 1960), and Nancy Lopez (1978).
7. In more than half (58%) of the photos, the sportswomen were depicted in passive, nonathletic portraits that captured their "personality" rather than their active athleticism. By contrast, only 44% of the photographs of male athletes were so depicted.

These patterns of stereotypic visual portrayals of women in sport are supported by other research data that examined the coverage of written content in *Sports Illustrated* (Felshin, 1974a, pp. 261-265). In her analysis of the coverage of women in this magazine, Corrigan (1972) reports that every article she surveyed contained descriptions of the sportswomen's physical attributes, with special attention given to height, weight and hair and eye color. A more recent study (Zang, 1976) contains supporting data that reflects the disproportionately small coverage given to women's sport in *Sports Illustrated* and the overemphasis on socially approved, individual sports.

In a major exception to this general trend, *Sports Illustrated*, in 1973, published a ground-breaking three-part series on the status of women's sports. Co-authored by Bill Gilbert and Nancy Williamson (1973), this national overview of sexual inequality in sport won the 1974 National Magazine Award for Outstanding Editorial Achievement in Service to the Individual. By documenting both the growing involvement of women in sport and the social and institutional barriers to women's full participation, this series had a significant impact on public awareness. The wealth of descriptive and statistical data interwoven with Gilbert and Williamson's analysis reached beyond the readers' hands and became a national document of both rising expectations and increasing impatience with conventional barriers to equal participation by women. According to Nancy Williamson, the series also had an impact on *Sports Illustrated's* approach to the issue: "The wide response to the series changed our managing editor's thinking at the time, and S.I. started covering women more often" (Hogan, 1976).

As the above data indicate, however, this national sports weekly still lags far behind the emerging patterns of female participation in sport. Its visual and written coverage of the sportswoman is still embedded in stereotypical imagery and readers, especially female readers, who want an exposure to the full range of options and issues that pertain to women in sport will have to look elsewhere.

The Extent and Nature of Coverage: Women's Magazines

Females at different stages of the life cycle can find magazines especially suited to their perceived interests and needs. According to Tuchman (1978, p. 17) "Some, like *Seventeen,* whose readers tend to be young adolescents, instruct on contemporary fashions and dating styles. Others, like *Cosmopolitan* and *Redbook,* teach about survival as a young woman—whether as a single woman hunting a mate in the city or a young married coping with hearth and home." These magazines are aimed at a predominantly white, middle-class, heterosexual population; other magazines of smaller circulation are devoted to different segments of the female population. For example, *True Story, Essence,* and *Ms.* are designed for the working–class, black woman and the liberal feminist, respectively. However, the minimal research that has been done on magazine coverage of woman in sport concentrates primarily on the first group, the white, middle-class female.

One of the earliest studies of how magazines portray women in sport was carried out by Slatton (1970). She analyzed the content of advertisements for five magazines, covering the period 1900-1968, and her data reveal that women in sport were seldom used as themes in magazine advertisements. The changes in women's sport participation since Slatton's study are reflected in the increased coverage given to women's sports in a variety of women's magazines. A recent study, reported in *womenSports* magazine (Leavy, 1977b, pp. 53-57), surveyed the sports coverage provided by *Seventeen, Cosmopolitan, Redbook* and *Ms.* for the period 1970-1976. The data indicate that all four magazines have increased their coverage of women's sports. In terms of average editorial space given to women's sports, the findings show that, for the time period surveyed, *Redbook* devoted 1% of its editorial coverage to women's sports, *Cosmopolitan* 1.5%, *Ms.* 2.5%, and *Seventeen* 4.6%.

However, as Leavy (1977b, p. 53) cautions, "the figures do not tell the whole story. All four magazines have been resourceful in finding ways to leave sports—and especially sports events—out of their sports articles. Many of their stories are sports–related articles on fashion, beauty, travel, or sex discrimination." Thus, just as other research shows a tentative, bland, and nonthreatening incorporation of feminist issues into women's magazines, this research indicates a similar pattern with respect to the inclusion of women's sports. Perhaps out of a mixture of editorial philosophy, advertisers' preferences, and a fear of reader rejection, the sports stories carried in these magazines attempt to merge conventional definitions of femininity and women's role with the changes occurring in women's sports.

This merger is accomplished by weaving sports into one or more of the following seven categories, identified by Leavy (1977b, pp. 53-57) as "Sports Chic": (a) women athletes as "Personalities"; (b) "How-To's" that stress sex or glamour, with a touch of sporting technique or information as a filler; (c) "A Pretty Face," with emphasis on the beauty and health benefits of sport; (d) "From Slim To Trim," which concentrates on diet and conditioning; (e) "Beautysports" that cater to sports fashion; (f) "The Issues," found mainly in *Ms.* Magazine, which stress prejudice and discrimination against women in sport; and, (g) "Muscle Phobia," which results in few photos or accounts of the stress and strain of sport. By employing the traditional editorial themes of women's magazines—fashion, beauty, diet, dating—women's sports is getting coverage in ways that are both subtle and safe but seldom sporting.

This pattern of women's sports coverage may be expected from magazines that cater to the large base of white, middle-class readers. Surprisingly, however, *Ms.*, the acknowledged feminist forum, is also vulnerable to pressures to include women's sports in socially approved ways. The traditional association of sport with masculinity, and the negative stereotypes that surround sportswomen, have made *Ms.* cautious about its coverage. As reported by Leavy (1977b):

According to Harriet Lyons (*Ms.* editor), *Ms.* has encountered the same prejudices simply in trying to provide sports coverage. Two women cyclists in short pants, with heavily muscled legs and pulled-back hair, appeared on the cover of the September 1974 issue devoted to 'The Sporting Life.' 'It got back to us,' Lyons said, 'that the issue was known in some circles as the 'dykes on bikes cover.' (p. 57)

If *Ms.* is vulnerable to these pressures to influence its coverage of women and sport, what chance of survival does a magazine have if its *entire content* is devoted to women's sport? The answer to this question is still unraveling, but a brief history of two such magazines may serve to illustrate some of the dilemmas embedded in media coverage of women and sport.

Magazine Production

In the Spring of 1973 the first issue of *The Sportswoman* appeared. With a staff of eight and a minimum budget, editor and publisher Marlene Jensen started off slowly, producing a quarterly magazine of approximately 30 pages. The content of the magazine included information about local and regional sporting news, interscholastic and intercollegiate competition, amateur athletics, and the lesser-known sports. While the magazine did cover the dominant women's sports, such as professional tennis, and the popular stars, such as Billie Jean King, it managed, from its very first issue, to give exposure to many of the diverse and emergent themes that shaped the expansion of women's sports in the seventies. The nature of its coverage was also consistently tied to issues that ranged across the continuum of feminist ideology, rather than limiting itself to only the more popular issues of the day, such as Title IX or equal salaries for professional athletes. Furthermore, in its approach to its audience, there was an assumption that its readers were knowledgeable about sports and active participants as well.

Approximately one year later, the first issue of *womenSports* magazine appeared and it provided strong competition for its sister publication. Published by Billie Jean King and her husband Larry King, the monthly magazine was produced by a considerably larger staff and with substantially greater financial support than *The Sportswoman*. While the covers of the first issues of both magazines carried a photograph of Billie Jean King, the 98–page inaugural issue of *womenSports* clearly signaled a difference between the two publications. Corporations with direct ties to women's products had purchased considerable advertising space; the quality of writing, color reproductions, and graphics were clearly professional; and the approach to sports was squarely in accord with white, middle-class, cosmopolitan, liberal feminism.

By 1975, both magazines had tentatively established themselves among a small segment of the general female population, with *womenSports'* circulation the greater of the two. Neither magazine, however, was on firm financial ground. The first of a series of changes in publishers occurred at *The Sportswoman* in 1975. In speaking of this shift in publishers and the difference between the two competing magazines, Marlene Jensen, who was then still the editor of *The Sportswoman*, said:

> Other sports magazines which feature women have begun publishing in the last year, and I think it's great the women finally have a choice of magazines. But the magazines being published have not presented the sportswoman as we have wanted her presented—with all the credit and respect for her accomplishments that society had previously reserved for the male. (Jensen, 1975, p. 4)

Slowly, the differences in style and tone of the two magazines were emerging. While *The Sportswoman* became more serious and sober in its coverage of women's sports, its rival magazine began to include more lighthearted, breezy articles on topics that were tangential to sports. *womenSports'* coverage still included attention to major professional, amateur, and intercollegiate sport, but, in tone and style, it began to resemble the coverage of women's sports presently found in women's magazines.

In 1976, both magazines experienced a change in ownership. Charter Publishing Company (which also published *Redbook*) took over control of *womenSports* in March of that year, at which time there were 100,000 subscribers (Dougherty, 1977, p. 60). According to Carlo Vittorini, the president of the new owners, "From the publishing point of view we had to start from scratch. We moved to New York from San Mateo (Calif.), changed editors, cover, design and art director" (Dougherty, 1977, p. 60). By 1977 subscriptions had been increased to 185,000 copies with plans to enlarge that figure the following year. As Vittorini saw it, "Our biggest single challenge is awareness that the magazine even exists. We haven't been able to use the tried and true methods that might have worked for other magazines" (Dougherty, 1977, p. 60). Some of those conventional methods of increasing awareness, according to Dougherty (1977, p. 60), "include circulation advertising, which proved inefficient because of the diffusion of the target audience."

The one element that *womenSports* did not have to contend with by 1977 was competition from *The Sportswoman*. It was no longer in existence. A year earlier, Allan Hanson had become the publisher of *The Sportswoman*. Two women, Molly Tyson and Annette Thompson, had come from the staff of *womenSports* to assume the respective positions of editor and art director and to help buttress the precarious *Sportswoman*, which had temporarily ceased publication in October, 1975.

When she assumed her new role as editor, Tyson was surprised by the tenacious and loyal reader response from *The Sportswoman's* subscribers. Even though many of the subscribers had not received their last three issues, and had experienced the frustrations of intermittent publication, many of them sent in subscription renewals, letters of encouragement and unsolicited manuscripts to help sustain their magazine. This unusually supportive response from subscribers was attributed by Molly Tyson to the nature of the magazine's coverage under former editor Marlene Jensen:

> Every issue featured prominent sportswomen. . . . But coverage wasn't limited to the Superstars. Every issue gave descriptions and results of the major collegiate and amateur championships that had taken place that month. The events weren't covered as phenomena but as sports events, and readers were addressed not as neophytes but as knowledgeable sportswomen. (Jensen, 1976, p. 4)

Apparently, enthusiastic reader response, a serious treatment of women's sports, and two subsequent changes in publishers and editors were not enough to insure the magazine's survival, and it ceased publication in 1977.

With no competition, *womenSports* became the only national vehicle for disseminating information and opinion to a women's audience. However, its own viability as a magazine was still precarious and in January, 1978 it, too, ceased publication. Billie Jean King, the original founder of the magazine, worked to insure its revival by having the newly-formed Women's Sports Foundation (which King helped to found) take over the circulation of *womenSports.*

In January, 1979 the premier issue of the magazine, now called *Women's Sports,* appeared on the newsstands as "the membership publication of the Women's Sports Foundation," with Margaret Roach as Editor and Douglas H. Latimer as Publisher. The revived magazine resumed and now intensified its chic, light, breezy approach to women's sports. Sophisticated graphics and photography, polished writing, and full-page color advertisements now enhanced the "respectability" of the magazine as a serious contender for corporate advertising dollars and readers' subscriptions.

Within that year, the changing nature and direction of *Women's Sports* coverage was accomplished. The most telling sign appeared on the cover of the December, 1979 issue. A full-face close-up photograph of skier Suzy Chaffee, framed by blonde hair and accentuated by detailed cosmetics, adorned the cover of this issue. To illustrate the approach *Women's Sports* had taken, the following description of Chaffee appeared on the editorial page: "Suzy Chaffee, alias 'Suzy Chapstick,' has always been full of surprises. Today she's into legislation, lip balm, rollerskates and much much more"(*Women's Sports,* 1979, p. 4).

The identification of Chaffee with her corporate sponsor and the trivialization of Chaffee's interest in legislation is part of the larger turn that the magazine had taken to bring it into the mainstream. In this same issue, Editor Margaret Roach correctly anticipated the surprise that veteran readers of the magazine would feel when seeing this new cover. Roach's letter from the editor was appropriately titled, "Hey! What's Going On Here?" Roach then explained that the cover, the new logo, and the shift in content were part of the changing policy that would shape *Women's Sports* in the future.

While Roach (1979, p. 4) reassures her readers that the magazine "will continue to be first and foremost a *sports* magazine" (original italics), she argues that reader response has resulted in "broadening our editorial philosophy to include more material that will benefit all active women—those who are primarily interested in recreational athletics as well as those whose main concern is organized competition." And what material will benefit all active women? What material is of concern to those mainly interested in recreational athletics? Roach tells us: health, fitness, nutrition, beauty, how-to articles, and sports fashion! If this list sounds familiar, it should. It is a list of the type of articles on sport presently appearing in women's magazines, as we discussed earlier. Ironically, in what may have been a prophetic article, the nature and implications of this patronizing coverage of women's sport first was discussed in *womenSports* magazine, in an article entitled "Sports Chic" (Levy, 1977, pp. 53-57). Although we believe it is important to reach out to "the active woman" who is mainly interested in noncompetitive, recreational sport, we must argue against the means and manner employed to reach this goal. When the means cater to stereotypical images of being female, we suspect that the end will result in a confirmation rather than an alteration of established conceptions of womanhood.

In her closing paragraph, Roach reveals the philosophical and ideological justification of the magazine's new policy:

> I would like to sum up by saying that the image of the female athlete is, unfortunately, often a negative one among both men and women. We at *Women's Sports* believe that there is in fact no conflict between femininity and athletics. We know that beauty and sports are not mutually exclusive, and we fully intend to provide evidence of this every month. We think this "new" issue is as beautiful as the active women who read it. We're sure you'll agree. (Roach, 1979, p. 4)

We're sure we do not. We believe that the present editorial philosophy of *Women's Sports* is a giant step backward for women. It caters to conventional stereotypes of both women and women in sport; it fails to challenge traditional definitions of femininity; it preys on homophobic fears among women; it maintains the insidious demand that all women conform to elitist, sexist images of women's proper involvement with sport. In sum, we believe that while this philosophy will insure the economic survival of *Women's Sports*, it signals the demise of a magazine that could have been a forum for reconstructing women's roles and their relations to sport as an institution. Instead, we have a magazine that flirts with liberal feminism, but leaves intact the sexist underpinnings of society's vision of both women and sport.

To illustrate our position in the concrete, we need only to examine the subsequent issues of this magazine. In 1980, the January cover celebrates women "dancing their way to fitness;" the February cover is a *Seventeen*-like photo of Linda Fratianne; and the March cover features a soft-focus, close-up photograph of "athlete turned actress—Cathy Lee Crosby." As Roach promised, the articles in these three issues include an increase in coverage of beauty, fashion, and other dimensions of sports chic—all designed to appeal to the cosmopolitan, affluent, upwardly mobile, young, white, heterosexual woman. Full-page ads have been purchased by major producers of women's products, such as Maybeline, Bonnie Bell, Bobbie Brooks, L'eggs, Stayfree, Avon, and Scott Paper Company.

The willingness of such corporations to invest advertising dollars in a woman's sport magazine supports Dougherty's (1977) observation, in his *New York Times* "Advertising" column, that "In some quarters there is the feeling that 'women's sports is the hottest topic since the Frisbee' " (p. 60). Perhaps the changing editorial policy in *Women's Sports* is not so much a function of reader response, as Editor Roach suggests. Rather, it may be a necessary strategy to acquire the corporate advertising dollars that are essential to a magazine's survival and profitable growth. As Tuchman (1978) notes, in discussing a women's magazine audience, that additional readers are only indirectly profitable

> because the cost of publication and distribution per copy far exceeds the price of the individual copy—whether it is purchased on the newsstand, in a supermarket, or through subscription. Instead a magazine realizes its profit by selling advertisements and charging its advertisers a rate adjusted to its known circulation. Appealing to advertisers, the magazine specifies known demographic characteristics of its readership. (p. 18)

Although we do not yet know the "demographic characteristics" of *Women's Sports* readership, our impression is that this magazine increasingly draws readers from the same pool as the readers of the major, white, middle-class women's magazines. They will see the same types of advertisements that grace these magazines, with their explicit emphasis on the cluster of traits presently defined as acceptable for "the liberated woman."

The degree to which corporate sponsorship determines a magazine's profit will determine the nature of the magazine's content, because such content will be shaped by its appeal to the interests and values of the corporate sponsors. Given the fact that circulation advertising depends on a known and identifiable target audience, rather than a diffuse one, this audience is being created by *Women's Sports*, intentionally or unwittingly, and it will function to insure that advertisers of "women's products" will find their appropriate audience. In the case of *Women's Sports*, we believe that the price of survival and growth has been too costly. Instead of standing apart as the only magazine devoted to alternative visions of the sporting woman, it can safely join *Ms.* at the newsstand, next to *Cosmopolitan*, *Seventeen*, and *Redbook*.

Notes

1. In fact, it is ironic that most of the anthologies on women and the mass media, including Tuchman et al. (1978), fail to consider the topic of women in sport.
2. Judge Motley's decision was a specific one and was not binding on other baseball clubs or sports commissioners.

Chapter 8/

Power Plays: Government and Public Policy

Public policy shapes the nature and processes of social life. The collective decisions about the goals of group life and the appropriate means to reach those ends—public policy—are clearly evident in the structure of such institutions as the military, the economy, and the school system. We are aware of the difficult and complex battles over public policy that confront society as it grapples with such problems as crime and justice, health and welfare, social order, and public dissent. Most people are sensitive to the competing interest groups that disagree over the nature of public policies and their effective implementation in such spheres as employment, foreign policy, urban development, public service and the like.

Ironically people who are willing to examine the impact of public policy in many areas of social life become curiously silent when it comes to sport. To many observers, the "purity of sport myth" (Johnson, 1978, p. 320) is accepted uncritically. This mythical view of sport encourages a vision that exempts sports from the influence of public policy. Sport is seen as immune to the forces, interest groups, and public decisions that shape the policies of society's other dominant institutions. This naive view has resulted in a neglect of the role of public policy as a *political context* in which sporting forms and processes are developed, maintained, or changed over time. It has also obscured the political nature of sporting activity, the use of sport for nationalistic ends, and the array of public policy choices that affect the quality of sport both within and among nations.

In an effort to address this issue, our aim in this chapter is to examine the ties between public policy and women's participation in sport. In order to give some structure to this complex topic, we shall devote separate attention to three general, albeit intersecting, issues. First, we want to investigate the historical and present patterns of female participation in the Olympic Games as a case study of *international public policy*. Specifically, we shall explore the changing nature of public decision making about "the proper role" of female Olympic participation and the political use of female athletes for the purpose of nationalism.

In the second section we will discuss *national public policy* by investigating specific US policies that directly affect sport. With some exceptions (e.g., Title IX, which we discussed in chapter 6) most American public policy is presently directed at men's sporting endeavors. Nevertheless, we believe that an examination of those public postures that regulate men's sports will provide us with a set of precedents, benchmarks, and potential problems that may arise as women's sports become an increasingly central item on the public agenda.

Third, we will look at the policy implications of the various models of feminism that have been developed throughout this work. At both the international and national levels of public policy and decision making, we shall explore the range of public choices available to those who espouse different approaches to feminism and divergent priorities regarding women's involvement in sport.

The Olympics: A Case Study of International Public Policy

No longer can anyone question the political nature of the Olympics. Naive pronouncements, as expressed by Avery Brundage, former President of the International Olympic Committee, that "The Olympic Movement appears as a ray of sunshine through clouds of racial animosity, religious bigotry and political chicanery" (Johnson, 1972, p. 24), all pale in the face of just a few Olympic facts. In 1980, US President Jimmy Carter ordered the boycott of the Moscow Olympics because of the

Soviet invasion of Afghanistan. In 1972 terrorists killed eleven Israeli athletes at the Munich Games. Between 1965 and 1976 China's representation at the Games was bitterly disputed. Dr. Ryotaro Asuma wrote of the 1964 Tokyo Olympics: "Our national prestige was tied to it and, yes, it was a *governmental policy* to make the Olympics our announcement to the world that Japan was no longer a beaten nation, that Japan had regained confidence in herself" (Johnson, 1972, p. 248, emphasis added). The participation of South Africa remains a hotly contested issue for African and other Third World nations. Three Olympics were cancelled because of world wars. And who could ever doubt Hitler's exploitation of the 1936 Olympics in Berlin?

This brief highlighting of the political and nationalistic use of the Olympics need not continue. Sports and politics are inextricably related, particularly at the international level. Thus, the question that is before the international community is how to minimize the negative consequences of political intrusion in sporting contests between and among nations. It is not our intent to explore this issue in any detail. Rather, we wish to underscore the fact that as long as athletic competition exists between and among nation-states, politics and public policies will color these contests.

Based on this vision of sport and politics, our purpose in this section is to utilize Olympic history as a case study for analyzing the international status of women in sport. Specifically, we wish to investigate the changing nature of international public policy regarding the "proper role" of female Olympic participation and to demonstrate the political and ideological basis for using women athletes for the purposes of nationalism.

Women and Olympic Competition

The first recorded Olympic Games (776 B.C.) barred women entirely from this religious and political event (Harris, 1972, p. 20). For these sacred celebrations only the public beings—men (Arendt, 1958, p. 24)—were allowed to be present. Women, the private beings, could not even view the Games and faced the death penalty for entering the sacred grounds.

After a hiatus of over 1500 years in 1896 the Olympics were revived. Although women were no longer put to death for merely being spectators, they once again were not included as participants. The original Games had been only for men and this policy continued. Indeed, scholars (Gilbert, 1980, p. 82; Mandell, 1971) have contended that the reintroduction of the Olympic Games was done in order to prepare the

French *male* population for "real war" through the simulated contests in the Olympic stadium. This public posture rendered the participation of women irrelevant and was uncritically accepted.

Efforts to overcome female exclusion have been slow and arduous. Indeed they continue today. In order to highlight these continuing efforts, we have compiled an abbreviated history of women's gradual inclusion in the Olympic Games. Beginning with 1908, the first relatively representative Olympics, the number of women participating in the Games has steadily increased, a fact indicated in Table 7.

Table 7
The Modern Summer Olympics

Date	Place	Countries Represented	Male Athletes	Female Athletes
1896 (April 6-15)	Athens	13	311	0
1900 (July 2-22)	Paris	22	1,319	11
1904 (Aug. 29-Sept. 7)	St. Louis	12	617	8
1908 (July 13-25)	London	22	1,999	36
1912 (July 6-15)	Stockholm	28	2,490	57
1916 No Olympics due to war—scheduled to be held in Berlin				
1920 (Aug. 14-29)	Antwerp	29	2,543	64
1924 (July 5-27)	Paris	44	2,956	136
1928 (July 28-Aug. 14)	Amsterdam	46	2,724	290
1932 (July 30-Aug. 14)	Los Angeles	47	1,281	127
1936 (Aug. 1-16)	Berlin	49	3,738	328
1940 Olympics (scheduled for Tokyo) cancelled due to World War II				
1944 Olympics cancelled due to World War II				
1948 (July 29-Aug. 14)	London	59	3,714	385
1952 (July 18-Aug. 3)	Helsinki	69	4,407	518
1956 (Nov. 22-Dec. 8)	Melbourne	71	2,958	384
1960 (Aug. 25-Sept. 11)	Rome	83	4,738	610
1964 (Oct. 10-24)	Tokyo	93	4,457	683
1968 (Oct. 12-27)	Mexico City	112	4,750	781
1972 (Aug. 26-Sept. 11)	Munich	122	6,077	1,070
1976 (July 17-Aug. 1)	Montreal	88	4,915	1,274

However, Tables 8 and 9 reveal that sheer numerical increases in Olympic competition did not result in women's equality as Olympic contestants. Let us look at the data in these two tables to see if they reflect a shared policy statement about women's "proper" place in the Games.

Table 8
Summer Olympics: Female and Male Individual Events

Events	Year Introduced for Men	Year Introduced for Women
Track and Field		
Individual Track Events		
100 meters	1908	1928
200 meters	1908	1948
400 meters	1908	1964
800 meters	1908	1960*
1,500 meters	1908	1972
5,000 meters	1912	----
10,000 meters	1912	----
110 meters hurdles	1908	1932(80m)
400 meters hurdles	1908	----
3,000 steeplechase	1908	----
Individual Road Events		
20 KM Walk	1908	----
Marathon	1908	----
Jumping Events		
High Jump	1908	1928
Long Jump	1908	1948
Triple Jump	1908	----
Pole Vault	1908	----
Throwing Events		
The Shot Put	1908	1948
The Discus	1908	1928
The Hammer	1908	----
The Javelin	1908	1932
Combined Events		
Decathlon	1912	----
Pentathlon	----	1964
Team Events		
4 X 100 meter relay	1912	1928
4 X 400 meter relay	1908	1972
Boxing		
Eleven Weight Categories	1908**	----

Table 8, continued

Canoeing		
500 Meter Events		
Kayak Singles	1976	1948
Kayak Pairs	1976	1960
Canadian Canoe Singles	1976	----
Canadian Canoe Pairs	1976	----
1,000 Meter Events		
Kayak Singles	1936	----
Canadian Canoe Singles	1936	----
Kayak Pairs	1936	----
Canadian Canoe Pairs	1936	----
Kayak Four Men	1964	----
Cycling		
Cycling Six Events	1908**	----
Fencing		
Individual Events		
Foil	1908	1924
Epee	1908	----
Saber	1908	----
Team Events		
Foil	1920	1960
Epee	1908	----
Saber	1908	----
Gymnastics		
Individual Events		
Floor Exercises	1932	1952
Pommel Horse	1924	----
Rings	1924	----
Horse Vault	1924	1952
Parallel Bars	1924	----
Uneven Bars	----	1952
Horizontal Bar	1924	----
Beam	----	1952
Combined Individual	1908	1952
Combined Exercises Team	1908	1928
Judo		
Six Weight Categories	1964**	----
Modern Pentathlon		
Individual Winners	1912	----
Pentathlon Team	1952	----
Rowing		
Single Sculls	1908	1976
Pair Oars Without Coxswain	1908	1976
Four Oars Without Coxswain	1908	----

Table 8, continued

Double Sculls	1920	1976
Pair Oars With Coxswain	1920	----
Four Oars With Coxswain	1912	1976
Eight Oars With Coxswain	1908	1976
Quadruple Sculls Without Coxswain	1976	----
Quadruple Sculls With Coxswain	----	1976
Swimming and Diving		
Individual Events		
100 meters freestyle	1908	1912
200 meters freestyle	1968	1968
400 meters freestyle	1908	1920
800 meters freestyle	----	1968
1,500 meters freestyle	1908	----
100 meters breaststroke	1968	1968
200 meters breaststroke	1908	1960
100 meters backstroke	1908	1924
200 meters backstroke	1964	1968
100 meters butterfly	1968	1956
200 meters butterfly	1956	1968
400 individual medley	1964	1964
Swimming Relay Events		
4 X 100 meters freestyle	----	1912
4 X 200 meters freestyle	1908	----
4 X 100 meters medley	1960	1960
Diving		
Springboard diving 3 meters	1908	1920
Platform diving	1908	1912
Weightlifting		
Nine Weight Categories	1920**	----
Wrestling		
Ten Weight Categories	1908**	----
Archery	1972	1972

* First held in 1928; removed until reintroduced in 1960
** The first appearance of these sports occurred in the year indicated; additional
  categories were introduced in subsequent Olympics.

Examining Table 8, one finds that men compete in far more individual events than women. Men engage in 114 separate events, while women have only 46; thus, men have 250% more individual events. Furthermore, there is *not one* category of competition in which women compete for which there is no male counterpart.[1]

Another pattern from Table 8 reveals that of the 13 types of individual events, women do not compete in 6 of them: boxing, cycling, judo, the modern pentathlon, weightlifting, and wrestling. Therefore, nearly one-half (46%) of the Summer Olympic[2] categories of events admit no female competitors. Each of the six events which exclude women possesses a trait that is considered "unfeminine" by the entire international community. Boxing, judo, and wrestling entail physical contact, a cross-cultural taboo for women. They, along with weightlifting, also emphasize strength, an attribute assigned to men alone.

The modern pentathlon (competition composed of five skills—riding, fencing, shooting, swimming, and a cross-country run) is also exclusively male. It promotes activities that are military in nature, "specifically, those which were required by a courier in the field" (How to. . ., 1975, p. 176). Of course, preparation for combat and participation in war, with rare exceptions, have been historically and culturally retained only for men.

The historical exclusion of cycling for women was based on more subtle sexist premises. The danger in the sport, as witnessed by frequent accidents and high speeds, accounts for some of the reluctance to allowing "fragile women" to participate. Additionally, women do not compete in events that occur outside the stadium. Road cycling, after many years of petitioning, has tentatively been scheduled for inclusion in the 1984 Los Angeles Olympic Games.

If we now compare events in which both sexes compete, we can still see the evidence of common international public policy that limits full female Olympic participation. First, the 1,500 meter race has been the longest track event for women. The International Amateur Athletic Federation (IAAF) refused, for many years, to have women run the longer distances. Despite continued petitions, it was only at the 1928 games that even the distance of 800 meters was first allowed. Nina Kuscsik (1976, p. 28) writes that the 800 meters race in the 1928 Olympics "set women's distance running back 50 years." She continues:

> The 800-meter race itself was highly competitive, and although some of the entrants were not properly trained and collapsed en route, the top six finished within 10 seconds of each other; the first three bettering the old world record.

> Isn't the point of racing to reach one's limit at the finish line? When male runners collapsed en route in the marathon, it was called drama, but when women reached this physiological level, it was labeled "frightful" and officials from several countries jumped on the IAAF to cancel the "frightful episode" from future Olympic games. (p. 28)

The 1928 "frightful episode" brought the cancellation of the 800 meters for the 1932 Games; it was not reintroduced again until 1960. Another two Olympics passed before the 1,500 meters was added. Women still have not competed in the 5,000 or 10,000 meters or the marathon. Despite repeated appeals to have the longer distances included, and the existence of non-Olympic international competition in these events, women remain relegated to the shorter distances in the Olympics; only the marathon will be added to the 1984 Olympic Games.

Other differences in the track and field events are noteworthy. The 20–kilometer walk is another road contest from which the women are excluded. In jumping, the highest and the longest events (the pole vault and the triple jump) are exclusively male. Thus, if one takes the Olympic motto "the fastest, the farthest and the highest" as one's goal, women have been categorically excluded from the events that would take them that far and that high. In the throwing events (shots, discus, javelin, and hammer), women participate in all but the hammer. The hammer, of the heavier objects, is propelled the farthest in distance. Finally, the male athlete is expected to be at least twice as proficient as the female since his overall individual championship (the decathlon) involves twice as many events (10) as the female championship (the pentathlon).

In Olympic canoeing, women are again excluded from the longer distance events. In fencing, women compete with only the lightest of the weapons, the foil. Less endurance and less strength are once again assumed to be attributes of women and these two Olympic events repeat this theme.

Gymnastics provides one of the most intriguing developments of Olympic history. During the 1972 and 1976 Games, the world marveled at the sporting exploits of Olga Korbut and Nadia Comaneci. Perhaps never before had two female athletes caught so much of the world's attention and interest. But what was being celebrated by media coverage? We do not wish to minimize the accomplishments of females in gymnastics, but the enormous social approval given these athletes must be explored. First, these two athletes were *girls*, not women. They captured worldwide attention, as did the youthful Cathy Rigby in the United States. The older and more mature gymnasts like L. Tourischeva and Nelli Kim went largely unnoticed. In fact, in 1972 it was L. Tourischeva, not Olga Korbut, who won the gold medal for the combined individual events.

Second, modern gymnastics separates the ancient Greek male ideal. The word "gymnastics" derives from the "Greek 'gymnasia'—an elaborate establishment where the young men of the upper classes worked out for the better part of the day. Physical prowess and beauty were considered very important" (How to. . ., 1975, p. 42). Today, gymnastics stresses physical prowess and strength for the men's events and beauty, grace, and finesse for the women's. Women do not take part in the strength events of the pommel horse, rings, parallel bars, and horizontal bar. The men do not compete in the uneven bars and the balance beam. These events, therefore, have structural differences that reflect what people consider appropriate gymnastic skill for each sex. Even common events, such as the floor exercises, do not demand the same behavior of the male and female participants. The required movements differ; the choreography differs; the moods differ; the marking systems differ; and what is titled the same proves not to be the same. Why? The conventional answer is, "because men and women are different"; thus, they are not allowed to occupy the same sporting space even when there is no intrinsic reason for them not to.

Swimming shares with women's gymnastics common attributes. Female swimmers peak at a very young age. Rare indeed, is the female gymnast or swimmer who is chronologically or physiologically a young adult. Thus, in a sport which has great social approval, age is a deterrent to athletic excellence. New winners and new challengers are mostly in their teens and, increasingly, in their very early teens. Acceptability is provided to the girl who will devote ten years of her life to intensive training and competition, but who by young adulthood, is expected to relinquish her athleticism. The very structure of the sport, the rules of evaluation, and the rigors of competition make the "retirement" age of the female swimmer and gymnast very young, considerably younger than that for men (Chourage, 1973).

Swimming and diving, like track events, find women accepted first, sometimes only, in shorter distances. The longest freestyle event for women is the 800 meters while the men swim 1,500 meters. The men's relay is 800 meters while the women's is only 400 meters. In each case, the men go nearly twice as far. It is noteworthy that mounting scientific evidence suggests that it is precisely in longer swimming and running distances that women's anatomy and physiology may give them an edge over men (Gerber et al., 1974, p. 414). Thus, for social reasons, not biological ones, women have been restricted from participating in longer events for which they have a better physiological predisposition.

Table 9
Summer Olympics Team Events

Single-sex Teams	Year Introduced for Men	Year Introduced for Women
Basketball	1936	1976
Field Hockey	1908	----*
Soccer	1908	----
Handball	1936	1976
Water Polo	1908	----
Volleyball	1964	1964

Table 9, continued

Mixed-sex Teams	Year Begun
Equestrian Sports	1912
Shooting	1908
Yachting	1956

* Added at the Moscow Olympics in 1980

Table 9 presents the Olympic team sports for women and men and shows the same basic patterns of policy decisions. Men compete in six single-sex team sports, whereas women compete in only three. In two of the common three (basketball and handball), the men began their Olympic competition considerably earlier than the women. Only volleyball, introduced in 1964 at the Tokyo Games, began simultaneously for both sexes. Furthermore, the two team sports which have no women's competition (soccer and water polo) involve greater physical contact, strength, and endurance than the sports in which women do compete.

The dates of inclusion of Olympic events provides yet another confirmation of sexist international public policy. Women received IOC approval for their sporting endeavors considerably later than men. We have used 1908 as the first Olympic year in which there was some degree of national representation. Using this as the base year, we found that of the 114 individual events men compete in, 57% were introduced in 1908 and almost all the events (82%) were in the program by 1936. In contrast, the very first official appearance by women occurred in 1912 and was restricted entirely to swimming. Of the 46 individual events in which women compete, only 30% appeared before 1936. Fully 70% of the female Olympic competitive events have appeared in the post-World War II period. International opposition to women's presence in the masculine domain of sports is apparently not quickly overcome.

This review of the history of women's participation in the Olympic Games reveals patterns of public policy and decision making that have been shared by the international community for the entire 20th Century. We summarize these patterns in the following way: first, international sports and sport competition is considered primarily a masculine domain. Second, the admission of women to the modern Olympics has been a slow and segmental process, only begrudgingly undertaken and, even today, far from possessing a structure that allows full and equal participation by women.

Third, in Olympic competition, the IOC has continued to emphatically perpetuate the belief that sports were invented by men for men. Any inclusion of women is accompanied by an alteration in the sporting event itself. Olympic decision-makers create an actual differentiation in the sports themselves (e.g. "feminine" and "masculine" versions of gymnastic floor exercises and different weights for the discus and the shot) so that there can be no confusion that the *real* sport is the activity men pursue. The altered, diminished, shortened, and "feminized" character of women's events is the best approximation for which a "truncated male" (Weiss, 1969, p. 219) is capable.

Finally, there are constant themes of female inferiority in the international arena: women are weaker and therefore should not compete in strength events; women are less aggressive; women are less likely to know the joys or desire the rigors of team competition; women are fragile and should avoid contact sports; women are better suited to the aesthetic sports; women should retire from sports during adolescence. Let us now look at the ways in which female athletes are used, in international sporting events, as one source of national success.

Nationalistic Use of Female Athletes

Beyond the cross-cultural policy agreements regarding women's role in sport that is evident in our case history of the Olympic Games, we must now consider the political use of female athletes for nationalistic goals. Indeed, nationalism may be the most serious threat to the continuation of the Olympic movement in our time. Ironically, women's achievements in the Games may serve to inadvertently exacerbate the extreme nationalism.

Fundamental Principle No. 7 of the Olympic Code laudably reads: "the Games are contests between individuals and not between countries." Of course, the reality of the Olympics is that they are political and nationalistic contests. Richard Mandell writes: "a trend that was strengthened by the results of the 1936 Olympics was to view athletes increasingly as national assets, procurable like fighter planes, submarines or synthetic rubber factories. After 1936 a stable of athletes became necessary for a national standing" (Mandell, 1971, p. 99).

Ideological hostilities have been carried into the sporting arena. Cumulative medal counts for nations, a practice officially frowned upon by the IOC, has become a major measure of national prestige and vigor. Increasingly, nations now gain acclaim and power from victories achieved in athletic competition.

Once social scientists abandoned the belief in the purity of sport, they began to investigate those national characteristics that contribute to Olympic success. Among the factors studied are religion, political institutions, and attributes of economic and social systems.[3]

We must critically examine the literature on the social and political factors behind Olympic success, because this entire body of research measures athletic success and prestige solely in terms of a national team's performance. It fails to distinguish between the contribution of the women and the men on that team. Researchers assume that the nation has but one sporting culture shared by all its Olympic athletes. Within one nation there are a series of subcultures and a variety of ideological supports for participation by different groups of citizens in all aspects of public life. Most importantly, at least one group division has had predominance in all cultures, that between women and men (Kelly & Boutilier, 1978, pp. 49-60). Therefore, any evaluation of national Olympic success should benefit from a separate analysis of the performance of male and female athletes on the nation's team.

Commenting on the use of international sports for nationalistic prestige, Brian Petrie writes that "nations compete with each other to secure, not only medals, but proof of their country's *virility* through the successful performance of its youth" (1975, p. 214, emphasis added). We will now argue that Olympic history demonstrates that many of the most "virile" nations are achieving this status through the feats of their *women* athletes—a fact that we uncover only when we do a separate analysis of the performance of male and female athletes on a given national team. Table 10 provides such an analysis.

A number of important findings emerge from the data provided by Table 10, including three significant patterns. First, if sexism did not exist, one should expect the female athletes in any nation to contribute approximately one-half of that nation's medals. However, the correlation between a nation's total gold medals and the percentage contributed by the females is only .465 (RS = .465 p < 02). There are 14 nations in which the female contribution reached the expected 50% level. These countries are: Australia, Austria, Bulgaria, Canada, Czechoslovakia, Denmark, East Germany, Great Britain, Hungary, The Netherlands, Romania, South Africa, USSR and West Germany. There are two nations which have won a substantial number of gold medals (above the total national mean of 20) which fall below the 50% level; Japan's women contributed only 13% and the US women only 36% to their nation's total number of gold medals.

A second finding concerns one of the variables traditionally used to explain national success in the Olympics—population. This correlation between population size and national Olympic success does hold for total gold medals and total population—.539 (RS = .539 p < .01). However, this factor is negligible in explaining women's success. The correlation for female success and size of population (population figures are from 1970) is only .189 (RS = .189 p > .10). The simple logic of the larger the population available to draw athletes from, the greater the probability of producing excellence *does not* hold true for female success.

Third, looking at those nations whose female athletes have obtained 50% or more of the total gold medals leads to some important observa-

Table 10
Women's Contributions to National Olympic Performances*
(Summer Olympics 1908-1976)

Country	Gold Medals Won	Gold Medals Won by Women	Percentage of Gold Medals Won by Women	Number of Categories Won**
Austria	3	3	100%	3
Bulgaria	3	3	100	2
Netherlands	12	12	100	3
South Africa	2	2	100	2
Czechoslovakia	14	13	93	3
Hungary	24	21	88	5
Denmark	7	6	86	3
East Germany	41	32	78	4
***Germany	22	17	77	5
Great Britain	12	9	75	4
Romania	9	6	67	2
West Germany	8	5	63	1
USSR	108	66	61	8
Australia	35	21	60	2
Canada	4	2	50	1
Poland	15	6	40	1
United States	227	81	36	3
Yugoslavia	3	1	33	1
Italy	16	5	31	3
New Zealand	4	1	25	1
France	17	3	18	1
Sweden	11	2	18	1
Finland	7	1	14	1
Japan	30	4	13	2
Argentina	1	0	0	0
Cuba	2	0	0	0
Jamaica	1	0	0	0
Kenya	1	0	0	0
Mexico	2	0	0	0
Norway	2	0	0	0
Switzerland	2	0	0	0
Trinidad	1	0	0	0

* This table includes only those sports events for which both men and women had competition. It starts the comparison from the first year that both sexes competed in the event; thus, the number of possible medals for each sex is the same.

** There are a total of nine possible sporting categories in which women could have won medals: track and field, canoeing and rowing, gymnastics, fencing, swimming and diving, volleyball, archery, basketball, and handball.

*** Germany competed as one nation until 1968. Since the 1968 Olympics, West Germany and East Germany have competed as separate nations.

tions. Of the 14 nations, 6 are Communist (43%) which form part of the Soviet bloc and 4 (29%) are members or former members of the United Kingdom. "Greater cultural acceptance in a sport generally yields greater number of competitors which, in turn, raises the performance levels in competition" (Gerber et al., 1974, p. 411). Cultural acceptance and public promotion of women athletes is a vital intervening factor in explaining female Olympic success. Six Communist countries have achieved extraordinary levels of female Olympic success. Bruce Bennett writes of that success:

> Some people have attributed this success to the masculine qualities of their women athletes. However, it is quite apparent that the Communist superiority has been due to giving their female athletes the same access as the men to excellent facilities, first-class coaching and extensive competition. (1975, p. 183)

Hungary and East Germany deserve special note in this Olympic *her*story. Both are relatively small countries, with populations of approximately 10 million and 17 million, respectively. Hungarian women have won 21 gold medals representing 88% of its national total. East Germany is even more astounding for it did not compete as a separate country until 1968. Thus, in just three Olympics it has accumulated 32 female gold medals which represents 78% of its national total. We can also cite Australia, which has a population of 12.5 million, for its contribution of 21 women's gold medals. However, Australia's medals are in only two of the nine possible categories in which women compete, while Hungary has medals in five of nine categories and East Germany in four of nine. Only the USSR, a country with over 20 times the population of Hungary and 17 times the population of East Germany, has a comparable record. With 61% of its gold medals contributed by women and with medals in eight of nine categories, the Soviet Union has demonstrated a consistent policy of ideological commitment to female Olympic success.

Recent Olympic history may illustrate a new twist in the pursuit of nationalism—the prestige of a nation and its way of life can be promoted simply by encouraging elite *female* athletes to assume the same roles the elite males so long have played. Since elitism is of longer duration in men's than in women's sports, nations facing the obstacles of a slow or late start in the Olympic sweepstakes have chosen to compete for prestige by *using their women*. Here, the race is not as far, as long, or as fast and the competitors "not as serious." Put bluntly, nations are learning that it is often easier to gain national recognition by deliberately concentrating their efforts on the rapid development of their female athletes. This is an excellent demonstration of how national public policy regarding female athletes can be altered when it suits the ideological purposes of the nation-state in the arena of international competition.

An even more blatant illustration of this willingness to use "the female presence" in sport to enhance national pride can be seen in the efforts of several countries to employ female impersonators and pseudohermaphrodites in the service of winning Olympic medals. According to Gerber et al. (1974), "Apparently, some of the middle European countries, in their zeal to have winning teams, either actively recruited these types of individuals, or at least, didn't discourage their participation" (p. 419).

The issue of female impersonators or pseudohermaphrodites competing in international competition came to a head in 1966 when the IAFF ordered all female track-and-field contestants to undergo a nude parade in front of female gynecologists before they were allowed to compete. At the 1966 Bucharest championships more than two hundred women had to remove their clothes and stand before a panel of judges to have their sex certified. As Tutko has noted, "It's a way of saying 'If you're this good in sports you can't be a real woman' " (Tutko, quoted in J. Kaplan, 1979a, p. 93).

Although the tests have been refined and made less personally embarrassing, female athletes in Olympic competition still must undergo this sex-test verification (Gerber et al., 1974, p. 420). These episodes continue to pose a number of crucial policy questions. Why are only women tested? If the gender of an athlete is of issue in international competition, why are the males not required to certify that they are males? The tests are primarily directed at track–and–field athletes and swimmers, not at gymnasts. Clearly this reflects a concern about the "masculinization" potential of particular sports and, conversely, the obvious "feminine" character of gymnastics.

These tests also come at the very moment when the psychological pressures of the competition itself are the greatest. Janice Kaplan relates one young competitor's reaction:

When Debbie Meyer was preparing for the Olympics at age sixteen, the idea of taking a sex test got her more panicked than any of her competitions. 'I hadn't had my period yet,' she says, 'and I started worrying that maybe there was something wrong with me.' She had her private doctor in California perform a chromosome evaluation before the Olympics, to reassure her that she hadn't *trained herself out of being female* (Kaplan, 1979a, p. 93, emphasis added).

A simpler and more humane solution would be for *all* athletes to have their private physicians complete these tests and make the results available to an official international committee.

The recounting of this sex-test controversy provides dramatic proof of the degree to which nationalistic concerns assume the highest priority in shaping sport policies.

The male impersonator is but one extreme attempt to gain national prestige in athletics. A more widely known and debated Olympic policy concerns the use and control of anabolic steroids. It is claimed that steroids "produce *virilization* in women so that menstrual trouble, hirsutism, and deepening of the voice may occur" (Gilbert, 1980, p. 196, emphasis added). The debate over anabolic steroids is not confined to women's sports, because they are employed by male athletes as well. Of note in this controversy is that reaction to the use of steroids is a function of the sex–stereotyping alteration presumably created by their use. The short–range effects of the use of anabolic steroids by men indicates an effect on "sex organs in men resulting in a reduction in spermatogamesos" [sic] (Gilbert, 1980, p. 196). As cited earlier, the use by women has the opposite effect, "virilization." The major concern seems to be the fears which steroids create about "men being men" and "women being women" rather than about certified medical ill-effects. One of the oddities of this controversy is that the East German sports scientists have discovered that for women "birth control pills, diet, and exercise have created virtually the same changes that can be managed with anabolic steroids without the danger of breaking the rules or coming back with a positive in the tests" (Gilbert, 1980, p. 205). What may be more disturbing is the fact that the use of the steroids is condemned mainly because it may confuse the sex identification of the user. Another artificial substance, a birth control pill, has the same athletic effects but does not produce the same objection because the sexual identity of the user is not confounded. The widespread feminist outrage over the long–term *health* implications of the massively used birth control pill is not even addressed. Apparently, birth control pills present less of a threat since birth control pills are only for *women*, even if those women are athletes.

Male impersonators and anabolic steroids are examples of the extreme use of women for national pride. The national sacrifice called forth by these political decisions results in extraordinary burdens on both female and male citizen–athletes. Practices such as these lead us to agree that "nationalism . . . is the villain, the lynch pin of international affairs and also of international sports" (Gilbert, 1980, p. 207). In the last section of this chapter, we will examine some international policy recommendations embedded in alternative visions of feminism. At present, we wish to underscore the serious implications of present sport policies which often go unnoticed when sport is viewed as essentially apolitical.

US Sports Policy: A Model for Women's Athletics?

Our focus in this section shifts from the international to the national level of sports policy as we briefly examine the public decisions that affect men's athletics in the US. Why men's athletics? The most obvious reply is that today, with the exception of Title IX and related legislation, almost all policy decisions regulating sport in the US has centered on men's sports. More importantly, we believe that if women's sports continue to expand at a significant rate and range of involvement, they will be subject to similar policy assumptions and decisions that already shape men's sports. That is, we expect that the historical practices and present political choices embedded in the national control of men's athletics will, consciously or otherwise, serve as guideposts and criteria for regulating women's sports programs. Our intent, therefore, is to cull together some of the major themes that reflect American public policy in men's athletics and to use them as a political context in which to make predictions about the path that women's sports is likely to take in the next decade. In order to give organization to our discussion, we will first look at policies at the national level and then examine those at the state and local levels.

US Presidents, the most widely recognized public officials, play a vital role in arranging national political priorities. By their leadership, they can place an issue before the public, make it an area of political concern, and surround it with a sense of national urgency and commitment. The presidents of the 20th Century have assumed this role in relation to physical fitness and sports. Presidents have issued proclamations and executive orders, have created councils and committees, and have used personal example to emphasize the value of physical fitness and sports for the nation's health (Zingale, 1973).

To illustrate our point, the following presidential actions reveal how pervasive has been presidential leadership in sports policy:

- In 1905 Theodore Roosevelt personally intervenes in the intercollegiate football controversy. His action leads to the formation of the NCAA.
- Two wartime presidents, Woodrow Wilson and Franklin D. Roosevelt, emphasize the importance of physical fitness for the national war effort. Roosevelt creates the Division of Physical Fitness in the Office of Defense, Health and Welfare Services.
- Dwight D. Eisenhower establishes the President's Council on Youth Fitness and endorses a nation-wide health test.
- John F. Kennedy extends the Youth Fitness Council to include adults and sets a personal example of sporting achievement and involvement.

- Lyndon B. Johnson broadens the function of the council on Fitness to include sports.
- Richard M. Nixon is identified as the nation's "Number One Fan;" he telephones coaches with suggested game strategies.
- Gerald Ford's football experiences at the University of Michigan are widely known and praised. He writes an article (Ford, 1974) about the value of sports participation.
- Jimmy Carter receives national media coverage for playing softball and jogging. The participatory trends of the late 70's and 80's are personally endorsed by the president of the United States.

These examples of the "chief policy-maker's" (Koenig, 1965) involvement with sports are just one testimony to sport's political importance and the perceived need or desire of our highest public official to shape policies affecting sport in the US.

National foreign policy also has been affected by sporting activity. The State Department frequently uses elite athletes and victorious teams as "goodwill ambassadors." Sports figures have toured the world in order to improve international relations. Sports as a vehicle of diplomacy perhaps reached its zenith in the case of the People's Republic of China. Public opinion and foreign policy were substantially altered by the "table-tennis diplomats." Ping–pong competition helped to legitimate a major political decision, one that marked a reversal of US foreign policy and lead to mutual diplomatic relations.

A major policy-making body in the US is the Congress. Not surprisingly, since 1950 over 300 pieces of legislation affecting sports have been introduced into Congress (Johnson, 1972, p. 102). However, little of this legislation ever has been enacted, primarily because of the "hands off" posture of legislators and the political and economic power of sports entrepreneurs to effectively prevent public debate about many of the policies and practices of American sports.

The primary use of the power to prevent legislative decision making and public debate occurs in the area of professional spectator sport. As Bachrach and Baratz (1968) so brilliantly argued, the ability of key interest groups to keep issues from arising in a public forum and generating public debate is a measure of their power. Professional sports entrepreneurs, syndicates, and league commissioners have become experts in the use of this form of power. The most noteworthy demonstration of this political power is the continued exemption of professional sports from the provisions of most of the antitrust legislation that was passed to prevent monopolies and cartels (Scully, 1978, p. 432). In effect, established business interests, with the support of government, have minimized competition, prevented the movement of franchises into "their" market area, and managed to incorporate or eliminate new leagues that might increase the competition for the consumer's (fan's) dollars and the worker's (player's) expertise. Corporate sport has been given a privileged status by the legislative policy makers, resulting in an erosion of the free enterprise system that allegedly rests at the heart of our political system.

A direct and dramatic result of the antitrust exemption enjoyed by professional sports is the continued existence of some version of a reserve clause. Indeed, no legislative actions ever were taken to alter the reserve clause. Rather, the recent changes in the reserve clause have occurred primarily as the result of the unionization of players. It has been their collective actions, their threatened and real strikes, and their union power which have eliminated some of the worst facets of the reserve clause. Ironically, the power of the "sports trusts" to mold political decisions and to control public policy has been countered only by the power of players' unions in private labor–management negotiations.

The courts of this country also are major sources of public decision making and policy formation. Judges do not merely interpret laws and public policies, they have a role in creating them (Dahl, 1957). Although the courts have reviewed various aspects of sport as a commercial enterprise, they also have been far too willing "to look the other way" and to allow the sporting industry to regulate itself. As early as 1922 (*Federal Baseball Club of Baltimore v. National League*, 259 U.S. 200), the courts exempted baseball from the provisions of the Sherman Anti-Trust Act. Subsequent court decisions have eroded some of the monopolistic characteristics of professional sports and diluted the "slave-like" nature of the reserve clause. However, sports too often have been treated by the courts as games rather than as the multi-million dollar businesses they are.

The national policy makers in sports, as in other spheres of public interest are more frequently the career bureaucrats, the regulatory officials, and the day-to-day administrators rather than the well-known and highly visible political elites. For example, when the Federal Communications Commission allows athletic commissioners to sell exclusive rights to broadcast sports for an entire league, to negotiate home town "blackouts," or to remove them once a stadium is sold out, they have relinquished their duty to preserve the public's access rights to view sports via the electronic media. The FCC was established in part to monitor and control the public airwaves. The Commission's action in many instances display the same "hands off" policy that pervades the courts and legislative bodies.

In general, the basic pattern of national sports policy regarding professional sports is one that allows powerful and organized groups of owners to regulate sports for primarily self-interests with minimum regard for the interest of athlete–workers and virtually no concern for the fan-citizen-taxpayer.

This pattern is repeated at the amateur level in the US. Few people today are unaware of the tremendous power exerted over amateur athletics by the NCAA, the AAU, and the USOC. These athletic bureaucracies are allowed to govern themselves and their sports programs without interference by official governmental bodies. The well-known scandals in intercollegiate athletics, the increasingly vocal complaints by amateur athletes against their governing bodies, and the perceived "failure" of American athletes at the Olympic Games has resulted in a comprehensive study of the status of amateur athletic policy in the US. In what may be a change in the direction of American sports policy, the Final Report of the President's Commission on Olympic Sports calls for more active involvement by the federal government in regulating amateur athletics. As Johnson (1978) notes in evaluating the Final Report:

> The report states that 'the federal government has never attempted to direct amateur athletics in this country nor should it.' . . . The report contains substantive recommendations—including significant public financial subsidy, the use of the armed forces to develop elite athletes, and the use of these athletes 'in service recruiting efforts, to promote the concept of a voluntary military' which tie together intimately the federal government and amateur athletics. (p.321)

We interpret this suggestion for increasing governmental involvement in amateur athletics as a measure of the continuing vulnerability of sports to be manipulated by powerful policy–making bodies, be they in the private or public sector. What is of central concern to us is the way in which certain powerful publics (e.g., TV networks, corporate advertisers, franchise owners, intercollegiate league officials, etc.) establish policies at the expense of less powerful publics (e.g., worker-athletes, student-athletes, citizen-fans).

This pattern seemingly holds true for policy making at the state and local levels as well. Indeed, given the diversity and range of public actors, settings, political units, and policy agenda items at these more local levels of government, we are disappointed by the meager efforts of political scientists to study the origins and maintenance of local sport policy. Nevertheless, even the casual student of sport and politics is aware that state and local governments often use tax revenues to fund sport stadia and other athletic facilities. We know that real estate and commercial interests mix with political forces in determining the geographical locations of sport arenas. We recognize that television coverage of local sports, on both commercial and public channels, is shaped by the resources of corporations, foundations, and other powerful interest groups. We suspect that the determination of which professional and amateur sports will have access to sports facilities is the result of a political process of establishing priorities and weighing powerful inducements and rewards. Even in small town recreational programs, we know that the pattern of access and use of community sports facilities is not random or haphazard but set by the town officials in alliance with the most "resourceful" group of organized citizens. In summary, even the most skeletal review of men's sports shows that certain "publics" are more powerful than others when it comes to shaping policy decisions. We can recognize that financial, commercial, media, political, and other special interests often dominate the ultimate content of sports policies.

To the extent that these trends in policy making are clearly part of men's sporting forms, we can anticipate some of the paths that women's sports may take in the near future. At present, few women's sports capture the public attention, the media's interest, or the advertiser's dollar to such a degree that significant government intervention has occurred. However, there already exists some parallels between the path men's sports has taken and the one women's sports is on. For example, the Connecticut Falcons Professional Women's Softball Team has been on a "goodwill ambassador tour" to the People's Republic of China; women's professional sports have been organized along similar lines as men's teams, with an even stricter reserve clause and greater owner monopoly over players; as we mentioned in chapter 6, the sluggish enforcement of Title IX and the recent co-option attempt of the AIAW by the NCAA are telling signals that women's sports will be vulnerable to similar political forces that presently govern men's programs. As women knock at the door of the sporting establishment, eager to enter and willing to play, we would strongly suggest that they not rush in blind to the political forces that will shape their participation. As we have indicated, sport is inextricably linked to political values, and public pressure. Thus, a richer grasp of the dilemmas facing the sporting woman must include a journey into the realm of public policy as it may affect women's sports. We will take the first steps of this longer journey in our final section, whose goals are to develop a feminist and humanist vision of public policy and to flesh out some of the policy implications that are embedded in varied models of feminism.

Feminist Implications for Sport Policy

We began this book by noting that there are different models of feminism, each with a unique image of woman, with an explanation of the sources of her oppression, and with a set of proposals to enlarge and enhance her personal and social existence. It is only appropriate that we end this work by exploring as concretely as possible the wide ranging and often competing social and political choices that confront women as they continue to press for full participation in the world of sport.

Before we discuss the various policy implications arising from different visions of feminism, we must address ourselves to a more fundamental task which involves a challenge to the conventional understanding of public policy and an invitation to rethink the taken–for–granted assumptions about the form and dynamics of policy making.

Feminist and humanist social thinkers have begun to recognize that the traditional political science definition of public policy as the "course of action that public officials take to try to deal with a particular area of concern" (Watson, 1981, p. 524) is a narrow and, to a degree, an inaccurate reflection of the realities of the public policy process and its outcomes. As Zillah Eisenstein argues, we must understand that this conventional view holds

> that the important political and social decisions are made within government, narrowly defined. This view does not understand *how* the governmental realm is connected to the power relations of patriarchy and capitalism, nor that many decisions that affect our lives are not made through the governmental party process. (Eisenstein, 1981, p. 180)

Specifically, we must be aware that the "public officials"—the authoritative decision makers who are identifiable to the people (e.g., elected representatives)—are not the sole, or even primary, source of public policies affecting our sporting endeavors. Most public policy is made by the unseen and unknown bureaucrats and functionaries who exercise a wide range of discretionary power. Thus, if women are to affect sport policy, they must be able to identify and influence the hidden, "street-level bureaucrats" (Lipsky, 1980) whose actions become the public policies directly affecting citizens.

A major implication of this view of public policy is the recognition that government policy will only be effectively implemented to the degree that nongovernmental institutions and their structures, processes, and values are also in tune with the policy aims of governmental bodies. We recognize this reality when, as social scientists, we explain the failure of three decades of civil rights legislation to successfully eliminate racism. This reality must also be grasped by those women and men who wish to reform or radically alter the sporting institution and women's place in it. We must remind ourselves that true changes in public policy can only mean a change in the way people, individually and collectively, act, think, and feel. No governmental policy, by itself, can accomplish this feat. As Eisenstein so accurately puts it:

Laws, however in and of themselves, cannot change women's lives. It is time to move beyond the vision that equality of opportunity and freedom of choice can be created by legal reform alone. It must be reinforced by structural changes as well. (Eisenstein, 1981, p. 196)

Furthermore, official public policy makers too often define as an "area of concern" only the demands of the more organized, powerful groups in society. The demands of these special interest groups are camouflaged as the public concern, the public interest. Public policy thus becomes a euphemism in which policy is seemingly separated from the realities and dynamics of politics and power. For example, organized groups such as professional sports franchises make demands on public resources which then get answered. These are important demands because the owners have the power, the influence, and the access to guarantee that official decision makers know they are a "public" which cannot be ignored. If women wish to influence public policy in sport or in other areas, they must recognize that the female sex has not been a "public being" very long, has had little experience with the realities of power, and has little knowledge of where and how to make demands that will initiate a response to their "areas of concern."

Public policy is also the failure to act. A decision not made, a demand not heard, a silent public, all afford policy makers the freedom to listen and to respond to those vocal and powerful interest groups. Our review of the history of women's sports testifies to this harsh reality. The sporting inequities within society have been and continue to be enormous. Yet women and girls do not constitute a vocal public. The sole national public agenda item still remains Title IX. Even that "breakthrough" is under attack. The Reagan Administration has begun "a new assault on this simple law of nondiscrimination" (Women's Sports Foundation, October, 1981, p. 42). The assault is not likely to take the form of a repeal of the act. Rather, the tactic is likely to be nonenforcement. A policy of inaction, (when action is called for) is nonetheless a policy, a public posture, a position which indicates the power of inactivity to override official legislative mandates.

Finally, we in the United States must remember that from its origins in the philosophy of John Locke and other liberal political thinkers, the official ideology of the liberal state emphasizes the inviolable separation of private life from "public intrusion." This ideological posture effectively separates the private and public realms, making them appear to be unconnected when in reality they are inextricably linked together; it encourages an exaggerated public concern with civil rights and legal reforms as the ultimate solution to social problems; it generates a "privatization" of public issues, suggesting that each individual must solve his or her private problems by making use of available personal resources. However, the personal problems facing citizens—employment, health, education, housing, discrimination, etc.—are anchored in larger cultural, social, and institutional arrangements. Legal and political changes alone will not result in equality in other spheres of life. The right to unionize did not give workers safe working conditions, the right to vote did not give women educational equality, the Civil Rights Act of 1964 did not give minorities occupational equality. Unless women and men remain conscious of the limitations that result from this artificial separation of the public and private realms, they will continue to remain frustrated by the failure of governmental policies to affect significant changes in their personal lives.

With these general criticisms of traditional views of public policy in mind, we can now turn our attention to the more specific application of them with reference to women's involvement in sport. To order our discussion, we will deal separately with the four visions of feminism that have supplied a framework for this book. In each case, we will pull out the likely sports policy recommendations emerging from the assumptions of each of the models. Specific reference will be made to international sport policy and, within the United States, to policies affecting the family, the school, and the mass media.

Liberal Feminist Sports Policy

For liberal feminists and their foremost theoretical proponent Betty Friedan (1981), the problem for women remains the acquisition of equal opportunity. The difficulty for the sporting woman, as for the political woman, or the working woman, is that she has not achieved her full rights as a citizen. Inhibited by governmental failure to enforce the basic political and economic rights of US citizenship, women must concentrate their efforts on equalizing access to these rights, including equal access to sporting opportunities. This view of the liberal position would lead to specific policy recommendations.

At the international level of public policy, the liberal feminists have demanded that women be added to the USOC and the IOC. With women on the policy-making bodies for international sports competition, liberal feminists believe that more women's events will be added, the number of female participants will be increased and the opportunities for an equal representation by women will be more likely. Women on such bodies will represent the interests of their athletic sisters and actively promote an international and national program which does not discriminate against women. These members may not always be successful in being heard; they may not lobby for the inclusion of sports like boxing or wrestling for women, but they will signal symbolically and substantively the arrival of women on the international sports scene.

If we turn to the family and consider public decisions to foster its equalization of sporting opportunities for males and females, most liberal feminists take a very cautious stance. Accepting the separation of the public and the private, the liberal feminist considers the family the primary link between the private individual and the public sphere. However, liberals for the most part believe that the public sector should maintain a "hands off" policy toward the family as an institution. Liberal feminists would encourage parents to be aware that game, toys, and equipment for sports should accommodate girls as well as boys; that parents should encourage equal amounts of athletic participation and spectatorship for their female and male children; that parents should expose children of both sexes to "heroic" stories of female athletic achievements; and that as role models both parents should celebrate the joy of sports. In short, liberal feminists believe that reflective adults can evaluate the merits and limitations of their children's involvement in sport and can present sports to their children in nonsexist ways.

For liberals the family is viewed as a private subunit of a political community. Parents, as residents and taxpayers, should be informed about the recreational and sports programs provided by the community in its parks, gyms, recreational centers, and especially its schools. Parents could organize to apply pressure on local decision makers to insure that sports programs and activities do not discriminate against girls and women.

A particularly crucial area of concern for liberal feminists is the school system. They argue that Title IX legislation must be implemented and enforced with the greatest rigor possible, including supporting legal action and withholding of funds from schools violating the spirit as well as the letter of the law. As far as school sports are concerned, liberal feminists' recommendations include support of "watch-dog" agencies to monitor compliance with Title IX, establishment of lobbying offices near the political decision making centers, representation of girls' and women's positions before regulatory agencies and official hearings, and a generally watchful stance to make sure that the advances which have been made in school sports programs are not eroded.

Liberal feminists are aware that the next two to three years in women's intercollegiate athletics may prove a crucial turning point. The opportunity of admission into the men's sports bureaucracies like the NCAA holds the danger of co-optation and a symbolic victory matched by a substantive defeat. If women choose the option of full participation in formerly all male sporting bureaucracies, as many liberal feminists would recommend, they must be able to insure that women's programs receive their "piece of the pie." Equality of resource allocation for coaching, salaries, facilities, travel, budgets, and schedules, to name just a few, will be assured only if women assume some of the positions of power in all school sports bureaucracies. They believe that the correction of past abuses and oversights is possible from within the present structures; they believe that nonsexist men, as well as women, will work to promote athletic programs which all recognize as equitable and just.

Liberal feminists, precisely because they do not see any inherent structural impediments to women's equality, can promote women in sport and fully expect other institutions—the family, school, media, business, and government—to support their just goals. Even now, liberals point to media coverage and corporate sponsorship of female athletic endeavors which generate the same interest within the viewing or buying public as men's endeavors do. They expect that corporate sponsorship, prize monies, and media coverage will naturally increase as girls and women achieve a longer history of participation, a wider range of sports involvement, and higher levels of athletic proficiency. For a liberal feminist there is no reason to suspect the aims, motives, or commitment of those who control the media, the business community, and the sporting establishment. They are simply responsive to market demands. Thus, liberals argue that now that most of the legal and social barriers for female athletes have been eroded in this "decade of women," the rise of the sporting woman is inevitable and the corporate and media attention will of necessity follow.

As we mentioned earlier, liberalism presupposes progress as an inevitable by-product of legal and political reform. It postulates the viability of working through the present political system to achieve equality of opportunity for all. It understands that public attitudes and values may lag behind the more progressive elements of the women's liberation movement, but it remains convinced of the educability of the public and optimistic about political support for policies that are self–evidently right and just. Liberal feminists caution that social change takes time, but they believe that in the long run the growing public demand for equal sport participation cannot be resisted.

As we now turn to the policy recommendations of Marxist, radical, and socialist feminists, we find neither the optimism about the inevitability of women's progress in sport nor the specificity of proposals that we found in liberal feminism. The sport policy recommendations of these perspectives must necessarily be more suggestive than illustrative. Since each framework requires a more fundamental change in the cultural and social arrangements within society than the liberal framework, the specific contours of new sporting forms will be necessarily difficult to anticipate or foretell. Nonetheless, we offer some general themes and directions for sport as it would evolve within each of these three more transforming frameworks.

Marxist Feminist Sports Policy

Feminists who adhere to Marxist tenets stress the crucial role of economic power in shaping all other features of societal life. Their understanding of the roots of women's oppression rests in a recognition of how the structural interest of economic elites serve to deny access to social resources and rewards by the economically less powerful. Marxist feminists identify the unequal distribution of wealth as the foundation for all other sources of social inequality. They hold the view that all public policy serves the interests of economic elites, and they predict that any changes in such policies will only be effected to the degree that these interests are not threatened. Thus, Marxist feminists believe that policy and institutional reforms constitute a cruel and tragic hoax; they argue that only a deep-rooted revolution of present societal and cultural arrangements will ever succeed in producing true equality.

Given these assumptions, we see that Marxist feminism contains substantially different strategies for altering sports policies. At the international level, Marxist feminists would point with satisfaction to the actions of Communist countries in promoting female Olympic success, due to a national policy grounded in Marxist ideology which encourages athletic achievements regardless of the class origin and sex of the athletes. Since Communist Olympic athletes are government–sponsored, the opportunity structure for all athletes is far greater, and the consequent ability to identify and to train those with exceptional talent is less restricted than in capitalist countries. For the Marxist feminist, the results of the Olympics speak for themselves. Once the true source of economic oppression is removed, the elite status of the Olympic athlete is based solely on performance, and women as well as men can achieve their full athletic potential. They compare this situation with that of capitalist nations which, as presently structured, give only athletes from the privileged class such opportunity for Olympic and international success.

Marxist feminists' sports policy recommendations at the national level follow inexorably from their economic class analysis. They argue that the family's sport environment is bound by its primary status as an economic unit. The male and female children of wealthy families will always have more games, superior facilities, coaching, and equipment than the children of the working classes. They note that sport has been and continues to be class–specific and that no amount of parental encouragement can eliminate the disadvantage that a female from a poor family can experience in such expensive and elitist sports as tennis, golf, swimming, and gymnastics. Only public policies aimed at the destruction of economic privilege can substantially improve the position of the working class female and male experience in sport. Children from elite families will always have greater access to sport and its rewards under the present system of economic inequality. Parents who wish to insure equal access to sport for their daughters should, according to this perspective, concentrate their efforts on redistributing economic privilege—equality in sports will inevitably follow.

The themes which dominate the Marxist feminist perspective of the family are repeated and heightened by a consideration of the educational sphere. The close link between sport and school in the United States is said to perpetuate and intensify the class bias that is integral to maintaining the capitalist society. School athletic programs afford more sporting opportunities for middle and upper class girls and boys, at all levels of education, than for working class students.

In a class-based society all schools are unequal. Schools which educate the youth of the working class do not have sports programs (to say nothing of educational programs) that are as well financed, equipped, or extensive as those for the upper class. Marxist feminists might seek to sever the link between sports and schools. Sports programs could, in an economically socialized nation, be structured into the work environment, the local community, and sporting clubs that give both sexes true opportunities to participate and excel in athletics.

A similar indictment of the media and commercial dimensions of sport follow from this Marxist feminist analysis. Female athletes, like their male counterparts, will receive corporate funding and media attention only to the degree that their sports achievements result in economic benefits to those who own and control these institutions. Thus, Marxist feminists would reject all sport policies which would only benefit economically profitable female sports; they would challenge the very connection between profit and sport as it is played out between big business and the mass media. Marxist feminists despair of any policy changes that merely adapt themselves to the present capitalist system, even if it means that some women will be able to participate more fully in sport. Since Marxist feminists locate women's oppression as a by-product of economic oppression, they argue for a revolutionary restructuring of the economy as the major change that will insure, among other things, equal sport participation for all women.

Radical Feminist Sports Policy

As we noted in chapter 1, radical feminism contains a more variegated and amorphous mix of assumptions, premises, and theoretical postures than the other three feminist frameworks. Some radical feminists stress the need for women to control the forms of biological reproduction as a solution to their oppression, some call for a woman-identified existence as the answer to male domination, and others demand a radical transformation of culture and social organization itself as the only path toward women's liberation. Although members of the radical feminist community do not share a unified set of ideas about the specific causes of and solutions to the problems of women's secondary status, they do agree that patriarchy is its root source. Unlike liberals, radical feminists reject the possibility that sexism can be eradicated by reforming the structures and dynamics of established social institutions. They believe that such reforms would merely co-opt women while leaving intact the cultural and ideological underpinnings of patriarchy which they see as the fundamental source of women's oppression. For similar reasons, they also reject the solutions of Marxist feminists, who assume that patriarchy is primarily a result of capitalism; radical feminists believe that patriarchy is easily adapted to any range of political and economic forms. Thus, radical feminists call for a rejection of patriarchy, including its ideological justification of male supremacy; its celebration of such "masculine principles" as domination, control, and rationality; and those social forms that support patriarchy, such as enforced heterosexuality, gender polarization, and the nuclear family.

What are the possible implications of this model of feminism for altering present sports policies for women? At the international level, radicals would reject the very idea of organizing the Olympics and other athletic contests around nation-states, with their stress on nationalism, militarism, and politics, and their exaggerated emphasis on the instrumental, standarized, rationalized, and quantifiable dimensions of sporting endeavor. Although some radical feminists would reject all organized, hierarchically structured athletic contests as essentially patriarchal, others would support the formation of alternative forms of athletic competition. We can only speculate as to the possible shape these contests would take, but it seems likely that participants would not compete in terms of their ascribed categories, such as sex, age, or national origin; that the sports themselves would be restructured to allow for the recognition of expressive and aesthetic attributes as well as technical and rational ones; that the aim of such contests would include sociability, self-actualization, health, and participation as well as the quantifiable score. Joining voices with those in the New Games Foundation movement and other humanist critics of the present status of international athletic competition, radicals would support those alternative approaches to play, games, and sport that transcend the patriarchal values and forms of contemporary international sports.

Perhaps the major national policy concerns that radical feminists have regarding sport can be stated as the need to create new sports or modify existing ones so that they celebrate and inform women's experience, women's world, and women's consciousness. As we have noted earlier, the present games and sports that dominate in the family, the school, and the media emerge out of the awareness and experience of the men who created and shaped them. A clear implication of radical feminist thought would be to challenge women, in conjunction with or in isolation from men, to claim their own games, to mold them more specifically to the female body, to have them resonate with newly experienced women's consciousness, or to have them better approximate the cluster of values that characterize women's experience in the world.

What might this mean on a concrete level? Again, we can only venture some guesses. For example, it might mean continued family encouragement of traditional girls' games such as hopscotch and double-dutch; it could include the development of synchronized swimming and rhythmic gymnastics as recreational and sporting options in the school; it might ask that media coverage of sport shift its attention to include a recognition of the expressive elements of both male and female athletics; it might reveal itself in the adaptations that women have made to traditional male sports such as body-building.

In general, we understand that the implications of radical feminism center on encouraging the widest diversity possible of women's sporting experience, insisting that sport become a human endeavor that captures the unique needs and interests of all types of women, and extending radical feminism to include those women who, by virtue of race, age, social class, weight, sexual preference, life-style, and so on, remain excluded, either by force or choice, from the world of sport. Although the philosophy of radical feminism does not lend itself as easily as the Marxist and liberal models to specific policy positions, we believe this is primarily due to its sweeping rejection of virtually all societal forms and forces as essentially patriarchal. Given this position, radical feminism requires that women virtually re-create social existence; as Mary Daly would say, "It is both discovery and creation of a world other than patriarchy" (1978, p. 1). Although this challenge may appear to be ludicrously utopian to some people, to others it opens up the only real possibility of ever uprooting the seeds of sexism. Indeed, the perceived weakness of radical feminism to provide a coherent and concrete list of policy recommendations may turn out to be its ultimate strength. Out of this open-ended dialogue within the radical community, out of radical feminism's call for the discovery and creation of personal and public choices for sport may come the catalyst for reclaiming our relationship to sport.

Socialist Feminist Sports Policy

The major contribution of socialist feminism is to call attention to the dual role of economic oppression and patriarchy as limiting women's full participation in social life. They argue that privilege based on class and privilege based on sex are interrelated and that both must be abolished. Their emphasis on the need to eradicate "the sexual-class structure" (Eisenstein, 1981, p. 231) serves to integrate the contributions of Marxist and radical feminist thought.

For socialist feminists, a major change in international sport policy would include the de-politicization of the Olympic Games, using it instead as a global forum to engender female (as well as male) athletic camaraderie and achievement. They would push for the extension of sporting opportunities to the widest range of the female population, not merely to those with greater economic resources. They would encourage the incorporation of women into all sporting contests and would challenge the present gender biases that confront women athletes from most parts of the world.

We can illustrate the tenets of socialist feminism at the national level by examining the controversy raised over the issue of women's "half-court" basketball. This version of basketball, which is a venerable tradition in Iowa, among other states, is an adaptation of the men's games; it is traditionally played with six players on a team, three forwards and three guards, each restricted to one-half of the court and to only offensive or defensive play respectively. This game, when compared to the contemporary version played by men and an increasing number of women, differs significantly in structure, rules, strategy, complexity, requisite skills, and the like. Some feminists have argued that this style of basketball is an inferior, truncated version of "real" basketball and schools should replace it as a symbolic affirmation of women's ability to play the "real" game. Other feminists have pointed to the fact that the communities, schools, and media that still sponsor the half-court game unwittingly limit the prospects of their best players to receive college basketball offers and the other rewards that attend such opportunities. Other feminists argue that half-court basketball should be preserved and supported as one of the few athletic forms that presents an alternative to the men's game and reflects women's unique approach to a sport.

Clearly, this one case illustrates the tensions and complexities that arise from trying to arrive at consistent policy recommendations within the feminist community. Socialist feminists would support the Marxist position that access to a college education should be structurally available to all citizens, not just those who can serve the athletic and economic interests of institutions of higher learning. They would also join the radical feminists in viewing the half-court game as part of the small tradition of female athletic experience that has been allowed to flourish, at least regionally, in this country. They would be less sympathic with the liberal approach, which assumes that progress is defined by accommodating to the inducements of present institutional arrangements and forces.

In the broadest terms, socialist feminists recognize the deep-rooted, complex, and often conflicting implications of alternative visions of feminism. They are acutely aware that any concrete policy changes might overlook significant "publics" that constitute the female half of the population. Their guiding principle for sport policy is a vigilant concern that any specific policy should reduce the class biases and gender restraints of the past. Thus, they see no victory in a revised community recreational program that ignores the needs of the women who are elderly or poor as it makes available a field for the high school varsity softball team; they doubt the wisdom of expanded college athletic budgets that allocate funds for female trainers but fail to recruit minority athletes to join varsity teams; they hesitate to support corporate policies that equalize prize money for male and female competitors but leave unprotected the rights of lesbians in sport.

To be a socialist feminist is to be humble in the face of the bewildering web of contradictions that surround any given policy suggestion; it is to be patient in the realization that policy changes will take longer than the enthusiasm that their proponents would have us believe; it is to be cautious about the unanticipated consequences of policy that is quickly implemented; and it is to be optimistic about the possibility that women can transform sport into something better for all its participants.

Notes

1. This fact has led some to argue that there are no such things as "female sports." To this Simri (1979) responds:

    until this very day we do not have a typical female sport on the Olympic program (if one is to ignore such events as the balance beam or the uneven parallel bars) which is to say a sport in which only women take part. Why, for instance, should modern gymnastics and synchronized swimming . . . be kept out of the Olympic program? One has to pose the question whether they are kept out to prevent a female majority in the Olympic gymnastics and swimming events, as some—sometimes fanatical—women claim, or whether the I.O.C. is reluctant, as Lord Killinan claims, to introduce additional events that cannot be judged objectively, in order to avoid the repetition of refereeing scandals of recent Olympic Games. In any case, the situation creates a dilemma as women excel in rhythmic movement and in aesthetic expression, yet these, which are one of their specific contributions to the world of sports, cannot be measured objectively. (p. 17)

    Of course, the other dilemma is why must such events be measured at all?

2. We have excluded the Winter Olympics since geographic location has a larger bearing on a nation's ability to compete and excel in the Winter Games than in the Summer ones.

3. Luschen (1967) found that citizens of predominantly Protestant countries were more likely to win medals than nationals of other religious affiliations. He also discovered that Protestants were more likely to be participants in individualistic elite sports. By contrast, team sports had a disproportionate number of Catholics. Seppanen (Note 16) found that peoples with "inner-worldly" religious orientations (e.g., Confucian, Islamic, Hebrew and Christian) fared better than "other-worldly" (e.g., Hindu and Buddhist). Within the "inner-worldly" groups Seppanen discovered the same Catholic-Protestant division as did Luschen.

Jokl (1964) found a high correlation between Olympic success and low national death rates, low infant mortality rates, and high per capita income. Novikow and Maximenko (1972) found similar correlations for per capita national income, caloric consumption, life expectancy, literacy, urbanization and total size of the population. Pooley et al. (Note 17) attributed success more directly to concrete political decisions: political elites mobilized, encouraged and subsidized athletes to achieve sporting success.

These are just a few of the social science studies which have explored the correlates of national success in the Olympic Games.

Epilogue

The place of women in sport will be influenced as much by the work of academicians as by public policy decisions. In fact, the body of theory and research generated by physical educators and scholars in the natural and social sciences has an impact far beyond the academic community.

Scientific knowledge about sport is slowly spreading throughout the society. For example, sport scholars write books, teach courses, testify at government hearings, are interviewed by the media, and act as consultants to athletic organizations. Their ideas and opinions become part of the accumulated wisdom concerning the nature and dynamics of sport in our society. As the scientific study of sport develops greater sophistication and gains more legitimation, we expect that sport scholars will be even more influential in shaping future public opinion. We will address the implications of this situation for women's sport with respect to the sociological study of sport, but our remarks are meant to apply to other disciplines as well.

It is perhaps fortunate for women that the sociological investigation of sport in North America is barely 15 years old. In that period we saw, as a result of the women's movement, a critical reexamination of sociological knowledge in more established subfields, a reexamination that seriously questions the validity and generalizability of sociological ideas about the family, social stratification, bureaucracy, social change, crime, and work, to name but a few (Millman & Kanter, 1975).

In a now-classic article, Jessie Bernard (1973) identified the sexist bias that pervades the way we organize our ideas about and study social phenomena. The novice status of sport sociology means that it has a chance to avoid the sexist shortcomings of its sister subfields and to engage in theory and research that includes women as social beings, that gives equal emphasis to the spheres of "women's world," and that critically examines the sexist assumptions of any sociological approach to sport.

As we indicated in chapter 4, this task involves a rethinking of the conceptual models, theoretical issues, and research techniques that inform sport sociology. As they venture into the world of sport, sociologists must be especially sensitive to the subtle and unconscious ways in which sexism pervades this scholarly enterprise.

However, sport sociologists with a humanist orientation confront a major dilemma as they attempt to bring to their subfield the legitimacy and prestige that the more established areas of academic inquiry enjoy. On the one hand, Andrew Yiannakis (1979, p. 1), responding to the present status of sport sociology, calls for a "paradigm war" involving a debate over different theoretical approaches to sport. He decries the "current obsession with 'piece-meal' quantitative research" (1979, p. 1) and courageously insists on an intellectual debate over the prevailing concepts, theories, and values embedded in sport sociology.

This request for an open-ended, honest, and wide-ranging exchange of theoretical ideas and research designs is especially critical for the emergence of nonsexist approaches to sport. Much of the present work in sport sociology (whether carried out by symbolic interactionists, functionalists, or conflict, Marxist, and systems theorists) still treats as unproblematic the nature of sport as a masculine domain. There is a general, unstated acceptance of sexist sporting structures and processes and a willingness to leave unexamined the full exploration of a feminist perspective in sport sociology.

The enormity of the task of elaborating a feminist approach to the social scientific study of sport has been suggested in the pages of this book. There are certainly more questions to be debated than answers offered. And the task probably will fall disproportionately greater on women sociologists (as it has, for different reasons, on other "outsiders" within the discipline) to articulate this perspective in sport sociology. In this regard, we should heed the warning of Daniels (1975) concerning sexism within sociology:

> Women appear (in sociology) only as they are relevant to a world governed by male principles and interests. To the extent that women sociologists accept that perspective, they are alienated from their own personal experience. *They speak a language, use theories, and select methods in which they are excluded or ignored.* (p. 346, emphasis added)

The other side of the dilemma concerns a valid desire that sport sociology assumes its rightful place within the discipline as a respected and contributing field of inquiry. In an assessment of the status of the sociology of sport, John W. Loy (1980) identifies some of the barriers to full and legitimate acceptance of this sub-field. According to Loy (1980),

> the low status of sport sociology is not going to rise unless the quality of the existent research literature greatly improves. The most prestigious sociology journals characteristically only accept first-rate articles; thus sport sociologists must do first-rate work *that is capable of being published in the elite sociological journals.* (p. 102, emphasis added)

We must, however, question this assumption that "the most prestigious sociology journals only accept first-rate articles." We must understand more fully the criteria used by these elite journals to determine the "publishability" of an article. Exactly what kinds of articles are most likely to be accepted for publication in these prestigious journals?

Fortunately, an answer to this question is provided in a significant study by Spector and Faulkner (1980) of five new journals that have appeared over the past three years in sociology: *Human Studies, Humanity and Society, Qualitative Sociology, Studies in Symbolic Interaction,* and *Symbolic Interaction.* These journals, according to Spector and Faulkner (1980):

> are *qualitative* in their preference for research methods using fieldwork, participant observation, and interviewing; *interactionist* in their preference of micro-sociological and situational analyses; *humanistic* in their interest in reflexive sociology, the ethical implications of social research, and their critique of positivism. (p. 477, emphasis added)

An analysis of the content of the two leading journals in sociology—the *American Sociological Review* and the *American Journal of Sociology*—shows that these journals actually publish very few works in qualitative, interactionist, and humanistic sociology. According to data provided by Spector and Faulkner (1980), "three out of every four articles in the two leading sociology journals were empirically based, noninteractionist pieces" (p. 478). The authors identify mainstream sociology's major source of data collection as "the interview survey, one-shot, large scale 'observation', supplemented by official yearbooks, statistics, and the census" (1980, p. 478). Thus, both in theoretical and normative orientation and in research methodology, there exist important differences between the kinds of articles being accepted for publication in the elite journals and those being published in the newly created qualitative journals.

These differences are best understood when we contrast the nature of mainline sociology with that of the "minority" perspectives in sociology (Lofland, 1976, p. 5)—the qualitative, interactionist and humanistic perspectives. According to Spector and Faulkner (1980):

> Mainline sociology in print is the sociology of complex design and multivariate analysis, statistical techniques that have led to the emphasis on distributions and relationships between *variables* rather than the structure between social actors. (p. 479, original italics)

In contrast, Spector and Faulkner (1980) describe the different emphases in qualitative sociology in this way:

> While qualitative research designs and modes of analyses may be less elaborate than those in the mainline journals, *the original data are of much higher quality and more closely tied to the reality under study.* They also necessarily bring the researcher into more intimate contact with the phenomenon of interest, the research 'subjects', and the environment in which transactions take place. (p. 479, emphasis added)

We believe that the emergence of qualitative journals represents a vigorous effort to extend avenues for publication to a way of doing sociology that steadily has been blocked by the dominant journals in the discipline. Further, we believe that the study of sport, of women in sport, and the elaboration of a feminist perspective in sport sociology cannot be gained by using the quantitative, large-scale, statistically sophisticated designs of mainstream sociology. Both Andrew Yiannakis (1979) in sociology and Rainer Martens (1979) in psychology have called for a halt to these premature, methodologically complex but theoretically vacant approaches to sport studies.

We strongly support this position and believe we should proceed with extreme caution in following the advice of Loy that sport sociologists should do work "that is capable of being published in the elite sociological journals" (1980, p. 102). Since elite journals tend to reject precisely the kinds of theory and research that would enhance our understanding of sport, we should fight for the inclusion of such works rather than doing the kinds of studies that are acceptable to these journals. We also should publish in journals that are open to the wide range of theoretical perspectives and research choices that characterize sociology as a complex, pluralistic and critical discipline.

Reference Notes

1. Theberge, N. *Some factors associated with socialization into the role of professional women golfer.* Paper presented at the 9th Canadian Symposium of the Psycho-Motor Learning and Sport Psychology Conference, Banff, Alberta, October 26-28, 1977.
2. Birrell, S. *Achievement related motives and sport participation in high school and college.* Paper presented at the Women and Sport Conference, Temple University, Philadelphia, 1976.
3. Harris, D.V. *The social self and competitive self of the female athlete.* Paper presented at the third international symposium on the sociology of Sport, Waterloo, Ontario, Canada, 1971.
4. Layman, E.M. *Attitudes toward sports for girls and women in relation to masculinity-femininity stereotypes of women athletes.* Paper presented at Symposium of the American Association for the Advancement of Science, Dallas, TX, December 17, 1968.
5. Hall, M.A. *Sport, sex roles and sex identity.* Paper presented at the 1st Annual Conference of the North American Society for the Sociology of Sport, Denver, CO, October 16-19, 1980.
6. Power, T.G., & Parke, R.D. *Toward a taxonomy of father-infant and mother-infant play patterns.* Papers presented at the Biennial Meeting of the Society for Research in Child Development, San Francisco, March 1979.
7. Kleiber, D.A. *Sex differences and leisure behavior.* Paper presented at Research Symposium of National Recreation and Park Association, New Orleans, LA, October 1979.
8. Kleiber, D.A., Barnett, L.A., & Wade, M.G. *Playfulness and the family context.* Paper presented at SPRE Research Symposium of National Recreation and Park Association, Miami, October 15, 1978.
9. Metheney, E. *Where will you go from here?* Paper presented at North Central Regional Conference of the Athletic and Recreation Federation of College Women, Des Moines, IA, March 1964.
10. Greendorfer, S.L. *A social learning approach to female sport involvement.* Paper presented at the American Psychological Association, Washington, DC, September 1976.

11. Greendorfer, S.L. *Female socialization into sport: An in-depth analysis.* Paper presented at Eastern Psychological Association, New York, April 24, 1981.

12. Orlick, T.D. *Family sports environment and early sports participation.* Paper presented at the Fourth Canadian Psychomotor Learning and Sports Psychology Symposium, University of Waterloo, Waterloo, Ontario, Canada, 1972.

13. Kenyon, G.S., & Knoop, J.C. *The viability and cross-cultural invariance of a reduced social role-social system model of sport socialization.* Paper presented at the 9th World Congress of Sociology, Uppsala, Sweden, August 14-19, 1978.

14. Greendorfer, S.L., & Lewko, J.H. *Children's socialization into sport: A conceptual and empirical analysis.* Paper presented at 9th World Congress of Sociology, Uppsala, Sweden, August 14-19, 1978.

15. Pudelkiewicz, E. *Sport consciousness as an essential component of involvement in sport and socialization.* Paper presented at the Third International Symposium on Sociology of Sport, Waterloo, Ontario, Canada, August 22-28, 1971.

16. Seppanen, P. *The role of competitive sports in different societies.* Paper presented at the 7th World Congress of the International Sociological Association, Varna, Bulgaria, September 1970.

17. Pooley, O. et al. *Winning at the Olympics: A quantitative analysis of the impact of a range of socio-economic, politico-military, growth rate and educational variables.* Presented at the annual conference of the APHERA, Charlottestown, Prince Edward Island, Canada, November 1975.

References

ABERLE, D.F. Culture and socialization. In F.L.K. Hsu (Ed.), *Psychological anthropology: Approaches to culture and personality.* Homewood, IL: The Dorsey Press, 1961.

ADLER, F. The United States. In F. Adler (Ed.), *The incidence of female criminology in the contemporary world.* New York: New York University Press, 1981.

ADRIAN, M., & Brame, J. (Eds.). *NAGWS Research Report* (Vol. 3). Washington, DC: American Alliance for Health, Physical Education and Recreation, 1977.

ALDERMAN, R.B. *Psychological behavior in sport.* Philadelphia: W.B. Saunders, 1974.

ALLEN, D. Self concept and the female participant. In D. Harris (Ed.), *Women and sport: A national research conference.* Penn State HPER Research Series No. 2, 1972.

ALPER, R.B., & Greenberger, E. Relationship of picture structure to achievement motivation in college women. *Journal of Personality and Social Psychology,* 1967, *7,* 362.

ANDERSON, A. Status of minority women in the association of intercollegiate athletics for women. Unpublished master's thesis, Temple University, 1979.

ANDERSON, K.B. Nobody bowls anymore. *Women's Sports,* March 1979, pp. 35-57.

ANGELL, R. Sharing the beat. *The New Yorker,* April 9, 1979, pp. 46ff.

ARDREY, R. *The territorial imperative.* New York: Atheneum, 1966.

ARENDT, H. *The human condition.* Chicago: University of Chicago Press, 1958.

ASSOCIATION for Intercollegiate Athletics for Women. *Information Sheet.* Washington, DC: AIAW, no date.

ATCHLEY, R. *The social forces in later life* (2nd ed.). Belmont, CA: Wadsworth, 1977.

ATKINSON, J.W. Motivational determinants of risk-taking behavior. In J.W. Atkinson & N.T. Feather (Eds.), *A theory of achievement motivation.* New York: Wiley, 1966.

ATKINSON, J.W. The mainsprings of achievement-oriented activity. In J.W. Atkinson & J.O. Raynor (Eds.), *Motivation and achievement.* New York: Halsted, 1974.

ATKINSON, J.W. & Feather, N.T. (Eds.), *A theory of achievement motivation.* New York: Wiley, 1966.

ATWELL, R.H. Some reflections on collegiate athletics. *Educational Record,* Fall 1979, **60**, 367-373.

BACHRACH, P., & Baratz, M. Two faces of power. In W.D. Hawley (Ed.), *The search for community power.* Englewood Cliffs, NJ: Prentice-Hall, 1968.

BALAZS, E.K. Psycho-social study of outstanding female athletes. *Research Quarterly,* 1975, **46**, 267-273.

BANDURA, A. Influence of model's reinforcement contingencies on the acquisition of imitative responses. *Journal of Personality and Social Psychology,* 1965, **1**, 589-595.

BANDURA, A. *Aggression: A social learning analysis.* Englewood Cliffs, NJ: Prentice-Hall, 1973.

BARRY, H. III, Bacon, M.D., & Child, I.I. A cross-cultural survey of some sex differences in socialization. *Journal of Abnormal Social Psychology,* 1957, **55**, 327-332.

BARTON, R. *Philippine pagans.* London: George Routledge, 1938.

BAUMRIND, D. From each according to her ability. *School Review,* February 1972, **80**, 161-195.

BECKER, H.S. Whose side are we on. *Social Problems,* 1967, **14**, 239-247.

BEISSER, A.R. Modern man and sports. In J.T. Talamini & C.H. Page (Eds.), *Sport and society.* Boston: Little, Brown, 1973.

BEM, S. The measurement of psychological androgyny. *Journal of Consulting and Clinical Psychology,* 1974, **42**, 155.

BEM, S.L. *Beyond androgyny: Some presumptuous prescriptions for a liberated sexual identity.* Keynote address for APA-NIMH conference on the research needs of women, Madison, Wisconsin, May 1975. (a)

BEM, S. Sex role adaptability: One consequence of psychological androgyny. *Journal of Personality and Social Psychology,* 1975, **31**, 634. (b)

BEM, S.L. Theory and measurement of androgyny: A reply to the Pedhazur-Tetenbaum and Locksley-Colton critiques. *Journal of Personality and Social Psychology,* 1979, **37**, 1047-54.

BEM, S., Martyna, W., & Watson, C. Sex typing and androgyny: Further explorations of the expressive domain. *Journal of Personality and Social Psychology,* 1976, **34**.

BEND, E. *The impact of athletic participation on academic and career aspiration and achievement.* New Brunswick: National Football Foundation and Hall of Fame, 1968.

BENNETT, A. Ladies in weightlifting: Women get a lift in a male bastion. *Wall Street Journal,* April 19, 1978, 1.

BENNETT, B., et al. *Comparative physical education and sport.* Philadelphia: Lea & Febiger, 1975.

BENTZEN, F. Sex ratios in learning and behavior disorders. *National Elementary Principal,* 1966, **46**, 13-17.

BERGER, B.G. *Relationships between the environmental factors of temporal-spatial uncertainty, probability of physical harm, and nature of competition and selected personality characteristics of athletes.* Unpublished doctoral dissertation, Teacher's College, Columbia University, 1976.

BERGER, P. *Invitation to sociology.* New York: Doubleday, 1963.

BERGER, P. Sociology and freedom. *The American Sociologist,* 1971, **6**, 1-5.

BERKOWICZ, L. Aggressive cues in aggressive behavior and hostility catharsis. *Psychological Review,* 1964, 71, 104-122.

BERLIN, P. The woman athlete. In E. Gerber, J. Felshin, P. Berlin, & W. Wyrick (Eds.), *The American woman in sport.* Reading, MA: Addison-Wesley, 1974.

BERNARD, J. *Women and the public interest: An essay on policy and protest.* New York: Aldine-Atherton, 1971.

BERNARD, J. My four revolutions: Autobiographical history of the ASA. *American Journal of Sociology,* 1973, **78**, 773-791.

BEUTER, R.J. Sports, values and society. *The Christian Century,* April 5, 1972, **89**, 389-92.

BILLER, H.B. Father absence, maternal encouragement, and sex role development in kindergarten-age boys. *Child Development,* 1969, **40**, 539-546.

BILLER, H.B. The father and personality development: Paternal deprivation and sex-role development. In M.E. Lamb (Ed.), *The role of the father in child development.* New York: Wiley, 1976.

BILLER, H.B. Father absence and the personality development of the male child. *Developmental Psychology,* 1979, **2**, 181-201.

BIRD, E. Personality structure of Canadian intercollegiate women ice hockey players. In G.S. Kenyon (Ed.), *Contemporary psychology of sport.* Chicago: Athletic Institute, 1968.

BIRRELL, S. Achievement related motives and the woman athlete. In C. Oglesby (Ed.), *Women and sport: From myth to reality.* Philadelphia: Lea & Febiger, 1978. (a)

BIRRELL, S. The need for achievement. In P. Donnelly & S. Birrell (Eds.), *Motivation and sport involvement.* Ottawa: CAHPER sociology of sport monograph series, 1978. (b)

BLAU, P.M. *Exchange and power in social life.* New York: Wiley, 1964.

BLAUFARB, M. Sex-integrated programs that work. *AAHPER Update,* November 1977, 4.

BLOCK, J.H. Debatable conclusions about sex differences: A critical review of "The Psychology of Sex Differences." *Merrill-Palmer Quarterly,* 1976, **22**, 283-308. (b)

BLUMER, H. Society and symbolic interactionism. In A. Rose (Ed.), *Human behavior and social progress.* Boston: Houghton Mifflin, 1962.

BOSTON women's health book collective. *Our bodies, ourselves.* New York: Simon & Schuster, 1976.

BRASCH, R. *How did sports begin?* New York: David McKay, 1970.

BROOKS-Gunn, J., & Fisch, M. Psychological androgyny and college students judgments of mental health. *Sex roles.* 1979.

BROOKS-Gunn, J., & Matthews, W. *He and she: How children develop their sex-role identity.* Englewood Cliffs, NJ: Prentice-Hall, 1979.

BROVERMAN, I., Broverman, D., Clarkson, F., Rosenkrantz, P. & Vogel, S. Sex role stereotypes and clinical judgments of mental health. *Journal of Consulting and Clinical Psychology*, 1972, **34**, 1-7.

BROWN, D. Sex-role development in a changing culture. *Psychological Bulletin*, 1958, 55, 232-242.

BROWN, M., Jennings, J., & Vanek, V. The motive to avoid success: A further examination. *Journal of Research in Personality*, 1974, **8**, 172-176.

BUCHANAN, H.T., Blankenbaker, J., & Cotten, D. Academic and athletic ability as popularity factors in elementary school children. *Research Quarterly*, 1976, **47**, 320-325.

BULLOUGH, V.L. *The subordinate sex*. Baltimore, MD: Penguin Books, 1974.

BUNCH, C. Lesbians in revolt. In A.M. Jaggar & P. Rothenberg-Struhl (Eds.), *Feminist frameworks*. New York: McGraw Hill, 1978.

BURCK, C. It's promoters vs. taxpayers in the superstadium game. *Fortune*, March 1973, **87**, 105.

BURTON, E.C. State and trait anxiety, achievement motivation and skill attainment in college women. *Research Quarterly*, 1971, **42**, 139-144.

BUSS, A.H. Physical aggression in relation to different frustrations. *Journal of Abnormal and Social Psychology*, 1963, **67**, 1-7.

CAILLOIS, R. *Man, play, and games*. New York: Free Press, 1961.

CALVERT, R., & Clarke, K. Injuries and collegiate athletics: Taking their measure. *Educational Record*, Fall 1979, **60**, 44-66.

CAPLAN, P.J., & Kinsbourne, M. Sex differences in response to school failure. *Journal of Learning Disabilities*, 1974, **7**, 232-235.

CARRON, A. Personality and athletics: A review. In B.S. Rushall (Ed.), *The status of psychomotor learning and sport psychology research*. Dartmouth, NH: Sport Science Association, 1975.

CHAFETZ, J.S. *Masculine/feminine or human?* Itasca, IL: Peacock, 1978.

CHILD, I., Potter, E., & Levine, E. Children's textbooks and personality development: An exploration in the social psychology of education. In M.L. Haimonitz & N.R. Haimonitz (Eds.), *Human development: Selected readings*. New York: Thomas Y. Crowell, 1960.

CHOURAGE, Z. The age factor in competitive sport. In O. Grupe et al., (Eds.), *Sport in the modern world: Chances and problems*. New York: Springer-Verlag, 1973.

CHORBAJIAN, L. The social psychology of American males and spectator sports. *International Journal of Sport Psychology*, 1978, **9**, 165-175.

CHRIST, C.P. & Plaskow, J. *Woman spirit rising*. New York: Harper & Row, 1979.

CLARK, A.H., Wyon, S.M., & Richards, M.P. Free-play in nursery school children. *Journal of Child Psychology and Psychiatry and Allied Disciplines*, 1969, **10**, 205-216.

COAKLEY, J.J. *Sport in society: Issues and controversies*. St. Louis: C.V. Mosby, 1978.

COLEMAN, J.C. *The adolescent society*. New York: The Free Press, 1961.

COLKER, R., & Widom, C. Correlates of female athletic participation. *Sex Roles*, 1980, **6**, 47-58.

CONDRY, J., & Dryer, S. Fear of success: Attribution of cause to the victim. *Journal of Social Issues*, 1976, **32**, 63-83.

CORRIGAN, M. Societal acceptance of the female athlete as seen through the analysis of content of a sports magazine. Unpublished paper, May 11, 1972.

COSER, L.A. Presidential address: Two methods in search of a substance. *American Sociological Review*, 1975, **40**, 691-700.

COURTNEY, A., & Whipple, T. Women in T.V. commercials. *Journal of Communications*, 1974, **24**, 110-18.

CRAIG, T.T. (Ed.). *The humanistic and mental health aspects of sports, exercise and recreation.* Chicago: American Medical Association, 1976.

CRANDALL, V.J. Achievement. In H.W. Stevenson (Ed.), *Child psychology: The sixty-second yearbook of the National Society for the Study of Education.* Chicago: University of Chicago Press, 1963.

CRANDALL, V., Dewey R., Katkovsky, W., & Preston, A. Parents' attitudes and behaviors and grade school childrens' academic achievements. *Journal of Genetic Psychology*, 1964, **104**, 53.

CRASE, D. Selected periodicals in sport and physical education. *Journal of Physical Education and Recreation*, May 1979, pp. 25-27.

CULLEY, J., & Bennett, R. Selling women, selling blacks. *Journal of Communications*, 1976, **26**, 160-174.

DAHL, R. Decision-making in a democracy: The Supreme Court as a national policy maker, *Journal of Public Law*, 1957, **279**, 310-322.

DAHRENDORF, R. *Class and class conflict in industrial society.* Stanford, CA: Stanford University Press, 1959.

DALY, M. *Beyond God the father.* Boston: Beacon, 1974.

DALY, M. *Gyn/ecology: The metaethics of radical feminism.* Boston: Beacon Press, 1978.

DAMON, W. *The social world of the child.* San Francisco: Jossey-Bass, 1977.

DANIELS, A.K. Feminist perspectives in sociological research. In M. Millman & R.M. Kanter (Eds.), *Another voice.* New York: Anchor Books, 1975.

DAUGERT, P. *Relationship of anxiety and to learning of swimming.* Unpublished doctoral dissertation, University of Michigan, 1966.

DAVIDSON, L., & Gordon, L.K. *The sociology of gender.* Chicago: Rand McNally, 1979.

DAVIS, E., & Cooper, J. Athletic ability and scholarship. *Research Quarterly*, December 1934, **5**, 68-78.

DAVIS, W. *NCAA General Round Table,* January 8, 1979.

DAVIS, W. The President's role in athletics: Leader or figurehead? *Educational Record*, Fall 1979, **60**, 420-430.

DAYRIES, J.L., & Grimm, R.L. Personality traits of women athletes as measured by the Edwards Personal Preference Schedule. *Perceptual and Motor Skills*, 1970, **30**, 229-30.

DEAUX, K. *The behavior of women and men.* Monterey: Brooks-Cole, 1976.

DEAUX, K., & Emswiller, T. Explanations of successful performance on sex linked tasks: What is skill for the male is luck for the female. *Journal of Personality and Social Psychology*, 1974, **29**, 80-85.

DEAUX, K., White, L., & Farris, E. Skill versus luck: Field and laboratory studies of male and female preferences. *Journal of Personality and Social Psychology*, 1975, **32**, 629-636.

DeBEAUVOIR, S. *[The second sex]* (H.M. Parshey, trans.). New York: Alfred A. Knopf, 1953.

DEBACY, D.L., Spaeth, R., & Busch, R. What do men really think about athletic competition for women? *Journal of Health, Physical Education and Recreation*, 1970, **41**, 28-29.

DeCOSTA, L. Pro softball's new pitch. *womenSports*, June 1977, pp. 38-58.

DEFORD, F. What makes Robyn ride. *Reader's Digest*, December 1972, pp. 102-106.

DEL REY, P. In support of apologetics for women in sport. *International Journal of Sport Psychology*, 1977, **8**, 218-223.

DEL REY, P. Apologetics and androgny: The past and the future. *Frontiers: A Journal of Women Studies*, Spring 1978, **3**, 8-10.

DENLINGER, K., & Shapiro, L. *Athletes for sale: An investigation into America's greatest sports scandal—Athletic recruiting.* New York: Crowell, 1975.

DOLLARD, J. *Criteria for the life history, with analyses of six notable documents.* Gloucester, MA: P. Smith, 1949.

DOMHOFF, G.W. The women's page as a window on the ruling class. In G. Tuchman, A.K. Daniels, & J. Benét (Eds.), *Hearth and home: Images of women in the mass media.* New York: Oxford University Press, 1978.

DOLLARD, J., Miller, N., Doob, L., Mower, O.H., & Sears, R. *Frustration and aggression.* New Haven, CT: Yale University Press, 1939.

DONNELLY, P. *A study of need for stimulation and its relationship to sport involvement and childhood environment variables.* Unpublished master's thesis, University of Massachusetts, 1976.

DONNELLY, P. The need for stimulation. In P. Donnelly & S. Birrell (Eds.), *Motivation and sport involvement.* Ottawa: CAHPER Sociology of Sport Monograph Review, 1978.

DOUGHERTY, P.H. Setting new goals for womensports. *The New York Times*, November 18, 1977, p. 60.

DOWLING, C. The hype report. *womenSports*, May 1977, pp. 65-71.

DOWLING, C. Women who race. *womenSports*, January 1978, **5**, 34-63.

DREXLER, R. The most powerful women in the world. *New York*, September 10, 1979, pp. 39-41.

DREZNER, K. I want to be Pelé when I grow up. *womenSports*, March 1977, p. 50.

DULLEA, G. Women angle for a line in the fishing world. *New York Times*, July 24, 1978, p. A15.

DUQUIN, M. *Institutional sanction for girls' sport programs: Effects on female high school students.* Unpublished doctoral dissertation, Stanford University, 1974.

DUQUIN, M.E. The androgynous advantage. In C.A. Oglesby (Ed.), *Women and sport: From myth to reality.* Philadelphia: Lea & Febiger, 1978.

DURSO, J. *The sports factory: An investigation into college sports.* New York: Quandrangle, 1975.

DWORKIN, A. *Woman hating.* New York: E.P. Dutton, 1974.

EDWARDS, H. *Sociology of sport.* Homewood, IL: Dorsey, 1973.

EDWARDS, H. Desegregating sexist sport. In S.L. Twin (Ed.), *Out of the bleachers.* New York: The Feminist Press and McGraw Hill Book Company, 1979.

EIDSMORE, R.M. The academic performance of athletes. *School Activities,* December 1961, **32**, 105-107.

EISENSTEIN, Z. *The radical future of liberal feminism.* New York: Longman, 1981.

EITZEN, D.S. Sport and social status in American public secondary education. *Review of Sport and Leisure,* Fall 1976, **1**, 139-155.

EITZEN, D.S. School sports and educational goals. In D.S. Eitzen (Ed.), *Sport in contemporary society: An anthology.* New York: St. Martin's Press, 1979.

EITZEN, D.S. (Ed.). *Sport in contemporary society.* New York: St. Martin's Press, 1979.

EITZEN, D.S. The structure of sport and society. In D.S. Eitzen (Ed.), *Sport in contemporary society: An anthology.* New York: St. Martin's Press, 1979.

EITZEN, D.S., & Sage, G.H. *Sociology of American sport.* Dubuque, IA: Wm. C. Brown, 1978.

ENTIN, E. Effects of achievement-oriented and affiliative motives on private and public performance. In J.W. Atkinson & J.O. Raynor (Eds.), *Motivation and achievement.* New York: Halsted, 1974.

EPSTEIN, C.F. The women's movement and the women's pages. In G. Tuchman, A.K. Daniels, & J. Benét (Eds.), *Hearth and home: Images of women in the mass media.* New York: Oxford University Press, 1978.

ERICKSON, E.J. Sex differences in the play configurations of preadolescents. *American Journal of Orthopsychiatry,* 1951, **21**, 667-692.

ESPECHSCHADE, A.S., & Eckert, H.M. *Motor development.* Columbus, OH: Charles E. Merrill, 1967.

FAGOT, B.I. Sex differences in toddlers' behavior and parental reaction. *Developmental Psychology,* 1974, **10**, 554-558.

FAGOT, B.I. The influence of sex of child on parental reactions to toddler children. *Child Development,* 1978, **49**, 459-465.

FAGOT, B.I., & Littman, I. Stability of sex role and play interests from preschool to elementary school. *Journal of Psychology,* 1975, **89**, 285-292.

FEATHER, N.T., & Raphelson, A.C. Fear of success in Australian and American student groups: Motive or sex role stereotype. *Journal of Personality,* 1974, **42**, 190-201.

FEATHER, N.T., & Simon, J.G. Fear of success and causal attribution for outcome. *Journal of Personality,* 1973, **41**, 525-542.

FELDMAN-Summers, S., & Kiesler, S.B. Those who are number two try harder: The effect of sex attributions on causality. *Journal of Personality and Social Psychology,* 1974, **30**, 846-855.

FELSHIN, J. The social view, In E.R. Gerber et al. (Eds.), *The American woman in sport.* Reading, MA: Addison-Wesley, 1974. (a)

FELSHIN, J. The triple option . . . for women in sport. *Quest,* 1974, **21**, 36-40. (b)

FELSHIN, J. The triple option—for women in sport. In M. Hart (Ed.), *Sport in the socio-cultural process* (2nd ed.). Dubuque: Wm. C. Brown, 1976.

FERGUSON, M. Imagery and ideology: The cover photographs of traditional women's magazines. In G. Tuchman, A.K. Daniels, & J. Benet (Eds.), *Hearth and home*. New York: Oxford University Press, 1978.

FESTINGER, L. *A theory of cognitive dissonance*. Stanford, CA: Stanford University Press, 1957.

FIELDS, C. Women's association to consider athletic scholarships, new diversions. *Chronicle of Higher Education*, December 12, 1977, p. A3-4.

FIRESTONE, S. *The dialectic of sex*. New York: William Morrow, 1970.

FISHEL, A., & Pottker, J. *National politics and sex discrimination in education*. Lexington, MA: D.C. Heath, 1977.

FLANERY, R.C., & Balling, J.D. Developmental changes in hemispheric specialization for tactile spatial ability. *Developmental Psychology*, 1979, **15**, 364-372.

FLING, S., & Manosevitz, M. Sex typing in nursery school childlren's play interests. *Developmental Psychology*, 1972, **7**, 146-152.

FORD, G.R. In defense of the competitive urge. *Sports Illustrated*, July 8, 1974, pp. 16-23.

FOUSHEE, H., Helmrich, R., & Spence, J. Implicit theories of masculinity and feminity: Dualistic or bipolar? *Psychology of Woman Quarterly*, 1979, **3**, 259-269.

FRANKS, L. See Jan run. In S.L. Twin (Ed.), *Out of the bleachers*. New York: The Feminist Press and the McGraw-Hill Book Co., 1979.

FRANZWA, H. Working women in fact and fiction. *Journal of Communication*, 1974, **24**, 104-109.

FREEMAN, J. *Women: A feminist perspective*. Palo Alto, CA: Mayfield, 1975.

FRENCH, E. Some characteristics of achievement motivation. In J.W. Atkinson (Ed.), *Motives in fantasy, action and society*. Princeton, NJ: Van Nostrand, 1958.

FRIEDAN, B. *The second stage*. New York: Summit, 1981.

FRISH, H.L. Sex stereotypes in adult-infant play. *Child Development*, 1977, **48**, 1671-1675.

FRODI, A., Macauley, J., & Thorne, P.R. Are women always less aggressive than men? A review of the experimental literature. *Psychological Bulletin*, 1977, **84**, 634-660.

GAA, J., Liberman, D., & Edwards, T. A comparative factor analysis of the Bem Sex Role Inventory and the Personality Attributes Questionnaire. *Journal of Clinical Psychology*, 1979, **35**, 592-598.

GAGNON, J. Physical strength, once of significance. In D.S. David & R. Brannon (Eds.), *The forty-nine percent majority: The male sex role*. Reading, MA: Addison-Wesley, 1976.

GALLUP (1978).

GARAI, J., & Scheinfeld, A. Sex differences in mental and behavioral traits. *Genetic Psychology Monographs*, 1968, **77**, 169.

GARBER, M. Mary Garber: Thirty-four years a sportswriter. *Editor and Publisher*, May 27, 1978, **111**, 44.

GENOVESE, P. *Perceptions of women in sport*. Unpublished master's thesis, Ithaca College, New York, 1975.

GERBER, E.R., Felshin, J., Berlin, P., & Wyrick, W. *The American woman in sport.* Reading, MA: Addison-Wesley, 1974.

GERBNER, G. The dynamics of cultural resistance. In G. Tuchman, A.K. Daniels, & J. Benét (Eds.), *Hearth and home: Images of women in the mass media.* New York: Oxford University Press, 1978.

GESCHWIND, N. The anatomical basis of hemisphere differentiation. In S. Dimond & J. Beaumont (Eds.), *Hemisphere function in the human brain.* New York: Wiley, 1974.

GILBERT, B. Gleanings from a troubled time. *Sports Illustrated,* December 25, 1972, **37,** 34-46.

GILBERT, B. & Williamson, N. Women in sport. *Sports Illustrated,* May 28, June 4, June 11, 1973.

GILBERT, D. *The miracle machine.* New York: Coward, McCann, Geoghegan, 1980.

GILMAN, K. The media's getting the message. *womenSports,* October, 1976, 37-42. (a)

GILMAN, K. TV sports producer Ellie Riger. *womenSports,* August 1976, 52-53. (b)

GILMAN, K. Sports. *Vogue,* February 1978, pp. 42-46.

GLEASNER, D. Margo Oberg. *WomenSports,* June 1977, pp. 11-12.

GOFFMAN, E. *Encounters.* Indianapolis: Bobbs-Merrill, 1961.

GOLDBERG, P. Are women prejudiced against women? *Trans-action,* 1968, **5,** 28-30.

GOLDBERG, S., & Lewis, M. Play behavior in the year-old infant: Early sex differences. *Child Development,* 1969, **40,** 21-31.

GOLDSTEIN, J., & Arms, R.L. Effects of observing athletic contests on hostility. *Sociometry,* 1971, **34,** 83-90.

GOLEMAN, D. Special abilities of the sexes: Do they begin in the brain? *Psychology Today,* November 1978, pp. 48ff.

GOODE, E. *Deviant behavior. An interactionist approach.* New Jersey: Prentice-Hall, 1978.

GOODENOUGH, E.W. Interest in persons as an aspect of sex difference in the early years. *Genetic Psychology Monographs,* 1957, **55,** 287-323.

GOODHART, P., & Chataway, C. *War without weapons.* London: W.H. Allen, 1968.

GOODMAN, L.W., & Lever, J. A report on children's toys. In J. Stacey, S. Bereaud, & J. Daniels (Eds.), *And Jill came tumbling after: Sexism in American education.* New York: Dell, 1974.

GORNICK, V. Watch out: Your brain may be used against you. *Ms.,* April 1982, pp. 14-20.

GOSLIN, D.A. (Ed.). *Handbook of socialization theory and research.* Chicago: Rand McNally, 1969.

GOULDNER, A.W. Anti-minotaur: The myth of a value-free sociology. In M. Stein & A. Vidich (Eds.), *Sociological trial.* Englewood Cliffs, NJ: Prentice-Hall, 1963.

GOULDNER, A.W. *The coming crisis of western sociology.* New York: Equinox, 1971. (a)

GOULDNER, A.W. Sociology today does not need a Karl Marx or an Isaac Newton: It needs a V.I. Lenin. *Psychology Today,* 1971, **5**, 53-57; 96-97. (b)

GRAHAME, A. The making of a non-sexist dictionary. *Ms.,* December 1973, **16**, 12-14.

GRANT, C. Institutional autonomy and intercollegiate athletics. *Educational Record,* Fall 1979, **60**, 409-419.

GREEN, L. Old Dominion does it! *Women's Sports,* May 1979, 46-51.

GREEN, R. *Sexual identity conflict in children and adults.* New York: Basic Books. 1974.

GREENDORFER, S.L. *The nature of female socialization into sport: A study of selected college women's sport participation.* Unpublished doctoral dissertation, University of Wisconsin, 1974.

GREENDORFER, S.L. Role of socializing agents in female sport involvement. *Research Quarterly,* 1977, **48**, 304-310.

GREENDORFER, S. Socialization into sport. In C.A. Oglesby (Ed.), *Women and sport.* Philadelphia: Lea & Febiger, 1978.

GREENDORFER, S.L. Childhood sport socialization influences of male and female track athletes. *Arena Review,* 1979, **3**(2), 39-53. (a)

GREENDORFER, S.L. Differences in childhood socialization influences of women involved in sport and women not involved in sport. In M.L. Krotee (Ed.), *The dimensions of sport sociology.* West Point, NY: Leisure Press, 1979. (b)

GREENDORFER, S.L. *Female socialization into sport: An in-depth analysis.* Unpublished paper, University of Illinois, 1980.

GREENDORFER, S.L., & Lewko, J.H. Role of family members in sport socialization of children. *Research Quarterly,* 1978, **49**, 146-152.

GREENSTEIN, F.I. *Children and politics.* New Haven: Yale University Press, 1965.

GRIFFIN, P.S. What's a nice girl like you doing in a profession like this? *Quest,* 1973, **19**, 96-101.

GUTTENTAG, M., & Bray, H. Teachers as mediators of sex-role standards. In A. Sargent (Ed.), *Beyond sex roles.* St. Paul, MN: West, 1977.

GUTTMAN, A. *From ritual to record: The nature of modern sports.* New York: Columbia University Press, 1978.

HAITCH, R. Women boxers. *The New York Times,* January 29, 1978, p. L31.

HALL, M.A. A 'feminine woman' and an 'athletic woman' as viewed by female participants and non-participants in sport. *British Journal of Physical Education,* 1972, **3**.

HALL, M.A. The sociological perspective of females in sport. In M. Adrian & J. Bame (Eds.), *NAGWS Research Report* (vol. 3). Washington, DC: American Alliance for Health, Physical Education and Recreation, 1977.

HAMMER, S. My daughter, the football star. *Parade,* August 5, 1979, pp. 6-8.

HANFORD, G. Controversies in college sports. *Educational Review,* Fall 1979, **60**, 351-366.

HARPER, L.W., & Sands, K.M. Preschool children's use of space: Sex differences in outdoor play. *Developmental Psychology,* 1975, **11**, 119.

HARRAGAN, B.L. *Games mother never taught you*. New York: Warner Books, 1977.

HARRES, B. Attitudes of students toward women's athletic competition. *Research Quarterly*, 1968, **39**, 278-284.

HARRIS, D.V. Psychosocial considerations. *Journal of Physical Education and Recreation*, 1977, **46**, 32-36.

HARRIS, D.V. It was as if all girls in phys. ed . . . were less than a she. Interview with D.V. Harris, *Mademoiselle*, August 1975, **81**, 231; 283.

HARRIS, D.V. (Ed.) *Women and sport: A national research conference*. Proceedings from the national research conference, women and sport. (Penn State HPER series no. 2.) Pennsylvania State University, August 13-18, 1972.

HARRIS, D.V. (Ed.) *DGWS research report: Women in sports*. Washington, DC: AAHPER, 1973.

HARRIS, H.A. *Sport in Greece and Rome*. Ithaca, NY: Cornell University Press, 1972.

HARRIS, M.B. Field studies of modeled aggression. *Journal of Social Psychology*, 1973, **89**, 131-129.

HART, M. On being female in sport. In M. Hart (Ed.), *Sport in the socio-cultural process* (2nd ed.). Dubuque, IA: Wm. C. Brown, 1976.

HART, R. *The child's landscape in a New England town*. Unpublished doctoral dissertation, Clark University, Worchester, MA. 1976.

HARTLEY, R.E. Sex-role pressures and the socialization of the male child. *Psychological Reports*, 1959, **5**, 457-468.

HARTLEY, R.E. A developmental view of female sex-role definition and identification. *Merrill-Palmer Quarterly*, 1964, **10**, 3-17.

HARTLEY, R.E. A developmental view of female sex-role identification. In B.J. Biddle & E.J. Thomas (Eds.), *Role theory: Concepts and research*. New York: Wiley, 1966.

HEILBRUN, A., Kleemeier, C., & Piccola, G. Development and situational correlates of achievement behavior in college females. *Journal of Personality*, 1974, **42**, 420-436.

HENNIG, M., & Jardim, A. *The managerial woman*. Garden City: Anchor Press, 1977.

HICKS, B. There's nothing powder puff about this derby. *womenSports*, January 1977, **4**, 53-54.

HICKS, B. Lesbian athletes. *Christopher Street*, October 1979, pp. 42-50.

HOCH, P. *Rip off of the big game: The exploitation of sports by the power elite*. Garden City, NY: Doubleday/Anchor, 1972.

HOFFMAN, L. Fear of success in males and females: 1965-1971. In M. Mednick, S. Tangri, & L. Hoffman (Eds.), *Women and achievement*. New York: Halsted, 1975.

HOGAN, C.L. Diamond and dust. *womenSports*, June 1976, pp. 39-41.

HOGAN, C.L. Title IX: From here to equality. *WomenSports*, September 1977, **4**, 16-24.

HOGAN, C. Title IX: From here to equality. In D.S. Eitzen (Ed.), *Sport in contemporary society: An anthology*. New York: St. Martin's Press, 1979.

HOKANSON, J., & Edelman, R. Effects of three responses on vascular processes.

Journal of Personality and Social Psychology, 1966, **3**, 442-447.

HOKANSON, J., Willers, K., & Koropsak, E. The modification of autonomic responses during aggressive interchange. *Journal of Personality*, 1968, **36**, 386-404.

HOMANS, G. *The human group.* New York: Harcourt, Brace and World, 1950.

HORNER, M.S. *Sex differences in achievement motivation and performance in competitive and non-competitive situations.* Unpublished doctoral dissertation, University of Michigan, 1968.

HORNER, M.S. Femininity and successful achievement: A basic inconsistency. In M.H. Garskof (Ed.), *Roles women play: Readings toward women's liberation.* Belmont: Brooks/Cole, 1971.

HORNER, M.S. Performance of women in noncompetitive and interpersonal competitive achievement-oriented situations. In J.W. Atkinson & J.O. Raynor (Eds.), *Motivation and achievement.* New York: Halsted, 1974.

HOW to watch the Olympics. ABC Production of the Olympics. New York: ABC Productions, 1975.

HOWE, F. Sexual stereotypes start early. *Saturday Review*, October 16, 1971, p. 81.

HUCKLE, P. Back to the starting line. *American Behavioral Scientist*, January 1978, **21**, 379-392.

HUDSON, J. Physical parameters used for female exclusion from law enforcement and athletics. In C.A. Oglesby (Ed.), *Women and sport: From myth to reality.* Philadelphia: Lea & Febiger, 1978.

HUIZINGA, J. *Homo ludens: A study of the play element in culture.* Boston: Beacon Press, 1950.

HULT, J. Different AIAW/NCAA eligibility rules: Tip of the iceberg. *Educational Record*, 1979, **60**, 12-16.

HUSTON, A.C. Sex-typing. Chapter prepared for P.H. Mussen & E.M. Hetherington (Eds.), *Carmichael's manual of child psychology* (Vol. 4, 4th ed.). In press.

HYMBAUGH, K., & Garrett, J. Sensation-seeking among skydivers. *Perceptual and Motor Skills*, 1974, **38**, 118.

JAGGAR, A.M., & Struhl, P.R. (Eds.). *Feminist frameworks: Alternative and theoretical accounts of the relations between women and men.* New York: McGraw-Hill, 1978.

JENSEN, A. How much can we boost IQ and scholastic achievement? *Harvard Educational Review*, 1969, **39**, 1-123.

JENSEN, M. Letter from the editor. *The Sportswoman*, May-June 1975, p. 4.

JOHNSON, A.T. Public sports policy. *American Behavioral Scientist*, January 1978, **21**, 319-344.

JOHNSON, W.O. *All that glitters is not gold.* New York: G.P. Putnam's Sons, 1972.

JOKL, E. Health, wealth, and athletics. In E. Jokl & E. Simon (Eds.), *International research in sport and physical education.* Springfield, IL: C.C. Thomas, 1964.

JORDAN, P. Designing woman. *Sports Illustrated*, August 4, 1975, pp. 49-57.

KAGAN, J., & Lewis, M. Studies of attention in the human infant. *Merrill-Palmer Quarterly*, 1965, **11**, 95-127.

KANE, J.E. Personality and physical abilities. In G.S. Kenyon (Ed.), *Contemporary psychology of sport*. Chicago: Athletic Institute, 1968.

KANE, J.E. Psychology of sport with special reference to the female athlete. In D. Harris (Ed.), *Women and Sport: A National Research Conference*. Penn State HPER Series No. 2, 1972.

KANE, J.E. Personality research: The current controversy and implications sports studies. In W.F. Straub (Ed.), *Sport psychology: An analysis athletic behavior*. Ithaca: Mouvement Publications, 1978.

KAPLAN, A.G. Clarifying the concept of androgyny: Implications for therapy. *Psychology of Women Quarterly*, 1979, **3**, 223-230.

KAPLAN, J. *Women and sports*. New York: Viking, 1979. (a)

KAPLAN, J. Women athletes are women, too. *The New York Times*, March 4, 1979, p. 25. (b)

KATZ, L.G., et al. *Sex role socialization in early childhood*. Urbana, IL: ERIC Clearinghouse on Early Childhood Education, 1977.

KELLY, R., & Boutilier, M. *The making of political women*. Chicago: Nelson-Hall Publishers, 1978.

KEMENER, B.J. *A study of the relationship between the sex of students and the assignment of marks by secondary school teachers*. Unpublished doctoral dissertation, Michigan State University, 1965.

KENNICKE, L. *Self profiles of highly skilled female athletes*. Unpublished master's thesis, Pennsylvania State University, 1972.

KENYON, G.S. Sociological considerations. *Journal of Health, Physical Education, and Recreation*, 1968, **39**, 31-33.

KENYON, G.S., & Loy, J.W. Toward a sociology of sport: A plea for the study of physical activity as a sociological and social psychological phenomenon. *Journal of Health, Physical Education and Recreation*, 1965, **36**, 24-25; 68-69.

KERLEY, M.R. Kitty O'Neil. *WomenSports*, April 1977, **4**, 17-19.

KIMBLE, D.P. *Psychology as a biological science*. Santa Monica: Goodyear, 1977.

KIMURA, D., & Durnford, M. Normal studies on the function of the right hemisphere in vision. In S.J. Dimond & J.G. Beaumont (Eds.), *Hemisphere function in the human brain*. New York: Wiley, 1974.

KINGSLEY, J., Foster, L., & Siebert, M. Social acceptance of female athletes by college women. *Research Quarterly*, 1977, **48**, 727-733.

KIRKPATRICK, C. Getting into the picture. *Sports Illustrated*, April 21, 1975, pp. 86-96.

KIRSHENBAUM, J. Steroids: The growing menace. *Sports Illustrated*, November 12, 1979, **33**.

KLAFS, C.E., & Lyon, M.J. *The female athlete: A coach's guide to conditioning and training*. St. Louis, MO: Mosby, 1978.

KOENIG, L. *Official makers of public policy: Congress and the president*. Chicago: Scott, Foresman, 1965.

KORT, M. Body politics: A *Chrysalis* sports report. *Chrysalis*, 1979, **7**, 84-87.

KOSLOW, S.P. Why do women want to be jocks. *Mademoiselle*, August 1975, **81**, 230-231; 293-294.

KROLL, W.P. Current strategies and problems in personality assessment of athletes. In A.C. Fisher (Ed.), *Psychology of sport*. Palo Alto: Mayfield, 1976. (a)

KROLL, W.P. Reactions to Morgan's paper. In G.M. Scott (Ed.), *The Academy papers, No. 10, Beyond research—Solutions to human problems*. Iowa City: American Academy of Physical Education, 1976. (b)

KUSCSIK, N. The history of women's participation in the marathon. *Road Runners Club*, 1976, pp. 28-31.

LAMB, M.E. Fathers: Forgotten contributors to child development. *Human Development*, 1975, **18**, 245-266.

LAMB, M. (Ed.). *The role of the father in child development*. New York: Wiley, 1976.

LANDERS, D.M. Birth order in the family and sport participation. In M.L. Krotee (Ed.), *The dimensions of sport sociology*. West Point, NY: Leisure Press, 1979.

LANGE, G.E. The most admired woman: Image-making in the news. In G. Tuchman, A.K. Daniels, & J. Benét (Eds.), *Hearth and home: Images of women in the mass media*. New York: Oxford University Press, 1978.

LANGLOIS, J.H., & Downs, A.C. Mothers, fathers, and peers as socialization agents of sex-typed play behaviors in young children. *Child Development*, 1980, **51**, 1237-1247.

LANSKY, L.M. The family structure also affects the model: Sex-role attitudes in parents of preschool children. *Merrill-Palmer Quarterly*, 1967, **13**, 139-150.

LAPIN, J. Ellie Riger. *The Sportswoman*, June 1976, pp. 44-45. (a)

LAPIN, J. Volleyball. *Women's Sports*, November 1976, pp. 20-23. (b)

LAPIN, J. Law without order: Trouble with Title IX. *Women's Sports*, January 1979, pp. 43-45.

LASSWELL, H. The structure and function of communication in society. In L. Bryson (Ed.), *The communication of ideas*, New York: Harper Brothers, 1948.

LEAVY, J. Whatever happened to Peaches Bartkowicz? *womenSports*, January 1978, **5**, 20-47.

LEE, A.M. *Toward humanist sociology*. Englewood Cliffs, NJ: Prentice-Hall, 1973.

LEEDS, W. *The toy market*. Unpublished manuscript, University of Pennsylvania, Philadelphia, 1976.

LEFEBVRE, L.M. Achievement motivation and causal attribution in male and female athletes. *International Journal of Sport Psychology*, 1979, **10**, 31-41.

LEONARD, G.B. Winning isn't everything, it's nothing. *Intellectual Digest*, October 1973, **4**, 45-47.

LEVENSON, H., Burford, B., Bouno, B., & Davis, L. Are women still prejudiced against women? *Journal of Psychology*, 1975, **89**, 67-71.

LEAVY, J. Sit-com sportscasting. *womenSports*, 1977, 4, 64. (a)

LEAVY, J. Sports Chic. *womenSports*, 1977, 5, 53-57. (b)

LEVER, J. Sex differences in the games children play. *Social Problems*, April 1976, **23**, 479-488.

LEVER, J. Sex differences in the complexity of children's play and games. *American Sociological Review*, 1978, **43**, 471-483.

LEVINE, A., & Cumrine, J. Women and fear of success: A problem in replication. *American Journal of Sociology*, 1975, **80**, 964-974.

LEVY, J. Psychological implications of bilateral asymmetry. In S.J. Dimond & J.G. Beaumont (Eds.), *Hemisphere function in the human brain.* New York: Wiley, 1974.

LEWIS, M. Culture and gender roles: There is no unisex in the nursery. *Psychology Today,* 1972, 5(12), 54-57. (a)

LEWIS, M. State as an infant-environment interaction: An analysis of mother-infant behavior as a function of sex. *Merrill-Palmer Quarterly,* 1972, **18**, 95-121. (b)

LEWIS, M. Parents and children: Sex role development. *School Review,* 1972, **80**, 229-240. (c)

LEWKO, J.H., & Ewing, M.E. Sex differences and parental influences in sport involvement of children. *Journal of Sport Psychology,* 1980, **2**, 62-68.

LINCOLN, M.L. Locker rooms: Equality with integrity. *The New York Times,* April 15, 1979, p. 52.

LIPSYTE, R. *Sports world: An American dreamland.* New York: The New York Times Book Co., 1975.

LIPSYTE, R. The varsity syndrome. *The Annals of American Academy of Political and Social Science,* September 1979, **445**, 18.

LISCIO, J. Woman athletes with femininity: Why not? *The New York Times,* June 19, 1977, p. 2.

LOCKHEED, M.E., & Hall, K.P. Conceptualizing sex as a status characteristic: Applications to leadership training strategies. *Journal of Social Issue,* 1976, **32**, 111-124.

LOCKSLEY, A., & Cotten, M. Psychological androgyny: A case of mistaken identity? *Journal of Personality and Social Psychology,* 1979, **37**, 1017-1031.

LOFLAND, J. *Doing social life: The qualitative study of human interaction in natural settings.* New York: Wiley, 1976.

LONG, B.H., & Henderson, E.H. Children's use of time: Some personal and social correlates. *Elementary School Journal,* 1973, **73**, 193-199.

LOPIANO, D.A. Solving the financial crisis in intercollegiate athletics. *Educational Record,* Fall 1979, **60**, 394-408.

LORANZ, K. *On aggression.* New York: Harcourt, Brace and World, 1966.

LOY, J. The nature of sport: a definitional effort. *Quest,* 1967, **10**, 1-15.

LOY, J.W. The nature of sport. In J.W. Loy & G.S. Kenyon (Eds.), *Sport, culture and society.* New York: Macmillan, 1968.

LOY, J.W. Sociology and physical education. In R.N. Singer et al. (Eds.), *Physical education: An interdisciplinary approach.* New York: Macmillan, 1972.

LOY, J.W. The emergence and development of the sociology of sport as an academic specialty. *Research Quarterly,* 1980, **51**, 91-109.

LOY, J.W., Birrell, S., & Rose, D.A. Attitudes held toward agonetic activities as a function of selected social identities. *Quest,* 1976, **26**, 81-93.

LOY, J.W., & Ingham, A.G. Play, games and sport in the psychosociological development of children and youth. In G.L. Rarick (Ed.), *Physical activity: Human growth and development.* New York: Academic Press, 1973.

LOY, J.W., McPherson, B.D., & Kenyon, G. *Sport and social systems.* Reading, MA: Addison-Wesley, 1978.

LOY, J.W., & Segrave, J.O. Research methodology in the sociology of sport. In

J.H. Wilmore (Ed.), *Exercise and sport sciences reviews*. New York: Academic Press, 1974.

LUSCHEN, G. The interdependence of sport and culture. *International Review of Sport Sociology*, 1967, **2**, 127-139.

LUSCHEN, G. Cheating in sports. In D.M. Landers (Ed.), *Social problems in athletics*. Urbana, IL: University of Illinois Press, 1976.

LYNN, D.B. A note on sex differences in the development of masculine and feminine identification. *Psychological Review*, 1959, **66**, 126-135.

LYPSKY, M. *Street-level bureaucracy*. New York: Russell Sage Foundation, 1980.

MACCOBY, E.E. (Ed.), *The development of sex differences*. Stanford, CA: Stanford University Press, 1966.

MACCOBY, E., & Jacklin, C. *The psychology of sex differences*. Palo Alto, CA: Stanford University Press, 1974.

MACCOBY, E., & Jacklin, C.N. Sex differences in aggression: A rejoinder and reprise. *Child Development*, 1980, **51**, 964-980.

MALUMPHY, T.M. Personality of women athletes in intercollegiate competition. *Research Quarterly*, 1968, **39**, 610-620.

MALUMPHY, T.M. The college woman athlete: Questions and tentative answers. *Quest*, 1970, **14**, 18-27.

MALUMPHY, T.M. Athletics and competition for girls and women. In D.V. Harris (Ed.), *DGWS research reports: Women in sports*. Washington, DC: American Association for Health, Physical Education and Recreation, 1971.

MANDELL, R. *The Nazi Olympics*. New York: Macmillan, 1971.

MARLOWE, M., Algozzine, B., Lerch, H.A., & Welch, P.D. The game analysis intervention as a method of decreasing feminine play patterns of emotionally disturbed boys. *Research Quarterly*, 1978, **49**, 484-490.

MARTENS, R. The paradigmatic crisis in American sport personalogy. *Sportwissenschaft*, 1975, 9-24. (a)

MARTENS, R. *Social psychology and physical activity*. New York: Harper and Row, 1975. (b)

MARTENS, R. Competitiveness in sport. *Proceedings of the International Congress of Physical Activity Sciences*, Quebec City, 1976.

MARTENS, R. About smocks and jocks. *Journal of Sport Psychology*, 1979, **1**, 94-99.

MATHES, S. Body image and sex stereotyping. In C.A. Oglesby (Ed.), *Women and sport: From myth to reality*. Philadelphia: Lea & Febiger, 1978.

MATZA, D. Position and behavior patterns of youth. In R. Faris (Ed.), *Handbook of modern sociology*. Chicago: Rand McNally, 1964.

McCABE, S. Jennifer Rowland: What you didn't read in *National Velvet*. *womenSports*, January 1977, **4**, 15-17.

McCLELLAND, D.C. *The achieving society*. New York: The Free Press, 1961.

McCLELLAND, D.C. *Power: The inner experience*. New York: Irvington, 1975.

McCLELLAND, D. Atkinson, J., Clark, R., & Lowell, E. *The achievement motive*. New York: Appleton-Century-Crofts, 1953.

McHUGH, M.C., Duquin, M., & Frieze, I. Beliefs about success and failure: Attribution and female athlete. In C.A. Oglesby (Ed.), *Women and sport: From myth to reality.* Philadelphia: Lea & Febiger, 1978.

McINTOSH, P.C. Mental ability and success in school sport. *Research and Physical Education*, 1966, **1**.

McPHERSON, B.D. Sport consumption and the economics of consumeries. In D. Ball & J.W. Loy (Eds.), *Sport and social order.* Reading, MA: Addison-Wesley, 1975.

McPHERSON, B.D. The child in competitive sport: Influence of the social milieu. In R.A. Magill, M.J. Ash, & F.L. Smoll (Eds.), *Children in sport: A contemporary anthology.* Champaign, IL: Human Kinetics, 1978.

MEAD, G.H. *Mind, self and society.* Chicago: University of Chicago Press, 1934.

MEAD, G.H. *George Herbert Mead on social psychology* (A. Strauss, Ed.). Chicago: The University of Chicago Press, 1956.

MEGGYESY, D. *Out of their league.* New York: Simon & Schuster, 1970.

MELNICK, M.J. A critical look at sociology of sport. *Quest*, Summer 1975, **24**, 34-47.

METHENY, E. *Connotations of movement in sport and dance.* Dubuque, IA: Wm. C. Brown, 1965.

METHENY, E. Symbolic forms of movement: The female image in sport. In M.M. Hart (Ed.), *Sport in the socio-cultural process* (1st ed.). Dubuque, IA: Wm. C. Brown, 1972.

MILLER, S.H. The content of news photos: Women's and men's roles. *Journalism Quarterly*, 1975, **52**, 70-75.

MILLET, K. *Sexual politics.* Garden City, NY: Doubleday, 1970.

MILLMAN, M., & Kanter, R.M. (Eds.), *Another voice.* New York: Anchor Books, 1975.

MILLS, C.W. *The sociological imagination.* New York: Oxford University Press, 1959.

MISCHEL, W. A social learning view of sex differences in behavior. In E.E. Maccoby (Ed.), *The development of sex differences.* Stanford, CA: Stanford University Press, 1966.

MISCHEL, W. Sex-typing and socialization. In P.H. Mussen (Ed.), *Carmichael's manual of child psychology* (Vol. 2, 3rd ed.). New York: Wiley, 1970.

MOLOTCH, H.L. The news of women and the work of men. In G. Tuchman, A.K. Daniels, & J. Benét (Eds.), *Hearth and home: Images of women in the mass media.* New York: Oxford University, 1978.

MOLOTCH, H., & Lester, M. News as purposive behavior: On the strategic use of routine events, accidents, and scandals. *American Sociological Review*, 1974, **39**, 101-113.

MONAHAN, L., Kuhn, D., & Shaver, P. Intrapsychic vs. cultural explanations of 'fear of success' motive. *Journal of Personality and Social Psychology*, 1974, **29**, 60-64.

MONEY, J.W., & Erhardt, A. *Man and woman, boy and girl.* Baltimore: Johns Hopkins University Press, 1972.

MONTAGU, M.F.A. Aggression and the evolution of man. In R.E. Whalen (Ed.), *The neuropsychology of aggression.* New York: Plenum, 1974.

MONTEMAYOR, R. Children's performance in a game and their attraction to it as a function of sex-typed labels. *Child Development*, 1974, **45**, 152-156.

MORAN, M. Grete Waitz sets record in park run. *The New York Times*, June 3, 1979, p. 59.

MORGAN, E. *The descent of woman*. New York: Stein & Day, 1972.

MORGAN, R. *Going too far*. New York: Random House, 1977.

MORGAN, W.P. Sport personalogy: The credulous-skeptical argument in perspective. In W.F. Straub (Ed.), *Sport psychology: An analysis of athlete behavior*. Ithaca: Mouvement Publications, 1978.

MORGAN, W.P. The trait psychology controversy. *Research Quarterly*, 1980, **51**, 50-76.

MORRIS, M. The public definition of a social movement: Women's liberation. *Sociology and Social Research*, 1974, **57**, 526-543.

MOSELEY, M.L. *The role of the female collegiate athlete in sports*. Honors paper for the Department of Sociology and Anthropology, Bowdoin College, 1979.

MRS. King says she had lesbian affair. *New York Times*, May 2, 1981, p. 9.

MUSHIER, C.L. Personality of selected women athletes. *International Journal of Sport Psychology*, 1972, **3**, 25-31.

MUSSEN, P.H. Early sex role development. In D.A. Gosline (Ed.), *Handbook of socialization theory and research*. Chicago: Rand McNally, 1969.

MUSSEN, P.H., & Hetherington, E.M. (Eds.). *Carmichael's manual of child psychology* (Vol. 4, 4th ed.). In press.

MUSSEN, P.H., & Rutherford, E. Parent-child relations and parental personality in relation to young children's sex-role preferences. *Child Development*, 1963, **34**, 589-607.

MYERS, A.M., & Lips, H. Participation in competitive amateur sports as a function of psychological androgyny. *Sex Roles*, 1978, **4**, 571-578.

NATIONAL Federation of State High School Associations. News release. Kansas City, MO, September 29, 1981.

NEAL, P. *Personality traits of U.S. women athletes who participated in the 1959 Pan American Games*. Unpublished master's thesis, University of Utah, 1963.

NEALON, N. *An analysis of the relationship between need for stimulation and differential sport involvement*. Honors thesis, University of Massachusetts, 1973.

NEVILLE, O.L. Sports—The ultimate challenge. *Do It Now*, January 1977, **10**, 4.

NIEDERMAN, T. Waitz sets world record. *New York Running News*, 1980, **21**, p. 54.

NOVIKOV, A., & Maximenko, A. The influence of selected socio-economic factors on the level of sports achievements in the various countries. *International Review of Sport Sociology*, 1972, **7**, 27-44.

NYQUIST, E.B. Win, women, and money: Collegiate athletics today and tomorrow. *Educational Record*, Fall 1979, **60**, 374-393.

O'CONNOR, R. Althea Gwyn: The changing American dream. *Sports Wise*, April-May 1979, pp. 45-46.

OGLESBY, C.A. *Women and sport: From myth to reality*. Philadelphia: Lea and Febiger, 1978.

OGLESBY, C.A. The masculinity/femininity game: Called on account of . . . . In C.A. Oglesby (Ed.), *Women and sport: From myth to reality*. Philadelphia: Lea & Febiger, 1978.

OGILVIE, B.C. What is an athlete? *Journal of Physical Education and Recreation*, 1967, **38**, 48.

OGILVIE, B.C. Psychological consistencies within the personality of high level competitors. In W. Morgan (Ed.), *Contemporary readings in sport psychology*. Springfield, IL: Charles C. Thomas, 1970.

OGILVIE, B.C., & Tutko, T. *Problem athletes and how to handle them*. London: Pelham, 1966.

O'KELLY, C., & Bloomquist, L. Women and blacks on T.V. *Journal of Communications*, 1976, **26**, 179-184.

OKNER, B. Taxation and sports enterprises. In R. Noll (Ed.), *Government and the sports business*. Washington, DC: The Brookings Institution, 1974.

ORLICK, T.D. Sport participation: A process of shaping behavior. *Human Factors*, 1974, **5**, 558-561.

ORWANT, J.E., & Cantor, M.G. How sex stereotyping affects perceptions of news references. *Journalism Quarterly*, 1977, **54**, 99-107.

OTTO, L.B., & Alwin, D. Athletics, aspirations and attainment. *Sociology of Education*, April 1977, **42**, 102-113.

PAGE, C.H. The world of sport and its study. In J.T. Talamini & C.H. Page (Eds.), *Sport and society*. Boston: Little, Brown, 1973.

PARKE, R.D. Perspectives on father-infant interaction. In J.D. Osofsky (Ed.), *The handbook of infant development*. New York: Wiley, 1979.

PARKE, R.D., & Suomi, S.J. Adult male-infant relationships: Human and non-primate evidence. In K. Immelmann, G. Barlow, M. Main, & L. Petrinovitch (Eds.), *Behavioral development: The Bielefeld interdisciplinary project*. New York: Cambridge University Press, 1980.

PECK, T. When women evaluate women nothing succeeds like success. *Sex Roles*, 1978, **4**, 205-213.

PEDHAZUR, E.J., & Tetenbaum, T.J. Bem Sex Role Inventory: A theoretical and methodological critique. *Journal of Personality and Social Psychology*, 1979, **37**, 996-1016.

PERRY, D.G., & Bussey, K. The social learning theory of sex differences: Imitation is alive and well. *Journal of Personality and Social Psychology*, 1979, **37**, 1699-1712.

PETERSON, H. Don't go near the water? Phooey! *Sports Illustrated*, May 13, 1974, pp. 54-58.

PETERSON, S.L., Weber, J.C., & Trousdale, W.W. Personality traits of women in team sports vs. women in individual sports. *Research Quarterly*, 1967, **38**, 686-690.

PETRIE, A. *Individuality in pain and suffering*. Chicago: University of Chicago Press, 1967.

PETRIE, B. Sport and politics. In D.W. Ball & J.W. Loy (Eds.), *Sport and social order: Contributions to the sociology of sport*. Reading, MA: Addison-Wesley, 1975.

PIAGET, J. *The moral judgement of the child*. New York: The Free Press, 1948.

PLUMMER, P.J. *A Q-sort study of the achievement motivation of selected athletes*. Unpublished master's thesis, University of Massachusetts, 1969.

POLLOCK, O. *The criminology of women.* Philadelphia: University of Pennsylvania Press, 1950.

PRESIDENT'S commission on Olympic sports: First report to the president. Washington, DC, 1976.

PUDELKIEWICZ, E. Sociological problems of sports in housing estates. *International Review of Sport Sociology,* 1970, **5,** 73-103.

PUTNAM, P. A case of volunteer — Or else. *Sports Illustrated,* July 23, 1973, **39,** 22-25.

PORTZ, E. Influence of birth order, sibling sex on sports participation. In D. Harris (Ed.), *Women and sport: A national research conference.* Penn State HPER Series No. 2, 1973.

RABINOWITZ, F.M., Moely, B.D., Finkel, N., & Clinton, S. The effects of toy novelty and social interaction on the exploratory behavior of preschool children. *Child Development,* 1975, **46,** 286-289.

RAPOPORT, R. Wham, bam thank you, ma'am. *womenSports,* November 1974, pp. 38-42.

REDMOND, G. A plethora of shrines: Sport in the museum and hall of fame. *Quest,* January 1973, **19,** 41-48.

RHEINGOLD, H.L., & Cook, K.V. The contents of boys' and girls' rooms as an index of parents' behavior. *Child Development,* 1975, **46,** 459-463.

RITZER, G. *Sociology: A multiple paradigm science.* Boston: Allyn & Bacon, 1975.

ROACH, M. From the editor. *Women's Sports,* December 1979, p. 4.

ROBBINS, L., & Robbins, E. Comment on 'Toward an understanding of achievement-related conflicts in women.' *Journal of Social Issues,* 1973, **29,** 133-137.

ROBERTS, G.C. Sex and achievement motivation effects on risk taking. *Research Quarterly,* 1975, **46,** 58-70.

ROBERTS, J., & Sutton-Smith, B. Child training and involvement. *Ethnology,* 1962, **1,** 166-185.

ROGERS, C. Sports, religion and politics: The renewal of an alliance. *Christian Century,* April 5, 1972, **89,** 392-394.

ROMER, N. The motive to avoid success and its effects on performance in school age males and females. *Developmental Psychology,* 1977, **11,** 689-699.

ROSENBERG, B.G., & Sutton-Smith, B. A revised conception of masculine-feminine differences in play activities. *Journal of Genetic Psychology,* 1960, **96,** 165-170.

ROSENKRANTZ, P., Vogel, S., Bee, H., Broverman, I, and Broverman, D. Sex role stereo-types and self-concepts in college students. *Journal of Consulting and Clinical Psychology,* 1968, **32,** 287-295.

RUBIN, L. *Worlds of pain: Life in the working class.* New York: Basic Books, 1976.

RUDIN, A.J. America's new religion. *Christian Century,* April 5, 1972, **89,** 384.

RUSHALL, B.S. An evaluation of the relationship between personality and physical performance categories. In G.S. Kenyon (Ed.), *Contemporary Sport Psychology.* Chicago: Athletic Institute, 1968. (a)

RUSHALL, B.S. Some practical applications of personality information to athletes. In G.S. Kenyon (Ed.), *Contemporary Sport Psychology*. Chicago: Athletic Institute, 1968. (b)

RYAN, E.D., & Foster, R. Athletic participation and perceptual reduction and augmentation. *Journal of Personality and Social Psychology*, 1967, **6**, 472-476.

RYAN, E.D., & Kovacic, C. Pain tolerance and athletic participation. *Perceptual and Motor Skills*, 1966, **22**, 383-390.

RYAN, J. Gynecological considerations. *Journal of Physical Education and Recreation*, 1975, **46**, 40.

SAARIO, T., Jacklin, C., & Tittle, C. Sex role stereotyping in the public schools. *Harvard Educational Review*, 1973, **43**, 386-416.

SAEGERT, S., & Har, R. The development of environmental competence in girls and boys. In M.A. Salter (Ed.), *Play: Anthropological perspectives*. West Point, NY: Leisure Press, 1978.

SAFILIOS-Rothschild, C. *Women and social policy*. New Jersey: Prentice-Hall, 1974.

SAGE. G.H., & Loudermilk, S. The female athlete and role conflict. *Research Quarterly*, 1979, **50**, 88-96.

SAGE, G. The collegiate dilemma of sport and leisure: A sociological perspective. In D.S. Eitzen (Ed.), *Sport in contemporary society: An anthology*. New York: St. Martin's Press, 1979.

SANGIOVANNI, L. *Ex-nuns: A study of emergent role passage*. Norwood, NJ: Ablex, 1978.

SANTROCK, J.W. Parental absence, sex-typing and identification. *Developmental Psychology*, 1970, **2**, 264-272.

SCANNELL, N., & Barnes, B. On unfeminine stigma. *The Washington Post*, May 15, 1974, pp. A1; A10.

SCHAFER, W.E., & Armer, J.M. Athletes are not inferior students. *Trans Action*, November 1968, pp. 21-26; 61-62.

SCHATTSCHNEIDER, E.E. *The semisovereign people: A realist's view of democracy in America*. New York: Holt, Rinehart & Winston, 1960.

SCHECHTER, L. *The jocks*. New York: Bobbs Merrill, 1969.

SCIMECCA, J.A. *Society and freedom: An introduction to humanist sociology*. New York: St. Martin's Press, 1981.

SCOTT, J. *The athletic revolution*. New York: Free Press, 1971.

SCOTT, J. Introduction. In P. Hoch (Ed.), *Rip off of the big game*. Garden City, NJ: Doubleday, 1972.

SCOTT, J. Sports and the masculine obsession. *The New York Times*, July 27, 1975, p. 2.

SCOTT, J. A radical ethic for sports. In S.L. Twin (Ed.), *Out of the bleachers: Writings on women and sport*. New York: The Feminist Press, 1979.

SCULLY, G. Binding salary arbitration in major league baseball. *American Behavioral Scientist*, January 1978, **21**, 431-450.

SEARS, R.R., Maccoby, E.E., & Levin, H. *Patterns of child rearing*. Evanston, IL: Row, Peterson, 1957.

SEARS, R.R., Rau, L., & Alpert, R. *Identification and child rearing*. Stanford, CA: Stanford University Press, 1965.

SELBY, R., & Lewko, J. Children's attitudes toward females in sports. *Research Quarterly*, 1976, **47**, 453-463.

SHAKLEE, H. Sex differences in children's behavior. In M. Wolraick & D. Routh (Eds.), *Advances in behavioral pediatrics* (Vol. 4). 1982.

SHAW, G. *Meat on the hoof: The hidden world of Texas football*. New York: St. Martin's Press, 1972.

SHAW, S., & Pooley, J. *National success at the Olympics: An explanation.* Paper presented at the 6th International Seminar on the History of Physical Education and Sport, Trois Rivieres, Quebec, July 1976.

SHERIF, C.W., & Rattray, G.D. Psychological development and activity in middle childhood. In J.G. Albinson & G.M. Andrew (Eds.), *Child in sport and physical activity.* Baltimore: University Park Press, 1976.

SHIELDS, S.A. Functionalism, Darwinism, and the psychology of women: A study in social myth. *American Psychologist*, 1975, 30.

SHOEMAKER, D.J., & South, D.R. White-collar crime. In C.D. Bryant, *Deviant behavior: Occupational and organizational bases.* Chicago: Rand McNally, 1974.

SIDELINES: S.I.'s silver anniversary. *Women's Sports*, November, 1979, p. 12.

SIMRI, U. *Women at the Olympic Games.* Netanya, Israel: The Wingate Institute for Physical Education and Sport, 1979.

SINGER, R., Harris, D., Kroll, W., Martens, R., & Sechrest, L. Psychological testing of athletes. *Journal of Physical Education and Recreation*, 1977, **48**, 30-32.

SLATTON, Y. La B. *The role of women in sport as depicted through advertising in selected magazines.* Unpublished doctoral dissertation, University of Iowa, Iowa City, 1970.

SLOAN, P. Bra-makers sprint to fill sport market. *Advertising Age*, December 25, 1978, **49**, p. 4.

SMITH, D.A. & Visher, C.A. Sex and involvement in deviance/crimes: A quantitative review of the empirical literature. *American Sociological Review*, 1980, **45**, 691-701.

SMITH, L.E. Personality and performance research: New theories and directions required. *Quest*, 1970, **13**, 74-83.

SMITH, R. TV Sports: Real or imagined. *womenSports*, May 1977, p. 72.

SMOLKIN, S. Racquetball: Stepchild to squash, cousin to handball. *Women Sports*, January 1977, **4**, 22-24.

SNYDER, E.E. Aspects of socialization in sports and physical education. In G.H. Sage (Ed.), *Sport and American society* (2nd ed.). Reading, MA: Addison-Wesley, 1974.

SNYDER, E.E. & Kivlin, J.E. Women athletes and aspects of psychological well-being and body image. *Research Quarterly*, 1975, **46**, 191-199.

SNYDER, E.E., & Kivlin, J.E. Perceptions of the sex role among female athletes and non-athletes. *Adolescence*, 1977, **45**, 23-29.

SNYDER, E.E., Kivlin, J.E., & Spreitzer, E. The female athlete: Analysis of objective and subjective role conflict. In D.M. Landers (Ed.), *Psychology of Sports and Motor Behavior.* University Park: Pennsylvania State University, 1975.

SNYDER, E.E., & Spreitzer, E. Family influences and involvement in sports. *Research Quarterly*, 1973, **44**, 249-255.

SNYDER, E.E., & Spreitzer, E. Correlates of sport participation among adolescent girls. *Research Quarterly*, 1976, **47**, 804-809.

SOFRANKO, A.J., & Nolan, M.F. Early-life experiences and adult sport participation. *Journal of Leisure Research*, 1972, **4**, 6-18.

SPECTOR, M., & Faulkner, R.R. Thoughts on five new journals and some old ones. *Contemporary Sociology*, 1980, **9**, 477-482.

SPENCE, J.T. *Guest lecture on research on androgyny.* University of Massachusetts, Department of Psychology, 1975.

SPENCE, J.T. & Helmreich, R. *Masculinity and femininity.* Austin: University of Texas Press, 1978.

SPENCE, J.T. & Helmreich, R. The many faces of androgyny: A reply to Locksley and Colton. *Journal of Personality and Social Psychology.* 1979, **37**, 1032-1046. (a)

SPENCE, J.T. & Helmreich, R. On assessing 'androgyny'. *Sex Roles*, 1979, **5**, 721-738. (b)

SPENCE, J., Helmreich, R., & Stapp, J. Likeability, sex role conference of interest and competence. *Journal of Applied Social Psychology*, 1975, **5**, 93-109.

SPREITZER, E., & Snyder, E.E. Socialization into sport: An exploratory path analysis. *Research Quarterly*, 1976, **47**, 238-245.

SPORTSWOMANLIKE conduct. *Newsweek*, June 3, 1974, pp. 50-55.

STAFFO, D.F. Survey report action in New York state to provide athletic opportunities to girls. *AAHPER Update*, December 1978, p. 3.

STAKE, J.E. The ability/performance dimension of self-esteem: Implications for women's achievement behavior. *Psychology of Women Quarterly*, 1979, **3**, 365-377.

START, K.B. Sporting and intellectual success among English secondary school children. *International Review of Sport Sociology*, 1967, **2**, 47-53.

STEFFENMEIR, D.J. Crime and the contemporary woman: An analysis of changing levels of female property crime. *Social Forces*, 1975, **57**, 566-584.

STEIN, A.H., Pohly, S., & Mueller, E. The influence of masculine, feminine and neutral tasks on children's achievement behavior, expectancies of success, and attainment values. *Child Development*, 1971, **42**, 195-208.

STOKES, R. The presidential role in community and junior college athletics. *Educational Record*, Fall 1979, **60**, 431-438.

STOLL, C., Inbar, M., & Fennessey, Jr. *Socialization and games: An exploratory study of sex differences* (Report No. 30). Baltimore: The Center for the Study of Social Organization of Schools. The Johns Hopkins University, 1968.

STORR, A. *Human aggression.* New York: Atheneum, 1968.

STRULLER, J. Gladys Heldman: A few words with the architect of women's pro tennis. *Women's Sports*, May 1979, pp. 29-32.

SULLIVAN, P.A. *A comparative study of self concepts and ideal self concepts of femininity between female athletes and non-athletes.* Unpublished master's thesis, Smith College, 1973.

SUTTON-Smith, B. The play of girls. In C.B. Koop & M. Kirkpatrick (Eds.), *Becoming female: Perspectives on development.* New York: Plenum, 1979.

SUTTON-Smith, B., Rosenberg, B.G., & Morgan, E.E. The development of sex differences in play choices during pre-adolescence. *Child Development*, 1963, **34**, 119-126.

SNYDER, E.E. Athletic dressing room slogans as folklore: A means of socialization. *International Review of Sport Sociology*, 1972, **7**, 89-102.

TALAMINI, J. School athletics: Public policy versus practice. In J. Talamini & C. Page (Eds.), *Sport and society: An anthology*. Boston: Little, Brown, 1973.

TASCH, R.G. The role of the father in the family. *Journal of Experimental Education*, 1952, **20**, 319-361.

TAUBER, M.A. Parental socialization techniques and sex differences in children's play. *Child Development*, 1979, **50**, 225-234.

TAYLOR, F.W. *The principles of scientific management*, 1911.

TAYLOR, S.P., & Epstein, S. Aggression as a function of the interaction of sex of the aggressor and sex of the victim. *Journal of Personality*, 1967, **35**, 473-486.

TIEGER, T. On the biological basis of sex differences in aggression. *Child Development*, 1980, **51**, 943-963.

TIGER, L. *Men in groups*. New York: Vintage Books, Random House, 1970.

TRESEMER, D. Fear of success: Popular but unproven. *Psychology Today*, March 1974, **7**, 82-85.

TUCHMAN, G. Objectivity as strategic ritual. *American Journal of Sociology*, 1972, **77**, 660-680.

TUCHMAN, G., Daniels, A.K., & Benét, J. *Hearth and home: Images of women in the mass media*. New York: Oxford University Press, 1978.

TUTKO, T., & Burns, W. *Winning is everything and other American myths*. New York: Macmillan, 1976.

T.V. and She. *New York Times*, February 12, 1979, **111**, p. 2.

TWIN, S.L. (Ed.). *Out of the bleachers*. New York: The Feminist Press and McGraw Hill, 1979.

TYLER, S. Adolescent crisis: Sport participation for the female. In D.V. Harris (Ed.), *DGWS research reports: Women in sports*. Washington, DC: American Association of Health, Physical Education and Recreation 1973.

TYLER, S.J. *Differences in social and sport self perception between female varsity athletes*. Unpublished master's thesis, Pennsylvania State University, 1973.

TYSON, M. Editorial. *Sportswoman*, March/April 1976, p. 4.

TYSON, M. No joy in Mudville. *womenSports*. January 1977, **4**, 48-52.

UNDERWOOD, J. Student-athletes: The sham, the shame. *Sports Illustrated*, May 19, 1980, **52**, 36-72.

VEBLEN, T. *The theory of the leisure class*. New York: The New American Library, 1953.

VEROFF, J., McClelland, L., & Ruhland, D. Varieties of achievement motivation. In M.T.S. Mednick, S.S. Tangri, & L.W. Hoffman, *Women and achievement*. New York: Wiley, 1975.

VEROFF, J., Wilcox, S., & Atkinson, J. The achievement motive in high school and college age women. *Journal of Abnormal and Social Psychology*, 1953, **48**, 108.

VIDA, G. (Ed.). *Our right to love: A lesbian resource book*. National Gay Task Force, 1978.

WALKER, J. Pain and distraction in athletes and non-athletes. *Perceptual and Motor Skills*, 1971, **33**, 1187-1190.

WALUM, L.R. *The dynamics of sex and gender: A sociological perspective.* Chicago: Rand McNally, 1977.

WARD, W.D. Variance of sex-role preference among boys and girls. *Psychological Reports*, 1968, **23**, 467-470.

WARNER, W.L., & Abegglin, J. *Big business leaders in America.* New York: Harper, 1955.

WATSON, G.G. Sex role socialization and the competitive process in little athletes. *The Australian Journal of Health, Physical Education and Recreation*, 1975, **70**, 10-21.

WATSON, R. *Promise and performance of American democracy* (4th ed.). New York: Wiley, 1981.

WEBB, H. Professionalization of attributes toward play among adolescents. In G.S. Kenyon (Ed.), *Aspects of contemporary sport sociology.* Chicago: The Athletic Institute, 1969.

WEBER, E. Revolution in women's sports. *womenSports*, 1979.

WEBER, M. *[Theory of social and economic organization]* (A.M. Kenderson & T. Parsons, trans.). New York: Oxford University Press, 1947.

WEINBERG, G. *Society and the healthy homosexual.* Garden City, NJ: Anchor Books, 1973.

WEINBERG, S., & Arond, H. The occupational culture of the boxer. *American Journal of Sociology*, 1952, **57**, 460-469.

WEISS, P. *Sport: A philosophical inquiry.* Carbondale, IL: Southern Illinois University Press, 1969.

WEISS, P. Women athletes. In J. Talamini & C. Page (Eds.), *Sport and society: An anthology.* Boston: Little, Brown, 1973.

WEITZMAN, L. Sex-role socialization. In J. Freeman (Ed.), *Women: A feminist perspective.* Palo Alto, CA: Mayfield, 1975.

WEITZMAN, L.J. *Sex-role socialization.* Palo Alto, CA: Mayfield, 1979.

WEST, P. Massive lobbying campaign seeks to gut Title IX. *National Now Times*, June 1979, **12**, pp. 1; 13.

WHEELER, E. Ms. women's volleyball. *womenSports*, May 1977, pp. 43-46.

WHITE, G.S. Volpe: Man behind the L.P.G.A. rise. *The New York Times*, June 10, 1979, p. 9.

WILLIAMS, J.M. Personality characteristics of the successful female athlete. In W.F. Straub (Ed.), *Sport psychology: An analysis of athlete behavior.* Ithaca: Mouvement Publications, 1978.

WILLIAMS, J., Hoepher, D., Moody, D., & Ogilive, B., Personality traits of champion level female fencers. *Research Quarterly*, 1970, **41**, 446-453.

WILLIAMSON, N. Red ink, rosey future. *Sports Illustrated*, May 14, 1979, pp. 64-68.

WILMORE, J.H. (Ed.). Research methodology in the sociology of sport. *Exercise and Sport Sciences Reviews*, 1974, **2**.

WINTER, D.G. *The power motive.* New York: Free Press, 1973.

WISE, G., & Cox, M.K. Public policy questions loom on the horizon as the consumer confronts selected aspects of major league baseball. *American Behavioral Scientist*, January 1978, **21**, 451-464.

WITELSON, S. Sex and the single hemisphere: Specialization of the right hemisphere for spatial processing. *Science*, 1976, **193**, 425-427.

WITTIG, A.F. Attitudes towards females in sport. *Proceedings, North American Society of Sport and Physical Activity*. Pennsylvania State University, 1975.

WOMEN in the sports media. *The Sportswoman*, March/April 1974, pp. 20-22.

WOMEN'S Sports Foundation. Closing the gap. *womenSports*, July 1977, pp. 23-24.

WOMEN'S Sports Foundation. Strides. *Women's Sports*, February 1980, p. 44.

WOMEN'S Sports Foundation. Title IX alert: Take action. *Women's Sports*, October 1981, p. 42.

YEARY, S. A comparison of achievement motive and anxiety level in college women athletes in selected sports. Unpublished master's thesis, University of Massachusetts, 1971.

YIANNAKIS, A. From the editor. *Newsletter: The North American Society for the Sociology of Sport*, July 1979, **1**, 1-5.

YIANNAKIS, A., McIntyre, T.D., Melnick, M.J., & Hart, D.P. (Eds.). *Sport sociology: Contemporary themes*. Iowa: Kendall-Hunt, 1976.

YOESTING, D.R., & Burkhead, D.L. Significance of childhood recreation experience on adult leisure behavior: An exploratory analysis. *Journal of Leisure Research*, 1973, **5**, 25-36.

YONGE, G.D. The Bem Sex Role Inventory: Use with caution if at all. *Psychological Reports*, 1978, **43**, 1245-1246.

YORBURG, B. *Sexual identity: Sex roles and social change*. New York: Wiley, 1974.

ZANG, K.M. An analysis of selected aspects of the treatment of sports as reflected in the content of *Sports Illustrated*, from the inception of the magazine, 1954-1975. Unpublished master's thesis, East Stroudsburg State College, 1976.

ZIEGLER, S. Self-perception of athletes and coaches. In D. Harris (Ed.), *Women and sport: A national research conference*. Pennsylvania State HPER Series No. 2. Pennsylvania State University, 1973.

ZINGALE, D.A. A history of the involvement of the American presidency in school and college physical education and sports during the 20th century. Unpublished doctoral dissertation, Ohio State University, 1973.

ZOBLE, J. Femininity and achievement in sports. In D.V. Harris (Ed.), *Women and sport: A national research conference*. Pennsylvania State HPER series No. 2. Pennsylvania State University, 1973.

ZUCKERMAN, M., & Wheeler, L. To dispel fantasies about the fantasy-based measure of fear of success. *Psychological Bulletin*, 1975, **82**, 932-946.

Index